THE RISE OF NEOLIBERALISM
AND INSTITUTIONAL ANALYSIS

THE RISE OF NEOLIBERALISM
AND INSTITUTIONAL ANALYSIS

Edited by John L. Campbell and Ove K. Pedersen

PRINCETON UNIVERSITY PRESS   PRINCETON AND OXFORD

Copyright © 2001 by Princeton University Press
Published by Princeton University Press, 41 William Street, Princeton,
New Jersey 08540
In the United Kingdom: Princeton University Press, 3 Market Place,
Woodstock, Oxfordshire OX20 1SY

Library of Congress Cataloging-in-Publication Data

The rise of neoliberalism and institutional analysis / edited by John L.
Campbell, Ove K. Pedersen.
p.   cm.
Papers presented at a conference at Dartmouth College in Aug. 1998.
Includes bibliographical references and index.
ISBN 0-691-07086-5 (alk. paper) — ISBN 0-691-07087-3 (pbk. : alk. paper)
1. Free enterprise—Congresses.   2. Liberalism—Congresses.
3. Institutional economics—Congresses.   4. Economic policy—Congresses.   I. Campbell, John L., 1952–   II. Pedersen, Ove Kaj, 1948–
HB95 .R56   2001
330.1—dc21   2001016374

This book has been composed in Electra

Printed on acid-free paper. ∞

www.pup.princeton.edu

Printed in the United States of America

10 9 8 7 6 5 4 3 2 1

(Pbk.)

10 9 8 7 6 5 4 3 2 1

Contents

List of Tables _____

List of Figures

Preface _____

THE GENESIS of this project stretches back to a series of conversations between the editors during the summer 1995 in which they recognized how little work in institutional analysis had been done that explored the possibilities for cross-fertilization among institutionalist paradigms. We wondered what would happen if proponents of various institutionalist camps were assembled to discuss their work and address this issue. Subsequently, we convened a conference outside of Copenhagen, Denmark, in August 1997 to which we invited representatives from these paradigms to share their work in progress and discuss the important issues in institutional analysis as they defined them. At that conference consensus emerged about what many of these issues were and that it would be constructive to hold a second, more focused meeting at which time each participant would present a paper that employed their particular theoretical approach to institutional analysis in order to analyze a common empirical phenomenon. This, then, would provide the basis for a more systematic comparison of the strengths and weaknesses of different paradigms and, hopefully, generate insights that would contribute to a second movement in institutional analysis. These papers were presented and discussed in August 1998 at a second conference at Dartmouth College and subsequently revised for this volume.

We decided to focus on neoliberalism for several reasons. First, the subject emerged frequently at the first conference and was clearly something in which we were all very interested. Second, neoliberalism has been a very important political project. Given its significance and institutional implications, neoliberalism is something with which institutional analysts should be concerned and something that they ought to be able to explain. Third, neoliberalism is a very complex, that is, multidimensional, project that involves changes in a plethora of institutional arenas: substantive and discursive; formal and informal; political and economic; public and private; global, national, and local. Given its complexity, all institutional analysts regardless of their theoretical orientations should find at least some aspect of neoliberalism suited to their intellectual tastes. Indeed, the contributors to this volume agreed to study this phenomenon in the first place because it was complex enough to accommodate everyone's interests, perspectives, and analytic tools. For all these reasons, neoliberalism provides an excellent lens through which to compare different approaches to the analysis of institutions.

At various stages of the project's development we benefited from the comments and suggestions of a number of friends and colleagues. To begin with, we thank all of the contributors to the volume, who committed to the project despite recognizing that it was a potentially risky one in the sense that it cut across so many intellectual paradigms and social science disciplines that it might never find enough eclectic reviewers to enable its publication. Additionally, we thank Michael Allen, Niels Å. Andersen, Peter Hall, Eva Halden, James March, Dorthe Pedersen, Woody Powell, Rune Premfors, Marc Schneiberg, Dick Scott, Jim Shoch, Rosemary Taylor, Alex Wendt, and the late Vincent Wright. We owe a special debt of gratitude to John Hall, who provided much encouragement, advice, and friendship along the way.

We gratefully acknowledge financial support from the Danish Social Science Research Council, which provided funds for the Copenhagen conference, and thank Marianne Lauersen, who helped organize it. Linda Fowler, Director of the Nelson A. Rockefeller Center for the Social Sciences at Dartmouth College, and Michael Mastanduno, Director of the John Sloan Dickey Center for International Understanding at Dartmouth College, were very enthusiastic supporters of the project and provided funding for the conference at Dartmouth. Margaret Brannen, Margot de l'Etoile, and Marcella Logue were instrumental in organizing that conference. Ove Pedersen benefited from a sabbatical at Stanford University's Scandinavian Center for Organizational Research. John Campbell benefited from a fellowship at Nuffield College, Oxford University, and several visits to Denmark sponsored by the Copenhagen Business School and the Institute of Political Science at the University of Copenhagen.

Finally, we thank Peter Dougherty at Princeton University Press for his early enthusiasm for the project and Ian Malcolm for his help bringing it into print.

John L. Campbell
Ove K. Pedersen

Contributors

Sarah L. Babb is Assistant Professor of Sociology at the University of Massachusetts–Amherst. She did her undergraduate work at the University of Michigan and received her Ph.D. from Northwestern University in 1998. She has written several articles in the areas of historical, political, and economic sociology, published in journals including the *American Sociological Review* and *Estudios Sociologicos*, and is currently completing a book on the economic profession in Mexico.

Ellen M. Bradburn completed her Ph.D. in sociology at Cornell University in 1994 and worked as Assistant Professor of Sociology at Coe College in Cedar Rapids, Iowa, for two years. She now works at the National Center for Education Statistics and will continue work in education research at MPR Associates, Inc., beginning in the fall of 2000. Her current research interests include the transitions and trajectories of community college students and faculty.

John L. Campbell is Professor and Chair in the Department of Sociology, Dartmouth College, and Adjunct Professor of Political Science in the Institute of Political Science, University of Copenhagen, Denmark. He has been a faculty member at Harvard University, Washington State University, and the University of Wisconsin and has held visiting positions at Oxford University (Nuffield College) and the Copenhagen Business School. His current research interests include institutional analysis, the political economy of tax policy, and the transformations of postcommunist Europe. His previous work includes *Collapse of an Industry* (Cornell University Press, 1988), *Governance of the American Economy* (Cambridge University Press, 1991), and *Legacies of Change: Transformations of Postcommunist European Economies* (Aldine de Gruyter, 1996).

Bruce G. Carruthers is Associate Professor in the Sociology Department at Northwestern University. He has written three books and numerous articles and is currently working on two projects: a historical study of the evolution of credit decision-making as a problem in the sociology of trust, and a study of global changes in bankruptcy law.

Terence C. Halliday is Senior Research Fellow at the American Bar Foundation. He has taught at the Australian National University and University of Chicago. His books on professions, law, and organizations include *Beyond Monopoly: Lawyers, State Crises, and Professional Empowerment; Rescuing Business: The Making of Corporate Bankruptcy Law in England and the United States* (with Bruce Carruthers); and *Lawyers and the Rise of Western Political Liberalism* (edited with Lucien Karpik). He is founder and former chair of the section on the sociology of law, American Sociological Association. Currently he is engaged with Bruce Carruthers in a study of international institutions and the global diffusion of insolvency regimes.

Colin Hay is Research Director and Senior Lecturer in the Department of Political Science and International Studies at the University of Birmingham, UK. In recent years he has been a visiting fellow in the Department of Political Science, Massachusetts Institute of Technology, and a research affiliate of the Center for European Studies at Harvard University. He has written widely on the theory of the state, the political sociology of postwar Britain, and the political economy of globalization. He is the author of *Re-Stating Social and Political Change* (Open University Press, 1996), which was awarded the British Sociological Association's Philip Abrams Memorial Prize and *The Political Economy of New Labour: Labouring under False Pretenses?* (Manchester University Press, 1999). He is also coauthor of *Postwar British Politics in Perspective* (Polity/Blackwell, 1999) and editor or coeditor of *Theorizing Modernity* (Longman, 1998), *Demystifying Globalization* (Macmillan/St Martin's, 2000) and *British Politics Today* (Polity, 2001). He is a member of the editorial board of *Sociology*.

Edgar Kiser is Associate Professor of Sociology at the University of Washington. He has published articles in sociology, political science, and economics journals on topics including the determinants of war, the development and decline of voting institutions, the evolution of systems of taxation, and the methodology of historical research.

Peter Kjær is Assistant Professor in the Department of Organization and Industrial Sociology at the Copenhagen Business School. He received his Ph.D. from the Department of Political Science at Stockholm University in 1996, where he wrote a dissertation on the institutional history of the Swedish furniture industry. His research interests include discourse and political communication, the Danish negotiated economy, and the history of management thought. He is working on projects on Danish political journalism and on management and social change in Denmark and Nordic countries between 1880 and 1960.

Jack Knight is Professor and Chair in the Department of Political Science at Washington University in St. Louis, where he is also a Resident Fellow at the Center for Political Economy and a member of the Committee on Social Thought and Analysis. His primary areas of interest are modern social and political theory, law and legal theory, political economy, and philosophy of social science. His publications include *Institutions and Social Conflict* (Cambridge University Press, 1992), *Explaining Social Institutions* (with Itai Sened) (University of Michigan Press, 1995), and *The Choices Justices Make* (with Lee Epstein) (CQ Press, 1997), as well as articles in various journals and edited volumes.

Aaron Matthew Laing is currently pursuing both his Ph.D. in Sociology and his J.D. in the Law of Sustainable International Development at the University of Washington. His research interests include social stratification, socioeconomic development, and sociological methodology and theory. Currently he is working on his dissertation, exploring the consequences of ethnic stratification on economic development, and coauthoring a methodologically oriented paper testing various diffusion models.

Ove K. Pedersen is Professor of Comparative Politics at the Institute of Political Science, University of Copenhagen, Denmark. He has been a member of the faculty at Roskilde and Aalborg Universities in Denmark; Director of the Center for Research in Public Organization and Management at the Copenhagen Business School; and has held visiting positions at Harvard, Stockholm, and Stanford Universities. His research interests include political and institutional theory, comparative politics, public administration, and the European Union. His internationally best known work is on the Scandinavian negotiated economy and institutional theory. His has published several books in Scandinavian languages and *Legacies of Change: Transformations of Postcommunist European Economies* (Aldine de Gruyter, 1996).

David Strang is Associate Professor of Sociology at Cornell University. His research interests include the study of organizations, political sociology, and models and methods for quantitative analysis. His current research focuses on the diffusion of managerial practices, examining the rise and fall of "quality" programs both within companies and the business community as a whole. Other work studies how new policies and programs spread across the American states.

Bruce Western is Professor of Sociology and a Faculty Associate at the Office of Population Research at Princeton University. His research interests include the comparative study of trade unions and labor markets, statistical methods, and the institutional sources of inequality in the U.S. labor market. His recent publications include *Between Class and Market: Postwar Unionization in the Capitalist Democracies* (Princeton University Press, 1997).

Chapter 1 _____

Introduction

THE RISE OF NEOLIBERALISM AND INSTITUTIONAL ANALYSIS

JOHN L. CAMPBELL AND OVE K. PEDERSEN

THE LAST two decades of the twentieth century have been marked by the election of conservative governments in North America and Western Europe, the pursuit of austere stabilization policies in Latin America, and the collapse of the communist regimes in Eastern Europe and the Soviet Union and their movement toward market economies. As a result, the period has been described as one of rising *neoliberalism* — that is, a time of market deregulation, state decentralization, and reduced state intervention into economic affairs in general (Albert 1993; Lash and Urry 1987; Przeworski 1995). Cast in these terms, neoliberalism has been a political project concerned with institutional changes on a scale not seen since the immediate aftermath of the Second World War and a project that has attempted to transform some of the most basic political and economic settlements of the postwar era, including labor market accords, industrial relations systems, redistributive tax structures, and social welfare programs. Integral to these changes has been a shift away from Keynesian economic ideas, which emphasized the political management of aggregate demand, to a more conservative discourse based on monetarist, supply-side, and rational expectations theories (Heilbroner and Milberg 1995). This has entailed a confrontation of ideas and rhetoric on a normative level regarding the sorts of institutional changes toward which societies ought to aspire and on a prescriptive level regarding the concrete policy recommendations deemed necessary to fix a variety of social and economic problems, notably economic stagnation and the dilemmas posed to national political economies by the forces of economic globalization. Much debate has occurred over how extensive these changes have been and over their causes, but few doubt that neoliberalism has become an important part of our world (Berger and Dore 1996; Boyer and Drache 1996; Crouch and Streeck 1997; Hirst and Thompson 1996; Kitschelt et al. 1999a).

Simultaneously, and not coincidentally, given the vast institutional changes associated with the rise of neoliberalism, there has been renewed interest since the mid-1970s in the analysis of institutions as critical determinants of political and economic performance as well as objects of inquiry in their own right.

This has occurred in Europe as well as North America and has involved the emergence of several new institutionalist paradigms, specifically *rational choice* (e.g., Knight 1992; North 1990), *historical* (e.g., Steinmo et al. 1992), *organizational* (e.g., Powell and DiMaggio 1991) and *discursive institutionalism* (Bourdieu 1998; Foucault 1969, 1991; Searle 1995).[1]

This volume compares the strengths and weaknesses of these new paradigms by turning them to an empirical analysis of the rise of neoliberalism. This is important for two reasons. On the one hand, as argued below, the rise of neoliberalism played an important role in the development of institutional analysis, so it is fitting that the theoretical perspectives that it helped foster should now be used to examine how extensive this phenomenon has become, how it emerged in the first place, and what some of its effects have been. On the other hand, until the mid-1990s scholars tended either to work within their own institutionalist paradigms or to engage in critical debates in which each side attacked the other's weaknesses (e.g., DiMaggio and Powell 1991; Kiser and Hechter 1991; Thelen and Steinmo 1992; for an exception, see March and Olsen 1989). Recently, however, there have been calls for what might be described as a *second movement* in institutional analysis, that is, a more constructive dialogue among paradigms in order to identify complementarities and explore the possibilities for rapprochement, cross-fertilization, and integration (Ethington and McDonagh 1995; Finnemore 1996; Fligstein 1998, chap. 5; Hirsch 1997, p. 1721; Hirsch and Lounsbury 1997; Peters 1999, chap. 9). This stems from the increasing recognition among scholars that institutions and institutional change are more complex than any paradigm portrays by itself and that it is time to begin exploring how paradigms complement and connect with each other in ways that might eventually generate new insights, if not a new problematic, for analyzing institutions. This volume seeks to advance that project by examining how different paradigms attack a common empirical problem, in this case the rise of neoliberalism.

To be sure, some of the chapters presented here embrace the principle of a second movement more wholeheartedly than others by trying to integrate insights from different paradigms in ways that shed new light on the rise of neoliberalism. Other contributors prefer to see how far their paradigm can go alone in explaining neoliberalism. They suggest, for instance, that those aspects of the phenomenon for which their approach cannot provide a satisfactory account may be explained better by one of the other paradigms. So, although not every chapter in this volume demonstrates or even aspires to the sort of paradigmatic cross-fertilization and integration that some scholars advocate, the volume does point the way toward more fruitful interactions among institutionalist paradigms — interactions that can further the second movement in institutional analysis.

In addition to the unique insights of each chapter, the volume as a whole makes several important points, which we elaborate in the concluding chapter. At an empirical level, it shows, first, that the concept of neoliberalism is more complex, diverse, contested, and open to interpretation than is often recognized. Several chapters demonstrate that neoliberalism is less a coherent totality, as is often assumed, than a loose conglomeration of institutions, ideas, and policy prescriptions from which actors pick and choose depending on prevailing political, economic, social, historical, and institutional conditions. The results can be either contradictory or complementary, and often vary across as well as within countries. Institutional analysis brings all of this clearly into view even though the process of picking and choosing can be viewed from many different angles, depending on the institutionalist paradigm at work. Second, it is a profound exaggeration to argue that there is widespread convergence toward a common set of neoliberal institutions, but it is also wrong to suggest that there is no convergence whatsoever. The truth is in between, rooted in the notion that neoliberalism does not so much involve *deregulation* as *re-regulation* of economic activity. Third, states are much less incapacitated by the rise of neoliberalism than is often appreciated. Instead, states can block, adapt to, mediate, and in some cases even reverse neoliberal tendencies. Finally, contrary to what the proponents of neoliberalism assert, market deregulation does not necessarily yield more efficient economic behavior than do other institutional arrangements.

At a theoretical level, the volume indicates that differences in methodological approach do not preclude a second movement in institutional analysis, as some have suggested, even though different approaches tend to be associated with different paradigms. As discussed in the conclusion, such a movement has begun recently and involves a variety of strategies: linking paradigms by specifying the contexts under which different causal processes operate; blending insights from different paradigms to show how the causal factors of one paradigm interact or are nested with those of another; identifying analytic problems shared by different paradigms; and subsuming arguments from one paradigm into those of another. More importantly, significant theoretical payoffs can be gained from a second movement. First, the fact that debates about the relative explanatory power of these paradigms keep recurring in the social science fields of political economy, historical sociology, comparative politics, international relations, organizational analysis, and others suggests that no paradigm has a monopoly on the truth.[2] By trying to transcend paradigmatic boundaries, scholars can discover a wider, more complex array of mechanisms of institutional change than each paradigm generally can alone. They can also identify areas where paradigms overlap, where they complement or supplement each other, and where paradigms describe different parts of the empirical world (Ruggie 1998, p. 885). Indeed, this volume yields all of these benefits, but particularly insights about the many mechanisms of institutional change — such as political struggle, diffusion, imitation, translation, learning and experimentation — that affected the rise of neoliberalism. Second, engaging in construc-

4

JOHN CAMPBELL AND OVE PEDERSEN

tive dialogue across paradigms can advance research agendas on all sides by raising new questions about the causes and effects of institutional development that have been neglected previously (Kahler 1998, p. 940). For instance, debates among advocates of these paradigms have spawned a wave of empirical studies that seek to adjudicate the manner in which cognitive, normative, and formal regulatory institutions — each representing a different institutionalist approach — affect policy, economic performance, and institutional change (e.g., Hall 1997). This is a theme in several of our chapters. Finally, advocates for a second movement have argued that the debate needs to be pushed from the level of theoretical polemic, of claims and counterclaims, to the level of empirical research in order to see how well each paradigm explains real-world phenomena (Kahler 1998, p. 922; Lichbach 1997, p. 266). In doing so, scholars are more likely to arrive at a better understanding and more accurate theoretical account of empirical reality (Keck and Sikkink 1998, pp. 210–11). Certainly, the empirical insights offered by contributors to this volume underscore this point.

Of course, several excellent volumes have been published in which scholars from a *single* institutionalist paradigm studied a *wide variety* of empirical phenomena in order to demonstrate the analytical power of their approach.[3] This was a necessary and constructive first step in the development of institutional analysis because it defined different approaches and established the terrain for debate among them. In the end, however, it also led more to the construction of barriers than to the building of bridges among paradigms.

This volume is much different because it presents work by authors operating from *different* paradigms who have agreed to focus their attention on a *common*, albeit complex, empirical subject. In doing so, it strives toward four goals. First, it represents the state of the art in using the new paradigms of institutional analysis. Second, it reveals the comparative virtues of each paradigm by turning them all to an analysis of a common empirical problem, the rise of neoliberalism. Third, it identifies possibilities for rapprochement, crossfertilization, and integration among paradigms. Finally, it contributes to our understanding of the rise of neoliberalism. In sum, this volume is both a *demonstration* of how scholars from different theoretical traditions practice their craft and an empirically based *comparison* of different approaches to the analysis of institutions that helps show how scholars might begin to contribute more systematically to the second movement in institutional analysis.

This volume is *not* an attempt to adjudicate which paradigm is somehow the "best." As it demonstrates, each paradigm has its own advantages and disadvantages, particularly when it comes to explaining a phenomenon as complex as the rise of neoliberalism. Nor does it claim that a second movement in institutional analysis is inevitable. This would be naive, if not utopian, insofar as it ignores how scholars thrive on carving out and defending various theoretical niches for themselves. Nevertheless, this volume indicates that theoretical headway can be made by considering the ways in which different paradigms may inform one another through empirical research.

Political-Economic Intersections with New Institutional Analysis

It seems particularly fitting to compare and evaluate different institutionalist paradigms by deploying them for an empirical analysis of neoliberalism. Neoliberalism is itself a heterogeneous set of institutions consisting of various ideas, social and economic policies, and ways of organizing political and economic activity that are quite different from others. Ideally, it includes formal institutions, such as minimalist welfare-state, taxation, and business-regulation programs; flexible labor markets and decentralized capital-labor relations unencumbered by strong unions and collective bargaining; and the absence of barriers to international capital mobility. It includes institutionalized normative principles favoring free-market solutions to economic problems, rather than bargaining or indicative planning, and a dedication to controlling inflation even at the expense of full employment. It includes institutionalized cognitive principles, notably a deep, taken-for-granted belief in neoclassical economics. In many ways it is the antithesis to the Fordist-Keynesian institutions that preceded it in the advanced capitalist countries during the three decades following the Second World War (e.g., Hall 1998, 1993; Locke and Thelen 1995; Piore and Sabel 1984). If the new institutionalist paradigms are worthwhile, they should be able to account for the emergence of this very important set of institutions. They should be able to show how nations adopted new ideas, pursued different policies, and ultimately reorganized political-economic activity in ways that were fundamentally different from what had previously been the case.

It also seems fitting to use institutional analysis to view neoliberalism because some versions of institutional analysis were developed to explain the same set of political and economic problems that triggered debates over the desirability of neoliberalism in the first place. Other versions of institutional analysis were not stimulated so directly by these problems, but still had profound theoretical implications for some of neoliberalism's core precepts.

More specifically, in an effort to understand why some advanced capitalist countries were more likely to suffer stagflation after the collapse of the Bretton Woods agreement in 1971 and the first oil embargo in 1973, scholars examined the different national institutions within which political and economic decision making was embedded. Building on earlier literature in comparative political economy (e.g., Shonfield 1965), many argued that differences in economic performance during the 1970s depended on whether liberal, statist, or corporatist institutions prevailed. Indeed, much of this literature maintained that corporatist arrangements were superior to the others insofar as they tended

to be associated with lower inflation, lower unemployment, and less labor unrest, as well as higher rates of productivity growth and technological innovation (Goldthorpe 1984; Gourevitch 1986; Hibbs 1987; Katzenstein 1978;
Lindberg and Maier 1985). Much of this literature laid the foundation for what
later came to be known as *historical institutionalism*.

As this literature began to emerge, scholars, particularly in the Scandinavian countries, who recognized that complex and important institutional differences existed *among* the corporatist countries and, by implication, among
liberal and statist ones as well, voiced concern that the emergent comparative
literature overemphasized the formal aspects of institutions at the expense of
others. Having been influenced by the development of discourse and linguistic analysis in Europe (e.g., Foucault 1991, 1969; Latour and Woolgar
1986; Ricouer 1983; Wagner, Wittrock, and Whitely 1991), they argued that
the comparativists neglected how institutions also consist of discursive elements that shape political and economic perceptions, the definition of actors'
interests and, ultimately, behavior. Moreover, they believed that differences
in the discursive side of institutions helped explain variation in public policy
and economic performance among corporatist countries. For example, they
credited Denmark's remarkable success in reducing its budget deficits during
the mid-1980s to the ability of its leaders to utilize the principles of a well-
institutionalized discourse, stressing social cooperation and consensus building, which enabled the major social partners to redefine their interests in terms
of bringing the budget under control. This critique represented another body
of work that also sought to explain the relative success of corporatist arrangements, but with a more multidimensional approach to institutional analysis
(e.g., Nielsen and Pedersen 1991; Pedersen 1991, 1993). We refer to this literature as *discursive institutionalism*. Eventually, scholars from other theoretical
traditions in political economy began to incorporate the discursive approach
into their work, often in their accounts of the rise of neoliberalism (e.g., Block
1996; Bourdieu 1998; Schmidt 1999, 2000).

As stagflation persisted and in some cases worsened, doubts emerged in the
late 1970s and early 1980s about the efficacy and desirability of corporatism
and political space opened up for neoliberal experiments (Kitschelt et al.
1999b). This was exacerbated by the growing belief that economic activity was
becoming more globally oriented; that the capacities of nation-states to manage their economies were being subverted accordingly; that the competitive
position of advanced countries required more institutional flexibility, especially in the organization of labor markets and production, in order to better
respond to global economic imperatives; and that institutional rigidities were
contributing to economic problems (e.g., Ohmae 1990; Piore and Sabel 1984;
Reich 1991). In turn, some governments began to reduce welfare-state programs and abandon centralized corporatist bargaining and the indicative planning that had flourished earlier in so many countries (Lash and Urry 1987).

Institutions drew attention once again but this time as impediments to international competitiveness. Scholars had created the intellectual justification for this neoliberal turn years earlier through public choice theory, the Austrian school of economics, monetarism, and conservative liberalism (Kelley 1997, chap. 2). An especially important and related literature gained prominence during the 1980s and early 1990s that focused on how rational economic actors pursuing their short-term interests tend to build political and economic institutions that often stifle technological innovation, economic efficiency, and long-term economic growth (e.g., North 1990; Ostrom 1990). Some of this work was directly concerned with explaining stagflation and other economic problems of the late 1970s (e.g., Olson 1982). Of course, rational actor models had been around for years, and the impetus for *rational choice institutionalism* came as much from academic debates as it did from concerns with contemporary economic problems (e.g., Swedberg 1990, chaps. 6, 9). Nevertheless, its development intersected and often provided insights into the problems that precipitated neoliberal experiments.

Early work in *organizational institutionalism* was not concerned with problems of stagflation, market deregulation, and the like. Instead, it was done by scholars who were interested in showing how organizations such as schools, museums and hospitals changed their institutional practices as new cultural scripts and schema diffused through organizational environments, often at the international level, and served symbolic and ceremonial purposes at least as much as utilitarian ones (DiMaggio and Powell 1983; Meyer et al. 1977; Meyer and Rowan 1977; Thomas et al. 1987). However, these scholars reacted to the emergence of historical and rational choice institutionalism in ways that had significant implications for some of neoliberalism's central tenets.

Organizational institutionalists charged that both rational choice and historical institutionalism systematically neglected the importance of norms, cultural scripts, cognitive frames, and meaning systems. They argued that these factors heavily mediated whatever tendencies there might be for actors to build institutions on the basis of their self-interests (e.g., Dobbin 1994a; Fligstein 1990, 1998; Soysal 1994) and that these influences were often quite positive for the economic performance of firms, markets, and national political economies (Abolafia 1996; Baker 1984; Fligstein 1990, 1998; Nelson and Winter 1982). As a result, organizational institutionalism signified a double-edged critique of neoliberalism. On the one hand, neoliberalism assumed that actors were naturally driven by a self-interested, instrumental rationality, but organizational institutionalists showed that this rationality, like others, was socially constructed and culturally and historically contingent. In other words, there was nothing natural about it (Dobbin 1994b; Meyer, Boli, and Thomas 1987). On the other hand, neoliberalism maintained that if actors were left to freely pursue their self-interests, then the economy would yield optimal results. Yet organizational institutionalists showed that liberal market systems did not necessarily perform better than statist or corporatist forms of capitalism (Dobbin 1994a; Fligstein 1998) and that institutionally unbridled self-interest might actually undermine economic performance (Abolafia 1996).

During the 1990s world events continued to invigorate institutional analysis. First, the collapse of communism precipitated new experiments with neoliberalism as many new postcommunist governments distanced themselves from anything that resembled state economic intervention or planning. Poland's shock therapy program in the early 1990s was perhaps the most dramatic example, but other countries engaged in similar experiments. Of course, international organizations, such as the International Monetary Fund and the World Bank, encouraged these efforts, much as they continued to do in Latin America and East Asia (Greskovits 1998). However, when it became obvious that postcommunist societies lacked the institutional foundations required for the rapid development of capitalism and that this severely undermined neoliberal policies and created all sorts of problems in the region, institutional analysts moved into the breach to better explain what was going on and how to proceed (e.g., Amsden, Kochanowicz, and Taylor 1994; Campbell and Pedersen 1996; Elster, Offe, and Preuss 1998; Przeworski 1995; Stark and Bruszt 1998). Second, the Asian financial crisis in the late 1990s provoked much soul-searching among politicians and academics, some of whom had advocated neoliberalism earlier in order to promote economic development in the region but who in retrospect admitted publicly that more institutionally sensitive policies might have worked better (Kristof and Sanger 1999). Finally, recognition that neoliberal experiments in the advanced capitalist countries had contributed to rising unemployment, income inequality, and other problems generated increasing interest in the institutionalized discourses that continued to make neoliberalism so appealing politically despite its less attractive side effects (Block 1996; Bourdieu 1998).

The Paradigms

In sum, by the mid-1990s four distinct paradigms of institutional analysis had developed. They constitute the paradigmatic foundations upon which the remaining essays in this volume are built. Their characteristics have been described in great detail elsewhere (e.g., Campbell 1997b; Finnemore 1996; Hall and Taylor 1996; Lichbach 1997; Pedersen 1991; Peters 1999; Thelen 1999; Scott 1995). Nevertheless, we briefly highlight below some of their most relevant features insofar as our project is concerned. This discussion is summarized in table 1-1. However, it is important to understand that table 1-1 represents these paradigms as ideal types, each of which really represents a somewhat *heterogeneous family* of theories. Like all families, there are often disagreements *within* each paradigm over theoretical and other issues (e.g., Hechter and

Kanazawa 1997; Hall and Taylor 1996, 1998; Hay and Wincott 1998; Knight in this volume; Schneiberg and Clemens forthcoming; Strang and Bradburn in this volume). For example, rational choice institutionalism encompasses transaction-cost theory, principle-agent theory, game theory, and even some versions of traditional pluralist theory insofar as they all assume that actors pursue their self-interests and build political and economic institutions accordingly. As a result, attempts at brief characterization necessarily provide a glimpse of only the rough contours of each paradigm beneath which much important variation may exist, not to mention fuzziness at the boundaries between paradigms.[4] Still, we provide such a sketch in order to alert readers to the most important theoretical and methodological issues at stake throughout this volume.

To begin with, at its most basic level each paradigm is motivated by a different *problematic*. The rational choice view is concerned with how rationally motivated actors build institutions to solve problems of exchange, such as reducing transaction costs and managing principle-agent relations, and the production of collective goods (North 1990, 1981; Ostrom 1990; Williamson 1985). Historical institutionalists are more often concerned with how variations in political or other institutions shape actors' capacities for action, policy making, and institution building (Steinmo, Thelen, and Longstreth 1992). Organizational institutionalists are often interested in how rationality and the rationalization of institution building are culturally and cognitively constituted and legitimized (Thomas et al. 1987). The principal concern of discursive institutionalists is in how institutions are constituted, framed, and transformed through the confrontation of new and old discursive structures — that is, systems of symbolic meaning codified in language that influence how actors observe, interpret, and reason in particular social settings (Kjær and Pedersen, this volume).[5] This is important because, as this volume illustrates, these problematics influence the sorts of questions that researchers find interesting and worth studying. As a result, when they set out to study an empirical phenomenon like the rise of neoliberalism, they may end up examining different parts of it and thus making discoveries that other paradigms might miss given the different questions they tend to ask. This is certainly true of the contributions to this volume.

For example, different paradigms theorize different *conditions of change*. Rational choice institutionalists posit that actors transform institutions when material factors, such as prices or transaction costs, shift and they perceive that the benefits of doing so will exceed the costs (e.g., Moe 1987; North 1990). Historical institutionalists concur that institutional change occurs when actors perceive that it is in their political or economic interests to pursue it — notably, in the face of major crises or other shocks like depression, civil unrest, or war — and that institutions shape the capacities and therefore the strategies with which actors pursue change (e.g., Gourevitch 1986). However, they also main-

TABLE 1-1
Comparison of Rational Choice, Historical, Organizational, and Discursive Institutionalism

	Rational Choice Institutionalism	Historical Institutionalism	Organizational Institutionalism	Discursive Institutionalism
Problematic	How do institutions solve problems of exchange and collective goods production?	How do institutions shape capacities for action and institution building?	How are institutions culturally constituted, rationalized and legitimized?	How are institutions constituted, framed, and transformed through discourse?
Conditions of Change	Shift in costs and benefits	Crisis and exogenous shock Contradictory institutional logics	Increased environmental uncertainty Political-cultural shifts	Perceived political-economic crisis Presence of alternative discourses
Mechanisms of Change	Interest-based struggle, conflict, bargaining, strategic gaming	Interest, idea, and ideologically-based struggle, conflict, bargaining Learning, feedback, and experimentation	Imitation, diffusion, translation	Translation, displacement, bricolage
Epistemology and Methodology	Positivist deductive search for general theory	Comparative inductive search for historically specific theory	Positivist deductive search for theory Interpretive inductive search for historically specific explanation	Interpretive inductive search for historically specific explanation Archaeology of texts

tain that because different institutions may operate according to different logics and that these logics may occasionally contradict each other, the impetus
for institutional change may also be endogenous to an existing constellation of
institutions (Thelen 1999; see also Schneiberg 1999). Organizational institutionalists suggest that institutional change occurs under conditions of environmental uncertainty where actors, often confused about what the most
rational or cost-effective strategy should be, adopt whatever culturally appropriate or legitimate practices and models they find around them. As a result,
institutional change is driven more by a logic of appropriateness than a logic
of instrumentality (Dobbin 1994a; Fligstein 1990). Moreover, and in sharp
contrast to the other paradigms, some organizational institutionalists also argue
that in addition to changes in material conditions, political-cultural shifts — in
particular the emergence of new models of appropriate political, organizational, or economic behavior — often stimulate institutional change (Boli and
Thomas 1999; Soysal 1994; Thomas et al. 1987). Discursive institutionalists
maintain that perceptions of institutional crisis coupled with the presence of
alternative discourses, through which actors define and interpret crises in new
ways and propose new solutions to them, are essential conditions for institutional change (Wittrock and Wagner 1996). Subsequent chapters reveal that
all of these factors helped foster neoliberalism.

Paradigms also take different positions on the *mechanisms through which
change occurs*. Rational choice theorists generally see interest-based struggle,
conflict, bargaining, or strategic gaming as the chief mechanisms of change.
For example, ruling elites struggle with each other and the citizenry to build
political institutions to extract taxes and other resources from society (Levi
1997b, 1988). Historical institutionalists also view struggle and conflict as the
primary mechanism through which institutional change occurs, although they
see that ideas and ideologies as well as interests drive these struggles (Hattam
1993; Peters 1999; Rueschemeyer and Skocpol 1996). Recently, they have also
begun to pay close attention to how institutional change may stem from trial-
and-error experimentation, learning, and the effects of policy feedback (Hall
1993; Pierson 1993). For both rational choice and historical institutionalists,
outcomes may vary considerably across cases, depending on prevailing institutional, historical, and political conditions. In contrast, much organizational
institutionalism suggests that because institutional change is largely a process
of modeling appropriate behavior, it is a much less conflictual process of imitation through which new institutional forms diffuse through fields of organizations or across nation-states — a process whose outcome is described in terms
of institutional isomorphism, homogeneity, or convergence (DiMaggio and
Powell 1983; Strang and Meyer 1993). More recent proponents of organizational institutionalism view the process of change more as one of translation,
where organizations or polities adopt new models, but in ways that are heavily
mediated by prevailing institutional conditions that result in somewhat more

differentiated institutional outcomes (Soysal 1994). Similarly, discursive institutionalists focus on how elements of one discourse are translated into another and displace older definitions of problems and solutions. Thus, old and new discursive elements are combined in innovative ways that facilitate institutional change through discursive alliances or bricolage (Wittrock and Wagner 1996; see also Douglas 1986, pp. 66–67; Campbell 1997a). Whether these mechanisms are mutually exclusive is a question that we address in chapter 10 based on the analyses provided by our contributors, but the important point here is that specifying and examining these processes sheds light on the degree to which neoliberalism has spread and penetrated in different countries and cases around the world.

Finally, each paradigm tends to adopt different *epistemological and methodological conventions*. Rational choice institutionalists subscribe to a positivist approach that emphasizes deducing hypotheses from theories based on the microanalytic principles of methodological individualism and tests them by studying bargaining and exchange relations in order to develop general theories that hold across time and space (e.g., Bates et al. 1998; Kiser and Hechter 1998). In contrast, although historical institutionalists are not averse to hypothesis testing, they often compare cases of similar types, such as groups of advanced capitalist economies or democratic states, in order to inductively generate theories about political economic systems that are more specific to particular times and places (Katznelson 1997; Hall 1997). For many years organizational institutionalists have taken a positivist approach, although deducing hypotheses from much different theoretical principles from those of rational choice. However, more recent practitioners have adopted far more interpretive and inductive strategies in order to better identify the processes and mechanisms through which actors try to make sense of their situations and attribute meaning to their institutions (Schneiberg and Clemens forthcoming). This very inductive approach is also typical of discursive institutionalism, which hails from a hermeneutic tradition, particularly insofar as it requires that researchers perform an archaeology of archival or textual material. In the extreme, the concern is for developing historically specific descriptions and explanations, not causal theories in a conventional sense (Bourdieu 1998; Foucault 1991, 1969; Pedersen 1991). The fact that organizational institutionalism, if not representatives of the other paradigms, appears to be adopting an especially varied set of methodologies in order to advance their theoretical position is important because it suggests that perhaps the rather stark methodological differences that often appear to separate these paradigms do not, in fact, pose insurmountable obstacles to theoretical cross-fertilization and integration, another issue tackled in chapter 10.

Of course, each paradigm has unique theoretical roots too complex to review here in detail. Rational choice evolved from neoclassical economics as indicated, notably, by the fact that both embrace the principles of methodological individualism. However, it largely eschewed the neoclassical obses-sion with formal modeling at the expense of empirical analysis and insisted in-creasingly on theorizing how institutions affect the strategic calculations and information costs of individuals (Levi 1997a). Historical institutionalists re-jected methodological individualism as well as excessively broad, often func-tionalist, analyses of society by adopting Weber's comparative political econ-omy approach, including an interest in the potential autonomy of state actors and institutions, and Marxism's concern with crisis theory and class struggle (Katznelson 1997). Organizational institutionalism developed in critical reac-tion to both the behavioralism and functionalism of the social sciences after the Second World War and rational choice theory more recently, and was heav-ily influenced by the social constructionist theories of phenomenology, sym-bolic interactionism, and cognitive psychology (DiMaggio 1997; DiMaggio and Powell 1991). Discursive institutionalism was influenced, on the one hand, by linguistics, hermeneutics, and the anthropological structuralism of Claude Levi-Strauss, Mary Douglas, John Searle, and others and, on the other hand, by the critical social philosophy of theorists like Paul Ricouer and Michel Foucault (Pedersen 1991). It represented a rejection of empiricism, positivism, behavioralism, and Marxist materialism, particularly the French structuralist variety, and was more concerned with social criticism.

Yet despite these widely varying theoretical origins, all four of these per-spectives share a common concern for locating human behavior in institu-tional context. What makes these paradigms "new" and, indeed, what con-tributed to their origins at a theoretical level was a rejection of excessively general theories of social structure and individual behavior. As a result, they all stress the importance of more middle-range explanation than did their fore-runners. Even rational choice institutionalists, who strive for broad theoretical generalizations more than do theorists of other institutionalist paradigms, take history and context much more seriously than do neoclassical theorists (e.g., Kiser and Hechter 1998; Knight 1992; Levi 1988; Ostrom 1990). Notably, many rational choice theorists now advocate using a methodological approach known as *analytic narratives*, where researchers blend the analytic tools of game theory with thick historical descriptions of empirical cases, carefully specify the scope conditions of their theory, and only later, once the theory has been refined in light of the empirical cases, test it against "out of sample" cases in order to generalize more broadly (Bates et al. 1998; Levi 1999, 1997b).

This is an important point. One of the reasons why institutional analysis has become so important is that it fills a vacuum left by other scholars who had de-veloped a variety of much different paradigms, which in the end turned out not to be very good for explaining empirical reality. Two examples will suffice. First, structural functionalism made sweeping predictions in the 1950s about the gradual, evolutionary development of increasingly well integrated indus-trial societies, the inevitability of modernization, and the like. Yet the social up-

heavals of the 1960s and the failure of many developing countries to really
"modernize" and become independent democratic societies discredited this
approach, as dependency theory, world systems theory, and recent versions of
development theory have all shown (Haggard and Kaufman 1992; Wallerstein
1976). Second, neo-Marxism's determination to theorize universal laws associated with the capitalist mode of production was also flawed in that it could
not adequately account for wide variations in the organization and performance of different societies within advanced capitalism. Indeed, during the
late 1970s several prominent neo-Marxists began to incorporate rudimentary
institutional analyses into their work precisely to grapple with these problems
(e.g., Jessop 1982; Poulantzas 1978). Nor was neo-Marxism able to account for
the empirical realities of state socialist societies, particularly the persistent in-
equalities and flagging economic performance of both the Soviet Union and
East European countries prior to the collapse of their communist regimes
(Konrad and Szelenyi 1979).

Eventually, scholars became dissatisfied with such "grand theory" (Mills
1959) and began to return to the classical roots of sociology, political economy,
and political science by rediscovering institutions (e.g., March and Olsen
1989; Evans, Rueschemeyer, and Skocpol 1985). Max Weber, Emile Durkheim, Karl Polanyi, and others whose work focused sharply on how political
and economic behavior was firmly embedded in institutions became the hub
of an intellectual renaissance — the new institutional analysis. By adopting a
middle-range approach to theory, scholars found that institutional analysis offered an escape from the quagmire of grand theory and provided the kind of
analytic leverage necessary to account for both historical and cross-national
variation in political and economic activity. Of course, we must guard against
the possibility that the old debates that distracted us from these classical traditions and created the opportunity for the ascendance of grand theory do not
recur and undermine the institutionalist project that has blossomed. Slipping
back into arguments about whether structure or agency ought to enjoy pride
of place in our theories or whether macrolevel analysis is more appropriate
than microlevel analysis may present just such dangers. By sticking to middle-
range theorizing, institutional analysis provides ways to avoid these pitfalls.

Outline of the Volume

Contributors to this volume represent all of the major approaches to the study
of institutions. In chapter 2, Jack Knight develops a game theoretic account of
the spread of neoliberalism through Latin America that relies on rational
choice theory to adjudicate among a variety of more specific theories of institutional change and development. Edgar Kiser and Aaron Laing also adopt a
rational choice perspective in chapter 3 but question how extensively the

spread of neoliberalism has really been insofar as government taxation and spending policies are concerned. Indeed, they provide evidence that neither policy area has changed in the advanced capitalist countries in ways predicted in standard accounts of the rise of neoliberalism. They also offer a rational choice explanation for this anomaly.

In chapter 4, Bruce Western adopts a historical institutionalist view to examine how among OECD countries neoliberal institutions mediate and affect labor market outcomes. He too suggests that the shift toward neoliberalism may not have been as extensive as is sometimes assumed and that neoliberal outcomes may not be as efficient as often claimed. In chapter 5, Bruce Carruthers, Sarah Babb, and Terence Halliday use historical institutionalism to show that although central bank institutions have gained more autonomy from governments, thereby shifting monetary policy in a neoliberal direction, this has created a much harsher competitive environment for firms, so governments have compensated by softening their bankruptcy laws in very non-neoliberal directions. Again, the degree to which neoliberalism results in more efficient institutional outcomes is drawn into question.

In chapter 6, David Strang and Ellen Bradburn explore how neoliberal reforms in U.S. health care institutions emerged through processes of diffusion and imitation that are typically theorized by organizational institutionalists. In chapter 7, John Campbell shows how the rise of neoliberalism in the United States involved a contest between essential neoliberal principles, notably supply-side economics, and alternative industrial policy models that called for more, not less, political intervention and institutional innovation. He argues that neoliberalism's eventual victory during the early 1980s stemmed in part from its cognitive and normative advantages. His argument deliberately blends insights from organizational institutionalism with historical institutionalism.

Colin Hay seeks in chapter 8 to explain neoliberal reforms in Britain before and after Margaret Thatcher came to power. He finds that the adoption of neoliberalism followed a pattern of "punctuated evolution," in which some discursive elements of the neoliberal model were adopted long before others. This is another effort to work near the edges of two paradigms by exploring how discursive and historical institutionalism might inform each other. Chapter 9, by Peter Kjær and Ove K. Pedersen, is located more centrally within discursive institutionalism. They investigate how policy makers translated certain neoliberal concepts and principles into industrial policy in order to facilitate institutional change in Denmark during the 1970s and 1980s. As a result, Danish neoliberalism stemmed from the combination of old and new discursive elements.

The fact that some contributors represent the mainstream of their paradigms while others gravitate toward the margins, exploring how theirs might intersect with others, is a crucial point to keep in mind. Chapter 10 addresses this and other issues by taking stock of all the chapters. It examines the methodological approaches that contributors have utilized and argues that methodological differences per se do not preclude a second movement in institutional analysis, as others have suggested. It discusses the payoffs to a second movement by identifying areas of complementarity, overlap, and cross-fertilization and comparing how different paradigms explain the conditions and mechanisms of change, noted above, that are associated with neoliberalism. It also suggests several strategies for promoting a second movement in institutional analysis. Finally, it considers some of the most important empirical payoffs that these chapters offer about the rise of neoliberalism itself.

Notes

1. For comparisons of "old" and "new" institutional paradigms in sociology, economics, and political science, see, for example, DiMaggio and Powell 1991; Hirsch and Lounsbury 1997; Nee 1998; Peters 1999, chap. 1; and Stinchcombe 1997. We use the term "paradigm" cautiously, recognizing that it is often associated with the work of Thomas Kuhn (1962) and his particular philosophy of science, which has been heavily criticized. Without implying a particular philosophy of science, we understand a paradigm to be simply an analytic approach to social scientific inquiry that provides model problems, questions, and solutions based on a set of ontological, epistemological, and methodological principles. Different paradigms are based on different principles. Whether or not paradigms can or should be merged, blended, or transcended by evolutionary or revolutionary empirical breakthroughs, a subject dear to Kuhn, remains an open question for us.

2. For examples of these debates in the field of international relations, see *International Organization* 1998; in comparative politics, see Lichbach and Zuckerman 1997; in political economy, see Hall 1997; in political science, see Peters 1999; in historical sociology, see the *American Journal of Sociology* ("Symposium" 1998); in organizational sociology, see Scott 1995.

3. For example, see Evans, Rueschemeyer, and Skocpol 1985; Katzenstein 1978; and Steinmo, Thelen, and Longstreth 1992 for historical institutionalism; see Alt and Shepsle 1990 and Hechter, Opp, and Wippler 1990 for rational choice institutionalism; see Powell and DiMaggio 1991; Scott and Christensen 1995; Scott and Meyer 1994; and Thomas et al. 1987 for organizational institutionalism.

4. Although heterogeneity *within* paradigms is often the more difficult problem for building typologies, fuzziness *between* paradigms can be too. For example, considering how systems of meaning affect how actors interpret their problems and seek to transform policies and institutions has long been a preoccupation for organizational institutionalists, who insist that cognitive and normative scripts influence institution building (e.g., Dobbin 1994a). Similarly, it has long been a concern for discursive institutionalists who seek to understand how local intellectual differences do the same (Wittrock and Wagner 1996). However, the issue has also become important lately for historical institutionalists, who are interested in the effects of "ideas" on policy making (Berman 1998; Hall 1993; Hattam 1993; McNamara 1998), and rational choice insti-

tutionalists, who want to understand how cognitive structures help actors define their interests and strategies (Knight and North 1997). Convergence of this sort is one indication of the second movement in institutional analysis.

5. Organizational and discursive institutionalism share a strong interest in the effects that cognitive structures have on institution building, change, and policy making. However, organizational institutionalism generally takes these structures as given and seeks to explain how effects emanate from them. Discursive institutionalism is also interested in this but also pays close attention to how these structures are socially constructed in the first place.

References

Abolafia, Mitchel. 1996. *Making Markets.* Cambridge: Harvard University Press.

Albert, Michel. 1993. *Capitalism vs. Capitalism.* New York: Four Walls, Eight Windows.

Alt, James A., and Kenneth A. Shepsle, editors. 1990. *Perspectives on Positive Political Economy.* New York: Cambridge University Press.

Amsden, Alice H., Jacek Kochanowicz, and Lance Taylor. 1994. *The Market Meets Its Match.* Cambridge: Harvard University Press.

Baker, Wayne. 1984. "The Social Structure of a Securities Market." *American Journal of Sociology* 89:775–811.

Bates, Robert, Avner Grief, Margaret Levi, Jean-Laurent Rosenthal, and Barry Weingast. 1998. *Analytic Narratives.* Princeton: Princeton University Press.

Berger, Suzanne, and Ronald Dore. 1996. *National Diversity and Global Capitalism.* Ithaca: Cornell University Press.

Berman, Sheri. 1998. *The Social Democratic Moment: Ideas and Politics in the Making of Interwar Europe.* Cambridge: Harvard University Press.

Block, Fred. 1996. *The Myth of the Vampire State.* New York: New Press.

Boli, John, and George M. Thomas. 1999. *Constructing World Culture: International Nongovernmental Organizations since 1875.* Stanford, CA: Stanford University Press.

Bourdieu, Pierre. 1998. *Acts of Resistance: Against the Tyranny of the Market.* New York: New Press.

Boyer, Robert, and Daniel Drache. 1996. *States against Markets: The Limits of Globalization.* London: Routledge.

Campbell, John L. 1997a. "Mechanisms of Evolutionary Change in Economic Governance: Interaction, Interpretation and Bricolage." Pp. 10–32 in *Evolutionary Economics and Path Dependence,* edited by Lars Magnusson and Jan Ottosson. Cheltenham, UK: Edward Elgar.

——— . 1997b. "Recent Trends in Institutional Political Economy." *International Journal of Sociology and Social Policy* 17(7/8)15–56.

Campbell, John L., and Ove K. Pedersen, editors. 1996. *Legacies of Change.* New York: Aldine de Gruyter.

Crouch, Colin, and Wolfgang Streeck, editors. 1997. *Political Economy of Modern Capitalism.* Thousand Oaks, CA: Sage.

David, Paul A. 1985. "Clio and the Economics of QWERTY." *American Economic Review* 75(2)332–37.

DiMaggio, Paul J. 1997. "Culture and Cognition." *Annual Review of Sociology* 23:263–87.

DiMaggio, Paul J., and Walter W. Powell. 1983. "The Iron Cage Revisited: Institutional Isomorphism and Collective Rationality in Organizational Fields." *American Sociological Review* 48:147–60.

———. 1991. "Introduction." Pp. 1–40 in *The New Institutionalism in Organizational Analysis*, edited by Walter W. Powell and Paul J. DiMaggio. Chicago: University of Chicago Press.

Dobbin, Frank. 1994a. *Forging Industrial Policy*. New York: Cambridge University Press.

———. 1994b. "Cultural Models of Organization: The Social Construction of Rational Organizing Principles." Pp. 117–42 in *The Sociology of Culture*, edited by Diana Crane. Cambridge: Blackwell.

Douglas, Mary. 1986. *How Institutions Think*. Syracuse, NY: Syracuse University Press.

Elster, Jon, Claus Offe, and Ulrich K. Preuss. 1998. *Institutional Design in Postcommunist Societies*. New York: Cambridge University Press.

Ethington, Philip J., and Eileen L. McDonagh. 1995. "The Common Space of Social Science Inquiry." *Polity* 28(1)85–90.

Evans, Peter, Dietrich Rueschemeyer, and Theda Skocpol, editors. 1985. *Bringing the State Back In*. New York: Cambridge University Press.

Finnemore, Martha. 1996. "Norms, Culture, and World Politics: Insights from Sociology's Institutionalism." *International Organization* 50(2)325–47.

Fligstein, Neil. 1990. *The Transformation of Corporate Control*. Cambridge: Harvard University Press.

———. 1998. *Ruling Markets: An Economic Sociology of Capitalist Economies*. Department of Sociology, University of California—Berkeley. Manuscript.

Foucault, Michel. 1969. *The Archaeology of Knowledge and the Discourse on Language*. New York: Harper Colophon.

———. 1991. "Politics and the Study of Discourse." Pp. 7–26 in *The Foucault Effect: Studies in Governmentality*, edited by Graham Burchell, Colin Gordon, and Peter Miller. London: Harvester Wheatsheaf.

Goldthorpe, John, editor. 1984. *Order and Conflict in Contemporary Capitalism*. Oxford: Clarendon Press.

Gourevitch, Peter. 1986. *Politics in Hard Times*. Ithaca: Cornell University Press.

Greskovits, Bela. 1998. *The Political Economy of Protest and Patience: East European and Latin American Transformations Compared*. Budapest: Central European University Press.

Haggard, Stephan, and Robert R. Kaufman, editors. 1992. *The Politics of Economic Adjustment*. Princeton: Princeton University Press.

Hall, Peter A. 1993. "Policy Paradigms, Social Learning, and the State: The Case of Economic Policymaking in Britain." *Comparative Politics* 25(3)275–96.

———. 1997. "The Role of Interests, Institutions, and Ideas in the Comparative Political Economy of Industrialized Nations." Pp. 174–207 in *Comparative Politics: Rationality, Culture, and Structure*, edited by Mark Lichbach and Alan Zuckerman. New York: Cambridge University Press.

———. 1998. "Organized Market Economies and Unemployment in Europe: Is It Finally Time to Accept Liberal Orthodoxy?" Paper presented at the Eleventh International Conference of Europeanists, Baltimore, MD.

Hall, Peter A., and Rosemary C. R. Taylor. 1996. "Political Science and the Three New Institutionalisms." *Political Studies* 64:936–57.

———. 1998. "The Potential of Historical Institutionalism: A Response to Hay and Wincott." *Political Studies* 48(5)958–62.

Hattam, Victoria C. 1993. *Labor Visions and State Power*. Princeton: Princeton University Press.

Hay, Colin, and Daniel Wincott. 1998. "Structure, Agency, and Historical Institutionalism." *Political Studies* 46(5)951–57.

Hechter, Michael, and Satoshi Kanazawa. 1997. "Sociological Rational Choice Theory." *Annual Review of Sociology* 23:191–214.

Hechter, Michael, Karl-Dieter Opp, and Reinhard Wippler, editors. 1990. *Social Institutions*. New York: Aldine de Gruyter.

Heilbroner, Robert, and William Milberg. 1995. *The Crisis of Vision in Modern Economic Thought*. New York: Cambridge University Press.

Hibbs, Douglas A. 1987. *The Political Economy of Industrial Democracies*. Cambridge: Harvard University Press.

Hirsch, Paul M. 1997. "Sociology without Social Structure: Neoinstitutional Theory Meets Brave New World." *American Journal of Sociology* 102:1702–23.

Hirsch, Paul M., and Michael Lounsbury. 1997. "Ending the Family Quarrel: Toward a Reconciliation of 'Old' and 'New' Institutionalisms." *American Behavioral Scientist* 40(4)406–18.

Hirst, Paul, and Grahame Thompson. 1996. *Globalization in Question*. London: Polity.

International Organization. 1998. (special issue on Theoretical Perspectives in International Relations). 52(4).

Jessop, Bob. 1982. *The Capitalist State*. New York: New York University Press.

Kahler, Miles. 1998. "Rationality in International Relations." *International Organization* 52(4)919–41.

Katzenstein, Peter, editor. 1978. *Between Power and Plenty*. Madison: University of Wisconsin Press.

Katznelson, Ira. 1997. "Structure and Configuration in Comparative Politics." Pp. 81–112 in *Comparative Politics: Rationality, Culture, and Structure*, edited by Mark Lichbach and Alan Zuckerman. New York: Cambridge University Press.

Keck, Margaret E., and Kathryn Sikkink. 1998. *Activists beyond Borders: Advocacy Networks in International Politics*. Ithaca: Cornell University Press.

Kelley, John L. 1997. *Bringing the Market Back In*. New York: New York University Press.

Kiser, Edgar, and Michael Hechter. 1991. "The Role of General Theory in Comparative-Historical Sociology." *American Journal of Sociology* 97:1–30.

———. 1998. "The Debate on Historical Sociology: Rational Choice Theory and Its Critics." *American Journal of Sociology* 104:785–816.

Kitschelt, Herbert, Peter Lange, Gary Marks, and John D. Stephens. 1999a. *Continuity and Change in Contemporary Capitalism*. New York: Cambridge University Press.

———. 1999b. "Introduction." Pp. 1–10 in *Continuity and Change in Contemporary Capitalism*. New York: Cambridge University Press.

Knight, Jack. 1992. *Institutions and Social Conflict.* New York: Cambridge University Press.

Knight, Jack, and Douglass North. 1997. "Explaining Economic Change: The Interplay between Cognition and Institutions." *Legal Theory* 3:211–26.

Konrad, George, and Ivan Szelenyi. 1979. *The Intellectuals on the Road to Class Power.* New York: Harcourt Brace Jovanovich.

Kristof, Nicholas D., and David E. Sanger. 1999. "How U.S. Wooed Asia to Let Cash Flow In." *New York Times,* February 16.

Kuhn, Thomas S. 1962. *The Structure of Scientific Revolutions.* Chicago: University of Chicago Press.

Lash, Scott, and John Urry. 1987. *The End of Organized Capitalism.* Madison: University of Wisconsin Press.

Latour, Bruno, and Steve Woolgar. 1986. *Laboratory Life: The Construction of Scientific Facts.* Princeton: Princeton University Press.

Levi, Margaret. 1988. *Of Rule and Revenue.* Berkeley and Los Angeles: University of California Press.

———. 1997a. "A Model, a Method, and a Map: Rational Choice in Comparative and Historical Analysis." Pp. 19–41 in *Comparative Politics: Rationality, Culture, and Structure,* edited by Mark Lichbach and Alan Zuckerman. New York: Cambridge University Press.

———. 1997b. *Consent, Dissent, and Patriotism.* New York: Cambridge University Press.

———. 1999. "Producing an Analytic Narrative." In *Critical Comparisons in Politics and Culture,* edited by John Bowen and Roger Petersen. New York: Cambridge University Press.

Lichbach, Mark I. 1997. "Social Theory and Comparative Politics." Pp. 239–76 in *Comparative Politics: Rationality, Culture, and Structure,* edited by Mark Lichbach and Alan Zuckerman. New York: Cambridge University Press.

Lichbach, Mark I., and Alan Zuckerman, editors. 1997. *Comparative Politics: Rationality, Culture, and Structure.* New York: Cambridge University Press.

Lindberg, Leon N., and Charles S. Maier, editors. 1985. *The Politics of Inflation and Economic Stagnation.* Washington DC: Brookings Institution.

Locke, Richard M., and Kathleen Thelen. 1995. "Apples and Oranges Revisited: Contextualized Comparisons and the Study of Comparative Labor Politics." *Politics and Society* 23(3)337–67.

March, James G., and Johan P. Olsen. 1989. *Rediscovering Institutions.* New York: Free Press.

McNamara, Kathleen R. 1998. *The Currency of Ideas: Monetary Politics in the European Union.* Ithaca: Cornell University Press.

Meyer, John W., John Boli, and George M. Thomas. 1987. "Ontology and Rationalization in the Western Cultural Account." Pp. 12–38 in *Institutional Structure: Constituting State, Society, and the Individual,* edited by George M. Thomas, John W. Meyer, Francisco O. Ramirez and John Boli. Newbury Park, CA: Sage.

Meyer, John W., Francisco O. Ramirez, Richard Rubinson and John Boli-Bennett. 1977. "The World Educational Revolution, 1950–1970." *Sociology of Education* 50:242–58.

Meyer, John W., and Brian Rowan. 1977. "Institutionalized Organizations: Formal Structure as Myth and Ceremony." *American Journal of Sociology* 83:340–63.

Mills, C. Wright. 1959. *The Sociological Imagination.* New York: Oxford University Press.

Moe, Terry M. 1987. "Interests, Institutions, and Positive Theory: The Politics of the NLRB." *Studies in American Political Development* 2:236–99.

Nee, Victor. 1998. "Sources of the New Institutionalism." Pp. 1–16 in *The New Institutionalism in Sociology,* edited by Mary C. Brinton and Victor Nee. New York: Russell Sage Foundation.

Nelson, Richard R., and Sidney G. Winter. 1982. *An Evolutionary Theory of Economic Change.* Cambridge: Harvard University Press.

Nielsen, Klaus, and Ove K. Pedersen. 1991. "From the Mixed to the Negotiated Economy: The Scandinavian Countries." Pp. 145–68 in *Morality, Rationality, and Efficiency,* edited by Richard M. Coughlin. New York: M. E. Sharpe.

North, Douglass. 1990. *Institutions, Institutional Change, and Economic Performance.* New York: Cambridge University Press.

———. 1981. *Structure and Change in Economic History.* New York: Norton.

Ohmae, Kenichi. 1990. *The Borderless World.* New York: HarperCollins.

Olson, Mancur. 1982. *The Rise and Decline of Nations.* New Haven: Yale University Press.

Ostrom, Eleanor. 1990. *Governing the Commons.* New York: Cambridge University Press.

Pedersen, Ove K. 1991. "Nine Questions to a Neo-Institutional Theory in Political Science." *Scandinavian Political Studies* 14(2)125–48.

———. 1993. "The Institutional History of the Danish Polity: From a Market and Mixed Economy to a Negotiated Economy." Pp. 277–300 in *Institutional Change: Theory and Empirical Findings,* edited by Sven-Erik Sjostrand. New York: M. E. Sharpe.

Peters, B. Guy. 1996. "Political Institutions, Old and New." Pp. 205–20 in *The New Handbook of Political Science,* edited by Robert Goodin and Hans-Dieter Klingemann. New York: Oxford University Press.

———. 1999. *Institutional Theory in Political Science: The "New Institutionalism."* New York: Pinter.

Pierson, Paul. 1993. "When Effect Becomes Cause: Policy Feedback and Political Change." *World Politics* 45:595–628.

Piore, Michael, and Charles Sabel. 1984. *The Second Industrial Divide.* New York: Basic Books.

Poulantzas, Nicos. 1978. *State, Power, Socialism.* London: New Left Books.

Powell, Walter W., and Paul J. DiMaggio, editors. 1991. *The New Institutionalism in Organizational Analysis.* Chicago: University of Chicago Press.

Przeworski, Adam. 1995. *Sustainable Democracy.* New York: Cambridge University Press.

Reich, Robert. 1991. *The Work of Nations.* New York: Vintage.

Ricouer, Paul. 1983. *Time and Narrative.* Vol. 1. Chicago: University of Chicago Press.

Rueschemeyer, Dietrich, and Theda Skocpol, editors. 1996. *States, Social Knowledge, and the Origins of Modern Social Policies.* Princeton: Princeton University Press.

Ruggie, John Gerard. 1998. "What Makes the World Hang Together? Neo-Utilitarianism and the Social Constructivist Challenge." *International Organization* 52(4)855–85.

Schmidt, Vivien A. 1999. "Discourse and the Legitimation of Economic and Social Policy Change in Europe." Paper presented at the Sixth Congress of the French Association of Political Science, Rennes.

———. 2000. "Democracy and Discourse in an Integrating Europe and a Globalizing World." *European Law Journal* 6(3)277–300.

Schneiberg, Marc. 1999. "Political and Institutional Conditions for Governance by Association: Private Order and Price Controls in American Fire Insurance." *Politics and Society* 27:67–103.

Schneiberg, Marc, and Elisabeth Clemens. Forthcoming. "The Typical Tools for the Job: Research Strategies in Institutional Analysis." In *How Institutions Change*, edited by Walter W. Powell and Dan L. Jones. Chicago: University of Chicago Press.

Scott, W. Richard. 1995. *Institutions and Organizations*. Thousand Oaks, CA: Sage.

Scott, W. Richard, and Søren Christensen. 1995. *The Institutional Construction of Organizations*. Thousand Oaks, CA: Sage.

Scott, W. Richard, and John W. Meyer. 1994. *Institutional Environments and Organizations*. Thousand Oaks, CA: Sage.

Searle, John. 1995. *The Social Construction of Reality*. New York: Free Press.

Shonfield, Andrew. 1965. *Modern Capitalism*. New York: Oxford University Press.

Soysal, Yasemin. 1994. *Limits of Citizenship*. Chicago: University of Chicago Press.

Stark, David, and Laszlo Bruszt. 1998. *Postsocialist Pathways*. New York: Cambridge University Press.

Steinmo, Sven, Kathleen Thelen, and Frank Longstreth, editors. 1992. *Structuring Politics: Historical Institutionalism in Comparative Analysis*. New York: Cambridge University Press.

Stinchcombe, Arthur L. 1997. "On the Virtues of the Old Institutionalism." *Annual Review of Sociology* 23:1–18.

Strang, David, and John W. Meyer. 1993. "Institutional Conditions for Diffusion." *Theory and Society* 22:487–511.

Swedberg, Richard. 1990. *Economics and Sociology*. Princeton: Princeton University Press.

"Symposium: Historical Sociology and Rational Choice Theory." 1998. *American Journal of Sociology*. 104(3)722–871.

Thelen, Kathleen. 1999. "Historical Institutionalism in Comparative Politics." *Annual Review of Political Science* 2:369–404.

Thelen, Kathleen, and Sven Steinmo. 1992. "Historical Institutionalism in Comparative Politics." Pp. 1–32 in *Structuring Politics*, edited by Sven Steinmo, Kathleen Thelen, and Frank Longstreth. New York: Cambridge University Press.

Thomas, George M., John W. Meyer, Francisco O. Ramirez, and John Boli. 1987. *Institutional Structure*. Newbury Park, CA: Sage.

Wagner, Peter, Björn Wittrock, and Richard Whiteley, editors. 1991. *Discourse on Society: The Shaping of Social Science Disciplines*. New York: Kluwer Academic.

Wallerstein, Immanuel. 1976. *The Modern World-System*. New York: Academic Press.

Williamson, Oliver. 1985. *The Economic Institutions of Capitalism*. New York: Free Press.

Wittrock, Björn, and Peter Wagner. 1996. "Social Science and the Building of the Early Welfare State: Toward a Comparison of Statist and Non-Statist Western Societies." Pp. 90–114 in *States, Social Knowledge, and the Origins of Modern Social Policies*, edited by Dietrich Rueschemeyer and Theda Skocpol. Princeton: Princeton University Press.

Part I

RATIONAL CHOICE INSTITUTIONALISM

Chapter 2

Explaining the Rise of Neoliberalism

THE MECHANISMS OF INSTITUTIONAL CHANGE

JACK KNIGHT

FOR THIS volume we have been asked to assess how well various approaches to the study of institutions explain the emergence of neoliberalism in the 1980s. In this chapter I focus on rational choice accounts of institutional emergence and change. My primary goal is to illustrate how rational choice approaches to institutional change can help us distinguish the relative merits of various claims about what explains the rise of neoliberal institutions. In doing so I want to lend support to the argument that the most important task in the social sciences is the development of middle-range theories and explanations that build on an identification of the basic causal mechanisms of social life (Merton 1967; Boudon 1991; Elster 1999).

The emphasis on social mechanisms owes much of its impetus to the early work of Robert Merton. Merton advocated an approach to social-scientific research that adopted a middle ground between grand theorizing and description of specific events. The task was to identify "social processes having designated consequences for designated parts of the social structure" (Merton 1968, p. 43). More recent advocates of this middle-range approach have given greater specificity to what counts as a social mechanism. Representative of these are the alternative, but related, definitions offered by Thomas Schelling (1998, pp. 32–33): "a social mechanism is a plausible hypothesis, or a set of hypotheses, that could be the explanation of some phenomenon, the explanation being in terms of interactions between individuals and some other individuals, or between individuals and some social aggregate. . . . Alternatively, a social mechanism is an *interpretation*, in terms of individual behavior, of a model that abstractly reproduces the phenomenon that needs explaining."

The motivating idea here is that social mechanisms are the basic building blocks of social processes and that the goal of explanation should be to identify and account for these underlying mechanisms. Although the focus is on individual level analysis, a mechanism-based approach is not committed to a rigid methodological individualism. While some advocates of the approach, such as Elster (1999) and Gambetta (1998), limit the concept to explanations of individual action, others, such as Boudon (1991) and Schelling (1998), extend the concept to include both interactions among social actors and the effects of social institutions. Hedstrom and Swedberg (1998) have proposed a helpful typology of social mechanisms. Building on a scheme developed by Coleman (1990), Hedstrom and Swedberg identify three types of social mechanisms: (1) situational mechanisms, which focus on the effects of social context on individual actors, (2) action-formation mechanisms, which focus on "how a specific combination of individual desires, beliefs, and action opportunities generate a specific action" (1998, p. 23), and (3) transformational mechanisms, which focus on how the interactions of various individuals produce collective outcomes. The common feature of each type of mechanism is that an explanation in terms of social mechanisms requires an account of how the social phenomena to be explained is related to the actions of individuals. In the analysis of neoliberal institutions, which follows, I will focus on both type (2) and type (3) mechanisms.

A primary focus on social mechanisms entails a more modest project than the traditional claim that the goal of social-scientific research is the production of general laws. Much has been written about the strengths and weaknesses of the traditional approach, and I will not rehearse those arguments here.[1] For my purposes I rest my support for a mechanism-based approach on its practical benefits. Hedstrom and Swedberg (1998, pp. 8–9) contrast the practical differences between the two approaches:

> The covering law model provides justification for the use of "black-box" explanations in the social sciences because it does not stipulate that the mechanism linking *explanans* and *explanandum* must be specified in order for an acceptable explanation to be at hand. This omission has given leeway for sloppy scholarship, and a major advantage of the mechanism-based approach is that it provides (or encourages) deeper, more direct, and more fine-grained explanations. The search for generative mechanisms consequently helps us distinguish between genuine causality and coincidental association, and it increases the understanding of why we observe what we observe.

But here it is important to note that the more modest aspirations of the mechanism-based approach do not reduce to ad hoc accounts fitted to particular sets of facts. The mechanism-based approach is beneficial precisely because it focuses our attention on basic mechanisms that are prevalent in a wide variety of social situations. Peterson (1999, p. 62), for example, incorporates the generality requirement into his definition of a mechanism: "specific causal patterns, which explain individual actions over a wide range of settings." The task, as I will show in the following analysis, is to identify (1) the underlying mechanisms and (2) the social conditions under which these mechanisms are most likely to operate.

Institutional Consequences of the Emergence of Neoliberalism

Neoliberalism is a complex phenomenon. It emerged in various parts of the world and involved changes in policies, institutions, and ideas throughout the social, political, and economic spheres. One could thus take various approaches to trying to explain neoliberalism. My focus will be on the changes in various political and economic institutions that were fundamental to the neoliberal policy agenda. To ground this analysis in some particular empirical examples, I will concentrate on those institutional changes that occurred during efforts of several Latin American governments to implement neoliberal economic reforms.

I begin by offering a sketch of the dynamic of institutional development and change during the neoliberal reform period. In doing so I draw on several accounts of the rise of neoliberalism in Latin America (Conaghan and Malloy 1994; Roberts 1995; Teichman 1995; Otero 1996; Weyland 1996; Griffin 1997; Smith and Korzeniewicz 1997; Veltmeyer, Petras, and Vieux 1997). Although some of the historical particulars differ across the countries that attempted neoliberal reforms, a common picture can be discerned.

In the 1970s authoritarian states played a central role in the management of the economy throughout Latin America. The economy was characterized by substantial public ownership of enterprises, close ties between state bureaucrats and private owners of capital, a significant emphasis on exports as the primary source of economic growth, state policies to protect predominately export sectors, and social and economic policies that protected consumers and workers. For a time this state-managed export-oriented approach fostered significant economic growth.

But by the beginning of the next decade, the economic picture had undergone several important changes. Export earnings decreased dramatically, accounting in large part for a subsequent decline in domestic investment. The negative effects of the loss of domestic investment were exacerbated by a decrease in foreign investment due to a credit crisis in the international financial system. Domestically, the drop in economic growth created significant social conflict as people throughout the society faced declines in individual earnings and income. In the face of these tensions all parties looked to the state to see how it was going to confront the basic problem of how to generate sufficient investment to revive economic growth.

It was in the context of these declining economic conditions that governments throughout Latin America began to consider neoliberal economic reforms. The basic goals of these reforms were, in the words of Adam Przeworski (1991, p. 136), "to organize an economy that rationally allocates resources and in which the state is financially solvent." This involved a fundamental transformation of the economic sphere from state-oriented protections, controls, and planning to decentralized market-based economic decision making. To accomplish this, state officials had to address both short-term and long-term concerns. In regard to the short term, state officials implemented a set of economic stabilization policies such as currency devaluation and the curtailment of various price control, consumer subsidy, and worker protection programs. These policies in and of themselves had a significant impact on the domestic economies in these countries. But the long-term policies envisioned a fundamental neoliberal change in basic economic (and, in the case of these Latin American countries, political) institutions. First, the institutional foundations of a market economy had to be established or strengthened or both. This included the following types of changes: the dismantling of state bureaucratic procedures, the liberalization of trade and foreign investment practices, the enhancement of domestic market infrastructure, and the diminution of the power and influence of many private associations (corporate monopolies, labor unions, consumer associations, etc.) that had successfully influenced economic policy making under the state-oriented procedures. Second, the property rights in various sectors previously owned or controlled by the state had to be privatized. While attempting to do all of this, state officials were also trying to shore up the financial status of the state by decreasing public expenditures and increasing government revenues. The sale of publicly owned corporations was an important factor in these latter efforts.

Here it is important to note that the efforts to implement neoliberal economic policies took place at the same time that many of these same countries were undergoing efforts to establish constitutional democracies in the political sphere. By pointing out the simultaneous nature of the political and economic reforms, I do not mean to imply that the neoliberal policies necessarily required democratic political institutions. I take this to be an open and contestable question in terms of the long-run dynamics of a society. It seems possible that the economic liberalization in Latin America during this period could have occurred without the move toward democracy. But a complete understanding of the institutional changes associated with neoliberalism in Latin America requires us to take account of the fact that political and economic institutions were, in fact, being transformed at the same time. Furthermore, the Latin American experience suggests that the efforts to implement neoliberal economic changes had significant implications for the attempt to establish a democratic form of public decision making. Therefore, the changes in the institutions governing public decision making should serve as a third major aspect of the institutional changes to be explained in the assessment of neoliberalism.

The implementation of these neoliberal reforms produced varied consequences. Economists and other scholars of Latin America continue to debate the long-term merits of these reforms. But few would deny that the economic effects of the various policy and institutional changes have been substantial. Hyperinflation followed from the initial stabilization policies. This produced significant costs, and the costs were borne disproportionately by some social groups (e.g., capitalists in disfavored economic sectors, the working class, and the poor). Over time some countries did experience significant economic growth, but the benefits of that growth continued to be distributed in ways that favored property ownership in certain economic sectors.

For my purposes I want to distinguish the economic consequences of neo- liberal reforms from the institutional consequences. The economic conse- quences are primarily relevant for this analysis to the extent that they might have engendered a response in terms of changes in political and economic in- stitutions; although the neoliberal reforms involved substantial institutional changes in the three areas under consideration (market institutions, property rights, and democratic decision making), the economic costs associated with the various economic policy changes produced institutional responses. In re- sponse to the political demands generated by these costs, some states backed off of a strict neoliberal plan and reimplemented various control and subsidy protection programs. Other states attempted to sustain the basic neoliberal agenda, but they did so at the expense of democratic reform efforts. State offi- cials developed new institutional procedures for implementing economic poli- cies, seeking to insulate economic policy decision making from the effects of democratic politics.

This dynamic of institutional change associated with neoliberalism in Latin America forms the basis of my analysis of rational choice theories of institu- tions. Scholars of economic policy in Latin America during this period have proposed several explanations for these neoliberal reforms. Their proposals are instructive because they identify various causal factors that might be relevant to a rational choice account of these institutional changes. Let me briefly high- light here some of the more prominent explanations:

1. The economic crisis facing the Latin American countries was so severe that political leaders had no choice but to adopt neoliberal reforms (Naim 1993).

2. Pressure from international financial organizations forced politicians to adopt stabilization policies and neoliberal reforms (Stallings 1992).

3. Governments implemented radical neoliberal programs because they sought to enhance aggregate economic growth and the "shock" strategy was more efficient than more gradual approaches (Morales and Sachs 1989; Lipton and Sachs 1990).

4. The international diffusion of neoliberal economic ideas reached Latin Amer- ica at an especially important time and was embraced by government officials (Kahler 1990).

5. Neoliberal reforms were the product of the state's efforts to further the inter- ests of the capitalist class (Veltmeyer, Petras, and Vieux 1997).

6. In the face of the economic crisis, politicians enacted stabilization adjustment

policies early in their terms of office as an electoral strategy to remain in office (Prze-worski 1991).

7. The development of neoliberal reforms were the product of a complex politi-cal competition among domestic capitalists (Conaghan and Malloy 1994).

Although most of these explanations make no specific reference to rational choice theory, we can find among the various proposals several factors that might be incorporated in a rational choice account of neoliberal institutional change. A number of explanations treat the neoliberal programs as intentional reform efforts, highlighting the role of preferences in the determination of these changes. Others emphasize the importance of contextual factors, such as international pressure and competition, factors that might influence the choices of political and economic actors. Finally, one proposal emphasizes the importance of the diffusion of ideas, a factor that can influence both the pref-erences and beliefs of the relevant actors.

The various factors identified in these proposals constitute claims about the causal processes that govern neoliberal institutional change. Some are com-patible and some conflict, but there is very little effort in most of these accounts to assess the relative merits of the different explanations. In the next section I will discuss two alternative theories of institutional change. Each theory is grounded in a claim about the primary social mechanisms that generate pro-cesses of change. In the course of the discussion I will delineate the sets of so-cial conditions that make each of the theories plausible accounts of institu-tional change and highlight the types of empirical evidence we would need to support each theory's claims about the relevant social mechanisms. This analy-sis of the relationship between the analytical models and empirical evidence allows us to assess in a particular historical case the relative importance of dif-ferent social mechanisms that may underlie the process of institutional change. In doing so I will show how each of the factors proposed in the various accounts of neoliberalism in Latin American is relevant to at least one of the two theo-ries of institutional change that I consider. Through this analysis I hope to show how the mechanisms highlighted in these rational choice theories can serve as tools to help us clarify and make more explicit the ways in which these various proposed factors would enter into explanations of neoliberal institutional change.[2]

Rational Choice Theories of Institutional Change

Rational choice theories of institutional emergence and change take many forms.[3] They all share an initial premise that social actors pursue some set of preferences in a rational way. This means that social actors seek to achieve their most-preferred outcome in the least costly manner. But from this initial assumption, rational choice theorists develop quite different explanations about how social institutions emerge and change. In this chapter I will assess two alternative theories of institutional creation and change: a transaction cost theory of contract and selection through market competition and a bargaining theory that explains the emergence of institutions in terms of the asymmetries of power in a society. On each of these accounts social institutions resolve the strategic problems inherent in social interactions characterized by multiple equilibria: each of the equilibria could serve as the resolution of the social interaction, but the actors need to identify a common equilibrium to pursue. That is, institutions are rules that structure social interactions in ways that allow social actors to gain the benefits of joint activity. The process of institutional development culminates in the establishment of one of these rules as the common institutional form in a community.

To identify the analytical differences that distinguish the two theories, I want to employ a simple two-person game that is intended to model the basic social interaction out of which social institutions emerge. I use the game merely as a heuristic device and do not present it as an adequate representation of the complexity of the social interactions that we seek to explain. Nonetheless, it is sufficient to clarify the differences in the two theories and the implications of these differences for empirical analysis. The requirements of the model are straightforward. Each of the social actors must have at least two choices of action in his feasible set. At least two of the outcomes produced by the interdependent choices of the actors must be characterized by payoffs that incorporate the benefits of joint activity. In both of the theories that I consider here, these outcomes take the form of Nash equilibria; that is, there are at least two strategy combinations that would produce an outcome that the actors would accept as the resolution of the game. The task for the actors in the interaction is to find a way to produce one of the equilibrium outcomes. In this model, a social institution is a rule of action that would identify and induce compliance with one of these equilibrium strategy combinations.

These requirements are met by the game in figure 2-1. The two actors, players 1 and 2, have two choices of action, X and Y. This produces four possible outcomes in the game, and the outcomes can be characterized by their strategy combinations (X,X; X,Y; Y,X; Y,Y). The payoffs are characterized by the variables a and b. If $a_{1,2} > b_{1,2}$, then there are two Nash equilibria in the game, (X,X) and (Y,Y). The strategic problem for the players rests in the fact that without more information about the social context in which the interaction takes place, they do not know on which equilibrium to focus their strategic choice. In this situation, two possible institutional rules could emerge: either one that recommends a strategy choice of X or one that recommends a strategy choice of Y.

With this simple model I can illustrate which features of the social interaction the different approaches choose to give primary emphasis. As a shorthand,

Player 2

	X	Y
X	a_1, a_2	b_1, b_2
Y	b_1, b_2	a_1, a_2

Player 1

Fig. 2-1. Two-Person Strategic Game

I will refer to the approaches in terms of the primary social mechanism that underlies the different explanations: *contract* (for the exchange and selection through competition approach) and *bargain* (for the bargaining approach.) First, both approaches rely on the assumption that $a > b$. This is simply a claim that the benefits of living in a world with social institutions are greater than from living in an anarchic world without them.

Second, from this initial assumption the bargain approach differs from the contract approach in terms of the additional features of the social interaction it emphasizes. The contract approach emphasizes the following relationship: $a_1 + a_2 > b_1 + b_2$. This relationship emphasizes the following feature of the outcomes induced by the social institution: the aggregate benefits produced by the rule exceed the aggregate benefits of failing to produce a rule. The comparison is between social outcomes induced by a social institution and social outcomes without social institutions. This emphasis on the collective gains produced by social institutions is found in explanations that emphasize characteristics such as social efficiency, Pareto superiority, the minimization of transaction costs, and the like.

The bargaining approach, on the other hand, incorporates directly into the payoffs additional assumptions about the social context in which the social interaction takes place. This approach emphasizes the following relationship: the two equilibria are distinguished by the fact that $a_1 > a_2$ in one equilibrium and $a_2 > a_1$ in the other. This relationship emphasizes the following feature of the outcomes induced by social institutions: the institutions have distinctive distributional consequences (that is, the institutions affect the distribution of benefits of joint activity). The bargaining approach shifts the focus from aggregate effects to the effects on the benefits of the individual social actors. Here the comparison is between the outcomes induced by the different social institutions.

Thus, in seeking to explain how the institutional rule emerges to direct the choices of the actors to either the (X,X) or the (Y,Y) equilibrium, the two approaches model the basic social interaction somewhat differently. The contract approach emphasizes the $a_1 + a_2 > b_1 + b_2$ relationship. The bargaining approach gives primary emphasis to the relationship that characterizes the differences in the values of a_1 and a_2 for the different equilibria. In doing so, the two approaches give primary explanatory emphasis to different features of the social situation out of which social institutions emerge. These features are reflective of the different effects of institutions on social life. The significance of this emphasis should not be underestimated. The choice of emphasis is an important part of the process of interpreting a rational choice model. The choice represents a substantive claim about what the proponents think are the primary factors relevant to explaining the emergence of social institutions. This emphasis is central to subsequent claims about the importance of social context and about the mechanisms for resolving the strategic problem of multiple equilibria.

The Transaction-Cost Approach

The logic of contracting has been the source of many explanations of institutional development and change (e.g., Brennan and Buchanan 1985; Heckathorn and Maser 1987; Williamson 1975, 1985; North 1990; Ostrom 1990). In order to identify the relationship between the analytical model and the mechanisms of institutional selection invoked in the process of explanation, it is helpful to focus separately on the two main components of the contracting explanation: the individual exchange and the competition over alternatives.

Consider first the contracts produced by individual exchanges. The logic of the exchange relationship is one of mutual benefit. The motivation for the development of the contract is quite simple. When any two social actors perceive that they can achieve benefit from mutual exchange, they must agree on the terms of that exchange. Among these terms are the rules governing the actions of the parties during the course of the exchange relationship.

In the context of the general theory, these contracts constitute the social institutions produced by social actors to facilitate the achievement of socially beneficial outcomes. The main mechanism that explains the selection among possible contracts is voluntary agreement. Social actors create these institutional rules because they can achieve benefits that they would not enjoy without them. Hence the importance of the $a > b$ relationship. But the contracts produced by voluntary agreement can take many forms, so the mechanism of voluntary agreement is constrained by an assumption about the kinds of contracts social actors will try to produce. The dominant answer builds on Coase's (1960) insights into the effects of transaction costs.

Consider, for example, North's (1990) explanation of the development of property rights in a society. Say that two actors share an interest in a common piece of property. Their task is to determine the best way to structure their use of that property. There are a range of possible choices, from some form of shared or common property rights to various divisions into private property shares. North (1990, pp. 37–43) argues that these actors will contract for rights that minimize the transaction costs involved in the ongoing exchange, subject to a set of constraints on their ability to identify the most efficient contract (e.g., ideology, lack of knowledge, lack of capacity). They minimize transaction costs in order to maximize the benefits gained from the property. The contracting problem is one of structuring incentives in such a way that the person who has the greatest incentive to maximize the benefits from a piece of the property has the rights to that parcel. The emphasis on cost minimization or benefit maximization or both highlights the central importance of the $a_1 + a_2 > b_1 + b_2$ relationship.

On this contract approach, once the actors have established the property rights according to the minimization standard, they will maintain them as long as the relevant external circumstances remain stable. But there is always the possibility that some factors external to the exchange relationship will change in such a way as to affect the enjoyment of the benefits of the property. North (1990, p. 109) lists several changes in relative prices, which will affect benefits: in the ratio of factor prices, in the costs of information, and in technology. If any of these changes is substantial, it will affect the relative value of the different ways of institutionalizing property rights. If the result of these changes is that a new property rights scheme would produce greater aggregate benefits than the existing system, the contracting parties will consider the following cost-benefit calculation: do these additional benefits exceed the costs involved in changing the present contract? If the answer is yes, then the actors enter into a new contract institutionalizing new rights (North 1990, p. 67).

Note that at this point this is merely a discussion of the motivations of the actors in an individual exchange. As Eggertsson (1990) clearly points out, the more sophisticated versions of the transaction cost approach invoke more than the intentions of the actors in an individual exchange to explain the emergence of social institutions. Individual exchanges merely produce the variety of possible institutional forms; the second selection mechanism invoked by the contract approach is competition. Many explanations of institutional development and change situate the decision to establish social institutions in the context of a market or a marketlike environment. The main influence of the market on the choice of institutional form rests in the competitive pressure it supposedly exerts on the institutionalization process.[4]

Competition can serve as a dynamic selection mechanism, which determines the survival of various institutional forms on grounds of reproductive fitness. This is the logic behind the Alchian (1950) model of evolutionary competition employed by most economic analyses of institutional emergence. The existence of a large number of firms seeking profits from a common pool of consumers produces pressure for survival. Over time those firms that employ less efficient techniques will lose profits to those that are more efficient. Losing profits eventually translates into extinction. As the competitive process continues, only those firms that employ efficient techniques will survive.

The logic of this dynamic effect forms the basis of the theory of exchange and competition. On this account, competition selects the institutional form that maximizes $a_1 + a_2$. The invocation of competition as a selection mechanism draws on a particular conception of the social context in which these social interactions take place. It is important to remember that competition is not an either/or phenomenon; there are degrees of competition and therefore degrees of competitive effect. The extent to which competitive pressure will serve as a selection mechanism for efficient institutions depends on the degree to which the social context manifests the requisite empirical conditions under which competition will emerge. The variability of competitive pressure highlights an important feature of the transaction cost approach: it adopts different mechanisms in explaining change for different types of political and economic institutions. For economic institutions, competitive selection is normally invoked as the primary causal mechanism; for political institutions, the competitive selection constraint is often inoperative, so the intentions of the actors serve as the basis for the explanation of change.

The Theory of Bargaining and Distribution

The logic of bargaining has been used as the basis of a number of recent efforts to explain the intentional creation of political and economic institutions (e.g., Heckathorn and Maser 1987; Bates 1989; Ensminger 1992; Miller 1992). A bargaining approach to institutional emergence and change seeks to explain the emergence of social institutions primarily in terms of the characteristics that distinguish different institutional forms. Rather than seeking an explanation of institutional selection in a comparison of the differences between social outcomes induced by institutional rules and those outcomes that lack an institutional basis (the logic of the transaction cost approach), this approach places primary emphasis on a comparison of the different outcomes induced by the possible institutional alternatives. Given the reliance on an assumption of rational self-interest as the basis of the theory, the main focus of the analysis of institutional differences is the distributional effect of the alternatives. The theory builds its explanation on the distributional relationship highlighted in the basic analytical model: the two equilibria are distinguished by the fact that $a_1 > a_2$ in one equilibrium and $a_2 > a_1$ in the other.

On this bargaining account, social institutions are a by-product of strategic conflict over substantive social outcomes. By this I mean that social actors produce social institutions in the process of seeking distributional advantage in the conflict over substantive benefits; the development of institutional rules is merely a means to this substantive end. The mechanism of selection among the possible institutional alternatives is bargaining competition among the actors over the various alternatives. I developed a theory (Knight 1992) that identified the asymmetries of resource ownership in a society as the main factor explaining the resolution of bargaining over social institutions. The main thrust of the argument is that asymmetries in resource ownership affect the willingness of rational self-interested actors to accept the bargaining demands of other actors. Here the asymmetries of resource ownership serve as an ex ante measure of the bargaining power of the actors in a social interaction.[5] In explaining the establishment of particular social institutions, bargaining demands become claims about commitments to particular rules of behavior. The relevant question becomes: what will cause a social actor to accept the commitment of another actor to a particular course of action and thus a particular social outcome?

In bargaining interactions the most important resources are those available to the actors in the event that bargaining is either lengthy and costly or ultimately unsuccessful. For any particular bargaining interaction, many factors may determine the availability of these resources. We can think of these as the existing resources, which an actor might retain after the effort to achieve a bargain breaks down. Or we might think of them as the other options available to the actors if they are left to achieve a bargain with some other party. In the model in figure 2-1, these resources determine the values of $b_{1,2}$ — values which can be interpreted as a measure of the costs of noncoordination on an equilibrium outcome. If $b_1 = b_2$, then the costs are equal and we can conclude that there are no key resource asymmetries in the game. But if either $b_1 > b_2$ or $b_1 < b_2$, then we have an example of an asymmetry in resources and thus asymmetric bargaining power. Here we see an additional analytical relationship, which the bargaining approach emphasizes, but which the transaction cost approach does not: the possibility that the b values are not equal.

The standard view in bargaining theory is that if A has greater bargaining power than B, A will usually get a greater share of the benefits of the bargaining outcome (Maynard-Smith 1982, p. 105; Osborne and Rubinstein 1990, pp. 88–89). We can capture the underlying intuition of this view through the effects of differences in the values of b. Here the mechanism by which asymmetries of resource ownership influence social outcomes is in its effect on the credibility of the commitments in the bargaining interaction. To see this, consider a game in which $a_1 > a_2$ in the (X,X) equilibrium, $a_2 > a_1$ in the (Y,Y) equilibrium, and $b_1 > b_2$. Now the costs of noncoordination are greater for player 2 than for player 1. If player 1 is now able to communicate to player 2 that she will choose X regardless of what 2 does, what will 2 do? That is, what will this information do to 2's choice? The answer depends on how credible 2 finds 1's commitment to be. There are important reasons to believe that 2 will accept the credibility of the commitment in this case and respond by choosing X.

The principal idea here involves the relationship between available resources and attitudes toward risk.[6] Resource ownership influences one's attitude toward risky situations. There is a positive relationship between ownership of resources and risk acceptance, a negative relationship between ownership and risk aversion. Considered from the perspective of player 2, this relationship suggests two related reasons why he would find 1's commitment credible and choose X. First, since 1 will suffer fewer costs of failing to coordinate, then she is more likely to accept the risk and attempt the commitment to X. As Maynard-Smith (1982, p. 153) puts it in his analysis of asymmetric evolutionary games, "[a] player who has less to lose from a breakdown is more likely to risk one." If 2 is aware of the asymmetry, then he has good reason to believe that 1 is sincere in the commitment. Second, since 2 will suffer greater costs of noncoordination, then he is more likely to be risk averse and is, therefore, less likely to challenge 1's commitment. The risk aversion leads to a willingness to accept the commitment and to choose X. The greater the differences in resources between the actors, the stronger the relationship between costs of noncoordination and risk attitudes should be. That is, the greater the differential between b_1 and b_2, then the higher the probability that 2 will choose X.

Through its emphasis on asymmetries in resource ownership, the approach grounds its mechanism of rule selection in an important feature of many social interactions: social actors suffer significant costs for the failure to coordinate on equilibrium outcomes, yet those costs need not be suffered uniformly. When social actors are aware of these differentials, this awareness can influence the credibility of certain strategies. Those who have either fewer alternatives or less beneficial ones will be more inclined to respect the commitments of those who have them. In this way, the existence of resource asymmetries in a society can significantly influence the choice of equilibrium alternatives.

Explanations of Neoliberal Institutional Change

These two theories are grounded in quite different claims about the actual empirical conditions under which social institutions emerge and change. We can see this by turning explicitly to the question of how they would explain the institutional changes associated with the emergence of neoliberalism in Latin America. I will structure this comparison around the following question: Given the initial assumption that the relevant decision makers are motivated by individual self-interest, what are the conditions under which the different proposed mechanisms seem most relevant and thus most plausible as an explanation of the various neoliberal changes?

Contracts

The contract approach emphasizes the greater efficiency of outcomes induced by social institutions over outcomes that are produced without institutional assistance. There are two components of the mechanism of selection in the contract approach: (1) the voluntary contract and (2) the pressure of competition. According to the transaction costs approach, the parties will agree to that contract which minimizes costs, subject to the constraints on their knowledge and capacities. A transaction cost explanation of neoliberal institutional change will focus initially on (1) the preferences of the relevant social actors and (2) the efficiency effects of the resulting economic and political institutions. Here the central empirical questions are: (1) did the new neoliberal institutions enhance the efficiency of economic and political activity? (2) were there other institutional possibilities that would have had even greater efficiency effects if they had been established? and (3) were the new neoliberal institutions the ones that were most preferred by all of the relevant economic and political decision makers? Of the explanations of neoliberalism that have been previously proposed, the "shock therapy" alternative of Sachs and associates comes closest to approaching the voluntary contract version of the transaction costs theory. On this account the argument is that political and economic decision makers preferred those institutions that minimized transaction costs and thus maximized aggregate economic benefits.

From the perspective of individual self-interest, the plausibility of the voluntary selection by contract mechanism is open to question in those situations in which the institutions affect the distribution of benefits. In those cases rational self-interested actors will prefer a contract that maximizes their individual benefits over a contract that maximizes aggregate benefits. Only in the cases in which one contract satisfies both criteria will the contract mechanism provide an adequate explanation of selection. Thus, the argument at the level of voluntary contract is most likely to explain the emergence of social institutions under the condition $a_1 = a_2$.

Two types of evidence from the Latin American countries call any claim about the satisfaction of this criteria into question. First, there was considerable diversity in the form that the neoliberal institutions took in the different countries. This variety was characterized by significant distributional effects, not only between capitalists and noncapitalists, but also among the capitalists in different economic sectors. While this evidence alone does not undermine the transaction cost approach, it does raise questions about our ability to satisfy the claims that (1) the resulting institutions were the most efficient among the available alternatives and (2) the resulting institutions were the ones most preferred by all relevant decision makers. Second, the changes in both political and economic institutions that resulted from the political demands for relief from the initial economic consequences of the neoliberal reforms were not the most efficient alternatives. Those latter changes clearly cannot be explained by a preference for the transaction cost minimizing alternative; those changes were redistributive in nature.

When there are distributional effects, the second mechanism, competitive selection, serves as the primary source of explanation. The argument here rests on claims about the nature of the social context in which contracts are made. If the conditions of competition exist in a society, then those conditions will have two important, and related, effects on the selection of institutions. The first is the pressure for survival: competition selects out those joint activities that fail to maximize $a_1 + a_2$ in the long run. The second is the effect on the bargaining power of the actors: competition diminishes the differences in resource ownership among social actors. When the conditions of competition exist, the asymmetries in the levels of resources and opportunities available to the actors in case an agreeable contract cannot be reached diminish. In such cases the bargaining power necessary for an actor to achieve a distributionally favorable contract is absent. Then bargaining over distributional consequences will not adequately explain the selection of institutions and the contract approach becomes a more plausible explanation of the emergence of social institutions. Therefore, given the assumption of rational self-interested behavior, the transaction cost approach will best explain institutional emergence when the actual empirical conditions are such that $b_1 = b_2$.

The Naim argument that the economic crisis was so severe that political leaders had no choice but to adopt neoliberal reforms invokes factors consistent with the competitive selection version of the transaction cost argument. And there is evidence to support the idea that international competitive pressure had a role to play in the initiation of neoliberal institutions. Both the decline in export earnings and the unavailability of foreign investment and credit served as constraints on domestic political and economic decision making. But the latter factor is open to more than one plausible interpretation. While the pressure exerted by international financial organizations can be seen as competitive pressure for foreign resources from the perspective of an individual country vis-à-vis other countries in need of similar resources, the actions of these international organizations can also plausibly be interpreted as strategic initiatives on behalf of various domestic political actors engaged in an internal competition for the neoliberal reforms. The viability of the transaction cost explanation of neoliberalism in Latin America depends in part on which of these interpretations is deemed more plausible.

Combine these questions with evidence of (1) the significant institutional variation across countries, (2) the substantial political conflict throughout Latin America over the nature of the institutional reforms, and (3) the subsequent responses to political pressure after the initial period of reform, and there is good reason to conclude that the competitive selection mechanism will not adequately account for the nature of neoliberal institutional change.

Bargains

The bargaining approach emphasizes the fact that social institutions determine the ways in which the benefits of joint activity are distributed and can thus be distinguished by their distributional consequences. The mechanism of selection involves bargaining over the alternative distributional arrangements. The bargaining is resolved by the asymmetries of resource ownership in a society. Here the social context enters the analysis in the form of the asymmetries of resources that exist in a society in which social actors are involved in repeated interactions. Context is captured in the model by varying the values of b_1 and b_2 so that they reflect the idea that some actors will have more resources than others. From the perspective of individual self-interest, rational actors will be most concerned about the individual benefits that they derive from social institutions. If the institutions have distributional consequences, they will seek those institutions that provide them the highest value of a. The argument in support of the bargaining approach suggests that those actors with the higher b values will be able to cause the selection of more favorable social institutions.

As long as the institution is such that $a > b$ for those actors with the lowest b values (an assumption that both approaches share), the bargaining approach provides a plausible mechanism for institutional selection. Given the assumption of rational self-interested behavior, the bargaining approach will best explain institutional emergence when the actual empirical conditions are such that $a_1 \neq a_2$ and $b_1 \neq b_2$. The greater the differences in these values, the more likely it is that the bargaining approach will provide the best explanation of institutional emergence and change.

The bargaining explanation of neoliberal institutional change will focus on (1) the preferences of the relevant social actors, (2) the distributional consequences of the resulting economic and political institutions, and (3) the existence of asymmetries in bargaining power that translate into advantages in the political and economic competition over institutional creation and change. The primary empirical questions are (1) did the new neoliberal institutions create significant asymmetries in the distribution of the benefits of political and economic interactions? (2) did the relevant social actors have conflicting preferences over the possible institutional alternatives? (3) was the process of institutional change characterized by substantial conflict? and (4) did the resulting neoliberal institutions favor those political actors who had an ex ante advantage in the relevant measure of bargaining power?

Several of the proposed explanations of Latin American neoliberal reform invoke either conflicts of interest, political competition, or distributional consequences as important causes of institutional change. The evidence from the Latin American experience demonstrates the importance of these factors, and thus lends considerable support to the bargaining approach. A good example of this can be found in the Conaghan and Malloy (1994) comparative account of the rise of neoliberalism in Bolivia, Ecuador, and Peru. They argue that the dynamic of neoliberal reform in these countries was primarily a product of the ongoing political competition among domestic capitalists, politicians, and state economic planners. Other accounts (e.g., Veltmeyer, Petras, and Vieux 1997) emphasize a conflict that includes these actors but also portrays an important role for labor unions.

Two features of the dynamic of neoliberal institutional change add additional support to the bargaining argument. The first is the aforementioned variety in the form that political and economic institutions took during the rise of neoliberalism. The second is the sudden change in both political and economic institutions that occurred as a response to the political reaction to the initial reforms. Both of these features highlight the importance of the distributional consequences of neoliberal institutions. To the extent that the factors associated with political and economic conflict and the distributional consequences of the resulting institutions can be documented in the Latin American cases, the bargaining approach promises an explanation of aspects of the process of institutional change missing in the transaction costs account.

Conclusion

In this analysis I have tried to demonstrate that contrary to much of the criticism of the approach, rational choice analyses of political and economic institutions can offer a variety of explanations of institutional change. And the primary causal mechanisms that form the basis of these explanations are often the same ones proposed by other social science accounts that make no explicit mention of any form of rational decision making. One of the benefits of these rational choice theories is that they can serve as analytical tools for assessing the relative importance of various social factors for processes of institutional change.[7] This follows from the fact that the different theories correlate specific sets of social conditions with particular types of institutions and with particular social mechanisms that generate institutional change.

The substantial evidence of political and economic conflict and the existence of distributional differences among the variety of neoliberal institutional reforms suggests that bargaining is an important causal mechanism of change in these Latin American countries. But the evidence of the importance of political conflict for explanations of neoliberal institutional change, while lending support to the bargaining approach, does not completely undermine the relevance of the other theory: a complete explanation must take account of the extent to which international pressure constrained the choices of domestic actors. Nonetheless, what the evidence from Latin America does highlight is that the real explanatory power of the transaction cost approach lies in the competitive selection mechanism, not in the claims about individual contracting in order to minimize transaction costs. Here it is important to emphasize a point that is often lacking in many rational choice accounts: competitive pressure as a selection mechanism is an empirical question and not an a priori theoretical assumption.

The mechanism-based approach to social explanation is a potentially rich and fruitful one.[8] While the focus is on mechanisms that connect social phenomena to individual-level action, the methodology need not be limited to the rational choice approach adopted in this chapter.[9] But the focus provided by a strategic analysis such as the one undertaken here can help to identify how other mechanisms and other methodologies might enter into a comprehensive explanation of the rise of neoliberalism. To further illustrate this, let me conclude by discussing the relationship between the rational choice approach and two alternative approaches to institutional analysis, historical institutionalism and epistemic communities. By focusing on the different mechanisms that form the basis of the alternative approaches, we can better see that the approaches that are usually described as conflicting are, in fact, often complementary.

Rational choice accounts, as variants of intentional explanations, build on the relationship between the preferences of social actors and the effects of social institutions. But this relationship is a complex one, primarily because institutional choice is a strategic one. As the evidence from Latin America shows, this strategic choice takes place in a context of social, economic, and political conditions that make the choice more difficult than that of merely establishing one's most individually preferred alternative. This highlights the importance of paying attention to questions of uncertainty, knowledge, and belief formation as we seek to explain institutional change.

When social actors attempt to create and maintain political and economic institutions that will further their own interests, they often do so with at best an incomplete understanding of the relationship among their preferences, their actions, and the long-term consequences of the institutional alternatives. These actors will often be disappointed, as the beliefs that they have about the consequences of social institutions will often be mistaken. In such cases the beliefs and preferences on which they base their efforts at institutional change will not match the ultimate effects of those institutions. For those who seek to explain institutional change by invoking the preferences of relevant decision makers, the problem of unintended consequences complicates their efforts.[10]

This fact highlights the importance of identifying the social mechanisms that affect the formation of individual and social beliefs, type (1) mechanisms in the Hedstrom and Swedberg typology. The literature on epistemic communities provides one approach to the question of belief formation through its primary emphasis on the role of governmental learning in policy formation. Consider, for example, Haas's account (1989) of how groups of experts can substantially affect the knowledge base of state policy decision making. Haas's substantive focus was on the process by which environmental experts significantly affected the emergence and maintenance of the Mediterranean Action Plan, an international regime established to control pollution in the Mediterranean Sea. On his account, the regime established and legitimized a community of experts who then used their expertise (1) to affect the knowledge base of existing governmental decision makers and (2) to independently gain power within the various governments in the region. The experts used this power to establish convergent state policies in many of the domestic states in the region.

Haas's general theoretical point is that experts can gain control of important decision-making bodies, affecting the beliefs and interests that fashion state policy. A mechanism-based approach to social explanation clarifies both the primary benefits of the epistemic community literature as well as its relationship to rational choice approaches. On the one hand, the focus on governmental learning highlights the importance of knowledge and belief formation on state policy. In doing so, it identifies one important type (1) mechanism: the influence of experts. In this way the epistemic community approach complements the rational choice focus on type (2) and (3) mechanisms.

But, on the other hand, it is a mistake to see the epistemic community literature as a competitor of the rational choice approach because it relies on type (2) and (3) strategic mechanisms for an important feature of its own explanation of state policy. As Haas's account of the Mediterranean pollution problem shows, the influence of the experts does not rest entirely on their ability to affect social beliefs. It also rests on their ability to use their expertise as bargaining leverage to acquire governmental authority to set policy. This latter bargaining process involves a mechanism central to the rational choice approach, bargaining competition among interest-based strategic actors. In this way, the epistemic community literature relies on the strategic approach to complete its explanation of state policy formation.

The problem of unintended consequences also highlights a pervasive weakness in most accounts of institutional change. One of the most significant mistakes made by proponents of rational choice explanations of institutional change is the practice of working back from identifiable institutional effects to determine the initial preferences of the actors involved in the institutionalization process. This inappropriately conflates the ex ante uncertainty of the relevant actors with the ex post knowledge of the social-scientific analysts. Greater attention to the nature of preferences and the processes by which preferences are established is needed in substantive explanations based on rational choice mechanisms.

This calls attention to one feature of the close relationship between rational choice approaches to institutional change and the historical institutionalism literature (e.g., Hall and Taylor 1996; Pierson 1994). The greatest strength of the historical institutionalism literature is its emphasis on the historical processes by which actors come to have their economic and political preferences.[11] This historical research emphasizes the importance of type (1) mechanisms.

But, like the literature on epistemic communities, the approach is often complementary to, not conflicting with, rational choice accounts. To the extent that it focuses on type (1) preference formation mechanisms, it provides important insights that are lacking in most rational choice accounts. However, once the historical approaches move beyond preference formation to explanations of how preferences translate into policy outcomes, they tend to rely on type (2) and (3) mechanisms, like bargaining competition, that are at the core of the strategic approach to both policy and institutional formation.

More generally, the problem of uncertainty reminds us that the plausibility of any intentional account rests on our ability to identify both ex ante preferences and ex post institutional effects. Then the task is to analyze how the existing social conditions affect strategic choice and thus the various interactions from which political and economic institutions emerge. This requires an analysis that is attentive to all three types of mechanisms in the Hedstrom-Swedberg typology. It is through such an analysis of the contextual effects on choice that we come to understand the relative merits of the alternative explanations of the determinants of institutional change.

Notes

1. See Elster 1998 and 1999 for a persuasive argument that the search for general covering laws is an unattainable goal.

2. Here I want to emphasize that the primary purpose of this chapter is analytical in nature. I assess here the ways in which rational choice models can help to identify the causal mechanisms that form the basis of substantive historical explanations of the rise of neoliberalism. I am not attempting to present a fully adequate account of such events. But the fact that I do not offer such an account in this chapter does not suggest that rational choice approaches are unable to form the basis of such accounts. Examples can be found in the emerging "analytic narratives" literature (e.g., Bates et al. 1999).

3. The discussion in this section draws heavily on Knight 1995.

4. In the next section I consider a second potential effect of competition on institutional emergence: the implications of competition for the effects of bargaining power on the emergence of institutions.

5. The introduction of bargaining power as an explanatory concept has been the subject of great debate in the social sciences. I want to stress that the bargaining model that I propose here does not fall prey to the standard objection that power is introduced as an ex post explanation of social phenomenon and thus produces merely a tautological description of that phenomenon. The explanation requires an ex ante identification of the relevant asymmetries in resource ownership. This allows for a subsequent assessment of whether the asymmetry does serve to resolve the bargaining conflict and lead to the selection of a particular institutional rule.

6. There is a related argument in Knight 1992 that emphasizes the relationship between available resources and time preferences. Drawing on Rubinstein's analysis (1982) of the effects of time preferences on bargaining, I argue that the implications of differentials in time preferences for the resolution of a bargaining conflict over institutions are substantially the same as that of differentials in risk aversion.

7. See Johnson 1996 for a cogent and persuasive argument to the effect that the primary benefit of rational choice theory in the social sciences is in the identification of social mechanisms. On this point, see also Knight and Johnson 1999.

8. See Petersen 1999 for a sympathetic discussion of some of the potential weaknesses of the mechanism approach.

9. For examples that extend the approach beyond the standard rational choice framework, see Boudon 1997, 1998; Elster 1999; and Petersen 1999.

10. For a more detailed discussion of this problem, see Knight and North 1997.

11. This is not to say that many historical institutionalist accounts do not fall prey to the same weakness that I have attributed to strategic analyses: the attribution of ex post institutional effects to the ex ante preferences of the actors. The main point is that the historical institutionalist approach emphasizes the importance of explaining preference formation and has the methodological tools to appropriately answer the question.

References

Alchian, Armen A. 1950. "Uncertainty, Evolution, and Economic Theory." *Journal of Political Economy* 58:211–21.

Bates, Robert. 1989. *Beyond the Miracle of the Market: The Political Economy of Agrarian Development in Kenya.* Cambridge: Cambridge University Press.

Bates, Robert H., Avner Greif, Margaret Levi, Jean-Laurent Rosenthal, and Barry R. Weingast. 1998. *Analytic Narratives.* Cambridge: Cambridge University Press.

Boudon, Raymond. 1991. "What Middle-Range Theories Are." *Contemporary Sociology* 20:519–22.

———. 1997. "The Present Relevance of Weber's Theory of *Wertrationalitat.*" Pp. 27–31 in *Methodology of the Social Sciences, Ethics, and Economics in the Newer Historical School: From Max Weber and Rickert to Sombart and Rothacker,* edited by Peter Koslowski. Berlin: Springer.

———. 1998. "Social Mechanisms without Black Boxes." Pp. 172–203 in *Social*

Mechanisms: An Analytical Approach to Social Theory, edited by Peter Hedstrom and Richard Swedberg. Cambridge: Cambridge University Press.

Brennan, Geoffrey, and James Buchanan. 1985. *The Reason of Rule*. Cambridge: Cambridge University Press.

Coase, Ronald. 1960. "The Problem of Social Cost." *Journal of Law and Economics* 3:1–44.

Coleman, James. 1990. *Foundations of Social Theory*. Cambridge: Harvard University Press.

Conaghan, Catherine, and James Malloy. 1994. *Unsettling Statecraft*. Pittsburgh: University of Pittsburgh Press.

Eggertsson, Thrainn. 1990. *Economic Institutions and Behavior*. Cambridge: Cambridge University Press.

Elster, Jon. 1998. "A Plea for Mechanisms." Pp. 45–73 in *Social Mechanisms: An Analytical Approach to Social Theory*, edited by Peter Hedstrom and Richard Swedberg. Cambridge: Cambridge University Press.

———. 1999. *Alchemies of the Mind: Rationality and the Emotions*. Cambridge: Cambridge University Press.

Ensminger, Jean. 1992. *Making a Market: The Institutional Transformation of an African Society*. Cambridge: Cambridge University Press.

Gambetta, Diego. 1998. "Concatenations of Mechanisms." Pp. 102–24 in *Social Mechanisms: An Analytical Approach to Social Theory*, edited by Peter Hedstrom and Richard Swedberg. Cambridge: Cambridge University Press.

Griffin, Clifford E. 1997. *Democracy and Neoliberalism in the Developing World*. Aldershot, England: Ashgate Publishing.

Haas, Peter M. 1989. "Do Regimes Matter? Epistemic Communities and Mediterranean Pollution Control." *International Organization* 43:377–403.

Hall, Peter A., and Rosemary C. R. Taylor. 1996. "Political Science and the Three New Institutionalisms." *Political Studies* 64:936–57.

Heckathorn, Douglas D., and Steven M. Maser. 1987. "Bargaining and Constitutional Contracts." *American Journal of Political Science* 31:142–68.

Hedstrom, Peter, and Richard Swedberg. 1998. "Social Mechanisms: An Introductory Essay." Pp. 1–31 in *Social Mechanisms: An Analytical Approach to Social Theory*, edited by Peter Hedstrom and Richard Swedberg. Cambridge: Cambridge University Press.

Johnson, James. 1996. "How Not to Criticize Rational Choice Theory." *Philosophy of the Social Sciences* 26(1)77–92.

Kahler, Miles. 1990. "Orthodoxy and Its Alternatives." In *Economic Crisis and Policy Choice*, edited by Joan Nelson. Princeton: Princeton University Press.

Knight, Jack. 1992. *Institutions and Social Conflict*. Cambridge: Cambridge University Press.

———. 1995. "Models, Interpretations, and Theories: Constructing Explanations of Institutional Emergence and Change." Pp. 95–120 in *Explaining Social Institutions*, edited by Jack Knight and Itai Sened. Ann Arbor: University of Michigan Press.

Knight, Jack, and James Johnson. 1999. "Inquiry into Democracy: What Might a Pragmatist Make of Rational Choice Theories?" *American Journal of Political Science* 43(2)566–89.

Knight, Jack, and Douglass North. 1997. "Explaining the Complexity of Institutional

Change." Pp. 211–26 in *The Political Economy of Property Rights*, edited by David L. Weimer. Cambridge: Cambridge University Press.

Kreps, David M. 1990. *A Course in Microeconomic Theory*. Princeton: Princeton University Press.

Lipton, D., and Jeffrey Sachs. 1990. "Creating a Market Economy in Eastern Europe." Pp. 75–133 in *Brookings Papers on Economic Activity*, edited by W. Brainard and G. Peters. Washington, DC: Brookings Institution.

Maynard-Smith, John. 1982. *Evolution and the Theory of Games*. Cambridge: Cambridge University Press.

Merton, Robert. 1967. "On Sociological Theories of the Middle Range." Pp. 39–72 in *On Theoretical Sociology*. New York: Free Press.

———. 1968. *Social Theory and Social Structure*. New York: Free Press.

Miller, Gary. 1992. *Managerial Dilemmas: The Political Economy of Hierarchy*. Cambridge: Cambridge University Press.

Morales J., and Jeffrey Sachs. 1989. "Bolivia's Economic Crisis." Pp. 57–80 in *Developing Country Debt and Economic Performance*, edited by Jeffrey Sachs. Chicago: University of Chicago Press.

Naim, Moises. 1993. "Latin America: Post-Adjustment Blues." *Foreign Policy* 92:133–50.

North, Douglass C. 1990. *Institutions, Institutional Change, and Economic Performance*. Cambridge: Cambridge University Press.

Osborne, Martin J., and Ariel Rubenstein. 1990. *Bargaining and Markets*. San Diego: Academic Press.

Ostrom, Elinor. 1990. *Governing the Commons*. Cambridge: Cambridge University Press.

Otero, Gerardo. 1996. *Neoliberalism Revisited: Economic Restructuring and Mexico's Political Future*. Boulder, CO: Westview Press.

Pierson, Paul. 1994. *Dismantling the Welfare State?* New York: Cambridge University Press.

Petersen, Roger. 1999. "Mechanisms and Structures in Comparisons." Pp. 61–77 in *Critical Comparisons in Politics and Culture*, edited by John Bowen and Roger Peterson. Cambridge: Cambridge University Press.

Przeworski, Adam. 1991. *Democracy and the Market*. Cambridge: Cambridge University Press.

Roberts, Kenneth M. 1995. "Neoliberalism and the Transformation of Populism in Latin America: The Peruvian Case." *World Politics* 48:82–116.

Rubenstein, Ariel. 1982. "Perfect Equilibrium in a Bargaining Model." *Econometrica* 50:97–109.

Schelling, Thomas. 1998. "Social Mechanisms and Social Dynamics." Pp. 32–44 in *Social Mechanisms: An Analytical Approach to Social Theory*, edited by Peter Hedstrom and Richard Swedberg. Cambridge: Cambridge University Press.

Smith, William C., and Roberto Patricio Korzeniewicz. 1997. *Politics, Social Change, and Economic Restructuring in Latin America*. Miami, FL: North-South Center Press.

Stallings, Barbara. 1992. "International Influence on Economic Policy." Pp. 41–88 in *The Politics of Economic Adjustment*, edited by Stephan Haggard and Robert Kaufman. Princeton: Princeton University Press.

Teichman, Judith A. 1995. *Privatization and Political Change in Mexico*. Pittsburgh: University of Pittsburgh Press.

Veltmeyer, Henry, James Petras, and Steve Vieux. 1997. *Neoliberalism and Class Conflict in Latin America*. New York: St. Martin's Press.

Weyland, Kurt. 1996. "Risk Taking in Latin American Economic Restructuring: Lessons from Prospect Theory." *International Studies Quarterly* 40:185–208.

Williamson, Oliver. 1975. *Markets and Hierarchies*. New York: Free Press.

———. 1985. *The Economic Institutions of Capitalism*. New York: Free Press.

Chapter 3

Have We Overestimated the Effects of Neoliberalism and Globalization?

SOME SPECULATIONS ON THE ANOMALOUS STABILITY OF TAXES ON BUSINESS

EDGAR KISER AND AARON MATTHEW LAING

IT IS very rare in the social sciences to find neoclassical economists, political scientists, and Marxist sociologists in agreement, or to find a convergence of opinion between theorists stressing the causal importance of culture and ideas and those focusing more on material constraints and interests. So when they all predict the same thing, regardless of the differences in their assumptions and political biases, our confidence in the veracity of that prediction should be unusually high.

This is exactly what we find on the issue of business taxation in advanced capitalist countries over the past couple of decades. Whether it is explained as a consequence of the rise of neoliberal ideas or the increasing mobility of capital due to globalization, scholars of all theoretical stripes have confidently asserted that taxes on business should be declining (Steinmo 1993, p. 17; Frenkel, Razin, and Sadka 1991; McKenzie and Lee 1991, p. 1; Cohen 1996, p. 287; Hallerberg 1996; Helleiner 1994; Kurzer 1993; Dehejia and Geschel 1999, p. 403). It is interesting that this consensus exists in spite of the lack of systematic evidence;[1] most scholars seem to assume that the only real question remaining is the relative weight of political, cultural, and economic causal factors.[2]

It is thus quite surprising to find out that the theoretical consensus is wrong. As figure 3-1 shows, in Organization for Economic Cooperation and Development (OECD) countries,[3] the predicted effects of neoliberalism and globalization on business taxation are nowhere to be found. Total taxes on capital in OECD countries have not only not decreased over the past two decades, but have increased slightly. Most of the increase can be accounted for by employer social security contributions, pushed higher by demographic pressures (see Williamson and Pampel 1993). But corporate income taxes have not declined either; figure 3-1 shows that they have remained remarkably stable. To be more specific, marginal corporate tax rates have gone down in the past couple of decades in many countries, but various exemptions and deductions have been reduced or eliminated as well. The net effect is very little change in corporate income taxes (Swank 1998). Scholars who have looked only at marginal tax rates have thus often reached the incorrect conclusion that taxes on business have declined (e.g., Wallerstein and Przeworski 1995, p. 425).

This sort of anomaly is one of the best sources of progress in science — it forces us to think about things in new ways, and it helps us see which theories provide the most useful tools for explaining the unexpected. This paper will explore the extent to which a rational choice version of institutionalism can account for this anomaly. We begin with a short discussion of theoretical arguments about the effects of globalization/capital mobility and the rise of neoliberalism on business taxation. Since no existing theories provide obvious explanations of the stability of taxes on business in the developed world, we then turn to two means of resolving the anomaly: more detailed explorations of the data and further elaboration of the theory.

Theoretical Expectations of Declining Taxes on Business

There are two general types of arguments about state policy formation that lead to the conclusion that taxes on business should have been declining in the past couple of decades. Although these arguments are often mixed in practice, we outline fairly pure forms of the theories in order to stress their differences (cf. Campbell 1998 for an alternative strategy, developing a synthesis of two forms of institutionalism). The first, often referred to as organizational or cultural institutionalism, explains policy formation primarily in terms of general cultural, ideological, or intellectual trends that shape the worldviews and cognitive frames of policy makers (Meyer et al. 1997; DiMaggio and Powell 1983; Heclo 1974).[4] Things like how leaders understand and interpret the world, the information and the "mental models" that tell them about basic causal relations and processes, are seen as major determinants of their policy choices. For example, an early modern ruler who believes in mercantilist ideas about the relationship between trade and national prosperity will choose different policies than will one who has been convinced by the ideas of Smith and Ricardo.

The application of this argument to business taxation focuses on the shift from the Keynesian economic ideas that had shaped policy formation since the 1930s to the neoliberal ideas that became dominant among academic experts, powerful institutions (such as the IMF and World Bank), and influential political leaders (such as Thatcher and Reagan) in the late 1970s and 1980s. Neoliberal arguments suggested that several policy changes could increase the wealth of nations: privatization of state industries, deregulation of markets, cuts in state spending (especially on transfer payments to the poor), and cuts in taxes, especially taxes on business (the increased investments made as a result

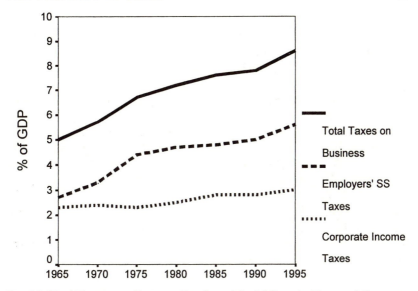

Fig. 3-1. Total Taxation on Business: Employers' Social Security Taxes and Corporate Income Taxation in OECD Countries as a Percentage of GDP (OECD 1997, pp. 80–83)

of the latter would create more wealth, which proponents argued would "trickle down" to the middle and lower classes).

Although their influence was clearly strongest in Britain and the United States, these neoliberal ideas influenced politics throughout the developed world — even the social democratic welfare states were not entirely immune. The central prediction of this theoretical perspective is clear: as neoliberal ideas began to influence political leaders in the late 1970s and 1980s, taxes on business should have declined.[5]

More materialist arguments from Marxism, rational choice, and historical institutionalism seem to fare no better. Lindblom (1977) and Block (1977) argue that states are dependent on capitalists because economic growth (and thus the tax base) is determined by the private investment decisions of owners of capital. Therefore, the threat of disinvestment or capital flight can have significant effects on state policy — state policy will tend to reflect the interests of business. The power of capitalists comes as much from threats of "exit" as it does from "voice" (Hirschman 1970); the ruling class does not have to rule (Block 1977).

This line of argument has been revitalized by recent economic changes. Several scholars have argued that with the globalization of economies the costs of exit have declined, thus further increasing the power of business and the likelihood that state policies will be in their interests (see Cohen 1996 for a good review of this literature).[6] As a result of this, policy makers will find it increasingly difficult to fund social welfare programs, use redistributive taxation, and tax business (Steinmo 1993). The specific prediction following from this is that as potential and actual capital movements increase (they increased moderately beginning in the early 1970s and at a more rapid pace beginning in the mid-1980s [Swank 1998]), taxes on capital should decrease (Frenkel, Razin, and Sadka 1991; Hallerberg 1996; Dehejia and Genschel 1999).

Although this argument is compelling theoretically, it has not fared well empirically. Jacobs (1988), Quinn and Shapiro (1991), Garrett (1998), and Swank (1998) find no support for the hypothesis. These theories also have a hard time accounting for the specific nature of tax reforms in recent decades. Not all capital is equally mobile — we can differentiate roughly between international businesses that can make credible exit threats and domestic businesses (defined as those with especially high costs of exit) that generally cannot. States interested in maximizing their revenue would be expected to treat the two groups differently. Since only international capitalists have increased power with globalization, they should be the only group to get tax breaks — domestic businesses have no leverage. Theorists would thus predict that tax reform would take the form of particularistic tax cuts, exemptions, or deductions for international capitalists. Overall, exactly the opposite has happened — there have been across-the-board tax cuts, but these have been balanced by the elimination of most particularistic tax breaks (Swank 1998). Moreover, Hallerberg (1996) argues that domestic (immobile) capitalists such as farmers often get lower tax rates due to their political power.

In an effort to account for the anomalous stability of business taxation, we use rational choice institutionalism to generate two potential explanations. First, tax rates on business across the developed world are expected to converge as capital mobility increases, and this will lead to a decline in capital mobility over time (and thus in its effects on business taxes). Collusion between states could speed this process, and could produce a higher tax rate equilibrium.

Second, we move beyond the sole focus on taxes to include variations in the bundle of services provided to capitalists by the state. Exchanges between business and the state can be altered on two dimensions: the amount of tax paid by business and the quantity of services provided by the state. Even though businesses are not paying less tax, they may be getting more services from the state for the same amount of taxation. If so, the argument that globalization has increased the power of business over the state may be right after all.

A third explanation can be more briefly discussed and rejected. Hirschman (1970) argues that there are two main reactions to an unfavorable situation: "exit" and "voice." Perhaps the increase in the exit power of capitalists has been counterbalanced by a decline in their power of voice. The voice power of business in the United States has been operationalized in two main ways, campaign contributions and collective action capacity. Studies of the relationship between campaign contributions and state policy have produced contradictory findings (Domhoff 1998; Quinn and Shapiro 1991; Williams and Collins 1997). However, there is good reason to believe that the influence of business measured in this way has increased over time. Until legislation in 1971 and 1974, corporate campaign contributions were illegal. As a result, "the great majority of corporations engaged in limited or no overt involvement in national politics before the late 1960s" (Quinn and Shapiro 1991, p. 855). Compared to the total absence of corporate contributions prior to the 1970s, over half of the Fortune 500 firms contributed to political action committees (PACs) in 1980 (Quinn and Shapiro 1991, p. 855). A second possibility, followed by Jacobs (1988), is to try to measure the collective action capacity of capital. He argues that the greater the concentration of assets within the capitalist class, the greater the likelihood that it will be able to overcome free riding problems and affect state policy (Olson 1965). Although his data analysis supports the hypothesis, Quinn and Shapiro (1991) find no association. Overall, then, it seems unlikely that the voice power of business has decreased substantially in the United States and, presumably, in the rest of the OECD countries over the past few decades.

Since the arguments about globalization and neoliberalism refer not to particular states, but to the world economy and polity as a whole, we will focus primarily on overall trends in the OECD, using aggregated data. However, in order to explore the effects of institutional differences across societies, we also (1) look at certain trends within the European Union (has there been greater convergence of tax policies within the EU?) and (2) examine variations in political institutions by comparing the most neoliberal states (United States and Britain) to the Scandinavian social democracies (Sweden, Norway, Finland, Denmark).

Have Tax Rates on Business Converged over Time?

Will increasing cultural and economic ties between societies lead to a convergence of policies, or will institutional differences inhibit these effects? As Milner and Keohane (1996, Pp. 19–20) note, this question requires further research. Taxes on business provide an apposite research site to address this issue, since they are important policies and relatively easy to measure quantitatively.

This section addresses four related questions: (1) To what extent have tax rates on capital converged over time? (2) Have globalization and neoliberalism facilitated convergence? (3) Have international organizations like the European Union increased the pace of convergence? (4) Has convergence occurred across even the most institutionally different developed states (comparing neoliberal Britain and the United States to the Scandinavian social democracies)?

When the mobility of capital is costly and thus infrequent, taxes on business are likely to vary significantly between countries. The situation is roughly analogous to large differences in profits across sectors of the economy when barriers to entry are high. If an exogenous change in some factor (such as the improvements in communications, data processing, and data storage techniques that have facilitated globalization) makes capital mobility less costly, mobility from high-tax to low-tax states will increase.[7] This movement will be expected to put pressure on high-tax states to lower their taxes on capital to prevent further capital flight that will deplete their tax base (Lindblom 1977; Block 1977). Just as profits are expected to equalize when barriers to entry are removed, so too should taxes on capital equalize as the costs of mobility decrease.[8]

More theoretically, in an increasingly global economy, states face a classic collective action problem (a multiple player prisoner's dilemma game) with respect to business taxation (Frey 1990; Hallerberg 1996; but cf. Dehejia and Genschel 1999). All states would prefer stable, fairly high levels of taxation (not so high as to "kill the goose," of course), but they can do so only if other states do likewise. The collective interest of states would thus be best served by all agreeing to maintain similar high levels of taxes on business. The problem is that individual states could benefit by free riding on this agreement, lowering their tax rates in order to attract capital from the others. Since all states know this, they are expected to begin a "race to the bottom," in which tax rates will cascade downward. The outcome is the worst one for their collective interests: a convergence of all states on low taxes on capital (Frey 1990, p. 89).

Whereas previous studies have tested the argument about capital flight and business taxes by looking only at variations over time within countries, we instead look at the variation across countries at the same time. If the argument about increasing capital mobility leading to convergence is correct, the standard deviation across countries should decrease. Since capital movements have increased moderately from the early 1970s, and more rapidly from the mid-1980s, we can test the following convergence hypothesis: *The variance in tax rates on business across developed countries will decrease moderately beginning in the early 1970s and more rapidly beginning in the mid-1980s.*

Convergence can be created by one of two causal mechanisms: market forces (as discussed above) or collective action by states. If it is due entirely to market forces, we would expect a low tax equilibrium, resulting from the race to the bottom. However, since the leaders of states are aware of this as a possible (even likely) outcome, and since they are involved in a repeated game with other state leaders, they may decide to collude to prevent it. Agreements along these lines have been discussed in a wide variety of international groups, including the OECD and the European Union, but they have thus far produced no formal agreements (Dehejia and Genschel 1999). It is difficult to know, however, whether these talks have resulted in informal pacts affecting tax rates. If states can make binding agreements to maintain similar high rates of taxation on business, and if the enforcement costs do not exceed the tax revenues, all of them will be better off. Thus, *if the causal mechanism is collective action, we would expect to find convergence of tax rates without a drop in the level of taxation.*[9] More specifically, we would expect more convergence in the states belonging to the most organized group in the OECD, the European Union.

Figure 3-2 shows the degree of variance (measured by the standard deviation) in the two most common taxes on business (corporate income taxes and employer social security contributions) across both OECD and EU countries for the past thirty years. At first glance, these data provide little support for the convergence hypothesis. In most cases, the variance across countries is greater now than it was in 1965 — so neither globalization nor neoliberal ideas seem to have produced the predicted convergence. The variance in social security contributions is much higher, and has increased since 1965 in what looks like a fairly predictable step function. This, however, could be due to demographic differences across these countries.

A closer look at the trend in the degree of variance in corporate income taxes does provide limited support for the convergence hypothesis. It increased fairly

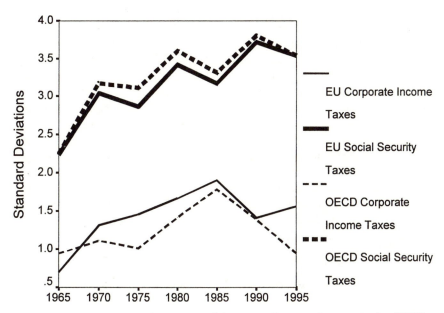

Fig. 3-2. Variance in Social Security and Corporate Taxes on Business in the OECD and EU (OECD 1997, pp. 80–83)

steadily between 1965 and 1985, but has declined sharply since. By 1994, it had declined to about its 1965 level. Since capital mobility began to increase dramatically around the mid-1980s, this change provides some evidence for convergence driven by globalization.

As noted above, the fact that this limited convergence has occurred without a decline in tax levels (and even with a slight increase; see fig. 3-1) lends support to collusion between states as the causal mechanism. Of course, collusion of this sort is often difficult to verify empirically. In an attempt to do that, we looked at the most highly organized group within the OECD, the European Union (EU) member states. Since they make up a large part of the OECD, maybe collective action within the EU is mostly responsible for this recent trend toward convergence. However, figure 3-2 shows that the trend toward convergence is much less pronounced in the EU than in the OECD as a whole. In fact, the variance in corporate income taxes within the EU increased between 1990 and 1994, while it was declining in the OECD as a whole. Therefore, the largest and most organized group within the OECD does not seem to be responsible for the collective action producing convergence. The OECD discussions (Dehejia and Genschel 1999) could have had some effect, but more detailed research would be necessary before coming to that conclusion.

Figure 3-3 shows the limits of convergence and the importance of national political institutions clearly. The increase in capital mobility in the early 1970s affected neoliberal states and social democratic states in very different ways (see Garrett 1998 for a detailed discussion of these differences). In fact, it seems clear that globalization decreased the extent of convergence across these states — the difference in their taxation of business is almost three times as great in 1995 as it was in 1965! Taxes on business have been relatively stable in the United States and Britain — increasing slightly until around 1985, with a minor decline following that. In sharp contrast, business taxes in Scandinavia rose sharply between 1970 and 1980, and have increased moderately since then. If we focus on the period between 1980 and 1995, it looks as if there are two tax regime equilibria, a social democratic strategy with high capital taxes and a neoliberal strategy with lower capital taxes, both of which have been relatively stable for fifteen years. This supports arguments made by Esping-Andersen (1990) and Garrett (1998) about the lack of convergence between different types of political regimes, which raises an interesting question: How have the social democratic states been able to prevent capital flight to low-tax states and remain economically competitive?

Has State Spending for Business Increased with Globalization?

Although everyone recognizes that the relationship between businesses and the state is complex and multifaceted, quantitative studies of the effects of glob-

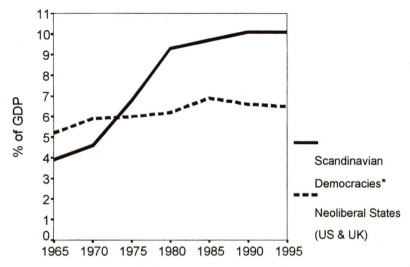

Fig. 3-3. Total Taxes on Business in Neoliberal States and Scandinavian Social Democracies. *Denmark, Finland, Norway, and Sweden (OECD 1997, pp. 80–83)

alization on business tax rates have tended to focus only on one part of the relationship—how much businesses pay in taxes (Quinn and Shapiro 1991;
Williams and Collins 1997; Swank 1998; Garrett 1998 is a notable exception).
We have also been making this assumption in the prior two sections. This
makes sense pragmatically for researchers, since tax rates are easy to quantify.
The problem is that taxes are only one side of the coin—the other is state
spending, the bundle of state services that these payments fund. Looking only
at how much businesses have to pay without also addressing what they get in
return leads to a one-sided and misleading picture — it is analogous to viewing
consumers as concerned only with price and not with the quality of the product they are buying (from that perspective, it would be impossible to understand why anyone would buy German cars or French wine instead of their
cheaper American counterparts).

Business decisions about where to locate are based not just on minimizing
taxes, but on finding the "best buy"—the best services for the tax "price."[10]
Therefore, in order to adequately measure the extent to which globalization
has increased the power of business relative to the state, and thus their ability
to shape policies in their interests, we need to look not only at what has happened to their tax payments, but at how the money the state spends for them
has changed, as well. Even though the taxes on business have not declined,
they could now be getting more services for the same tax bill.[11] If so, the anomaly would not be due to the theory being wrong, but to its operationalization
(focusing only on taxation) being too narrow.

A focus on only taxes and "services" may be too narrow as well. States could also respond to increased bargaining power of capitalists by decreasing various restrictions on business activity that decrease profits, such as environmental regulations or labor relations, for example. These restrictions on the activities of business can be viewed as "taxes" on business, since many of them have the same effect on the bottom line. Looking in some detail at variations in the overall level of restrictions on business (however that could be measured) is also probably necessary to fully test the argument about the effect of capital mobility on state-business relations.

Given that the state can respond to the increased bargaining power of international business by either lowering their taxes or increasing spending for them, which is the more likely outcome?[12] There are a few reasons to expect that the state, and to a lesser extent business, would prefer increased service provision to lower taxes. First, if the state is the most efficient producer of a commodity (such as highways, for example) for which there is high demand from business, then both the state and the consumers of that commodity would prefer more of it rather than paying less for the same amount. If there are economies of scale to the production of the commodity, the preference for additional services over tax relief will be even stronger. Many government-provided goods and services could be marked by such economies of scale. The cost per mile of highways should decline with their length, for example. This should be true until diminishing returns make an additional unit of the commodity less appealing to the consumer than the monetary equivalent.

Second, many services that the state provides for business, such as infrastructure, benefit other citizens as well. So when political leaders provide extra services for business, they are simultaneously increasing the number of votes they are likely to get in the next election. Whereas a tax cut to business may seem like an uncompensated loss to many voters, they may be more willing to increase their tax bill to pay for services from which they (as well as capitalists) will benefit.[13] To the extent that these services are public goods, the fact that business also benefits will not affect their utility.

Having argued that increased service provision is a more likely consequence of an increase in the power of business due to globalization, we face the same problem that has caused others to ignore this and focus only on taxation: how can we quantify state services to business? Luckily, there is a great deal of agreement among scholars from different disciplines and theoretical perspectives about what types of state spending will benefit capitalists. Most fundamentally, law and order must be maintained and property rights must be protected, but within the developed OECD states studied here these factors are roughly constant (this would certainly not be true of many other parts of the world). Beyond that, proponents of the New Growth Theory in economics (Barro and Sala-I-Martin 1995), historical institutionalists in political science (Garrett 1998), and Marxist sociologists (O'Connor 1973) agree that a state's expenditures on infrastructure, direct subsidies to business, and educational spending (building human capital) can all increase productivity and profits. As Garrett (1998, p. 8) argues, "government spending on human and physical capital is unlikely to provoke capital flight."

Figures 3-4, 3-5, and 3-6 document various types of spending on business in the OECD, and in neoliberal and social democratic states. The central questions concern whether these types of spending have increased as a consequence of globalization and neoliberalism, and whether patterns vary in states with different political institutions.

Figure 3-4 shows the most direct spending for business in OECD countries: infrastructure/capital spending and direct subsidies. Subsidies to industry are roughly stable until 1975, and decline slightly over the next fifteen years. This finding is contrary to what one would expect from globalization and capital flight—subsidies in particular would be expected to increase, since they are the most direct way of paying capitalists to stay. The decline does provide some evidence of the effects of neoliberal ideas, however, since these subsidies conflict with free market principles. Also providing no evidence for globalization effects, OECD capital spending increases slightly between 1965 and 1980, and remains stable after that.

Figure 3-5 looks at the same two types of spending for business, but this time contrasting neoliberal and social democratic states. Subsidies to capital have been declining in both types of states, showing that the process documented

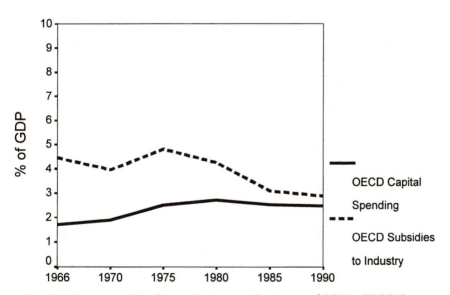

Fig. 3-4. Government Spending on Business as a Percentage of GDP in OECD Countries (Fourteen Country Average) (Garrett 1998)

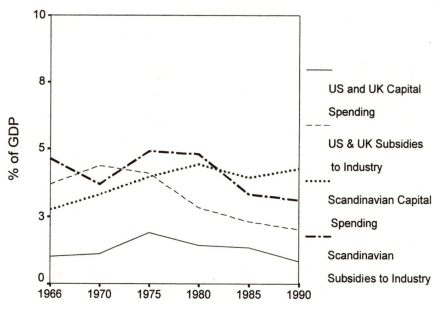

Fig. 3-5. Government Spending on Business as a Percentage of GDP in Neoliberal States and Scandinavian Social Democracies (Garrett 1998)

for the OECD as a whole is fairly widespread. The fact that the level of subsidies is lower and declines faster in neoliberal than in social democratic states lends further support to the argument that neoliberal ideas are important. Perhaps the most interesting finding in the figure is the consistent difference between the levels of capital spending by the state in the two types of regimes. Capital spending is consistently and significantly higher in social democratic than in neoliberal states. This answers the question posed at the conclusion of the preceding section — capitalists stay in social democratic states even though they pay higher taxes because they get a higher level of services in return (Garrett [1998] comes to a similar conclusion).

Figure 3-6, documenting government spending on human capital (education), reinforces these themes. There is again little evidence of strong globalization effects. Educational spending, like other types of spending for business, does not increase in the OECD with increases in capital flows in the 1970s or mid-1980s, but is relatively stable throughout. However, we again see major differences between social democratic and neoliberal regimes. The divergence between the two seems to begin around the middle of the 1970s, and they have diverged increasingly since. Spending on human capital by the state, as with physical capital, is significantly higher in social democracies.

Another feature of the taxes-services exchange would be worth exploring in

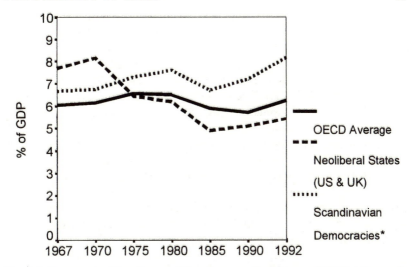

Fig. 3-6. Government Spending on Education as a Percentage of GDP. *Denmark, Finland, Norway, and Sweden (*UN Statistical Yearbook*, various years)

future research. One reason for the failure of taxes on business to decline further could be that they have already reached the floor set by the costs of providing services to capital. If taxes are seen as payments for services, no state will stay "in business" long if it sells these services below their cost. Perhaps the power of capitalists prior to globalization and neoliberalism was already great enough to allow them to force their taxes down to this floor. If that threshold was already reached, further ideological or economic changes would not push tax rates on capital down further. Testing this hypothesis will be very difficult, however, since it would entail knowing the actual costs of all state services and goods provided to business.

Conclusion

Anomalies are often very difficult to resolve, as the anomalous stability of taxes on business illustrates. No existing theory explains it, and the strategies suggested by rational choice theory that we have explored in this chapter have produced a few leads, but not much more.

There is some limited evidence of convergence, and evidence that it has been the result of collective action by states to decrease the variance in taxes on business while holding tax levels constant (although the collective action has apparently not been in the EU). This suggests that the answer to the anomaly may be found in repeated game theory, and collective action theory more generally. Empirically, more in-depth methods, such as detailed case studies of various international agreements and organizations, may be useful next steps.

Our second attempt at resolving the anomaly, viewing taxation as a payment for services and trying to see if service provision has changed, also failed to clearly resolve it. Although there are hints of globalization and neoliberalism effects in these data, no trend is strong or consistent.

Neoliberal and social democratic states are clearly characterized by very different tax regimes (Esping-Andersen 1990; Garrett 1998). The main thing that the comparison between neoliberal and social democratic states shows is that the market for capital is becoming increasingly differentiated. Instead of thinking that there is one optimal tax rate and one optimal bundle of services associated with it on which all states would be expected to converge, perhaps we would find it useful to view the market for capital as more differentiated. If businesses are now becoming increasingly diverse, what they need from the state, and what they are willing to pay for it, may also be more varied. Perhaps the lack of decline in rates and the lack of convergence are due to this increasing differentiation. Based on their different attributes (comparative advantages), states could each be trying to put together *unique* bundles of services at different prices in order to attract or keep *particular* types of capitalists.

It would be interesting to explore whether combining ideas from different types of institutionalism might provide a better explanation of this anomaly. There are some indications that useful synthesis might be possible (e.g., Campbell 1998). For example, arguments about the effects of exit strategies (capital flight) on business taxes (and relations between capital and the state more generally) have been made in fairly similar terms by historical institutionalists, Marxists, pluralists, and rational choice theorists. In this case, as in many others, these theories are overlapping at least, and sometimes (in the case of rational choice and some of the more materialist versions of historical institutionalism) almost indistinguishable (see Immergut 1998 for a detailed argument stressing the similarities of varieties of institutionalism). It is interesting to note that probably the most influential rational choice institutionalist opens his preface with this sentence: "History matters" (North 1990). Moreover, it would be wrong to view even organizational institutionalism as strictly opposed to rational choice. Since few rational choice models outside economics (and increasingly few within economics) assume perfect information, the beliefs actors hold about the world (their information) are important determinants of their actions. Some rational choice theorists have even begun to incorporate causal "mental models" into their explanations (see esp. North 1990).

The fact that taxes on capital have not declined recently, in spite of fundamental economic and ideological transformations, suggests that we may have overestimated the effects of both globalization and neoliberalism (both Garrett [1998] and Wade [1996] provide interesting arguments along these lines). These factors did not lead to the dismantling of the welfare state, as Pierson (1994) has pointed out. Moreover, Campbell and Allen (2001) show that the current tax regime in the United States began in the early 1950s — globalization and neoliberalism do not seem to have affected U.S. tax regimes (at least up to 1986). Perhaps we have overestimated their effects in other areas, as well.

Notes

This paper was initially presented at the conference "Comparative Institutional Analysis: The Rise and Development of Neoliberalism in the 1980s and 1990s," August 1998. We would like to thank all conference participants, and Terry Boswell, Yong Cai, April Eaton, and Josh Kane for helpful comments.

1. It is not that rare to find examples of widely accepted "facts" about taxation that turn out on closer examination to be misconceptions. As Steinmo (1993, p. 1) puts it, "not only do we know little about tax policy, but what we think we know is often wrong." His book provides several interesting illustrations of incorrect "conventional wisdom."

2. A somewhat embarrassing personal story illustrates the extent to which the claim that taxes on business have been declining recently was assumed to be true. Over dinner at a small conference last spring, I began to discuss my ideas about a paper on why taxes on business were declining — was it due to culture (the rise of neoliberal ideas) or material factors (globalization and the increasing mobility of capital)? Several people began to offer their ideas about the relative importance of these two causes, how they might be related, and how I might be able to adjudicate between them. Before the conversation got too far along, Paul Pierson pointed out that my premise was wrong — taxes on capital have not been declining — and suggested some things I should read that documented that fact. I can't thank him enough for saving me from writing a paper debating the causes of something that didn't happen.

3. The OECD consists of twenty-eight countries in Europe, North America, and Asia. Our data set consists of seventeen of those countries (Australia, Austria, Belgium, Canada, Denmark, Finland, France, Germany, Ireland, Italy, Japan, Netherlands, Norway, Sweden, Switzerland, United Kingdom, and United States). We left out all of the Eastern European postsocialist countries because they would not have experienced much of either capital mobility or neoliberalism prior to 1989. We also had to drop a few additional cases due to missing data — they tended to be biased toward the poorer countries in the OECD. Following Garrett 1998, we use unweighted averages in all figures.

4. Heclo (1974) may seem miscategorized here, since he is usually coded as a historical institutionalist. We tend to see the more culturally oriented historical institutionalists, such as Heclo (1974), as closer to organizational institutionalism. Campbell (1998) shows that the arguments of these two camps can be usefully combined.

5. Some other features of tax reforms have reflected neoliberal principles. As Swank (1998) puts it, there has been a shift in most countries from a "market-regulating" policy rule based on higher tax rates along with many particularistic deductions and exemptions to a "market-conforming" rule based on lower rates but fewer specific ex-

emptions. Since this shift decreases state control of the market through business taxes, it could be argued that neoliberalism had some effect on business taxes.

6. Since capitalists can decrease investments without leaving (or by moving to a different location within the same country, if the state has a federal structure), the arguments made by Lindblom (1977) and Block (1977) are not entirely dependent on globalization. The increasing global mobility of capital is, however, one of the main causal mechanisms.

7. There are of course many reasons other than taxation for moving or staying (labor costs being primary among them). We explore some of these below, but for simplicity we will ignore them for now.

8. Economists have long argued that rates of profit will equalize across different industries. Capital will move from low-profit to higher-profit sectors, increasing competition and thus driving down profits in the latter (unless there are very high barriers to entry). However, the analogy to the situation discussed here is only partial, since the causal process is more complicated. In the case of capital mobility across sectors, the causal mechanism works directly through the "invisible hand" of the markets (a simple aggregation of individual investment decisions), whereas the argument we develop here requires that the leaders of states recognize the situation and take explicit actions as a result.

9. The nature of the relationship between capital mobility, convergence, and rates of business taxation could also vary over time. Capital moves to take advantages of differences across states, such as differences in their rates of business taxation. The extent of convergence thus affects the incentives for capital mobility (the greater the convergence, the lower the incentive to move). Therefore, capital mobility could be a self-limiting process — as a result, its ability to drive business taxes downward could decrease over time. Once tax rates have converged, the threat of capital flight will be less credible, and the power of capitalists relative to the state will be diminished.

10. Different types of businesses will of course require and value different types and amounts of services, but we ignore that complication here.

11. O'Connor (1973) argues that the increase in state services to business is due to the shift from competitive to monopoly capitalism in the post–World War II period. It would be interesting to compare O'Connor's prediction of a large increase in services to business after World War II with the prediction of globalization arguments that the increase would come in the 1970s and especially in the 1980s.

12. This is a subset of a much larger question about the relationship between suppliers of commodities and consumers. In order to increase sales, producers can either lower the price or provide more of the commodity at the same price — which is likely to be the profit-maximizing strategy?

13. There are significant differences across countries in the willingness of voters to pay extra taxes for extra services — Swedish voters are much more willing to do so than those in the United States, for example.

References

Barro, Robert, and Xavier Sala-I-Martin. 1995. *Economic Growth*. New York: McGraw-Hill.

Block, Fred. 1977. "The Ruling Class Does Not Rule." *Socialist Revolution* 33:6–28.

Campbell, John L. 1998. "Institutional Analysis and the Role of Ideas in Political Economy." *Theory and Society* 27:377–409.

Campbell, John L., and Michael Patrick Allen. 2001. "Identifying Shifts in Policy Regimes: Cluster and Interrupted Time-Series Analyses of U.S. Income Taxes." *Social Science History* 25(2)37–65.

Cohen, Benjamin J. 1996. "Phoenix Risen: The Resurrection of Global Finance." *World Politics* 48:268–96.

Dehejia, Vivek, and Philipp Genschel. 1999. "Tax Competition in the European Union." *Politics and Society* 27(3)403–30.

DiMaggio, Paul J., and Walter W. Powell. 1983. "The Iron Cage Revisited." *American Sociological Review* 48:147–60.

Domhoff, G., William. 1998. *Who Rules America? Power and Politics in the Year 2000.* Mountain View, CA: Mayfield Publishing Company.

Esping-Andersen, Gosta. 1990. *Three Worlds of Welfare Capitalism.* Cambridge: Polity Press.

Frenkel, Jacob, Assaf Razin, and Efraim Sadka. 1991. *International Taxation in an Integrated World.* Cambridge: MIT Press.

Frey, Bruno. 1990. "Intergovernmental Tax Competition." Pp. 88–101 in *The Influence of Tax Differentials on International Competitiveness,* edited by Charles McLure, Hans-Vemer Sinn, Richard Musgrave, and Klaus Vogel. Deventer: Kluwer Law and Taxation Publishers.

Garrett, 1998. *Partisan Politics in the Global Economy.* New York: Cambridge University Press.

Hallerberg, Mark. 1996. "Tax Competition in Wilhelmine, Germany, and Its Implications for the European Union." *World Politics* 48(3)324–57.

Heclo, Hugh. 1974. *Modern Social Politics in Britain and Sweden: From Relief to Income Maintenance.* New Haven: Yale University Press.

Helleiner, Eric. 1994. *States and the Reemergence of Global Finance: From Bretton Woods to the 1990s.* Ithaca: Cornell University Press.

Hirschman, Albert O. 1970. *Exit, Voice, and Loyalty: Responses to Decline in Firms, Organizations, and States.* Cambridge: Harvard University Press.

Immergut, Ellen. 1998. "The Theoretical Core of the New Institutionalism." *Politics and Society* 26:5–34.

Jacobs, David. 1988. "Corporate Taxation and Corporate Economic Power." *American Journal of Sociology* 93:852–81.

Kurzer, Paulette. 1993. *Business and Banking: Political Change and Economic Integration in Western Europe.* Ithaca: Cornell University Press.

Lindblom, Charles E. 1977. *Politics and Markets: The World's Political-Economic System.* New York: Basic Books.

McKenzie, Richard, and Dwight Lee. 1991. *Quicksilver Capital: How the Rapid Movement of Wealth Has Changed the World.* New York: Free Press.

Meyer, John W. 1979. "The World Polity and the Authority of the Nation-State." Pp. 109–97 in *Studies of the Modern World-System,* edited by Albert J. Bergensen. New York: Academic Press.

Meyer, John W., John Boli, George M. Thomas, and Francisco O. Ramirez. 1997. "World Society and the Nation-State." *American Journal of Sociology* 103:144–81.

Milner, Helen, and Robert Keohane. 1996. "Internationalization and Domestic Politics: An Introduction." Pp. 3–24 in *Internationalization and Domestic Politics*, edited by Robert Keohane and Helen Milner. New York: Cambridge University Press.

North, Douglass C. 1990. *Institutions, Institutional Change, and Economic Performance*. New York: Cambridge University Press.

O'Connor, James. 1973. *The Fiscal Crisis of the State*. New York: St. Martin's Press.

OECD. 1997. *Revenue Statistics, 1965–1995*. Paris: OECD Publications.

Olson, Mancur. 1965. *The Logic of Collective Action*. Cambridge: Harvard University Press.

Pierson, Paul. 1994. *Dismantling the Welfare State? Reagan, Thatcher, and the Politics of Retrenchment*. New York: Cambridge University Press.

Quinn, Dennis P., and Robert Y. Shapiro. 1991. "Business Political Power: The Case of Taxation." *American Political Science Review* 85:850–74.

Steinmo, Sven. 1993. *Taxation and Democracy: Swedish, British, and American Approaches to Financing the Modern State*. New Haven: Yale University Press.

Swank, Duane. 1998. "Funding the Welfare State: Globalization and the Taxation of Business in Advanced Market Economies." *Political Studies* 46(4)671–92.

United Nations. Various years. *U.N. Statistical Yearbook*. New York: United Nations.

Wade, Robert. 1996. "Globalization and Its Limits: Reports of the Death of the National Economy are Greatly Exaggerated." Pp. 60–88 in *National Diversity and Global Capitalism*, edited by Suzanne Berger and Ronald Dore. Ithaca: Cornell University Press.

Wallerstein, Michael, and Adam Przeworski. 1995. "Capital Taxation with Open Borders." *Review of International Political Economy* 2:425–45.

Williams, John T., and Brian K. Collins. 1997. "The Political Economy of Corporate Taxation." *American Journal of Political Science* 41:208–44.

Williamson, John, and Fred Pampel. 1993. *Old-Age Security in Comparative Perspective*. New York: Oxford University Press.

Part II

HISTORICAL INSTITUTIONALISM

Chapter 4

Institutions, Investment, and the Rise in Unemployment

BRUCE WESTERN

THE SINGLE most striking sign of the end of the postwar golden age is the massive rise in unemployment throughout the advanced capitalist countries. In the 1950s and 1960s, most of the affluent capitalist economies maintained full employment. Inflation was the dominating concern of macroeconomic policy. For policy makers and researchers of the 1970s, sustained high unemployment was unimaginable because of its anticipated political costs (Crouch 1985). By the mid-1990s, unemployment in France, Italy, and Germany exceeded 10 percent. Moreover, high unemployment had been persistent throughout most of the OECD area for over a decade. A large-scale catastrophe in the advanced capitalist labor markets had become an ongoing reality.

Persistently high unemployment contrasts with institutional trends in Europe and North America. By a variety of indicators, labor markets of the advanced capitalist countries are becoming more deregulated. Unionization is falling, and collective bargaining is becoming decentralized (Wallerstein and Western 2000). As the organization of industrial relations weakens, standard economic accounts would predict the elimination of debilitating inefficiencies. If emerging neoliberalism in the OECD labor markets spells greater efficiency, we would expect a fall in unemployment, rather than an increase.

An alternative account that is more consistent with the stylized facts of deregulation and rising joblessness emphasizes the institutionalized influence of organized labor movements. To explain the general rise in unemployment, comparative researchers have detailed institutional theories that highlight the role of organized labor movements. Through a data analysis of unemployment trends in eighteen OECD countries between 1966 and 1992, this chapter studies two distinct but related institutional theories. The first, corporatist theory, focuses on state and industrial relations institutions that secure the encompassing representation of workers. In this approach, classwide representation of workers in centralized unions and labor governments is instrumental for low unemployment. The second, coordination theory, revises the corporatist account by claiming that cooperative institutions that raise productivity growth in export industries offer a recipe for national economic success.

While the general rise in OECD unemployment is intrinsically important, this chapter also provides a case study in institutional analysis. The corporatist and coordination theories view institutions as nonmarket mechanisms for economic allocation. Although rational action animates the model, both theories offer fundamental macrosociological challenges to standard economic accounts that share similar microfoundations. Economic theories view relations between workers and employers as fundamentally conflictual, but this conflict is resolved with corporatist and coordinating institutions. Theories based on rational action are often charged with evading empirical scrutiny (Shapiro and Green 1994). In this case, however, the data analysis below yields only modest support for the institutional theories, and theoretical revisions are outlined in the conclusion.

The Rise in Unemployment

Why study unemployment rates? The unemployment rate is a highly aggregated measure of labor market performance that reflects a variety of causal processes. Individual decisions about labor force participation, the possibilities of part-time work, work in the informal economy, and a host of other factors all influence the unemployment rate in ways that fall outside the theories of macrocomparative research. Ideally, we would prefer individual-level data that could be used in a highly disaggregated analysis, which might detail the microlevel process of job loss. Unfortunately, no data are available for a large number of countries over a long time series. Consequently, this study, as well as a long line of macrocomparative research (see, e.g., the review of Flanagan 1999), has focused on aggregate movements in the unemployment rate.

In any event, unemployment rates do tell us something valuable about the economic status of a workforce. The standardized unemployment rates used here are based on a common concept, where people are counted as unemployed if they are not working but have actively sought work in the last month. The data used to calculate these statistics have also been collected with a common methodology — large-scale labor force surveys. In short, the variation we see in unemployment rates captures real differences in labor market conditions in advanced industrialized countries. What is more, to the extent that unemployment rates reflect stable but idiosyncratic features of a national labor force, changes in the unemployment rate over time are informative about the improvement or decline in the economic fortunes of a workforce, regardless of national idiosyncrasies. Finally, the key empirical implications of the institutional theories under study here are at the aggregate level. We are interested in evaluating whether national labor market institutions can make a difference, not just for some section of the labor force, but for wage earners as a whole. Individual workers may feel these effects, on their training or wage levels for example, but we expect these microlevel effects to be sufficiently comprehensive that they can be observed in the aggregate.

Recent unemployment trends in eighteen OECD countries are shown in table 4-1. The table indicates the general growth in unemployment over the last thirty years. The old full employment standard of around 1 or 2 percent was common in the 1960s, but only two countries maintained this level be-

TABLE 4–1
Average Standardized Unemployment Rates in Eighteen OECD Countries, 1966–1992

	1966–1975	*1976–1984*	*1985–1992*
Australia	2.4	6.7	7.5
Austria	1.5	2.6	3.4
Belgium	2.8	9.6	9.2
Canada	5.4	8.9	9.2
Denmark	1.7	8.4	7.4
Finland	2.5	5.3	5.9
France	2.7	6.7	9.9
Germany	1.4	4.6	5.6
Italy	5.6	7.8	10.5
Ireland	5.7	10.1	16.2
Japan	1.3	2.2	2.4
Netherlands	2.1	7.9	8.4
New Zealand	0.3	2.8	6.6
Norway	1.7	2.2	3.9
Sweden	2.1	2.6	2.8
Switzerland	0.0	0.5	1.1
United Kingdom	3.3	8.2	9.3
United States	5.0	7.5	6.3
Average	2.6	5.8	7.0

Source: Data are taken from OECD 1996.
Note: Standardized unemployment rates are used for all countries except for Austria, Denmark, Ireland, and Switzerland because data are unavailable. In these cases, unemployment series are constructed from OECD unemployment and civilian labor force figures.

tween 1985 and 1992. Unemployment over 8 percent could be found in ten of the eighteen countries during this same period. Historically strong employment performers like Germany and Sweden now have a tenth or more of their labor forces out of work. Even the full employment regimes of Austria, Japan, and Switzerland currently face historically high jobless rates.

In addition to illustrating the general rise in OECD unemployment, table 4-1 also shows some interesting variation. Unemployment is highest among longstanding members of the European Union. Italy, Ireland, France, and Belgium fill the top slots in the table. Outside of Europe, the United States and Japan, in different ways, illustrate paths to labor market success. The Japanese unemployment rate was among the lowest of all OECD countries in the early 1970s, and has remained low in the 1990s. U.S. unemployment has been much higher, but, unlike any of the other countries surveyed here, the United States experienced a significant fall in unemployment in the late 1980s and again in the mid-1990s. Strong labor market recoveries in the United States were fueled by rapid job creation. Roughly 40 million new jobs were created in the United States between 1966 and 1990, providing a 50 percent increase in total employment. Job creation was dramatically slower in OECD Europe, where employment expanded by only 14 million, a 15 percent rise.

Lest the neoliberal enthusiasts take too much heart from the encouraging U.S. employment figures, it should also be noted that some of the decline in American unemployment is due to a coercive state intervention through the penal system. The labor supply among men in the United States was restricted by a threefold growth in the penal population through the 1980s and 1990s. By the end of the 1990s around 2 million working-age men were incarcerated in the United States, compared to around 200,000 in Europe. Estimates suggest that U.S. male unemployment would have trailed the European average from 1975 to 1994 if prison and jail inmates were included in the unemployment count (Western and Beckett 1999).

Two Institutional Theories of Low Unemployment

For many comparative researchers, variation in unemployment is closely tied to variation in state and labor market institutions. We can distinguish two generations of institutional theories. The first generation focused on highly centralized, or corporatist, bargaining arrangements that joined employers, union leaders, and state actors in an effort to control labor costs. The second generation of theories provided a basic amendment. While corporatist bargaining was held to be important, it was just one part of a broader system of institutions that coordinated economic actors to improve national economic performance.

Corporatism

Standard economic theories view unions as monopolists that undermine labor market efficiency. From this angle, unions use their monopoly control of the labor supply to maximize their members' wages, raising them above the competitive level. Labor markets fail to clear, and unemployment results (e.g., Rees 1989). Self-interested behavior by unions in wage bargaining thus leads to an inefficient outcome in the labor market.

The theory of corporatism provided a powerful antidote to this story. Corporatist theorists argued that if labor organization was sufficiently encompassing, unions could not force the cost of their wage demands on nonmembers (Olson 1982; Crouch 1985; Calmfors and Driffill 1988). Encompassing unions thus exercised wage restraint in order to achieve low unemployment. By drawing the fringes of the labor market into the labor movement, corporatism supported a solidaristic brand of wage bargaining that protected those at risk of joblessness.

Encompassing representation is often defined by three institutional characteristics. First, union leaders are more inclined to weigh the employment effects of their wage demands where collective bargaining is highly centralized (Schmitter 1981). With decentralized bargaining, unions serve narrow constituencies who are less likely to be driven out of work by their wage claims. Second, high unionization indicates that a large proportion of the labor force is integrated into the organized labor movement (Cameron 1984). If bargaining were centralized but unions represented few workers, the unemployment externality resulting from the union wage premium might still be large. Corporatist theories also claimed that labor or social democratic governments are important for wage restraint because they can offer tax or social welfare guarantees in return for wage discipline (Crouch 1985; Alvarez, Garrett, and Lange 1992). In essence, corporatist theory claimed that classwide organization of labor in state and industrial relations institutions provides a more efficient capitalism that can sustain low unemployment.

Despite similar microfoundations to the union monopoly approach, corporatist theory featured two main differences. First, corporatist theory denied the basic conflict of interest between unions and employers that was central to standard economics. Under corporatist bargaining, conflict could be transformed into cooperation. With encompassing labor representation, the wage behavior of self-interested unions became consistent with the common good of low unemployment. Second, corporatist theory could resolve the inconvenient fact of low unemployment in the highly institutionalized labor markets of Sweden and Austria. Unbridled union monopoly in these countries should have led to persistently high unemployment. Instead, unemployment in the corporatist countries was extremely low, underlining the importance of highly regulated labor markets.

Coordination

The key to the corporatist approach was labor costs. Centralized bargaining re-strained wage growth to produce low unemployment. However, with encom-passing labor representation, all employers faced the same wage schedule. If wages were taken out of competition, why restrain wage growth? In many of the corporatist countries, export industries occupied a central role in industrial relations. Thus key employers in the corporatist countries perceived intense competitive pressures — not from other domestic employers, but from abroad (Katzenstein 1985; Flanagan, Soskice, and Ulman 1983; Swenson 1989).

Taking international economic conditions into account placed the corpora-tist story in a different light. Low labor costs were not the only key to economic success in small economies heavily dependent on trade. Through the 1970s and 1980s, the volume of trade grew and international markets became more volatile following the deregulation of exchange rates. Under these conditions, strong national economic performance also depended on the production of high-quality export goods and rapid responses to fluctuating international de-mand. For the second generation of institutional theory, low unemployment thus appeared linked not just to low labor costs, but also to high productivity.

For revisionists emphasizing the influence of economic globalization, cor-poratist institutions contributed more to the economy than simply restraining wage growth. In corporatist countries, unions were often involved in industrial restructuring and planning for technological change (Swenson 1989). On the shop floor, labor-management relations tended to be cooperative, in contrast to the adversarial shop steward model of union representation (Thelen 1991). This was partly due to statutory forums for worker representation: works coun-cils (Rogers and Streeck 1994). In addition, unions in export industries took a leading role in industrial relations. Metals industry unions formed pattern-setting agreements on wages, working time, and employment levels. Govern-ment policy was also supportive. Spending on active labor market policy and industry subsidies was high in the corporatist countries (Garrett and Lange 1991; Janoski, McGill, and Tinsley 1997).

In short, corporatism appeared to involve much more than national bar-gaining, high unionization, and labor government. Corporatist countries also featured an interdependent system of institutions that coordinated labor and capital to promote the export competitiveness of the national economy and the productivity of the entire national labor market (Soskice 1990a, 1998; Hicks and Kenworthy 1998). Soskice (1990a) called these countries "coordinated market economies," arguing that low unemployment depended not just on wage restraint, but also on export success.

The empirical relationship between corporatism and export-oriented coor-dination is only approximate, however. Several researchers have identified an institutionalized commitment to international economic success in a few countries where organized labor is not strong. Katzentsein's (1985, p. 90) analysis of Switzerland underlined the highly centralized organization of employers and a strong orientation to flexible adjustment in export industries. Soskice (1990b) has argued that the highly coordinated approach to wage bargaining found in Japan also approximates the corporatist model. Japanese manufacturers, of course, have also famously pioneered flexible production systems and cooperative labor relations in the large-firm sector (Piore and Sabel 1984; Cole 1989). Swiss and Japanese institutions resemble the corporatist in another respect: large employers in both countries also provide strong employment guarantees to workers. Coordination theorists claim that these employment guarantees contribute to the productivity coalition between business and labor. With systems of long-term or, sometimes, lifetime employment, employers have strong incentives to make high investments in worker productivity (Streeck 1992). Far from creating economic inefficiency, as standard economic theory would claim, employment guarantees provide firms with incentives to improve human capital.

Table 4-2 reports a variety of institutional indicators of economic coordination. Here coordination is measured in a range of areas, including industrial relations, public administration, and firm-level organization. The corporatist variable indicates countries with highly centralized systems of collective bargaining. Works councils are measured by the presence of statutory provisions mandating worker representation within plants. The indicator for state employment service identifies countries with high coverage of public employment offices, union representation in these offices, and rules for employer notification of layoffs and vacancies. Firm-level commitments to employment security are indicated by the measure of employment guarantees. The final column of the table uses the institutional indicators to classify countries as either coordinated or noncoordinated market economies. In this sample of eighteen OECD countries, ten show strong evidence of institutionalized coordination. The constituent institutions of the coordinated market economies combine to improve the performance of export industries, and unemployment is low as a result.

So far the discussion has focused on the direct effect of institutionalized coordination on unemployment: we expect unemployment to be low in the coordinated market economies. However, coordination theory also suggests that institutions not only lower unemployment; they also shape the impact of market forces on unemployment. In the coordinated market economies, the influence of surrounding economic conditions on unemployment is relatively weak. For example, strong prohibitions on layoffs or plant closings in Germany encourage large investments in worker training (Streeck 1992, chap. 1). Under these institutional conditions, the labor market can withstand, at least tem-

TABLE 4–2
Institutional Indicators of Economic Coordination, Eighteen OECD Countries

	Corporatism	Works Council	State Employment Service	Employment Guarantees	Coordinated Market Economy
Australia	0	0	0	0	0
Austria	1	1	1	1	1
Belgium	0	1	1	1	1
Canada	0	0	0	0	0
Denmark	1	0	1	1	1
Finland	1	0	0	1	1
France	0	0	1	0	0
Germany	1	1	1	1	1
Ireland	0	0	0	0	0
Italy	0	0	0	1	0
Japan	0	0	—	1	1
Netherlands	1	1	0	1	1
New Zealand	0	0	0	0	0
Norway	1	1	1	1	1
Sweden	1	0	1	1	1
Switzerland	1	0	0	1	1
United Kingdom	0	0	1	0	0
United States	0	0	0	0	0

Sources: Corporatist data are from Crouch 1985. Works council data are from Western 1997. State employment service is a dichotomization of the index of Janoski, McGill, and Tinsley 1997 for the period 1985–89. Data for employment guarantees are a dichotomization of index reported by Hicks and Kenworthy (1998) for the period 1975–89.

porarily, the pressures of declining investment, accelerating prices, or rising competitive pressures from abroad. Similarly, works councils in concert with centralized bargaining can assist in work reorganization in response to the demands of industrial restructuring (Turner 1991; Thelen 1991). In general, workers in the coordinated market economies are insulated from the economic shocks that drive unemployment in less-regulated settings.

The Slow Growth Era and Neoliberalism

The year of 1973 provides a decisive watershed in postwar economic history. An unprecedented period of unbroken economic improvement ended with the first OPEC oil crisis. Protracted recession, increasing economic inter-dependence between countries, and rapid structural change signaled the end of the golden age. The slow growth era that followed the oil crisis presents new explanatory challenges to corporatist and coordination theories.

One version of the corporatist account readily generalizes to the slow growth era. Corporatist institutions eroded and unemployment increased as a result. Three developments are particularly important here. First, collective bargaining became more decentralized. Second, unionization fell in nearly all OECD countries. Third, long-standing social democratic governments throughout Europe lost office in the 1980s. The fragmentation of wage-setting institutions is a common theme in recent research on comparative industrial relations. From the late 1970s, comparativists have observed that collective bargaining has become more decentralized (Katz 1993; Streeck 1993; Western 1997). Few corporatist-style bargaining forums have survived into the 1990s. The paradigmatic Swedish case dissolved corporatist bargaining in 1983 (Lash 1985). Where industry-bargaining predominated, local wage talks within firms became more important. In decentralized countries, union coordination through multifirm agreements or pattern-bargaining also became less common (Kochan, Katz, and McKersie 1986). Even where there is significant formal continuity in collective bargaining institutions — as in Germany and Norway — local industrial relations increasingly influence wages and conditions (Thelen 1991; Røsdeth and Holden 1990). Without centralized bargaining, the possibility of union wage restraint becomes less likely.

The fall in unionization was even more general than bargaining decentralization. While bargaining decentralization does not involve the proliferation of individual employment contracts, declining unionization may. Accelerated declines in union density can be found in nearly all the mature capitalist democracies of the OECD area (Western 1997; Visser 1992). Britain offers the most radical example. While unions grew to represent more than half of the British workforce in the mid-1970s, unionization fell to below 40 percent by the mid-1990s. Where unionization had fallen throughout most of the postwar period — in France, Japan, and the United States — the pace of union decline quickened in the 1980s.

Just as unions became weaker on the industrial front, the political power of labor was also curtailed by a general "decline of social democracy" (Pontusson 1995). Evidence of this decline was reflected most prominently in the electoral victories of Thatcher, Reagan, and Kohl. The broad rejection of social democratic politics can also be seen in the growing success of parties of the radical right throughout Western Europe (Kitschelt 1995). Scandinavian tax revolt

movements, nativists in France, and regional separatists in Italy all point to a
rightward shift in the center of gravity of European politics. More generally, in
five out of the nine OECD countries surveyed by Pontusson (1995), the social
democratic vote declined in the 1980s, compared to the 1970s. These electoral
developments undermine the capacity of government to offer tax and social
welfare guarantees in exchange for wage restraint.

Although corporatist decline provides a plausible account of the general rise
in unemployment in the 1980s, coordination theory helps explain growing
variation in unemployment experiences. Partly developed in response to many
of the symptoms of slow growth, coordination theory offers both an account of
low unemployment in the contemporary period and a strategy for economic
renewal. With volatile international markets, wage restraint is too weak a policy instrument to sustain low unemployment. It is under precisely these conditions that institutionalized coordination contributes to national economic
performance. The coordinated market economies are able to raise productivity to compete on quality, not price (Soskice 1990a). Under institutionalized
coordination, workers thus play a very broad role in national economic performance. Through participation in industry policy and firm-level productivity coalitions, unions are actively engaged in the creative destruction of structural change and economic innovation. In contrast to the corporatist model,
unions in the coordinated market economies take on part of the entrepre-
neurial function previously monopolized by owners. This allows labor markets
to remain tight through extreme economic adversity.

Institutional Analysis of Capitalist Economies

While the empirical focus here examines the influence of institutions on
OECD unemployment, some more general lessons can also be taken that
speak to institutional analysis more broadly. For coordination and corporatist
theory, institutions are authoritative mechanisms for economic allocation that
provide alternatives to pure market exchange. Under corporatism, central
union leaders compel their members to restrain their bargaining power. With
coordination, employers are forced to support long-term employment relationships and training programs, while unions slow the pace of market-driven
structural change to ease the social costs of structural unemployment. Institutions thus influence labor market outcomes by structuring interests and providing capacities for action. Corporatist and coordinating institutions transform
the conflicting interests of owners and workers into cooperation. They provide
capacities for action by establishing the authority of central union leaders.

In the language of the rational action model that drives the institutional theories, corporatism and coordination essentially concern externalities, rent seeking, and public goods. For corporatism, union wage claims have the undesired

external effect of unemployment. Corporatist bargaining internalizes this external effect by drawing marginal workers into the union constituency. Coordination within firms through works councils and at the industry level in collective bargaining limits union rent seeking. With coordination, wage and employment gains for union members are paid out of the profits of export industries. In addition, coordinated market economies provide a range of public goods, including training and active labor market policy, that grease the wheels of the labor market and expand the stock of human capital.

The rational action microfoundations also help advance a larger macro-sociological argument. The institutional theories show how union egoism can, under the right conditions, contribute to a more humane brand of capitalism. Institutionalized representation of workers' interests can yield economic improvements that provide more security and higher living standards in the long run. Corporatist and coordinated unions thus link their narrow objectives to collective goals; self-interest is reconciled with the common good. In this analysis, instrumental rationality is consistent with a substantively rational capitalism that provides for the satisfaction of needs. This implication resonates with an old Marxist tradition in political economy, in which unemployment is an important tool for disciplining working-class militancy. From this approach — associated most famously with Kalecki ([1943] 1971) — high unemployment was politically favored by industry leaders as a means for stemming dissent. Modern institutional theories turn Kalecki on his head. Unemployment remains politically determined, in the sense of being subject to institutional control. Now, however, low unemployment follows from the institutionalized power of organized labor movements.

The methodology of institutional analysis follows from the theory. To study the effects of corporatist and coordinating institutions on unemployment, we take nations as the unit of analysis, then make measurements on national institutional characteristics and associate these with the unemployment trends. Because coordinating institutions are viewed as an important source of contextual effects—shaping the influence of market forces—this analysis goes farther than simply correlating institutional variables with economic outcomes. The analysis also studies how effects vary with the institutional setting.

Economic Sources of Unemployment

Institutional understanding of capitalist labor markets can be contrasted with the economic approach that emphasizes the influence of supply and demand in the labor market. In the analysis below, I take account of the effects of prices, labor costs, trade, and investment. Investment effects are of special interest because changes in the structure of financial markets suggest that large disinvestment shocks have contributed substantially to the rise in unemployment.

Movements in labor costs and prices are staples in the economic account of unemployment (see Bean 1994 for a review). Growth of labor costs in excess of productivity gains can prevent labor markets from clearing. In the historical context of recent unemployment trends, wage growth outstripped productivity in the 1970s, triggering a rise in joblessness. A long empirical tradition also shows a negative association between inflation (or growth in money wages) and unemployment (e.g., Phillips 1958). The apparent trade-off between inflation and unemployment has been interpreted in several ways, through aggregate demand in some theories, labor supply in others.

Interest in trade and investment effects shifts attention to the international origins of market forces. Although a variety of analysts agree that trade is important, the direction of its influence on unemployment is hotly disputed. Neoclassical theory claims that trade is basically good, promoting the comparative advantage of trading partners. Critics counter that trade forces high-wage workers in the North into competition with low-wage workers in the South. As a result, the demand for labor in the affluent capitalist democracies declines and unemployment increases. Wood (1994) has provided some empirical evidence for the negative economic effects of foreign trade in the core countries.

The effect of trade clearly captures the role of international economic forces, but this is less obvious in the case of investment. To see the influence of foreign pressures, we need to place investment patterns in historical context. Capital markets today are much more open than in 1970. Controls on capital mobility have been significantly relaxed from the late 1970s, and technological change has contributed to the massive increase in the volume of international financial transactions (Simmons 1998). The sheer number of internationally traded financial instruments has also risen dramatically, draining investment in fixed capital. To stem capital outflows, governments became more inflation averse. Some researchers thus argue that financial liberalization reduces state capacity by undermining traditional Keynesian demand-management. Mitterand's reflationary experiment of 1982 is often taken as an important watershed in the turn away from an activist role for government in macroeconomic management (e.g., Hall 1986). The ensuing capital flight in France demonstrated the risks of countercyclical policy.

Deflationary pressure in Europe is compounded by the European Exchange Rate Mechanism (ERM) and monetary union. By effectively pegging European currencies to the deutsche mark, the ERM has diffused low German inflation and the deflationary policies that sustain it. Gomes (1993, p. 306) thus describes the ERM as a "low-inflation–high-unemployment regime." The push for monetary union has had a similar effect. Membership in the monetary union depends on a number of economic targets that European Union countries must have satisfied by 1998. Included among these is a relatively low budget deficit of 4 percent of GDP. The drive for monetary union in many countries has thus involved cuts in government spending and the further abandonment of traditional demand-management (Cameron 1998). Taken together, the globalization of financial markets and tight monetary policy are claimed to have promoted a lengthy disinflation that has choked investment and prevented job creation.

The investment explanation of unemployment offers a fundamentally different logic from the corporatist and coordination theories. First, and most obviously, low unemployment for the institutional theories is a deliberate objective of institutionally powerful labor movements. The unemployment rate is not subject to such control in the economic account. Instead, it follows as an unintended consequence of investment patterns. (Indeed, the unemployment rate is an unintended consequence in all the economic explanations.) Second, investment effects highlight the role of the demand-side of the labor market. Corporatist and coordination accounts stress the supply-side. Investment is important because it affects employers' demand for labor. In contrast, coordination and corporatist theories focus on the job creation effects of lower labor costs and higher productivity, features of the labor supply. Contrasting institutional and economic theories thus raises two basic questions: (1) To what degree is Kalecki's insight true, and unemployment is subject to the political control of powerful economic actors? and (2) Has the recent rise in unemployment been determined chiefly on the demand-side or the supply-side of the labor market?

Data and Model Specification

We can pull together the institutional and economic accounts of OECD unemployment in a hierarchical model. The model is hierarchical in the sense that the effects of longitudinal variables measuring economic and institutional conditions are written as a function of a dummy variable indicating the coordinated market economies. This captures the idea that the economic and institutional determinants of unemployment vary depending on a broader institutional commitment to export success through coordination.

Table 4-3 describes the time-series data used for analysis. Because unemployment series are highly nonstationary (the mean of the unemployment changes over time), the unemployment equation is written in first differences. The annual change in unemployment is written as a function of variables measuring market conditions and encompassing institutions for labor representation. For the corporatist theory, these include unionization, the level of collective bargaining, and the proportion of cabinet seats held by labor or social democratic parties. The impact of economic conditions is measured by inflation, the growth in labor costs (real wage growth minus real productivity growth), and the the growth of trade dependence outside the OECD area. All the predictors are written in differenced form, except the left government and

TABLE 4–3

Time-Series Variables Used in Analysis of Unemployment, Eighteen OECD
Countries, 1966 — 1992

Variable Name	Description	Mean (s.d.)
Dependent Variable		
Δu	Annual change in the standardized unemployment rate[a]	.23 (.91)
Encompassing Institutions		
Bargaining Level	A 4-point index (from 0 to 1) indicating the highest level at which wages are de-termined: (1) plant-level wage-setting, (2) industry-level wage setting, (3) sectoral wage-setting without sanctions, and (4) sectoral wage-setting with sanctions (i.e., wage bargains include no-strike clauses)[b]	.49 (.32)
Left Government	The proportion of cabinet seats held by labor, social democratic, socialist, or communist parties[c]	.37 (.40)
Union Density	Annual change in union density defined as the number of union members as a percentage of all workers, including the unemployed[d]	.24 (1.60)
Market Conditions		
Investment Growth	Real growth in gross fixed capital formation as a proportion of GDP[a]	2.32 (7.26)
Trade Growth	Annual change in the total value of trade with non-OECD countries as a proportion of GDP[a]	.13 (1.22)
Inflation	Annual change in the inflation rate measured by the consumer price index[a]	−.03 (2.66)
Labor Costs	Percentage increase in real manufacturing wages minus real productivity growth measured by real GDP growth per employed person[e]	−.19 (2.96)

Note: A lagged dependent variable is also included in the model as a predictor.
[a]OECD 1997.
[b]Golden, Lange, and Wallerstein 1997.
[c]Western 1997.
[d]Visser 1996.
[e]Western and Healy 1999.

bargaining level variables. These change discretely and very slowly over time. Writing these variables as levels tests the idea that social democracy and centralized bargaining help prevent unemployment shocks.

If the time-series variables and an intercept for country i ($i = 1, \ldots, 18$) are collected in the matrix X_i, then the change-in-unemployment vector, Δu_i, is given by

$$\Delta u_i = X_i b_i . + e_i,\qquad (1)$$

where $b_i .$ is a vector of regression coefficients and e_i is a normal error term. Because of residual autocorrelation, a lagged dependent variable is also included in the model, giving a total of 9 time-series coefficients, including the intercept. Notation indicates that $b_i .$ is taken from row i of a (18×9) matrix, containing coefficients for each country. Columns of this matrix, $b ._j$, are vectors of eighteen country-level coefficients for time-series variables, j ($j = 1, \ldots, 9$). The coefficient vector,

$$b.j = a_{0j} + a_{1j} C + u_j,\qquad (2)$$

where C is a dummy-variable vector indicating the coordinated market economies (see table 4-2). This formalizes the idea that institutionalized coordination is a relatively time-invariant feature of national economies that shapes the impact of time-series variables. With this model, the average effect of time series variable j in the noncoordinated market economies is a_{0j}, the difference between the coordinated and noncoordinated countries is a_{1j}, and the average effect in the coordinated market economies is $a_{0j} + a_{1j}$. Also note that equation (2) contains a macrolevel error term, u_j, which reflects country-specific effects like, for example, the impact of reunification on the German economy.

Results

Estimates of the average economic and institutional effects from equation (2) are reported in table 4-4. Looking first at the average effects in the noncoordinated market economies, we find modest evidence for the corporatist theory. The left government coefficient indicates that unemployment has risen less when labor parties are in power. The effect for bargaining level also suggests that unemployment has risen less in countries with centralized industrial relations. Contrary to theory, union growth is significantly associated with rising unemployment in the less-regulated OECD labor markets. Union density may be capturing the effect of local wage pressure rather than the effect of centralized wage restraint, providing some evidence for the union monopoly ap-

TABLE 4–4

Institutional Effects in a Model of Unemployment, Eighteen OECD Countries, 1966–1992

	Average Non-CME Effect (a_0)	CME Effect (a_1)	Average CME Effect $(a_0 + a_1)$
Intercept	.29 [.16, .42]	−.26 [−.41, -.12]	.02 [−.07, .12]
Lagged Δu	.12 [.03, .20]	.14 [.03, .26]	.26 [.18, .34]
Encompassing Institutions			
Bargaining Level	−.11 [−.29, .06]	.22 [-.01, .48]	.11 [−.09, .29]
Left Government	−.11 [−.29, .07]	.07 [−.17, .30]	−.04 [−.18, .10]
Union Density	.06 [.00, .13]	.04 [−.03, .12]	.11 [.06, .15]
Market Conditions			
Investment Growth	−.10 [−.13, −.08]	.05 [.02, .08]	−.06 [−.07, −.04]
Trade Growth	-.17 [−.25, −.08]	.09 [−.01, .18]	-.08 [−.13, −.03]
Inflation	−.06 [−.40, .29]	.00 [−.44, .44]	−.06 [−.34, .24]
Labor Costs	−.14 [−.40, .13]	.44 [.09, .78]	.30 [.07, .53]

Note: Numbers in parentheses are 80 percent confidence regions. Inflation and labor cost effects have been multiplied by ten. These estimates are obtained from a pooled analysis of all eighteen countries over the full 1966–92 time-series.

proach. For the economic effects, interest centers on the influence of investment growth. As expected, growing investment in fixed capital provides a powerful deterrent to rising unemployment. This effect is consistent with the recent European deflation. A falling rate of investment growth is estimated to significantly raise unemployment. While these results suggest the negative effects of financial globalization, the data also support the positive influence of trade dependence. On average, growing trade outside the OECD area has accompanied falling unemployment. In general, the weakly coordinated labor markets of the Romance- and English-speaking countries provide mixed support for the effects of the encompassing institutions of corporatist theory. In contrast, there is strong evidence for the impact of market conditions, particularly investment and trade growth.

The determinants of unemployment are strikingly different in the coordinated market economies. The large negative intercept term shows that there was virtually no unemployment growth in the coordinated market economies between 1966 and 1992. Over the two decades from 1973 unemployment was, on average, more than 5 points lower in countries with strongly coordinated labor markets, controlling for differences in other institutional and economic conditions. Interestingly, the data analysis yields little support for other institutional effects. This suggests unemployment is low in the coordinated market economies, largely regardless of variation in encompassing labor representation. The analysis also provides strong evidence for the buffering effects of institutionalized coordination. While trade and investment effects were strong in many countries, these market conditions exert relatively little influence in the coordinated market economies. Trade and investment effects in the coordinated market economies are statistically significant, but approximately half the size or less than in the noncoordinated market economies. Thus it seems that weak investment growth has put upward pressure on unemployment rates in Germany and Austria, for example, but this pressure was much stronger in Britain and France.

Figure 4-1 explores more general features of the model fit. This figure reports observed and predicted mean unemployment growth in the sample of eighteen OECD countries. The top panel shows that the model provides a very good fit in the qualitative sense of capturing prominent, substantively important patterns of variation. The three recessions of 1975, 1983, and 1991 are indicated by peaks in the observed time series. Model predictions capture these recessionary patterns, although the extent of rising unemployment is underestimated.

The bottom panel of figure 4-1 studies whether encompassing institutions or investment growth are more important for explaining OECD unemployment since 1980. For this analysis, we use the model estimates to forecast the hypothetical rise in unemployment under two scenarios. Under the first, we assume that unions and labor parties retained their pre-1980 institutional strength through the 1980s and early 1990s. This is the "strong-labor" scenario. In the second scenario, we assume that investment growth remains at its pre-1980 level during the subsequent twelve years. We call this the "high growth" scenario. Under the strong-labor scenario, model forecasts show that unemployment trends would not be qualitatively different from those actually observed. If labor movements had maintained their organization, bargaining had remained centralized, and labor parties had remained electorally successful, average unemployment in the OECD area still would have grown signifi-

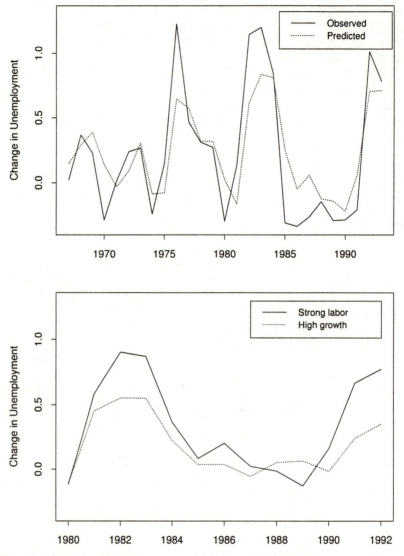

Fig. 4-1. Changes in Unemployment and Investment Growth. The top panel shows observed and predicted mean change in unemployment, 18 OECD countries, 1966–1992. The bottom panel shows forecast mean change in unemployment for labor power resources fixed at their pre-1980 levels and investment growth fixed at its pre-1980 level.

cantly. The high-growth scenario leads to a different conclusion. If strong investment growth had persisted through the 1980s, the recessions of 1983 and 1991 would have been substantially weaker. Under the strong-labor scenario, average unemployment is estimated to rise by about 4.5 percentage points between 1979 and 1992. Under the strong-growth scenario, unemployment would have risen by only 2.4 points. (The actual increase in unemployment was about 3.5 points.) In sum, this analysis suggests that declining investment growth had a stronger effect on the rise in unemployment than the declining organizational power of the OECD labor movements. Still, economic effects are patterned by institutions. Investment effects are generally strong everywhere, but weaker in the coordinated market economies than elsewhere.

Discussion

What, then, is the impact of institutions and labor market deregulation on unemployment? The data analysis provides several clear answers. The rise in unemployment is not strongly driven by the growing disorganization of the OECD labor movements. There is little joy here for the corporatist approach. On the other hand, union density effects offer some evidence that neoliberalism in OECD labor markets has reduced unemployment, but these effects were quite small. These results do not mean that there is no interesting institutional variation. Where the main economic actors are integrated into a systemic effort at maintaining high productivity growth and international competitiveness, unemployment is low and workers are insulated from the effects of market forces. Market forces themselves have also decisively driven the rise in unemployment. In particular, declining investment growth is powerfully associated with the rise in unemployment. The investment effects were the strongest and most consistent in the analysis.

Contrasting investment and institutional effects helps us evaluate the control of organized labor movements over labor market outcomes. Analysts of financial globalization argue that Keynesian demand management can no longer smooth inequities of capitalist economies without risking capital flight. The deregulation of financial markets thus removes a historically important weapon from the arsenal of organized labor movements. In this context, corporatist and coordination theory help answer the question "What's left for the Left?" (Garrett and Lange 1991). For these theories, the pursuit of union self-interest through the institutionalized perfection of the supply-side helps tame an iniquitous capitalism while responding to market necessity. While this view obtains some empirical support, the striking effect of the data analysis is on the demand-side — the impact of investment growth. If institutional control of the supply-side has only limited influence over patterns of unemployment, and investment has really been the decisive influence over the last twenty-five years, where does this leave our institutional theories? The empirical results provide two fundamental challenges.

First, ownership matters. The supply- and demand-sides of the labor market are not symmetric halves, equally influential. Ultimately, jobs originate with labor demand, endowing owners with a power over labor markets that stems fundamentally from their capital ownership. Workers are thus "structurally dependent" (cf. Przeworski and Wallerstein 1988). This is reflected empirically in the preeminent effect of investment growth — not labor market institutions — on unemployment. Although coordination theory charges unions with the entrepreneur's responsibility for economic innovation and niche marketing, the power of job creation resides mostly with the real owners. While we have good evidence for institutional effects, strong and consistent investment effects suggest that the basic property right of capital ownership expresses a power relationship that is largely unalterable by institutional mediation.

Second, regionalization matters. For the current analysis, the nation-state is the key research site. Institutions are measured at the national level, and we distinguish different national regimes of economic management. The key question that emerges, however, concerns the origins of the disinvestment shocks that fueled unemployment in the 1980s and 1990s. I argued above that slow investment growth is rooted in the widespread relaxation of capital controls, the transmission of deflationary policy through the European Exchange Rate Mechanism and the Maastricht targets. To the extent that slow investment growth is embedded in the economic institutions of the European Union, analysis should expand from examining processes within nations to examining relations between nations. Institutional explanation would still remain important in this context. Changes in the structure of financial markets that increase interdependence and the capital flows across national borders do not signal the triumph of markets over institutions. Instead it appears that the regulatory power of national institutions is challenged by a regional — in this case, European — institutional setting. Labor movements, by contrast, are contiguous with national boundaries. Thus, they increasingly bargain from a position of weakness, undermined by investment shocks emanating from abroad. Whatever the effects of neoliberalism in OECD labor markets, they appear overwhelmed by low rates of investment growth. While institutionalized coordination may offer some protection, the evidence reviewed here suggests the power of property rights is ultimately decisive.

Note

Research for this paper was supported by grant SBR95-11473 from the National Science Foundation. Thanks to Jonas Pontusson for providing the unionization data used in this analysis.

References

Alvarez, R. Michael, Geoffrey Garrett, and Peter Lange. 1992. "Government Partisanship, Labor Organization, and Macroeconomic Performance." *American Political Science Review* 85:539–56.

Bean, C. 1994. "European Unemployment: A Survey." *Journal of Economic Literature* 32:573–619.

Calmfors, Lars, and John Driffill. 1988. "Centralisation of Wage Bargaining and Macroeconomic Performance." *Economic Policy* 6:13–62.

Cameron, David R. 1984. "Social Democracy and Labor Quiescence: The Representation of Economic Interests in Advanced Capitalist Societies." Pp. 143–78 in *Order and Conflict in Contemporary Capitalism*, edited by John H. Goldthorpe. Oxford: Clarendon.

———. 1998. "European Monetary Union and Unemployment." Paper presented at the Conference of Unemployment in Southern Europe in Comparative Perspective, Princeton University.

Cole, Robert E. 1989. *Strategies for Learning: Small-Group Activities in American, Japanese, and Swedish Industry.* Berkeley and Los Angeles: University of California Press.

Crouch, Colin. 1985. "Conditions for Trade Union Wage Restraint." Pp. 105–39 in *The Politics of Inflation and Economic Stagnation: Theoretical Approaches and International Case Studies*, edited by Leon Lindberg and Charles Maier. Washington, DC: Brookings Institution.

Epstein, Gerald A., and Juliet B. Schor. 1992. "Structural Determinants and Economic Effects of Capital Controls in OECD Countries." Chap. 6 in *Financial Openness and National Autonomy: Opportunities and Constraints*, edited by Tariq Banuri and Juliet Schor. Oxford: Clarendon.

Flanagan, Robert J. 1999. "Macroeconomic Performance and Collective Bargaining: An International Perspective." *Journal of Economic Literature* 37:1150–76.

Flanagan, Robert J., David W. Soskice, and Lloyd Ulman. 1983. *Unionism, Economic Stabilization, and Incomes Policies: European Experience.* Washington, DC: Brookings Institution.

Garrett, Geoffrey, and Peter Lange. 1991. "Political Responses to Interdependence: What's 'Left' for the Left?" *International Organization* 45:539–64.

Golden, Miriam, Peter Lange, and Michael Wallerstein. 1997. *Master Codebook for NSF Data on 16 Countries.* University of California–Los Angeles. Typescript codebook.

Gomes, Leonard. 1993. *The International Adjustment Mechanism: From Gold Standard to the EMS.* New York: St. Martin's.

Hall, Peter. 1986. *Governing the Economy.* London: Polity Press.

Hicks, Alexander, and Lane Kenworthy. 1998. "Cooperation and Political Economic Performance in Affluent Democratic Capitalism." *American Journal of Sociology* 103:1631–72.

Janoski, Thomas, Christa McGill, and Vanessa Tinsley. 1997. "Making Institutions Dynamic in Cross-National Research: Time-Space Distancing in Explaining Unemployment." *Comparative Social Research* 16:227–68.

Kalecki, Michael. [1943] 1971. "Political Aspects of Full Employment." Reprinted in *Selected Essays on the Dynamics of the Capitalist Economy.* Cambridge: Cambridge University Press.

Katz, Harry C., Thomas A. Kochan, and Robert B. McKersie. 1990. "A Reaction to the Debate." Pp. 189–201 in *Reflections on the Transformation of Industrial Relations,* edited by James Chelius and James Dworkin. Metuchen, NJ: Institute of Management and Labor Relations.

Katz, Harry C. 1993. "The Decentralization of Collective Bargaining: A Literature Review and Comparative Analysis." *Industrial and Labor Relations Review* 47:3–22.

Katzenstein, Peter J. 1985. *Small States in World Markets: Industrial Policy in Europe.* Ithaca: Cornell University Press.

Kitschelt, Herbert. 1994. *The Radical Right in Western Europe: A Comparative Analysis.* Ann Arbor: University of Michigan Press.

Kochan, Thomas A., Harry C. Katz, and Robert B. McKersie. 1986. *The Transformation of American Industrial Relations.* New York: Basic Books.

Lash, Scott. 1985. "The End of Neo-Corporatism? The Breakdown of Centralised Bargaining in Sweden." *British Journal of Industrial Relations* 23:215–39.

OECD. 1996. *Historical Statistics, 1960–1994, on Diskette.* Paris: OECD.

Olson, Mancur. 1982. *The Rise and Decline of Nations: Economic Growth, Stagflation, and Social Rigidities.* New Haven: Yale University Press.

Philips, A. W. 1958. "The Relation between Unemployment and the Rate of Change of Money Wages in the United Kingdom, 1861–1957." *Economica* 25:283–99.

Piore, Michael and Charles Sabel. 1984. *The Second Industrial Divide: Possibilities for Prosperity.* New York: Basic Books.

Pontusson, Jonas. 1995. "Explaining the Decline of European Social Democracy: The Role of Structural Change." *World Politics* 47:495–533.

Przeworski, Adam, and Michael Wallerstein. 1988. "The Structural Dependence of the State on Capital." *American Political Science Review* 82:1–29.

Rees, Albert. 1989. *The Economics of Trade Unions.* 3d ed. Chicago: University of Chicago Press.

Rogers, Joel, and Wolfgang Streeck. 1994. "Workplace Representation Overseas: The Works Councils Story." Pp. 97–156 in *Working under Different Rules,* edited by Richard Freeman. New York: Russell Sage Foundation.

Røsdeth, Asbjørn, and Steinar Holden. 1990. "Wage Formation in Norway." Pp. 237–88 in *Wage Formation and Macroeconomic Policy in the Nordic Countries,* edited by Lars Calmfors. Stockholm: Oxford University Press.

Schmitter, Philippe C. 1981. "Interest Intermediation and Regime Governability in Contemporary Western Europe and North America." Pp. 287–330 in *Organizing Interests in Western Europe,* edited by Suzanne Berger. New York: Cambridge University Press.

Shapiro, Ian, and Donald P. Green. 1994. *Pathologies of Rational Choice Theory: A Critique of Applications in Political Science.* New Haven: Yale University Press.

Simmons, Beth. 1998. "The Internationalization of Capital." Pp. 36–69 in *Continuity and Change in Contemporary Capitalism,* edited by Herbert Kitschelt, Peter Lange, Gary Marks, and John Stephens. Cambridge: Cambridge University Press.

Soskice, David. 1990a. "Reinterpreting Corporatism and Explaining Unemployment: Co-ordinated and Non-co-ordinated Market Economies." Pp. 170–211 in *Labour Relations and Economic Performance*, edited by Renato Brunetta and Carlo Dell'Aringa. London: Macmillan.

———. 1990b. "Wage Determination: The Changing Role of Institutions in Advanced Industrialized Countries." *Oxford Review of Economic Policy* 6(4)36–61.

———. 1998. "Divergent Production Regimes: Coordinated and Uncoordinated Market Economies in the 1980s and 1990s." Pp. 101–34 in *Continuity and Change in Contemporary Capitalism*, edited by Herbert Kitschelt, Peter Lange, Gary Marks, and John Stephens. Cambridge: Cambridge University Press.

Streeck, Wolfgang. 1992. *Social Institutions and Economic Performance: Studies of Industrial Relations in Advanced Capitalist Economies*. London: Sage.

———. 1993. "The Rise and Decline of Neocorporatism." Pp. 80–101 in *Labor and an Integrated Europe*, edited by Lloyd Ulman, Barry Eichengreen, and William Dickens. Washington, DC: Brookings Institution.

Swenson, Peter. 1989. *Fair Shares: Unions, Pay, and Politics in Sweden and West Germany*. Ithaca: Cornell University Press.

Thelen, Kathleen. 1991. *A Union of Parts*. Ithaca: Cornell University Press.

Turner, Lowell. 1991. *Democracy at Work Changing World Markets and the Future of Labor Unions*. Ithaca: Cornell University Press.

Visser, Jelle. 1992. "The Strength of Union Movements in Advanced Capitalist Democracies: Social and Organizational Variations." Pp. 17–54 in *The Future of Labour Movements*, edited by Marino Regini. Newbury Park, CA: Sage.

———. 1996. "Unionization Trends Revisited." Research paper 1996/2. Center for Research on European Societies and Industrial Relations, Amsterdam.

Wallerstein, Michael, and Bruce Western. 2000. "Unions in Decline? What Has Changed and Why." *American Political Science Review* 3:355–77.

Western, Bruce. 1997. *Between Class and Market: Postwar Unionization in the Capitalist Democracies*. Princeton: Princeton University Press.

Western, Bruce, and Katherine Beckett. 1999. "How Unregulated Is the U.S. Labor Market: The Penal System as a Labor Market Institution." *American Journal of Sociology* 104:1030–60.

Western, Bruce, and Kieran Healy. 1999. "Explaining the OECD Wage Slowdown: Recession or Labour Decline?" *European Sociological Review* 15:233–49.

Wood, Adrian. 1994. *North-South Trade, Employment, and Inequality: Changing Fortunes in a Skill-Driven World*. Oxford: Clarendon.

Chapter 5

Institutionalizing Markets, or the Market for Institutions?

CENTRAL BANKS, BANKRUPTCY LAW, AND THE GLOBALIZATION OF FINANCIAL MARKETS

BRUCE G. CARRUTHERS, SARAH L. BABB, AND TERENCE C. HALLIDAY

MANY economic institutions function to ameliorate, regulate, or otherwise attenuate the dynamics and consequences of markets. Institutions act as buffers that protect people and organizations from the pressure of competitive markets (Polanyi 1944). They do so by making markets less competitive, by narrowing their scope, and by making selective criteria less exacting and, thus, less burdensome for firms and individuals. For example, labor market institutions like unions, protective labor legislation, and unemployment insurance help to protect workers from the uncertainties of the market, and so "decommodify" labor (Esping-Anderson 1990).

More fundamentally, institutions help to create markets. By establishing particular legal, social, and informational conditions, institutions make the production, distribution, and exchange of commodities possible. Thus, markets are "institutionalized" on the basis of specific organizational and institutional foundations. In causal language, institutions shape the markets they help to create.

This relationship is not one-sided, however, for institutions are themselves subject to market pressure. For instance, as organizations with personnel to pay, equipment to purchase, and physical plant to maintain, institutions need to mobilize economic resources. Insufficiency of resources constrains institutions (DiMaggio and Powell 1983). The rules that institutions promulgate to regulate markets can be undermined if economic actors flee to other, less-intrusive jurisdictions, thus shrinking the market. Through a mixture of exit (e.g., capital flight) and voice (e.g., political pressure from business groups), markets affect the institutions that govern them. In theory at least, exit and voice can combine to replace less efficient institutional arrangements with more efficient ones. Speaking loosely, one can posit a "market" for institutions, complete with entry, exit, and performance criteria.

Recent developments around the globe (referred to as *neoliberalism*) appear to reflect just this kind of selective process operating at the institutional level: widespread deregulation and globalization of commodity and capital markets, privatization of public industry, retrenchment of the welfare state, and so on. It seems that the political, legal, and economic institutions that formerly regulated markets are themselves being dismantled to allow unrestrained markets. In the battle between markets and institutions, markets appear to have won.

Rather than "deinstitutionalization" in general, neoliberalism involves the replacement of one set of institutions by another set — a process that is fundamentally political. By contrast, many economists see neoliberal reform as an instance in which the market dictates the replacement of inefficient institutions with more efficient ones. One influential argument about institutional change comes from Demsetz (1967). In his discussion of aboriginal land rights in eighteenth-century Quebec, Demsetz claims that communal property rights in land shifted to private property rights because as European demand for furs increased, private property became more efficient (thanks to the increased value of furs, the benefits of private property exceeded its costs). Market pressure forced institutional change. Similar arguments include Williamson's (1985) analysis of multidivisional corporations during the nineteenth and twentieth centuries, and Posner's (1986) account of the history of the English common law.[1] This general line suggests that the changes wrought by neoliberalism reflect a "weeding-out" process in which "efficient" economic and legal institutions replace "inefficient" ones.

Broad assertions about neoliberalism and institutional change are easy to make but hard to sustain without knowledge of how specific changes occur, and why. In this chapter, we focus on two institutions: corporate bankruptcy law and central banks. Both are created by the state; neither arises "naturally" or as the result of market forces. Furthermore, each institution is central to the operation of a modern market economy.

One advantage of these two institutions is that the meaning of *neoliberal* is fairly clear. For a central bank, neoliberal reform entails greater autonomy from politicians (which allows central banks to combat inflation). For bankruptcy law, it involves greater protection for debt contracts, and thus a preference for firm liquidation over reorganization and rehabilitation. Firms enter into contractual arrangements, and a law favoring liquidations leaves those as unchanged as possible (Baird 1986).

We can also gauge the "efficiency" of these institutions: an efficient bankruptcy law is one that quickly and cheaply liquidates firms that are hopelessly insolvent or reorganizes those that can be salvaged (Jackson 1986). "Good" bankruptcy laws consequently reduce the cost of capital and facilitate investment (McCauley and Zimmer 1989). An efficient central bank is one whose policies enhance monetary stability. If a "market" for institutions exists, central banks and bankruptcy laws will be weeded out according to how well they perform.

The differences between the two institutions also offer analytic advantages. Central banks are embedded in a strong network of international relationships and are subject to various influences from abroad (international institutions like the International Monetary Fund, the World Bank, and the financial communities of London and New York, knit central banks together), whereas corporate bankruptcy law is promulgated by nations more or less independently. A nation's bankruptcy legislation is seldom dictated by other countries, leaving more room for cross-national variation. As compared to bankers, bankruptcy experts from different nations do not interact on a regular basis. This means that central banks are more likely than bankruptcy laws to be subjected to the institutional effects (mimetic and normative isomorphism) identified by DiMaggio and Powell (1983). Central banks face a range of pressures to converge, but bankruptcy legislation, in contrast, is less vulnerable to such pressures.

Other important differences distinguish the two institutions: one is a legal institution and the other a financial organization; one is reactive (bankruptcy law), the other proactive (central banks); one involves more centralized decision making than the other; one involves fairly continuous market interventions (central banks), while the other acts intermittently, on a case-by-case basis. Central banks apply explicit theories derived from scholarly research about what they are supposed to do and why it works, while bankruptcy judges and lawyers operate on a more pragmatic basis. Furthermore, bankruptcy laws intervene in specific cases of insolvent firms, whereas central banks enact policy more broadly. In short, central banks enact the kind of visible, active, organizationally based policy that is usually identified as "government intervention." In contrast, corporate bankruptcy law exemplifies the latent, easily overlooked, property-rights-based regulation that Campbell and Lindberg (1990) highlight.[2] With such differences, it is not obvious that central banks and bankruptcy law will respond similarly to neoliberal forces.

Central banks and corporate bankruptcy law both affect the operation of markets and indirectly influence each other. On the one hand, central banks help to determine the macroeconomy. In particular, tight monetary policy intended to control inflation means high interest rates, which make credit scarce and consequently push more firms into insolvency. With money tight, bankruptcy law will be activated frequently. On the other hand, governments suffer politically from the consequences of tight monetary policy. But if bankruptcy law favors reorganizations over liquidations, or is seldom applied, then tight monetary policy need not lead to politically unfortunate events like insolvencies, closures, and liquidations. Liberal bankruptcy laws loosen budget constraints and ameliorate the political price of tight money.

Central banks and bankruptcy law are also linked because they both affect the same interest group: banks and bankers. Monetary policy determines the cost of capital; bankruptcy law influences how easily banks, as creditors, can recover their money from a defaulting customer. Such interconnections suggest that central banks and bankruptcy law may react similarly to the influence of neoliberal changes.

Below we consider these two institutions, describing first what they do and how they are changing in the neoliberal era. Our task is to determine whether these institutions are converging toward less government interference and freer markets. We will argue that recent trends in central banking legislation exemplify the neoliberal pattern of change. But we will also show that changes in bankruptcy law have functioned as a counterweight to neoliberalism. Bankruptcy law represents an "off-budget" form of government policy, and compensates for the decline in more traditional (and obvious) forms of intervention. Furthermore, the contrast between the two illustrates the unevenness of neoliberal developments — it would be a mistake to overgeneralize from one institutional sphere to the political economy as a whole. By analyzing the cases of France and Mexico, we provide two examples of how these institutions coevolved. The case studies make clear that institutional reform is driven as much by politics as by market pressures.

Central Banks

Monetary policy represents a common form of government intervention in modern capitalist economies, and operates primarily through the central bank. Throughout the nineteenth century in Europe, central banks were established and took on some of their modern functions. In 1920, the League of Nations' International Financial Conference resolved that all countries should establish a central bank, both to maintain domestic financial stability and to facilitate world cooperation. After World War II, a central bank became almost a universal symbol of independent nationhood. Whereas in the interwar period central banks were founded in preexisting nation-states (such as those of Latin America), central bank creation after the war followed the creation of new nation-states, particularly in Africa.

Central banks have traditionally been concerned with monetary stability. Their core functions are decidedly mundane, and include:

1. regulation of the currency;
2. performance of banking services for the government;
3. custody of the cash reserves of commercial banks;
4. management of the nation's international currency reserves;
5. provision of credit facilities to commercial banks, discount houses, bill brokers, and dealers, or other banking institutions, and acceptance of the responsibility of lender of last resort, and
6. settlement of clearance balances between banks, and provision of facilities for the transfer of funds between financial centers. (de Kock 1974, p. 14)

After the Great Depression, however, these activities were increasingly framed within the more glamorous goal of helping to promote economic growth and full employment. According to Keynesian doctrine, national economies could be at equilibrium and still have high unemployment and underutilized capacity. By injecting more money into the economy, governments could stimulate demand and thereby raise growth and employment. Phillips's famous curve showed a trade-off between unemployment and inflation, and implied that if governments endured higher inflation, they could stimulate economic growth through monetary expansion. This new role for central banks justified keeping monetary policy under direct government control. A mid-twentieth-century textbook on banking summarized this idea, pronouncing that "the fundamental business of a central bank is to control the commercial banks in such a way as to support the monetary policy directed by the state" (Sayers quoted in Deane and Pringle 1994, p. 110).

However, starting in the late 1980s governments reduced their control over monetary policy by making their central banks legally independent. This trend is documented in table 5-1 (see also Bernhard 1998).

Why have governments given up this tool for promoting economic growth and employment? Although different rationales exist, a common theme is that economic globalization reduces the efficacy of active monetary policy and increases the benefits of central bank independence. Two sets of factors militated in favor of central bank independence: one theoretical and the other historical. The first was the rise of the monetarist and rational expectations schools

TABLE 5-1
Central Bank Independence since 1989

Developed Countries	Developing Countries	Eastern Europe
Belgium (1993)	Algeria (1991)	Albania (1991)
England (1998)	Argentina (1992)	Belarus (1994)
France (1993)	Chile (1989)	Bulgaria (1991)
Greece (1993)	Colombia (1992)	Czech Republic (1993)
Italy (1992)	Ecuador (1992)	Estonia (1993)
New Zealand (1989)	Egypt (1992)	Hungary (1991)
Portugal (1992)	Mexico (1993)	Kazahkstan (1993)
Spain (1994)	Pakistan (1993)	Latvia (1992)
	Turkey (1989)	Lithuania (1994)
	Venezuela (1992)	Poland (1991, 1992)
	Vietnam (1992)	Romania (1991)
		Russia (1993)
		Slovak Republic (1993)
		Ukraine (1993)

Source: Maxfield 1997.
Note: This table depicts changes in statutory central bank independence.

in economics, which claimed to demonstrate that the manipulation of monetary policy could have no positive long-term effect on unemployment and would worsen inflation. In this view, the most important function of central banks was to ensure monetary stability, rather than attempt to foster growth through monetary expansion. Therefore, central banks needed independence from governments so that they could better carry out their anti-inflationary functions. The monetarist and rational expectations schools were strengthened by the combination of inflation and unemployment of the early 1970s ("stagflation"), which Keynesian policies seemed incapable of resolving.

Second, economic globalization seemed to diminish the benefits of active monetary policy. During the postwar period, international trade barriers were reduced through such multilateral policy initiatives as the General Agreement on Tariffs and Trade (GATT) and the European Common Market, making economies more open (McKeown 1999). At the same time, financial markets became more global through the growth of an offshore banking sector that was able to evade national regulations, as well as technological developments making international financial transactions easier and faster (Simmons 1999). Thus, policy makers could pursue only two out of three policy options: free capital flows, fixed exchange rates, and autonomous monetary policy (McNamara 1998, p. 44). But stable exchange rates are especially important for open economies, and so, for example, European nations quickly established the "Snake" (a European Community exchange rate regime) after the collapse of Bretton Woods (McNamara 1998, p. 98). Furthermore, postwar globalization meant freer trade, greater economic interdependence, and free capital flows (Simmons 1999, p. 40). As a result, when expansionary monetary policy led to currency devaluation, it raised the price of imports used as inputs in domestic production, and led to inflation rather than productivity growth (Goodman 1992, p. 17). This was particularly true for small, open economies like that of New Zealand, which had an enduring problem of high inflation in the decade leading up to central bank independence (Grimes 1996).

Goodman (1992, p. 18) observes that under the circumstances, Western European governments had only two choices: either to deglobalize through imposition of capital controls or to implement full-fledged monetary integration. Most European countries have chosen the latter course. The terms of European monetary integration in the adoption of a single currency, the euro, reflect the influence of the Bundesbank, one of the world's most independent and inflation-conscious central banks (Goodman 1992, pp. 217–18), and they ensure stable exchange rates among European Monetary System (EMS) members. In keeping with both Bundesbank influence and conventional wisdom among central bankers and economists, the primary aim of the new system is price stability and freedom from political interference. The new European Central Bank (ECB) will have an executive board selected "by 'common accord' of the participating governments, on the recommendation of the Council of Ministers after it had consulted with the European Parliament and the ECB's governing council" (Deane and Pringle 1994, p. 333). However, the European Parliament will not be empowered to amend ECB laws, leading some to question whether the Bank will be sufficiently accountable (p. 335). Among the conditions for joining the Union is central bank independence — hence the European trend depicted in table 5-1.

In the context of the European Monetary Union, central bank independence is only a way station on the road to an even more spectacular abdication of governments' ability to use independent monetary policy: namely, a single currency under the jurisdiction of a transnational central bank. For developing countries, central bank independence has served a somewhat different function that is also predicated on economic globalization. In the Third World, neoliberal policies — including privatization of state-owned industries and trade liberalization — were often linked to the Third World debt crisis and the declining power of Less Developed Countries (LDCs) with respect to foreign governments, international investors, and financial institutions (Kahler 1992; Stallings 1992). However, unlike such policy reforms as budget cuts and free trade, which in many cases were linked to IMF conditionality, central bank independence appears to have been voluntarily adopted by underdeveloped countries (albeit with the widespread approbation of Western economists and officials).

Why would LDC governments tie their own hands in such a way? According to Maxfield (1997), central bank independence has become a signaling device whereby Third World governments gain the confidence of investors. The fate of LDC governments was originally tied to that of international investors during the Third World lending boom of the 1970s. As Frieden (1991) shows, reglobalization of financial markets and the glut of "petrodollars" from oil-exporting nations gave banks a surplus of investable funds and encouraged heavy external borrowing by developing countries. Foreign financing in the 1970s provided Third World countries with new opportunities for productive investment, along with unprecedented opportunities for expensive white elephants, pork-barrel politics, and corruption.

When world interest rates rose in 1979, many Third World governments found themselves with enormous debts, tying these countries to international financial markets and making them extremely vulnerable to international fluctuations. In lieu of the radical solution of a debtors' cartel, these countries had to pay — and have been paying ever since. To give one example, in 1995 Mexico's external debt amounted to 65 percent of GDP; 11 percent of Mexico's export revenue for that year went toward interest payments on the debt (ECLA 1996, p. 248).

For our purposes, the rise of Third World indebtedness led to one critical consequence: it meant that more countries were vulnerable to balance-of-payments crises, capital flight, and devaluations (e.g., Mexico in 1994–95). Consequently, the need to foster the confidence of foreign investors was extremely pressing, since upon this confidence rested economic performance, the stability of the currency, and national solvency. Thus, the wave of central bank independence in the 1990s can be explained as a signal of creditworthiness to international investors (Maxfield 1997). This also helps explain why central bank independence has been so common in Latin America (where foreign indebtedness was high) and relatively uncommon in East Asia (where until recently indebtedness and dependence were lower).

What about the largest group of countries adopting central bank independence (in table 5-1), the Eastern European countries? It should not surprise us that Eastern European governments, in embracing capitalism, instituted central banks in accordance with conventional Western economic wisdom: the importance of independent central banks is unquestioned among mainstream economists, including "money doctors" like Jeffrey Sachs, who were invited to help remake socialist economies. Central banks are part of the same institutional package that includes bankruptcy law. In the context of Eastern Europe's need for foreign investment, central bank independence made sense, for the same reasons identified by Maxfield (1997) for LDCs: central bank independence is a good way to court foreign investors. For this reason, even countries with high levels of unemployment would probably still make their central banks more independent.

In fact, catering to the wishes of international investors seems everywhere more important than it used to be — whether in the First World, the Third World, or the formerly socialist world. As Deane and Pringle (1994, p. 18) point out, the decreased ability of central banks to use monetary policy to promote growth rather than simply to cause inflation means that governments must increasingly look to markets to help finance their spending: in lieu of printing more money, governments must borrow, and may get better terms if their central banks are independent and devoted to combating inflation. In general, it seems that economic globalization has widened the options of investors of all nations, who can now invest wherever they receive the highest return; conversely, it has tied the hands of governments — or led them to tie their own hands, in the hopes of courting the favor of foreign investors. Central bank independence represents one form of voluntary hand-tying; the European Monetary Union represents another.

Recent work on the effects of central bank independence shows that while independence is strongly correlated with low inflation, it has no significant effect on economic growth (Edison 1993; Eijffinger and Haan 1996; Maxfield 1997). Although this suggests that central bank independence does not hurt growth, it fails to support the stronger claim (often made by central bankers and Chicago-school economists) that central bank independence is good for growth. Moreover, when broken down into developed (OECD) and developing countries, the evidence shows that central bank independence does not have a significant effect on inflation in Third World economies (Maxfield 1997, p. 14).

Like any other policy, central bank independence generates winners and losers. For example, monetary independence may have social costs if it becomes harder for governments to finance social programs. Even if central bank independence is merely neutral for growth but good for monetary stability, some groups still stand to benefit more than others. Banks and other creditors are the primary beneficiaries of monetary stability, just as debtors still benefit from inflation.

Unfortunately, little research has been done on the interest groups involved in the recent wave of monetary independence. It seems that bankers and international investors favor monetary independence, but that there are no organized opponents. Labor movements generally exert upward pressure on wages, but rarely influence monetary policy. Soft money coalitions are rare in the late twentieth-century.[3]

Central bank independence is an abstract issue, and thus seems to be relatively cost-free in political terms. The political contention surrounding European monetary integration suggests that in democratic countries with an educated populace, issues like monetary independence may attract some attention. In comparison to other aspects of neoliberal reform, however, central bank independence is a political nonstarter. Consider, for example, the popular outrage at IMF austerity measures, which often lead to high interest rates, widespread layoffs, and cuts in government subsidies for basic foodstuffs. In contrast, nobody has ever heard of a "central bank independence riot."

The shift toward greater central bank independence appears to be general, although its causes and circumstances are not. The trend is consistent with the ascendant ethos of neoliberalism: less government management of the economy. Pushing in the direction of more independence is the increasingly internationalized community of financiers, investors, and bankers, who seem to be the winners (although it is not clear who loses). And the political and economic pressure of this community engenders a political response — a decision to endow central banks with more autonomy.

Now we turn to bankruptcy law, where the pattern and direction of change is very different. If central banks exemplify neoliberalism, bankruptcy law seems to change in response to neoliberalism, counterbalancing the shrinking ability of states to manipulate markets. Movement of the "less visible hand" of government in property rights offsets the diminishing "visible hand" of government intervention.

Corporate Bankruptcy Law

In a capitalist economy, bankruptcy law provides a legal answer to the question of what to do with insolvent firms.[4] The best indicators of insolvency are when a firm cannot pay its bills or when its liabilities exceed its assets. Two things can happen: an insolvent firm can be closed and liquidated to pay off creditors or it can be reorganized to become economically viable again. Bankruptcy law determines which of these two procedures occurs. In both outcomes, the property rights of debtors and creditors are evaluated and modified.

A bankruptcy law generally determines: (1) when companies may obtain court protection from creditors; (2) who may initiate legal proceedings; (3) the specific powers corporate managers retain after their company is declared bankrupt; (4) how much contractual commitments can be modified; (5) who gets priority in the distribution of assets; (6) the protections creditors have from further losses incurred by the company; (7) procedures for company reorganization; and (8) the terms for the repayment of debts or the reorganization of assets.

The first of the two bankruptcy options, organizational liquidation, occurs when the firm's situation is deemed hopeless. In a sense, the firm has become worth more dead than alive. With liabilities greater than assets, it is impossible to repay fully all the debts. The value of the company owners' claims can be zero (if owners have limited liability) or even negative (if they do not), and so they typically do not participate in the liquidation. Thus, a liquidation involves distributing assets to creditors whose claims cannot all be fully satisfied.

Creditors may anticipate a firm's insolvency and try to take back their money. In general, the prospect of bankruptcy sets off a "rush to the assets" among creditors. This destructive free-for-all can reduce the value of a firm's assets and seriously hurt those creditors not lucky enough to be in the first wave. To prevent this, bankruptcy laws frequently institute a legal "stay," which suspends all debt-recovery actions and allows for a more orderly distribution.

Several rules govern the distribution of assets in a straight liquidation. One is to allocate assets in proportion to the magnitude of claims. For example, if a corporation owes a total of $1 million to four creditors, and has assets worth $100,000, then each claimant receives 10 cents on the dollar. Another rule is to rank creditors temporally, where the oldest claims are satisfied first. Security offers yet another common rule. Creditors who obtained security for their loans (i.e., collateral) receive a higher ranking than unsecured creditors. Or claims may receive a statutory ranking, where the law gives some creditors priority over others.

Current bankruptcy laws typically combine these rules so that creditors are classified into different groups. Higher priority classes get repaid before the others, but assets are distributed proportionately within each class. Suppose, for example, that two of the debtor's four creditors are secured (owed $30,000 each) and two are unsecured (owed $700,000 and $240,000, respectively). Out of the $100,000 in assets, the two secured creditors receive full repayment. The remaining $40,000 is shared among the unsecured creditors on a proportional basis, so that one gets $29,787 and the other $10,213 (about 4 percent). Current laws also frequently favor particular creditors so that unpaid wages, for example, or unpaid taxes enjoy a high priority.

Liquidation of an insolvent corporation performs an important function in a market economy. A bankrupt firm is one that has become so unprofitable that its capital and credit are exhausted. Liquidation takes the firm's assets away from the unsuccessful managers and gives them to others. Thus, in neo-Darwinian fashion, the weak are weeded out and only the efficient survive. But this happy ending does not come without cost, for liquidation of a firm means that at least in the short run, management and workers will become unemployed and productive capacity will be underutilized.

A similar evaluative exercise occurs in a corporate reorganization. Saving an insolvent firm usually requires changing both the asset and liability side of the balance sheet. Consider the debtor's liabilities. It may have delinquent loans to banks, outstanding trade credit owed to suppliers, and a wage bill owed to its employees. To survive, the firm will have to lower its costs through some combination of lower interest on its loans, lower payments for supplies, and lower labor costs. Thus, for a reorganization to succeed, lenders, suppliers, and workers will have to reduce their claims. It will benefit all if the firm survives, but each group has an interest in seeing that the burden of cost reduction falls less on themselves and more on others. Workers, for example, prefer that banks reduce their interest rates, rather than have their wages cut drastically. The simple distributional rules that apply in liquidations do not apply in reorganizations, but negotiations nevertheless can be structured by the law to favor some over others.

Although liquidations and reorganizations are both distributional exercises, groups are not indifferent between them. In general, secured creditors do best in liquidations, since collateralization gives them first crack at the assets. Unsecured creditors frequently get very little, shareholders receive nothing, and the firm's employees simply lose their jobs. A reorganization, in contrast, resembles a calculated gamble. If the firm recovers, then creditors get repaid, shareholders retain their wealth, and employees keep their jobs. But if the firm fails again, the burden of the additional loss normally falls on the secured creditors, since it is their money that gets depleted during the unsuccessful reorganization. Thus, secured creditors generally prefer liquidations over reorganizations, while groups like employees, managers, and shareholders prefer reorganizations.[5]

Unlike liquidation, corporate reorganization "softens" budget constraints, for it gives those who have failed another chance. Reorganization weakens the neo-Darwinian operation of markets. By promulgating a bankruptcy law that encourages reorganizations, the state can help to sustain employment and production, at least in the short run. Unlike the soft budget constraints of command economies, however, corporate reorganization need not involve public financial subsidies, loans, or other forms of direct support. The additional money usually comes from the secured creditors.

Bankruptcy law provides the framework within which corporate liquidations and reorganizations occur, and determines the balance between them. Bankruptcy laws can be arrayed from the "hardest" (which protect creditor property rights, and so allow only liquidations) to the "softest" (which encourage reorganizations). Hard laws enshrine the most rigorous selective pressure, and so punish inefficient firms with extermination. Soft laws impose weaker selective criteria.

Changes in Bankruptcy Law

Corporate bankruptcy law seldom figures in discussions of neoliberalism, but consider that the following countries have passed new legislation since 1977: Denmark (1977), the United States (1978), Austria (1982, and again in 1997), the United Kingdom (1985), France (1985, and again in 1994), Norway (1986), Yugoslavia (1986), Chile (1987), China (1988), Columbia (1988–89), Poland (1990), the Czech Republic (1991, and again in 1993), Hungary (1991), Mongolia (1991), Australia (1992), Canada (1992, and again in 1997), Finland (1992), Japan (1992), Russia (1993), Vietnam (1993), Bulgaria (1994), Germany (1994), Argentina (1995), Romania (1995), Azerbaijan (1997), Kazakhstan (1997), Indonesia (1998), Thailand (1998), and South Korea (1998 and 1999). The last three countries revised their laws in response to IMF pressure in the wake of the Asian financial crisis (Vatikiotis 1998; Mertens 1997; Urapeepatanapong and Okanurak 1998). What connection is there between bankruptcy law and neoliberalism?

In some countries, the adoption of bankruptcy laws is part of a larger set of institutional changes that transform a command economy into a market economy (Legros and Mitchell 1995). To have capitalism, one must have a bankruptcy law (Mitchell 1993, p. 198). Market economies entail hard budget constraints: "Along with the maintenance of a hard-budget constraint by the state, bankruptcy legislation is the main channel for introducing market discipline to the enterprise sector" (OECD 1994, p. 7). Nevertheless, what in principle is a significant "hardening" of constraints, in practice gets watered down in several ways.

Eastern European countries face a problem familiar to capitalist nations: the firm that is too big to fail. Banks and other secured creditors generally favor liquidations because they can cut their losses and recover their money. But banks are less eager to liquidate large debtors who drag their creditors down with them. As the examples of Chrysler and Lockheed in the United States during the 1970s attest, even core capitalist nations may suspend bankruptcy laws and bail out a firm whose failure will set off a chain reaction of bankruptcies.[6] Transitional economies in Eastern Europe may have passed rigorous bankruptcy laws, but they became reluctant to enforce them rigorously: too many firms were insolvent, and their closure would result in even more economic dislocation (Blasi, Kroumova, and Kruse 1997, pp. 177–78; Rajak 1998; Rapaczynski 1996, p. 101).

Hungary's experience illustrates the problem. Hungary passed three laws in 1991 to help move toward capitalism (Okolicsanyi 1992): the Bankruptcy Act, the Accounting Law (which required the adoption of Western accounting procedures), and the Act on Financial Institutions (which put Hungary's banks on a Western footing). But these new laws unleashed a flood of corporate bankruptcies, and so many enterprises stopped payment that the banking sector was threatened with widespread insolvency (Stark 1996, p. 1010). The Hungarian government had to bail out the financial sector in 1992 and 1993. These interventions effectively "softened" the harder budget constraints that were supposed to accompany the new bankruptcy law. In 1993, the bankruptcy law was changed so as to encourage more reorganizations (Gray and Hendley 1997, p. 144).

Similarly in Russia, a new bankruptcy law was passed in 1993 (Demchenko 1993), but almost no firms were declared bankrupt. The new law remained more a legal possibility than an actuality (Yakovlev 1994, p. 143; Åslund 1995, pp. 264–65). Furthermore, the government passed a subsequent measure to water down the first law by favoring reorganizations over liquidations (Savateyeva 1994). As in Hungary, so many Russian firms were technically insolvent that to push them all into liquidation would destroy a large proportion of the Russian economy, massively increase unemployment, and shut down the nascent banking sector. Such a shock would be politically unacceptable, and so in practice budget constraints were relaxed. Thus, in many transitional economies new bankruptcy laws create the appearance of hard budget constraints. But were they enforced, many enterprises would fail. Even politicians who support economic reform do not want too many insolvent firms closed down (Bufford 1996, pp. 469–70). Consequently, either the laws are not enforced or they are subsequently modified so that corporate reorganization becomes the preferred outcome.[7]

Other cases involve capitalist countries. In 1978, the United States reformed its bankruptcy laws and introduced Chapter 11 to encourage corporate reorganizations. The intent was to reduce the number of corporate liquidations, whose economic and political costs were apparent to many, and give troubled firms a second chance. This shift from liquidation to reorganization offered a way to soften budget constraints. As secured creditors with the most to lose from reorganizations rather than liquidations, American bankers opposed the reorganization provisions of Chapter 11 but tolerated the changes as part of a larger deal that improved the standing and jurisdiction of bankruptcy courts (Carruthers and Halliday 1998, chap. 4).

Britain revised its insolvency laws in 1985. Reformers were well aware of the precedent set by Chapter 11 but chose not to follow the U.S. lead.[8] Pursuing the same end with different means, the British instituted a new procedure, the

Administrative Order, to help troubled firms reorganize. This change occurred despite the fact that British law historically sanctified and protected the rights of secured creditors (Ziegel 1994, p. xxv), and so seemed an especially unlikely place to witness any shift toward reorganizations.[9]

Some laws have not shifted to favor reorganizations. German bankruptcy law, for example, traditionally protected the rights of secured creditors and gave little thought to saving the debtor. Thus, the law focused more on liquidations than reorganizations, and this priority has been maintained through the last set of legal changes (Fialski 1994). Yet much of what might be accomplished in a bankruptcy court occurs outside of it (Kaiser 1996). German banks do their reorganizations outside of insolvency law, taking advantage of their strong ties to corporate debtors and their traditionally active role in corporate governance (Zysman 1983; "French Shareholders v. British Creditors" 1992).[10]

Some developing economies have also changed their laws. Thailand, for example, recently amended its 1940 Bankruptcy Act in response to pressure from the international financial community. It made reorganizations a legal alternative (under the old law, bankruptcy always led to liquidation), but reserved reorganization for larger firms (those with debts over Bt10 million). This allows small insolvent firms to be terminated while giving larger firms, whose liquidation would be more consequential, another chance (Urapeepatanapong and Okanurak 1998).

Many countries have altered their insolvency or bankruptcy laws in the last two decades. In general, the constraints introduced are de facto or de jure considerably "softer" than a simple survival-of-the-fittest picture of bankruptcy suggests. Whether bankruptcy law is simply not invoked, or when applied favors reorganizations, or whether reorganizations occur outside bankruptcy courts, no simple neo-Darwinian measure punishes inefficient firms with extermination. Poorly performing firms receive many additional chances to pull through. This pattern occurs, somewhat surprisingly, in the era of neoliberalism. The contrast with central banks seems especially dramatic.

We now consider two cases to examine in more detail these developments in bankruptcy law and central banking. The first is France, an advanced capitalist economy that passed a new bankruptcy law in 1985. The second is Mexico, a developing economy that very recently updated its bankruptcy law. Both countries granted formal autonomy to their central banks in 1993. Neither has been a leader in neoliberal reform, and so together they offer a chance to study institutional reform in both advanced and developing contexts where the impetus for change is both external and internal.

The post-1973 era posed a dilemma to capitalist democracies. The period after 1973 has been plagued by low economic growth, high unemployment, and frequently high inflation. Yet citizens continue to hold their governments responsible for the economy, and vote out of office those who fail to solve their nation's economic problems. Worse yet, Keynesian and social democratic

methods for managing the economy have been discredited or became ineffectual. High unemployment is no longer easily soluble through deficit spending, public subsidies, protective tariffs, social programs, or other traditional
measures. Thus, elected governments are held politically responsible for an
economy that they are finding harder to manipulate.

In the neoliberal era, governments must seek new tools to accomplish their
domestic political goals. The incentive to reduce unemployment is as strong
as ever, but the means are not so readily available. With fewer nationalized
assets to work with and less budgetary discretion, governments shift to "off-
budget" forms of economic intervention. Institutional change and legal innovation represent two alternatives, exemplified by modification of the central
bank and reform of bankruptcy law, respectively. By changing the law to favor
corporate reorganizations over liquidations, a government can protect jobs
without spending tax dollars or directly managing the economy. And by en-
hancing central bank autonomy, a government can send a favorable signal to
investors. The case of France shows how domestic political factors combined
with external economic forces to motivate legal and institutional change.

France

The Banque de France

After the Second World War, the Banque de France was conceived as a critical institution for the reconstruction of France's economy. As such, it was an
instrument of government policy rather than an autonomous "watchdog" dedicated to monetary stability. One motive for making the bank dependent on
the government stemmed from a fear that overly rigorous monetary policy
would lead to political support for the French left (Goodman 1992, p. 105).

Legislation passed on December 2, 1945, nationalized the central bank; it
also created a National Credit Council for regulating credit policy. Legislation
passed in 1973 gave the Banque de France broader powers, but did not increase
its independence (Goodman 1992, p.48). Under the 1973 law, the Banque de
France was run by a governor and a General Council with the governor and
two deputies appointed by the French president. The Banque was used by the
executive as a policy tool, and when the Banque questioned monetary policy,
its governor often "had the impression of not being heard" (p. 109).

Two changes—France's decision to join the European Union and the collapse of the Bretton Woods system—combined to make active monetary policy a less effective tool for promoting economic growth. Goodman argues that
the de jure dependence of the French central bank became less relevant over
time, as European economies became integrated with one another and with
the global economy. Thus, long before the French central bank became for-

mally autonomous in keeping with the Maastricht Treaty (1993), the French government had retreated from using monetary policy to stimulate growth: they had learned that in the context of global economic integration, a politically dependent central bank in an open economy had become an ineffectual anachronism.

This lesson took years to unfold. The political unrest of May 1968 reinforced French policy makers' belief that "increases in the workers' standard of living — even at the cost of inflation — were necessary to ensure social peace" (Goodman 1992, p. 110). After 1973, however, "France's continued emphasis on growth came into conflict with the restrictive policies pursued in both the United States and West Germany" (p. 111). With the United States and Germany pursuing courses of monetary austerity, it was difficult for France to pursue an expansionary course: in the long run, monetary expansion would stimulate imports as demand for French exports declined, leading to a trade deficit and pressure to devalue the franc. Devaluation would, in turn, lead to higher prices for imports and inflation, which would put pressure on the Banque de France to devalue even more. Furthermore, France's open economy made stability of the franc an ongoing priority.

In 1981, Mitterand's socialist government pursued monetary expansion during a world recession. This policy quickly failed and stood in marked contrast to the success of Germany's low-inflation policy (McNamara 1998, p. 135). The turning point occurred in the spring of 1983, when the increasingly unpopular Socialist government "abandoned economic expansion in favor of austerity and convergence" (Goodman 1992, p. 135). Three devaluations of the franc had only worsened inflation (without helping French exports), and so the government accepted the need to conform to the external constraints on French economic policy making (McNamara 1998, p. 137). Thus, de jure central bank dependence was recognized as a de facto anachronism. By the time France formally gave up control over its central bank (as part of European integration in 1993), such control had become essentially irrelevant: the French government gave up a tool it no longer used.

Bankruptcy Law in France

France also revised its insolvency law in 1985 under Mitterand's government. As compared with other bankruptcy statutes, this law institutionalized a strong bias toward reorganization rather than liquidation. As Kaiser (1996, p. 71) put it: "The legal text of the 1985 law . . . states that the objectives of the law, in order of priority, are to maintain firms in operation, preserve employment and, thirdly, to enforce credit contracts." It was a legal process "primarily concerned with saving the enterprise and, especially, the jobs it provides" (Beardsley 1985, p. 973).

The new law offered three procedures for troubled firms: a negotiated settlement, a judicial arrangement, and judicial liquidation. The first two were aimed at saving the firm, whereas the third performed a more conventional liquidation. Only the debtor could initiate a negotiated settlement, whereas debtor, creditors, or the court initiated judicial arrangements. And only if reorganization failed would the firm move to liquidation.

The 1985 law tried to engineer successful reorganizations by encouraging the management of a troubled firm to go into court sooner (when the firm was still salvageable) rather than later. The statute substantially reduced the risk that management would be held responsible for their firm's bankruptcy. It usually kept management in place, rather than firing or replacing them at the outset of formal proceedings (Koral and Sordino 1996, pp. 439–41). Managers could file for bankruptcy with greater assurance that they would keep their jobs and would not be blamed for failure.

Given that the new law was passed by a socialist government, it is no surprise that it put job preservation ahead of repayment of creditors. Socialist parties worry more about unemployment than about what concerns bankers. But it is not clear why Mitterand's government would turn to such an unlikely tool to pursue its goals. After all, socialist governments have traditionally used measures like nationalization of industry or social spending, not bankruptcy law.

Given the evolution of Mitterand's economic policy, however, it becomes clearer why bankruptcy law was used this way. French voters elected Mitterand president to solve France's economic problems (Hall 1985, p. 81; Smith 1998, p. 61). Through state control over domestic credit, France had enjoyed high levels of growth during the 1950s and 1960s, but over the 1970s this interventionist policy became decreasingly effective (Loriaux 1991, p. 4). After 1973, investment dropped faster and unemployment rose higher in France than in the other OECD countries.

In France's "overdraft economy," firms relied heavily on banks for capital. As compared to those in the United States or Britain, financial markets were underdeveloped and firms needing external funds went to their bank for a loan rather than sell bonds or issue stock (Loriaux 1991, p. 57). The banks were themselves indebted to the Banque de France, and given the dependence of the latter, the government was able to regulate the flow of credit into banks and eventually into industry (Loriaux 1991, p. 277). But firms became overly reliant on such credit, and (not without reason) expected that banks would always extend more loans. Although the credit system allowed the French government to funnel funds into targeted industries, it also institutionalized soft budget constraints (Kornai 1986).

On coming to power, the socialists made some dramatic changes: nationalizing the banks and large industrial firms, reducing the workweek, and supporting social programs. Among other things, the goal was to reduce unemployment and raise wages so as to set off a consumer-led boom. But this

stimulus package was put in place just as the world economy went into a recession, and while Mitterand was fighting unemployment inside France,
Margaret Thatcher and Ronald Reagan were fighting inflation outside. It
soon became clear that Mitterand's policies were not working, and the consumer boom did little but increase the trade deficit and weaken the franc
as French consumers rushed to buy German and Japanese goods (Smith
1998, p. 72).

By 1982–83, Mitterand's government had reversed course. Nationalized
firms soon required huge subsidies, and for budgetary reasons the government
had to pursue an austerity program. Unemployment rose from 8.1 percent in
1982 to 9.7 percent in 1984, even as the government tried to boost profits by
cutting wages and taxes (Hall 1985, p. 88). By 1984, severe budget cuts in the
coal and steel industry had alienated the Communist Party.

Besides reducing public spending and trying to boost corporate profits, the
government instituted another policy reversal, involving liberalization of the
financial sector, starting in 1983. As the overdraft economy system was dismantled, firms needed to attract foreign capital, and so more "marketlike" financial institutions were put in place.[11]

In general, the socialist government shifted from actively promoting specific
industries to a more conservative policy that addressed the general business climate (Smith 1998, p. 70). It made a very public about-face in abandoning its
Keynesian stimulus and in reversing the nationalization program. But the
French government did not relinquish its concern for the unemployed. As the
1985 bankruptcy law makes clear, new means could be deployed to pursue an
old end. Budget constraints that were hardened through deregulation of the financial sector and reduction of government subsidies could be softened again
by having a bankruptcy law that favored reorganizations.

A final motivation for the new law stemmed from the central role played by
French firms in the provision of social programs. Many social services mandated by the state were actually provided by and funded through employers.
Thus, liquidation of a firm represented an even greater problem for employees than just the loss of their jobs, for it meant that the provider of health care
benefits, child care, and educational programs ceased to function. Liquidation
could tear a hole in the social safety net.

The domestic political context of the 1985 French law goes some distance
in explaining its proemployment tendencies. In an open economy, the socialist government had rejected the policy tools it formerly used to pursue low unemployment, high wages, and economic growth. Furthermore, government
control over the central bank lapsed as active monetary policy became impossible. As a result, the government embarked on a more conservative program:
nationalization halted, industries were deregulated, and budget deficits were
reduced. But the reversal was not complete. A bankruptcy law that favored reorganizations could help protect jobs and reduce unemployment, but without

unbalancing the budget or requiring visible government intervention in the economy.

Mexico

The Banco de México

On April 1, 1993, the Mexican central bank acquired statutory independence — a move greeted with much fanfare in the international press. This development was only the latest chapter in the history of Mexican monetary policy, in which central bank autonomy has waxed and waned. Since its foundation in 1929, declines in Mexican central bank autonomy have corresponded roughly to increased power of domestic constituencies over government economic policy, while increases have corresponded to the greater influence of international creditors (Maxfield 1997).

The Great Depression markedly reduced international capital flows, which meant that countries like Mexico had less need to pursue policies favorable to international creditors: foreign investment was simply not forthcoming (Eichengreen 1994). For the next decade, Mexico's ruling party was concerned more with cultivating support among workers and peasants than with attracting foreign investment. As a result, the Banco de México was treated during the 1930s as something of "a subservient financier of an expensive process of political consolidation" (Maxfield 1997, p. 93).

In the 1954–70 period, the Mexican government combined developmentalist policies (such as import protection for domestic producers) with fiscal and monetary rectitude. This period, known as "stabilizing development," enjoyed high levels of economic growth (averaging over 6 percent per annum), and relatively low levels of inflation. Stabilizing development was also accompanied by a high level of de facto (although not de jure) central bank autonomy. Legally, the Mexican central bank was under the control of the president and the minister of finance. In practice, however, starting in the early 1950s the Banco enjoyed considerable independence. As a result, the Banco was directed by a single governor (Rodrigo Gómez) from 1952 until 1970.[12] Low inflation during the stabilizing development period reflected this de facto autonomy. Inflation in 1955–70 averaged a meager 4.71 percent per annum, as compared to over 10 percent during 1940–54 (Ayala 1988, pp. 315, 386). The policies of the stabilizing development era contributed greatly to Mexico's good reputation among international lenders. By the late 1960s private lenders competed for the privilege of having Mexico as a debtor: Mexico had acquired the Third World's highest credit rating (Thompson 1979, pp. 174–85).

During the 1970s, however, a sea change occurred in Mexican economic policy as developing countries began to rely on external financing made possible by globalized financial markets. In Mexico, most international borrowing was done by the public sector, and foreign loans were used by two successive presidential administrations to address Mexico's economic, political, and social problems. Easy credit was later supplemented by revenues from Mexico's rapidly expanding petroleum industry (Teichman 1988). With little need to satisfy international lenders, the Mexican government abandoned its prior emphasis on monetary stability. Domestic political demands for social justice and economic growth got priority, while bankers' concerns about inflation fell by the wayside.

During the so-called populist governments of 1970–82, the Banco found its semi-independent status threatened by an increasingly powerful presidency. In contrast to the stabilizing development period, there were three different central bank governors from 1976 to 1982. The loss of central bank authority in the 1970s and early 1980s was reflected in a drastic increase in inflation. Inflation averaged 24.5 percent in 1980–81, as compared to 4.8 percent in 1970–71.

This period of Mexican economic policy making ended unhappily. Increased government spending and rising demand led to inflation and capital flight; rising world interest rates and a fall in oil prices in 1981 caused a dramatic increase in Mexico's short-term external debt (Kraft 1984, pp. 34–35). In 1982, the finance minister announced that Mexico would not be able to meet its external debt payments, and a full-fledged crisis unfolded. After 1982, Mexican economic policy was no longer primarily concerned with satisfying domestic constituencies, but with meeting the increasingly stringent demands of international investors, U.S. policy makers, the World Bank, and the IMF.

As a result, the Mexican government moved back to fiscal and monetary austerity. The governments of De la Madrid (1982–88) and Salinas (1988–94) embraced orthodoxy more firmly than the governments of the postwar "stabilizing development" ever had, selling off state industries, removing tariff barriers with the United States and Canada, and liberalizing the financial sector. Among these neoliberal reforms was the implementation of statutory independence for the Banco de México in 1993.

Mexico's story of overborrowing in the 1970s followed by crisis and retrenchment in the 1980s, is typical of many developing countries (Frieden 1991). As Maxfield (1997) points out, since the outbreak of the 1982 debt crisis, there has been a strong incentive for developing countries to grant independence to their central banks. Central bank autonomy is a valuable signal to international investors, which can give Third World governments better access to external funding when it is desperately needed. Indeed, the Mexican government's voluntary relinquishment of the tools for conducting monetary policy is typical not only of developing countries, but also of many developed ones as well. Since the collapse of the Bretton Woods system in the 1970s, governments around the world have recognized the difficulty of trying to conduct independent monetary policies while simultaneously being dependent on highly mobile international capital flows (cf. McNamara 1998). With the efficacy of monetary policy so dramatically reduced, policymakers have believed that making central banks independent involves low costs and high gains, since independent central banks are thought to foster investor confidence.

Mexican Bankruptcy Law

The Banco de México was always a highly visible actor in Mexican economic policy making. In contrast, it was only during the last two years that bankruptcy law became a salient issue. In April 2000 the Mexican Congress passed new bankruptcy legislation, which encourages agreements that allow creditors to recover their money. The law is intended to make bankruptcy court decisions speedier and more efficient, and promotes reconciliation between debtors and creditors to help maintain the operation of firms at the highest possible level, thus protecting employment. The law also establishes a Federal Institute of Specialists, staffed with mediators who will function as arbitrators between creditors and debtors. From now on, when a firm declares bankruptcy, it will immediately be sold, both to preserve jobs and to guarantee the payment to creditors. After multiple revisions, the new law acquired cross-partisan support, and was approved by a wide margin by both lower and upper houses of the Mexican Congress (Finerin 2000).

This new legislation was supported by a widespread consensus that the previous bankruptcy law, which dated back to 1943, was no longer useful. The old law began to draw public criticism after the infamous "Fobaproa" debacle — a massive banking bailout that resembled the Savings and Loan bailout in the United States. Fobaproa, a government agency, bailed out Mexican banks after the 1994–95 financial crisis by purchasing 552 billion pesos (about $55 billion) in delinquent loans. Only a small proportion of the money will likely ever be recovered ("Mexico" 1998, p. 30).

Inadequate bankruptcy legislation was one of the key factors contributing to the Mexican banking disaster. The 1943 law allowed firms declaring themselves insolvent to stop making payments until the case was settled in court — a process that could take up to eight years ("La Ley de Quiebras y Sus Interpetaciones" 1998). There were no automatic provisions for the restructuring of bankrupt firms, and by declaring bankruptcy, a firm could stop accumulating interest on its debts; indeed, creditors did not even have the right to reclaim their collateral (La Porta and López-de-Silanes 1998, p. 11).

In theory, the law's goal was to give debtors a "breathing space" during which they could recover, without having to make payments to creditors. In practice, however, the law encouraged creditors to settle out of court with their debtors, since otherwise debtors could suspend payments for years by declaring insolvency (Krawiec 1997, p. 484). One Mexican judge claimed that between 1943 and 1998 there were no more than three thousand official bankruptcy cases, and that only a hundred lawyers specialized in bankruptcy law (Carrillo 1998). Its infrequent use meant that for most of its history, Mexican bankruptcy law was an obscure piece of legislation. In the 1990s, this inadequate law was exploited by Mexican companies that declared insolvency, and used the "breathing space" as a chance to loot their own firms; by the time creditors were allowed to enforce their claims, the assets were gone. This contributed to the insolvency of the Mexican banking system in the 1990s, leading to the government bailout ("Ley de Quiebras, Fortalezas y Debilidades" 1998).

To say that Mexican bankruptcy law has come under scrutiny because of its role in the banking crisis, however, still begs the question of why the issue did not arise earlier. If proper bankruptcy legislation is necessary to prevent opportunistic behavior, then why did it not lead to a crisis earlier? The reason is that for much of the twentieth century, bankruptcy law has been largely irrelevant to the Mexican economy. When the bankruptcy legislation was originally drafted, Mexico had an underdeveloped financial sector (Shelton 1964, p. 142). The Mexican state addressed this problem by establishing a development bank, which was the largest source of public credit in the postwar period. As late as 1961, credit from public institutions accounted for more than half of all long-term loans, bond holdings, and stock holdings in Mexico (Blair 1964, p. 195). Over the postwar period, most private lending occurred within business groups that used horizontal linkages between lenders and borrowers, and informal family ties, to solve problems of information and trust (Maxfield 1997, p. 48). Although the international lending boom of the 1970s brought new sources of financing, foreign loans mostly went to the government rather than to the private sector: as late as 1981, more than 80 percent of Mexican foreign debt was owed by the public, rather than the private, sector (Frieden 1991, p. 77).

However, neoliberal reforms in the 1980s and 1990s led to a dramatic change in this panorama. These reforms included deregulation of financial markets, privatization of state-owned banks, and the opening of the financial sector to international competition (Maxfield 1997, p. 103). As a result, foreign lending to the Mexican private sector skyrocketed during the 1990s (Gavito Mohar, Nava, and Escamilla 1998). In the context of Mexico's weak bankruptcy law, this credit boom ultimately led to the collapse of the Mexican banking system. The hope is that the new bankruptcy legislation will reactivate credit in a system that has been starved for liquidity since the 1995 financial crisis.

In contrast to central bank independence, which was always recognized by Mexican technocrats, international economists, and foreign investors as an important prerequisite to Mexican "economic modernization," bankruptcy reform has been slow in coming. Indeed, the new bankruptcy law appears to have resulted from a process of "social learning" (Hall 1993), as policy makers gradually came to recognize and adapt to dramatic historical changes. Since the 1970s, the governance regime of the Mexican economy has been transformed to become far more reliant on formal credit markets, international financing, and private (as opposed to public) firms. In other words, the Mexican economy has become like that of the United States. In the process of neoliberal reforms, the Mexican government has relinquished an impressive number of economic policy tools, including its control over central bank emissions. But bankruptcy law represents a new policy tool, suited to the new configurations of the Mexican economy. Significantly, the reform is not draconian in nature — it provides ample space for reorganization over liquidation — and is therefore supported by policy analysts and policy makers across the political spectrum (Fineren 2000). The trials and disastrous errors of the past ten years have led to a multiparty consensus that efficient bankruptcy legislation is a sine qua non of a functioning capitalist economy.

Conclusion

Together, these two institutions present a complex picture, providing insight into government policy in the neoliberal era. Among central banks, recent developments have generally been consistent with the pattern of government disintervention. The difference between de facto and de jure independence complicates matters, but increasingly autonomous central banks nevertheless resist the urge to meddle in financial markets, whether to inflate the economy or to achieve some other goal. Independent central banks send a credible signal to international bankers and investors that it is safe to invest, and assure them of monetary stability.

Changes in corporate bankruptcy law, by contrast, seem less favorable to bankers. A shift from liquidation toward reorganization hurts banks and other secured creditors, for they are the ones who pay for failed attempts to rehabilitate a firm. Whether the law facilitates reorganizations, or reorganizations occur outside the law, or insolvency law is simply not applied, failing firms can continue to operate. Bankers thus appear to be the political losers. And whatever role bankruptcy law plays in the legal framework of a capitalist economy, such a law need not entail hard budget constraints. Constraints may be firmer, to be sure, than under socialism, but they fall well short of the survival-of-the-fittest ideal.

In favoring reorganizations over liquidations, governments exploit their central role in the constitution and regulation of property rights. Even with the state's role shrinking in other respects, government remains the key actor for property rights. And neoliberal rhetoric notwithstanding, the problem originally posed by Polanyi (1944) remains: competitive markets threaten to undermine their own social and political foundations. As Rodrik (1997, p. 2) has argued more recently, "the most serious challenge for the world economy in the years ahead lies in making globalization compatible with domestic social and political stability."

The French case shows clearly that even within the neoliberal paradigm, states can weaken the pressures of the global market by softening bankruptcy law and creating an easier environment in which to survive. This is not old-style "decommodification," for it involves no additional public expenditures, no nationalization, no direct bureaucratic intervention. For one thing, it is a "passive" rather than "active" form of intervention — the state offers a bank-ruptcy law and debtors and creditors use it at their discretion. Furthermore, redistribution of assets occurs within the private sector (mostly from secured creditors to others), rather than between the public and private sectors. And the softening of budget constraints occurs within the very law that is supposed to distinguish a command economy from a market economy.

Bankruptcy legislation is an essential part of the Anglo-American "gover-nance regime," where markets are regulated through property law rather than direct bureaucratic control (Campbell and Lindberg 1990). As some have re-cently suggested, however, the Anglo-American version is only one of many "capitalisms" that exist around the world (Hollingsworth and Boyer 1997). Mexico's postwar regime involved substantial state intervention in the econ-omy, and it was the movement toward a more American brand of capitalism that made bankruptcy legislation more salient. Unfortunately, Mexico's recent transition to American-style economic governance was not immediately ac-companied by adoption of the full package of regulatory institutions — an over-sight that has hurt the Mexican economy. If other countries follow suit and em-ulate Anglo-American capitalism, bankruptcy law will continue to grow in importance.

In both central banks and bankruptcy law, we witness a measure of interna-tional convergence, but in offsetting directions. Convergence occurs among nations, but divergence happens between institutions. Bankruptcy laws are converging functionally, and against the neoliberal tide. In terms of the letter of the law, bankruptcy still manifests considerable cross-national variation: some countries have laws that favor liquidation, some do not. In practice, how-ever, bankruptcy laws evidence less variation. Some laws have formally shifted toward reorganizations, some are simply not applied, and sometimes reorga-nization occurs outside of a bankruptcy court. Functionally, most bankruptcy systems have shifted toward reorganization. The appearance of legal diver-gence may reflect the fact that, as compared to central banking, bankruptcy is not an area with strong cross-national connections and channels.[13] But func-tional convergence suggests that capitalist democracies still try to ameliorate market forces for political ends. In fact, neoliberalism seems to involve an un-even *reconfiguration* of state involvement in the market, rather than a simple *reduction*, a reinstitutionalization rather than a deinstitutionalization. As direct modes of government intervention decrease, indirect modes become more important.

Central banks also seem to be converging, but in the opposite direction from bankruptcy law. Both functionally and organizationally, central banks have become less interventionist, more insulated from political pressure, and better able to combat inflation using unpopular monetary policies. Central bank independence appears to be a political response to the increasing dominance of global capital markets and the dependence on foreign capital. In many countries, the credibility of this strategy derived from the combination of the post-1973 failure of Keynesianism, the success of Germany's hard money policy, and the availability of rational expectations and monetarist justifications for hard money (McNamara 1998, p. 6).

What might explain the divergent fates of these two institutions? Consider the domestic political coalitions that surround central banks and bankruptcy law — different political forces can lead to different outcomes. Banks play a key role in both cases and, outside of experts and professionals, are often the only political group to mobilize or express an interest.[14] Banks experienced mixed fortunes — "winning" in the case of central banks and "losing" in bankruptcy law, to put it simplistically. Yet these two outcomes are not equally mysterious. The fate of central banks is perhaps the easiest to account for. Consistent with recent neoliberal trends, central banks follow the pattern of state retrenchment. Central banks are densely linked with each other, and with the international financial community, so not surprisingly they converge to a more modest and less interventionist role.

Bankruptcy law is the real puzzle. Why are soft budget constraints problematic in a command economy, but acceptable if inserted as rehabilitative bankruptcy law inside the legal core of a "minimalist" state? Capitalist states are simultaneously hardening constraints with one hand and softening them with the other. We cannot offer a conclusive answer, but some of the differences between central banks and bankruptcy law qua institutions may account for the outcome. Central banks are highly visible, coherent, organizationally based institutions — bank policy is explicit and highly rationalized (both in the sense that policy derives from explicit theory and that policy is explained and justified post hoc). When a central bank intervenes in the market, the intervention soon becomes public knowledge. Neoliberalism as a political project addresses salient forms of government involvement in the economy, and seeks to reduce them.

By contrast, bankruptcy law is an implicit and passive form of intervention, hidden deep within the technicalities of property rights. It has no visible organizational manifestation and exemplifies the type of market intervention performed by "low-capacity" states (Campbell and Lindberg 1990). Among other things, this means that however sensitive international investors are to differences in central bank independence (preferring nations with independent banks), they react less sharply to differences in bankruptcy law. Furthermore, the shift from liquidation to reorganization is not always obvious, often being a de facto change rather than a de jure reform.

Bankruptcy law puts an acceptable face on soft budget constraints. It connotes an appropriately "minimalist" state that protects property rights, enforces contracts, and otherwise stays out of the economy. Such an image shapes the politics of bankruptcy reform, separating it from other, more controversial forms of public involvement in the market. Although neoliberal doctrines prevail today, politicians remain tempted to intervene in the economy: after all, voters still punish politicians who preside over economic decline. Bankruptcy law gets activated most frequently when times are bad, and so when designed to engineer reorganizations, it performs countercyclically to resuscitate failing firms.

The incentive to use bankruptcy law to intervene in the economy increases as other policy tools are set aside — deprived of other options, a neoliberal state becomes reluctant to jettison its few remaining tools. Independent central banks do not intervene to reflate the economy, but tight monetary policy becomes easier to tolerate if it does not always lead to widespread defaults and failures. Nationalization or subsidies to industry may no longer be acceptable ways to bolster employment, but jobs can still be saved with laws that encourage corporate reorganizations. In this sense, the changes in bankruptcy law help to dampen the shock of neoliberalism. Rather than simply contradicting or undercutting neoliberalism, the new bankruptcy regime helps to save neoliberalism from itself.

In contrast to bankruptcy law, which is important under some but not all forms of capitalism, central banks matter to a wide variety of governance regimes. Indeed, even the noncapitalist nations of the Eastern bloc had central banks, albeit highly dependent ones. Central banks seem to be part of the standard package of institutions adopted by modern nation-states (Meyer 1994; Meyer et al. 1997). Thus, central banking has been of much greater policy relevance, in more nations and over a much longer span of time, than has bankruptcy legislation. However, if neoliberal reforms cause more nations to adopt Anglo-American governance regimes, bankruptcy law will become increasingly important.

The story of these two institutions should also put to rest simplistic explanations of institutional change. Central banks have shifted in a less interventionist direction, but the economic pressure of global capital markets and mobile investors is mediated politically, and does not exert itself directly upon institutions. Governments make political choices about the autonomy of their central banks, although not under circumstances of their own choosing. The notion of direct market pressure on institutions seems equally problematic in the case of bankruptcy law, for that is the institution which constitutes the legal preconditions for market pressure! Indeed, bankruptcy laws are being altered so as to ameliorate the market pressures that distressed corporations face. This does not invalidate the idea of institutional efficiency, but it casts doubt on the idea that market pressures drive institutions in the direction of ever-greater efficiency.

Notes

Presented at the Comparative Institutional Analysis Conference, Dartmouth College, August 1998. Thanks to the conference organizers, John Campbell and Ove Pedersen, and participants for their helpful comments. We are also grateful to Michael Loriaux for his timely reading and to the Lochinvar Society for its warm support.

1. See, more generally, Eggertsson 1990.

2. For more on bankruptcy law and property rights, see Carruthers and Halliday 1998.

3. Although in Mexico (where enormous indebtedness combined with restrictive monetary policy have kept interest rates extremely high), there has been a recent movement of farmers and small businessmen against the banks known as "El Barzón" (Williams 1996).

4. Obviously, socialist economies have little need for a bankruptcy law. As countries shift from socialism to capitalism, they pass bankruptcy statutes (Åslund 1995, p. 265; S. Campbell 1994; Flaschen and DeSieno 1992; Sak and Schiffman 1994).

5. Bankruptcy therefore induces cross-class alliances (between workers and managers) and creates conflicts within classes (e.g., banks versus trade creditors).

6. Woo-Cumings (1997, p. 64) shows how the problem of "too big to fail" has affected corporate finance and insolvency in South Korea.

7. China's 1988 bankruptcy law has seldom been invoked (see Yaping 1994), and the Czech Republic's new bankruptcy law was suspended almost as soon as it was passed (Arbess and Varanese 1993; Stark and Bruszt 1998, p. 155). Later, in 1993, the Czech government softened its bankruptcy law to make reorganizations easier ("Czech Bankruptcy Law" 1993).

8. One important difference is that during reorganization in Chapter 11, incumbent management typically stays in place, whereas corporate insolvency in the United Kingdom entails "the implication of management culpability" (Segal 1994, p. 10).

9. Other examples include Australia's bankruptcy law, which instituted a new voluntary administration regime to maximize the chances of saving a firm, maintaining its assets, and protecting employment (Harmer 1994, p. 47). Although Australian law traditionally protected secured creditors, the law was changed to render organizational death less inevitable. A similar change occurred in Canada (Tay 1993).

10. The absorption of the East German economy put Germany in a position similar to that of Hungary or Russia: subjecting firms from a command economy to the rigors of bankruptcy. Rather than soften the bankruptcy law, the Germans created a special institution, the Treuhandanstalt, to reorganize East German enterprises.

11. Thanks to Michael Loriaux for underscoring this point.

12. Between 1950 and 1989, the Banco had lower than average turnover in its directorship (when compared to other central banks), similar to that of France and Swe-

den, and dramatically lower than the average among developing countries (Eijffinger and de Haan 1996, p. 28).

13. Historically it has lacked the equivalent of an IMF or BIS, although recently the United Nations Commission on International Trade Law has become interested in bankruptcy law.

14. This was true in the United States and England (Carruthers and Halliday 1998, chap. 4).

References

Arbess, Daniel J., and James Varanese. 1993. "Insolvency: Czechs Unlock the Bargain Basement." *International Corporate Law* 27:23–26.

Åslund, Anders. 1995. *How Russia Became a Market Economy*. Washington DC: Brookings Institution.

Ayala Espino, José. 1988. *Estado y Desarrollo: La Formación de la Economía Mixta Mexicana, 1920–1982*. México City: Fondo de Cultura Económica.

Baird, Douglas G. 1986. "The Uneasy Case for Corporate Reorganizations." *Journal of Legal Studies* 15:127–47.

Beardsley, James. 1985. "The New French Bankruptcy Statute." *International Lawyer* 19:973–80.

Bernhard, William. 1998. "A Political Explanation of Variations in Central Bank Independence." *American Political Science Review* 92:311–27.

Blair, Calvin P. 1964. "Nacional Financiera: Entrepreneurship in a Mixed Economy." Pp. 193–240 in *Public Policy and Private Enterprise in Mexico*, edited by Raymond Vernon. Cambridge: Harvard University Press.

Blasi, Joseph R., Maya Kroumova, and Douglas Kruse. 1997. *Kremlin Capitalism: Privatizing the Russian Economy*. Ithaca: Cornell University Press.

Bufford, Hon. Samuel L. 1996. "Bankruptcy Law in European Countries Emerging from Communism." *American Bankruptcy Law Journal* 70:459–83.

Campbell, John L., and Leon N. Lindberg. 1990. "Property Rights and the Organization of Economic Activity by the State." *American Sociological Review* 55:634–47.

Campbell, Steve. 1994. "Brother, Can You Spare a Ruble? The Development of Bankruptcy Legislation in the New Russia." *Bankruptcy Developments Journal* 10:343–95.

Carrillo, Lilia. 1998. "Inutil Ley de Quiebras." *Economista*, June 1.

Carruthers, Bruce G., and Terence C. Halliday. 1998. *Rescuing Business: The Making of Corporate Bankruptcy Law in England and the United States*. Oxford: Oxford University Press.

Castruita, Cesar. 1998. "Eduardo Fernández Impiden las Leyes . . ." *Economista*, May 21.

Caufield, Catherine. 1996. *Masters of Illusion: The World Bank and the Poverty of Nations*. New York: Henry Holt and Company.

"CNBV Ley Quiebras." 1998. *Servicio Universal de Noticias*, May 25.

Council of Europe. 1996. *Bankruptcy and Judicial Liquidation*. Strasbourg: Council of Europe Publishing.

Cukierman, Alex, Pantelis Kalaitzidakis, Lawrence H. Summers, and Steven B. Webb. 1993. "Central Bank Independence, Growth, Investment, and Real Rates." *Carnegie-Rochester Conference Series on Public Policy* 39:95–140.

"Czech Bankruptcy Law Softened." 1993. *East European Markets* 13(7)6.

Deane, Marjorie, and Robert Pringle. 1994. *The Central Banks.* London: Hamish Hamilton.

de Kock, M. H. 1974. *Central Banking.* London: Crosby Lockwood Staples.

Demchenko, Irina. 1993. "Law on Bankruptcy to Go into Effect Soon." *Current Digest of the Post-Soviet Press* 45(5)21–22.

Demsetz, Harold. 1967. "Toward a Theory of Property Rights." *American Economic Review* 57:347–59.

DiMaggio, Paul, and Walter W. Powell. 1983. "The Iron Cage Revisited: Institutional Isomorphism and Collective Rationality in Organizational Fields." *American Sociological Review* 48:147–60.

ECLA (Economic Commission for Latin America). 1996. *Economic Survey of Latin America and the Caribbean, 1995–1996.* Santiago, Chile: United Nations.

Edison, Hali J. 1993. "The Effectiveness of Central-Bank Intervention: A Survey of the Literature after 1982." *Special Papers in International Economics.* Vol. 18. Princeton: International Finance Section, Department of Economics, Princeton University.

Eggertsson, Thráinn. 1990. *Economic Behavior and Institutions.* New York: Cambridge University Press.

Eichengreen, Barry. 1994. "House Calls of the Money Doctor: The Kemmerer Missions to Latin America, 1917–1931." Pp. 110–32 in *Money Doctors, Foreign Debts, and Economic Reforms in Latin America,* edited by Paul Drake. Wilmington, DE: SR Books.

———. 1996. *Globalizing Capital: A History of the International Monetary System.* Princeton: Princeton University Press.

Eijffinger, Sylvester C. W., and Jakob de Haan. 1996. "The Political Economy of Central-Bank Independence." *Special Papers in International Economics.* Vol. 19. Princeton: International Finance Section, Department of Economics, Princeton University.

Esping-Anderson, Gosta. 1990. *The Three Worlds of Welfare Capitalism.* Princeton: Princeton University Press.

Fetter, Frank W. 1965. *Development of British Monetary Orthodoxy, 1797–1875.* Cambridge: Harvard University Press.

Fialski, Heiko. 1994. "Insolvency Law in the Federal Republic of Germany." Pp. 21–32 in *Corporate Bankruptcy and Reorganisation Procedures in OECD and Central and Eastern European Countries.* Paris: OECD.

Finerin, Dan. 2000. "Changes in Mexican Lending Laws May Ease Credit Some." *New York Times,* May 2.

Flaschen, Evan D., and Timothy B. DeSieno. 1992. "The Development of Insolvency Law as Part of the Transition from a Centrally Planned to a Market Economy." *International Lawyer* 26:671.

"French Shareholders v. British Creditors: Bankruptcy Laws in Japan, Germany, France and Britain." 1992. *Economist* 324:64.

Frieden, Jeffrey A. 1991. *Debt, Development, and Democracy: Modern Political Economy in Latin America, 1965–1985.* Princeton: Princeton University Press.

Gavito Mohar, Javier, Aarón Silva Nava, and Guillermo Zamarripa Escamilla. 1998. "Recovery after Crisis: Lessons for Mexico's Banks and Private Sector." Pp. 87–109 in *Mexico's Private Sector: Recent History, Future Challenges*, edited by Riordan Roett. Boulder, CO: Lynne Rienner.

Goodman, John B. 1992. *Monetary Sovereignty: The Politics of Central Banking in Western Europe*. Ithaca: Cornell University Press.

Gray, Cheryl W., and Kathryn Hendley. 1997. "Developing Commercial Law in Transition Economies: Examples from Hungary and Russia." Pp. 139–64 in *The Rule of Law and Economic Reform in Russia*, edited by Jeffrey D. Sachs and Katharina Pistor. Boulder, CO: Westview Press.

Greenhouse, Steven. 1993. "Central-Bank Gripes about a New World." *New York Times*, August 23.

Grimes, Arthur. 1996. "Monetary Policy." Pp. 247–78 in *A Study of Economic Reform: The Case of New Zealand*, edited by Brian Silverston, Alan Bollard, and Ralph Lattimore. Amsterdam: Elsevier Press.

Hall, Peter A. 1985. "Socialism in One Country: Mitterand and the Struggle to Define a New Economic Policy for France." Pp. 81–107 in *Socialism, the State, and Public Policy in France*, edited by Philip G. Cerny and Martin A. Schain. New York: Methuen.

———. 1993. "Policy Paradigms, Social Learning, and the State: The Case of Economic Policymaking in Britain." *Comparative Politics* 25(3)275–96.

Harmer, Ron. 1994. "An Overview of Recent Developments and Future Prospects in Australia (with Some Reference to New Zealand and Asia)." Pp. 39–60 in *Current Developments in International and Comparative Corporate Insolvency Law*, edited by Jacob S. Ziegel and Susan I. Cantlie. Oxford: Clarendon Press.

Hendley, Kathryn, Barry Ickes, Peter Murrell, and Randi Ryterman. 1997. "Observations on the Use of Law by Russian Enterprises." *Post-Soviet Affairs* 13:19–41.

Hollingsworth, J. Rogers, and Robert Boyer, editors. 1997. *Contemporary Capitalism: The Embeddedness of Institutions*. New York: Cambridge University Press.

Jackson, Thomas H. 1986. *The Logic and Limits of Bankruptcy Law*. Cambridge: Harvard University Press.

Kahler, Miles. 1992. "External Influence, Conditionality, and the Politics of Adjustment." Pp. 89–136 in *The Politics of Economic Adjustment*, edited by Stephan Haggard and Robert R. Kaufman. Princeton: Princeton University Press.

Kaiser, Kevin M. J. 1996. "European Bankruptcy Laws: Implications for Corporations Facing Financial Distress." *Financial Management* 25(3)67–85.

Koral, Richard L., and Marie-Christine Sordino. 1996. "The New Bankruptcy Reorganization Law in France: Ten Years Later." *American Bankruptcy Law Journal* 70:437–58.

Kornai, Janos. 1986. "The Soft Budget Constraint." *Kyklos* 39(1)3–30.

Kraft, Joseph. 1984. *The Mexican Rescue*. New York: Group of Thirty.

Krawiec, Kimberly D. 1997. "Corporate Debt Restructuring in Mexico." *New York Law School Journal of International and Comparative Law* 17:481–86.

Lafont, Hubert. 1994. "The French Bankruptcy System." Pp. 15–20 in *Corporate Bankruptcy and Reorganisation Procedures in OECD and Central and Eastern European Countries*. Paris: OECD.

La Porta, Rafael, and Florencio López-de-Silanes. 1988. "Capital Markets and Legal Institutions." Paper presented at Harvard University, May 15.

League of Nations. 1920. *International Financial Conference*. Brussels: League of Nations.

Lee, Charles S. 1998. "Broke but in Business: South Korea's Mediation Buoys Sinking Companies." *Far Eastern Economic Review* 161:55.

Legros, Patrick, and Janet Mitchell. 1995. "Bankruptcy as a Control Device in Economies in Transition." *Journal of Comparative Economics* 20:265–301.

"The Living Dead: Bankruptcy in Asia." 1998. *Economist* 346:71–72.

"Ley de Quiebras, Fortalezas y Debilidades." 1998. *Crónica*, June 14.

"Ley de Quiebras y sus Interpretaciones, La." *Crónica*, 1998. June 28.

Loriaux, Michael. 1991. *France after Hegemony: International Change and Financial Reform*. Ithaca: Cornell University Press.

Martinez, Eduardo R. 1997. "Mexican Bankruptcy Law: The Legal Effects of Bankruptcy and Suspension of Payments." *New York Law School Journal of International and Comparative Law* 17:297–305.

Maxfield, Sylvia. 1997. *Gatekeepers of Growth: The International Political Economy of Central Banking in Developing Countries*. Princeton: Princeton University Press.

McCauley, Robert N., and Steven A. Zimmer. 1989. "Explaining International Differences in the Cost of Capital." *Federal Reserve Bank of New York Quarterly Review* 14:7–28.

McKeown, Timothy J. 1999. "The Global Economy, Post-Fordism, and Trade Policy in Advanced Capitalist States." Pp. 11–35 in *Continuity and Change in Contemporary Capitalism*, edited by Herbert Kitschelt, Peter Lange, Gary Marks, and John D. Stephens. New York: Cambridge University Press.

McNamara, Kathleen R. 1998. *The Currency of Ideas: Monetary Politics in the European Union*. Ithaca: Cornell University Press.

Mertens, Brian. 1997. "Outdated Law Hinders Creditors." *Asian Business* 33(9)38–40.

"Mexico: Time to Settle Up." 1998. *Economist* 348:30.

Meyer, John W. 1994. "Rationalized Environments." Pp. 28–54 in *Institutional Environments and Organizations: Structural Complexity and Individualism*, edited by W. Richard Scott, John W. Meyer, and Associates. Thousand Oaks, CA: Sage Publications.

Meyer, John W., John Boli, George M. Thomas, and Francisco Ramírez. 1997. "World Society and the Nation-State." *American Journal of Sociology* 103(1)144–81.

Mitchell, Janet. 1993. "Creditor Passivity and Bankruptcy: Implications for Economic Reform." Pp. 197–224 in *Capital Markets and Financial Intermediation*, edited by Colin Mayer and Xavier Vives. New York: Cambridge University Press.

"Monetary-Policy Mysteries." 1996. *Economist* 340(7985)96–98.

Morales, Yolanda. 1998. "Para Reducir el Costo Fiscal . . . Aumentarian Reformas a la Ley de Quiebras, la Recuperacion de Cartera del Fobaproa." *Economista*, September 22.

Okolicsanyi, Karoly. 1992. "Two New Hungarian Laws Tighten Economic Discipline." *RFE/RL Research Report* 1(10)37–40.

OECD (Organization for Economic Cooperation and Development). 1994. *Corporate Bankruptcy and Reorganisation Procedures in OECD and Central and Eastern European Countries*. Paris: OECD.

"Perspectivas Aprobación Presupuesto Impulsaron Record Histórico." 1999. Spanish Newswire Services, December 9.

Polanyi, Karl. 1944. *The Great Transformation*. Boston: Beacon Press.

Posner, Richard. 1986. *Economic Analysis of Law*. 3d ed. Boston: Little, Brown.

"Propuestas Ley Quiebras." 1998. *Servicio Universal de Noticias*, May 25.

Rajak, Harry. 1998. "Rescue versus Liquidation in Central and Eastern Europe." *Texas International Law Journal* 33:157–72.

Ramírez Piña, Moises. 1998. "Actualizar Ley de Quiebras, Requisito Para Evitar Crisis Recurrentes." *Crónica*, July 14.

Rapaczynski, Andrzej. 1996. "The Roles of the State and the Market in Establishing Property Rights." *Journal of Economic Perspectives* 10:87–103.

Rodrik, Dani. 1997. *Has Globalization Gone Too Far?* Washington DC: Institute for International Economics.

Sak, Pamela Bickford, and Henry N. Schiffman. 1994. "Bankruptcy Law Reform in Eastern Europe." *International Lawyer* 28:927–29.

Salavert, Didier, and Richard Ortoli. 1986. "The Bankruptcy Laws of France." Pp. 55–73 in *European Bankruptcy Laws*, 2d ed., edited by David A. Botwinik and Kenneth W. Weinrib. Chicago: American Bar Association.

Sánchez Venegas, Adolfo. 1998. "Mayor Autonomia al Banxico . . ." *Excelsior*, November 24.

Savvateyeva, Irina. 1994. "Bankruptcy: Ruination or Salvation?" *Current Digest of the Post-Soviet Press* 46(26)16–17.

Schmidt, Vivien A. 1996. "Business, the State, and the End of Dirgisme." Pp.105–42 in *Chirac's Challenge: Liberalization, Europeanization, and Malaise in France*, edited by John T. S. Keeler and Martin A. Schain. New York: St. Martin's Press.

Segal, Nick. 1994. "An Overview of Recent Developments and Future Prospects in the United Kingdom." Pp.5–18 in *Current Developments in International and Comparative Corporate Insolvency Law*, edited by Jacob S. Ziegel and Susan I. Cantlie. Oxford: Clarendon Press.

"Senado Mexicano Aprobó Nueva Ley que Regulara Quiebra de Empresas." 1999. Spanish Newswire Services, December 8.

Shelton, David H. 1964. "The Banking System." Pp. 11–189 in *Public Policy and Private Enterprise in Mexico*, edited by Raymond Vernon. Cambridge: Harvard University Press.

Simmons, Beth. 1999. "The Internationalization of Capital." Pp.36–69 in *Continuity and Change in Contemporary Capitalism*, edited by Herbert Kitschelt, Peter Lange, Gary Marks and John D. Stephens. New York: Cambridge University Press

"Senate Approves Simplified Bankruptcy Law." 1990. SourceMex., December 15.

Smith, W. Rand. 1998. *The Left's Dirty Job: The Politics of Industrial Restructuring in France and Spain*. Pittsburgh: University of Pittsburgh Press.

Stallings, Barbara. 1992. "International Influence on Economic Policy: Debt, Stabilization, and Structural Reform." Pp. 41–88 in *The Politics of Economic Adjustment*, edited by Stephan Haggard and Robert R. Kaufman. Princeton: Princeton University Press.

Stark, David. 1996. "Recombinant Property in Eastern European Capitalism." *American Journal of Sociology* 101:993–1027.

Stark, David, and László Bruszt. 1998. *Postsocialist Pathways: Transforming Politics and Property in East Central Europe*. New York: Cambridge University Press.

Tay, Derrick C. 1993. "Canadian Bankruptcy Reform: The Move from Liquidation to Rehabilitation." *International Insolvency Review* 2:44–73.

Teichman, Judith A. 1988. *Policymaking in Mexico: From Boom to Crisis.* Boston: Allen and Unwin.

Thompson, John K. 1979. *Inflation, Financial Markets, and Economic Development: The Experience of Mexico.* Greenwich, CT: JAI Press.

Urapeepatanapong, Kitipong, and Chirachai Okanurak. 1998. "New Bankruptcy Act to Boost Thai Economy." *International Financal Law Review* 17:33–37.

Vallens, Jean-Luc. 1996. "The Law in France: Main Features." Pp. 21–24 in *Bankruptcy and Judicial Liquidation.* Strasbourg: Council of Europe Publishing.

Vatikiotis, Michael. 1998. "Legal Hurdle: Under IMF Pressure, Thais Debate New Bankruptcy Law." *Far Eastern Economic Review* 161(10)54–55.

Vernon, Raymond, editor. 1964. *Public Policy and Private Enterprise in Mexico.* Cambridge: Harvard University Press.

Williams, Heather L. 1996. *Planting Trouble: The Barzón Debtors' Movement in Mexico.* San Diego: University of California-San Diego Center for U.S.-Mexican Studies.

Williamson, Oliver. 1985. *The Economic Institutions of Capitalism.* New York: Free Press.

Woo-Cumings, Meredith. 1997. "Slouching toward the Market: The Politics of Financial Liberalization in South Korea." Pp. 57–91 in *Capital Ungoverned: Liberalizing Finance in Interventionist States,* edited by Michael Loriaux, Meredith Woo-Cumings, Kent Calder, Sylvia Maxfield, and Sofia Perez. Ithaca: Cornell University Press.

Yakovlev, V. F. 1994. "The Legislation of the Russian Federation Concerning Bankruptcy." Pp. 131–44 in *Corporate Bankruptcy and Reorganisation Procedures in OECD and Central and Eastern European Countries.* Paris: OECD.

Yaping, Jiang. 1994. "Five Years of China's Bankruptcy Law: Problems and Prospects." *Beijing Review* 37(6–7)21–22.

Ziegel, Jacob S. 1994. Introduction. Pp. ii–xxx in *Current Developments in International and Comparative Corporate Insolvency Law,* edited by Jacob S. Ziegel and Susan I. Cantlie. Oxford: Clarendon Press.

Ziegel, Jacob S., and Susan I. Cantlie, editors. 1994. *Current Developments in International and Comparative Corporate Insolvency Law.* Oxford: Clarendon Press.

Zysman, John. 1983. *Governments, Markets, and Growth.* Ithaca: Cornell University Press.

Part III

ORGANIZATIONAL INSTITUTIONALISM

Chapter 6 _____

Theorizing Legitimacy or Legitimating Theory?

NEOLIBERAL DISCOURSE AND HMO POLICY, 1970–1989

DAVID STRANG AND ELLEN M. BRADBURN

SINCE THE 1970s, public policy in the United States and other wealthy democracies has moved in a neoliberal direction, and we have seen the increasing application of market solutions to public problems. Privatization and the deregulation of natural monopolies are only the more extreme forms of this movement. Equally telling are efforts to reorganize social welfare, education, and health care along the lines of the private sector, with great emphasis on individual choice by consumers and market competition among suppliers.

This chapter examines one moment in this public policy shift: the emergence and spread of institutional support for health maintenance organizations (HMOs) in American health care. Federal and state HMO policy marks an important effort to insert market principles into a sector traditionally organized around professional authority. Analysis of this policy shift contributes to an understanding of the more general rise of neoliberalism.

The theoretical goal is to explore how institutional arguments about organizational legitimacy can be used to explain public policy. We contrast three lines of argument: an *ecological institutionalism* focusing on the size of the organizational population; a *structural institutionalism* focusing on alliances with other key players within the organizational field; and a *discursive institutionalism* focusing on how an organizational form is constituted and interpreted within public discourse. Arguments are considered qualitatively in an account of federal legislation, and quantitatively in an analysis of the timing and content of HMO legislation across the American states.

We distinguish two stages in the development of HMO policy. The first stage involves the formulation and passage of federal HMO legislation, and here we argue that discursive processes were absolutely central. Without appreciating the transformative power of neoliberal discourse, it is difficult to understand how a small, embattled organizational population could have garnered public support. But once HMOs had gained the public stage, the policy-making process became more complex. The diffusion and modification of HMO policy was shaped by institutional pressures for homogenization, by the interests of powerful actors in the health industry, and by HMOs themselves.

Three Lines of Institutional Argument

While we are accustomed to think of different versions of institutionalism as employing different logics and modes of inquiry (elaborated in this volume), related oppositions appear within the empirical field of organizational studies. Many types of institutional argument have entered organizational research, from Selznick's notions of adaptive systems to Meyer's notions of rationalized environments (for reviews, see Scott 1987; DiMaggio and Powell 1990; Strang 1994; Scott 1995). This chapter examines *ecological*, *structural*, and *discursive* lines of institutional argument. These three approaches provide distinct insights into the roots of organizational legitimacy, insights that are transposed here to formulate alternative predictions about how an organizational form gains legislative support.

Ecological Institutionalism

Ecological versions of institutionalism focus attention on the size and resources of the organizational population targeted by public policy. Hannan and Freeman's (1987) notion of density dependent legitimation poses this idea in a particularly clear way. As organizational populations grow, they become "taken for granted" (see Berger and Luckmann 1966; Meyer and Scott 1983). Taken-for-grantedness is both a diffuse orientation and a basis for concrete support. Hannan and Freeman (1987, p. 28) thus suggest that low density "presumably makes it difficult to convince key actors, such as banks and government agencies, to transfer material and symbolic resources to the organizations in the population."

Hannan and Freeman employ a cognitive logic, where simple prevalence leads an organizational form to be seen as natural. Others describe different mechanisms but assert the same conclusion. For example, Torres (1988) points to the way organizations push for public policies that serve their interests. Larger populations with more resources should be able to do so more forcefully. Tendencies toward the capture of regulatory bodies by the regulated (Stigler 1971) lead to the development of very similar ideas.

Structural Institutionalism

Structural versions of institutionalism point to relations of power and cooperation within "organizational fields," communities of exchange partners and competitors making up a recognized sector. DiMaggio and Powell's (1983) seminal discussion focuses attention on the way interaction within fields generates isomorphism. But we can also consider how interorganizational rivalry, exchange, and alliance condition state policy. Institutional support may depend on how organizations are situated within larger fields, particularly when the organizations at issue are small and the field is large.

To develop an argument along these lines, we need an analysis of the relevant structure of the health sector. Most revealing is the historical opposition of the medical profession to HMOs and other forms of "managed care." Prior to the 1970s, most physicians shunned HMOs, ostracized their fellows in prepaid practice, and sponsored legal restrictions that safeguarded the fee-for-service practice of the solo practitioner.

Much work argues that the "professional sovereignty" of the physician began to collapse under the enormous fiscal expansion of the health sector produced by Medicare and Medicaid. Imershein, Rond, and Mathis (1992) find that policies promoting negotiated competition (like HMO laws) emerge when health care purchasers mobilize and health providers fragment. Unified purchasers of care press for the opportunity to bargain with economizing providers, and disorganized health providers are unable to resist the pressure.

New actors may also disrupt the policy equilibrium to aid pariah organizational forms like HMOs. One example of this sort of analysis is the claim by many that the mobilization of business coalitions promoted neoliberal public health policy (Bergthold 1987; Imershein, Rond, and Mathis 1992). Long the silent partner in health care, corporate America felt the pinch of rising medical expenditures from the mid-1960s on. Linda Bergthold (1984) argues that the business-led Roberti Coalition engineered California's market oriented health reforms in 1982. In other states business coalitions advocated a variety of cost containment strategies that included managed care systems and HMOs (Bergthold 1987; McLaughlin, Zellers, and Brown 1989).

Discursive Institutionalism

Discursive versions of institutionalism develop a cultural analysis of the meanings attached to particular organizational arrangements (Meyer and Rowan 1977; Fligstein 1990; Dobbin 1994). Here, institutional support emerges not when organizations are powerful or well connected, but when they embody models of appropriate and effective action that make sense within larger systems of discourse.

The policy debate in American health care has traditionally revolved around a confrontation between "professional" and "bureaucratic" organizing principles. Since the turn of the last century, health care had been organized around professional authority (Freidson 1970; Starr 1982), with control in the hands of physicians socialized to technical mastery and a commitment to service. State policies conceived within this framework sought to reinforce professional standards and provide resources to physicians and hospitals.

The traditional alternative to professional control was the "bureaucratic" model, where health experts coordinated health care delivery to maximize access and equity. Under the aegis of an expanding welfare state, bureaucratic reforms were proposed at the national level in the 1920s, 1930s, 1940s, 1960s, 1970s, and 1990s without success (Starr 1982). Historically, HMOs (qua group prepaid practice) can be located within one wing of this movement, eschewing physician autonomy in favor of cooperation among doctors and between doctors and communities.

In the 1970s, however, a neoliberal or "market" model was gaining legitimacy in American health care discourse. Of course, this model may be understood as the taken-for-granted core of American approaches to political economy (Campbell and Lindberg 1990; Dobbin 1994). But market-liberal approaches were new to the field of health care, and generally resurgent in American policy circles. Under a market model, health entrepreneurs would integrate or spin off services to maximize productive efficiencies, and gain relatively unrestricted access to capital and labor markets. Competition for the consumer's health dollar would discipline entrepreneurs and ensure the provision of a better product at a lower price.

A discursive institutionalism notes the benefits accruing to organizational forms that could be linked to a neoliberal policy analysis. As described below, HMOs (along with other organizational forms, like for-profit hospitals) found themselves in just this position.

Federal HMO Policy

Federal support for HMOs began in the Department of Health, Education, and Welfare (Falkson 1980; Brown 1983). In February 1970, Dr. Paul Ellwood of the American Rehabilitation Foundation met with senior officials at HEW. He argued that mounting health care costs were the product of misaligned incentives in health care. Fee-for-service medicine gave the physician a financial incentive to engage in expensive, crisis-driven forms of care, and a relatively free hand to do so. The insurer footing the bill had the clearest incentive to economize on health care, but was poorly placed to manage the doctor-patient relationship.[1]

Ellwood argued that an organization that simultaneously insures and delivers health care would reconnect incentives and capacities. Such an organization would possess both the motive and the opportunity to find ways of economizing on health care. Efforts to build these sorts of plans in the past, the argument continued, had been crippled by the physicians jealous of their professional prerogatives. Elimination of political barriers should thus spark rapid organizational expansion. Ellwood christened such plans "health maintenance organizations" to emphasize the preventative strategy they might rationally embrace.[2]

The newly christened "HMO" was not made entirely out of whole cloth. HMO prototypes (as they came to be anachronistically called) could be recognized in community based groups such as the Elk City Cooperative and Group Health Cooperative, in corporate plans like Kaiser Permanente, in now extinct "union plans," and in physician alliances like the San Joaquin Medical Care Foundation. All of these forms of prepaid practice fit Ellwood's minimal definition of an integrated insurer and provider. And the good reputation enjoyed by the most successful of these "prototypes" (Kaiser, GHC, Group Health Association) added to the plausibility of Ellwood's argument.

All kinds of choice-theoretic arguments suggest, of course, that the health crisis felt by state regulators in the 1970s would produce proposals for reform. But a content-free model does not help explain why policy makers would promote health maintenance organizations and not some other reform strategy. Further, a model of adaptive search (Levinthal and March 1981) suggests that federal policy makers should have sought to replicate the highly successful Kaiser model across the country. Rather than basing policy on the specific organizational strategies adopted by successful prepaid plans in the past, health analysts and legislators constructed a new and highly generalized conception of prepaid practice that resonated with core cultural understandings about incentives, organizations, and markets. HMOs were theorized (Strang and Meyer 1993), not found.

The efficiency analysis advanced by Ellwood differed dramatically from the traditional case for prepaid practice, which revolved around consumer rights and the rationalization of medical care (MacColl 1966). Patient participation, cooperation among physicians, and elaborated quality control were seen as the great advantages of these groups — not cost savings. And prepaid practices did not view themselves as sharing a core identity until the federal government enacted one into law. Corporate and community plans had little in common. In fact, the HMO concept combines historical enemies: group plans like Kaiser and the medical care foundations that solo practitioners formed to keep the plans out of town (Starr 1982, pp. 324–25; Strang and Uden-Holman forthcoming).

The "HMO concept" jibed with the policy concerns and commitments of the Nixon administration. Health maintenance organizations provided a proactive response to the need to contain costs in the increasingly state funded health sector. They were attractive as an alternative to national health care reform proposed by Senator Ted Kennedy and others. And an HMO experiment was consistent with the larger policy repertoire of the American state, which works through the redefinition of property rights and the chartering of market competitors (Campbell and Lindberg 1990) much more than through explicit controls. In March 1970, Richard Nixon placed health maintenance organizations at the core of his health policy initiative.

In Congress, the analysis forwarded by Paul Ellwood resonated with the commonsense reasoning of legislators and the disciplinary training of health analysts. Like Ellwood, legislators and health policy experts presumed that individual self-interest drives most behavior, that markets discipline organizational outcomes, and that structural hurdles are easily overcome. Brown's (1983) detailed account of the legislative process points to the repeated and effortless deployment of these arguments throughout congressional deliberations.

An HMO act also received support from longtime health reformers like Ted Kennedy and William Roy. These lawmakers had motives in direct opposition to Nixon and HEW — they wanted HMOs to provide a first step toward a national health plan rather than to substitute markets for professional controls. To do so, they accepted the HMO vehicle but pushed for a law that would underwrite new startups in medically underserved inner cities and rural areas.

Existing prepaid practices were interested but lukewarm supporters of legislation. Kennedy's ideas worried Kaiser Permanente and other large, successful plans, who feared that federal support would lead to their ghettoization. And in any case, the nation's roughly one hundred prepaid practices boasted fewer than 3 million enrollees in the early 1970s, so their voices did not carry far.

Perhaps the most striking support for HMOs came from a wide variety of established players: commercial insurers, Blue Cross and Blue Shield (BC/BS) plans, nonprofit hospitals, for-profit hospitals, and trade unions. Many of these groups were longtime opponents of prepaid practice. For example, Blue Cross and Blue Shield had been initially formed to ward off earlier efforts at circumscribing professional sovereignty. But now Walter McNerney, president of the Blue Cross Association, testified before Congress: "You ask what is in it for us. I will make it real fast. We also live with seven of the largest 10 industries in this country, with management and labor, who want evidence that we are not just trading bugs, that we are interested in productivity and better delivery. That pressure is predominant" (U.S. House of Representatives 1972, p. 1014).

Influential players in health care were thus acutely sensitive to the Nixon administration's rationalizing discourse, viewed federal action as an opportunity rather than a threat, and positioned themselves as "potential HMO sponsors." In virtually lone dissent stood the American Medical Association, which argued that the federal government should conduct a modest experimental trial to investigate HMO performance.

One might think that so many advocates would generate a strong law. But multiple supporters with divergent agendas watered down the final product. Visions of the HMO as promoting market competition were inconsistent with visions of movement toward national health insurance. All kinds of existing and projected forms of prepaid practice campaigned to receive recognition as HMOs. Only the more extreme proposals were rejected, like the American Hospital Association's attempt to substitute publicly financed "health care centers" (i.e., hospitals) for HMOs.

The highly compromised federal HMO Act of 1973 was judged by many interested parties to be "unworkable" (McNeil and Schlenker 1975). It held out a number of attractions to HMOs that met federal standards, including a mandated dual choice provision that obliged employers to offer an HMO option if a plan operated in the area, a program of federal grants and loans, and the preemption of restrictive state laws. But to qualify under federal law, an HMO had to offer a rich benefits package, admit all consumers up to capacity during an open enrollment period, and apply uniform community rates rather than adjust premiums by prior medical history.

While federal monies and the prestige accorded by the 1973 act stimulated a small number of new ventures, established plans refrained from meeting federal standards. They pressed for revisions in the law instead, with substantial success (Falkson 1980, pp. 175–84; Brown 1983, pp. 346–57). Open enrollment was emasculated in 1976 and eliminated entirely in 1981; community rating was waived for many plans in 1976; and other requirements were progressively lightened. Over time, federal HMO policy became better aligned with the financial interests and conventional routines of the largest prepaid plans. One can thus usefully describe a policy dynamic of interest mobilization and even regulatory capture. But interest mobilization was triggered by federal law; it did not drive the law.

Elements of all three lines of institutional argument thus appear in the federal policy process. The legislative process was initiated and framed by a new interpretation of prepaid practice that made the HMO a poster child for market virtues. Neither existing prepaid practices nor their traditional enemies (now potential allies) were quick to mobilize or able to substantially define federal legislation. But over time, these groups awakened and gained the sort of law they desired.

The Spread of State Legislation

Congress provided in many ways the crucial legislative arena for HMO politics, but its analysis did not discriminate between causal arguments in a clear way. We thus turn to state HMO acts that defined and regulated HMOs on an everyday basis. Examination of state laws allows us to more concretely identify conditions that promoted or retarded public policy, and to model the spread of support for HMOs over time and across space.

State HMO laws are enabling acts that specify what organizations can, cannot, and must do to incorporate as HMOs. Such legislation reduces uncertainty about which state regulations will be applied, and decreases the likelihood that inappropriate regulations will be imposed.[3] State HMO laws generally went further, eliminating existing legal barriers and ensuring a receptive regulatory climate. Earlier "Blue Shield" laws requiring that prepaid plans be formed by physicians, controlled by physicians, or permit all inter-ested physicians to participate were replaced with laws facilitating HMO ac-cess to employers and eliminating restrictions on physician employment.

State HMO legislation supported the nationwide growth of the HMO pop-ulation. But as with federal policy, this support came at a price. Some enabling acts imposed structural or procedural requirements that threatened existing or-ganizational routines. Such requirements served as a quid pro quo for public endorsement; in order to receive institutional support, organizations had to ex-hibit concern for the public good. State reforms were thus initially attacked for the benefit packages and marketing practices they mandated (see fears of leg-islatively induced "Cadillac HMOs" in McNeil and Schlenker 1975).

The symbolic effect of HMO enabling acts may have been more important than their regulatory impact. Public legislation reversed the stigma that had at-tached to prepaid practice since the 1920s, presenting HMOs as visionary and progressive. For example, the preamble to the New York HMO Act of 1975 read: "Encouraging the expansion of health care services options available to the citizens of the state is a matter of vital state concern. Without such an ex-pansion, increased health insurance and other benefits will continue to esca-late the costs of medical care and overload the health care delivery system. The health maintenance organization concept . . . represents a promising new al-ternative for the delivery of a full range of health care services at a reasonable cost."

The first state HMO acts were passed by Connecticut and Tennessee in 1971, two years before federal legislation but a year after Nixon's proposal for a national HMO initiative. Within two years of the 1973 federal law, almost half of the states had passed HMO acts. By 1989 only Alaska, Hawaii, Oregon, and Wisconsin lacked explicit enabling legislation for HMOs. Figure 6-1 lists the years when states first passed HMO laws.

We analyze the passage of state HMO laws within an event history frame-work, where the quantity of interest is the hazard of legal enactment (see Tuma and Hannan 1984 for an explication of event history modeling). Analyses of state legislation develop explanatory measures tied to each of the three insti-tutional logics presented above, as well as consider models of the diffusion process itself. We examine measures first singly and then in combination. Ap-pendix A gives descriptive statistics and sources for all indicators.

Ecological Arguments

While ideas about population size and resources can be expressed in many ways, we follow the "density dependence" tradition of employing measures of organizational density and mass. Table 6-1 gives the impact of a variety of mea-sures of state HMO density on the passage of legislation; all are examined as bi-

1971	Connecticut, Tennessee
1972	Florida, Pennsylvania
1973	Arizona, Colorado, Iowa, Minnesota, New Jersey, Nevada, Utah
1974	Idaho, Illinois, Kansas, Kentucky, Michigan, South Carolina, South Dakota
1975	Arkansas, California, Maryland, Maine, North Dakota, Oklahoma, Texas, Washington
1976	Massachusetts, New York, Ohio
1977	North Carolina, New Hampshire, West Virginia
1978	Nebraska
1979	Georgia, Indiana, Rhode Island
1980	Virginia, Vermont
1981	—
1982	Delaware
1983	Missouri
1984	New Mexico
1985	Wyoming
1986	Alabama, Louisiana, Mississippi
1987	Montana

Fig. 6-1. First Passage of State Enabling Laws for Health Maintenance Organizations (Aspen Systems Corp.)

variate relationships within a maximum likelihood framework (horizontal lines distinguish each analysis).[4] We measure whether any HMO operated within the state, the number of operating HMOs, quadratic functions of density, and logarithmic functions of density. (Of these, only quadratic and logarithmic functions can [over any finite range of empirical values] demonstrate a declining monotonic effect of the sort described in ecological accounts.) We also examine measures derived from HMO size: total HMO enrollment and HMO enrollment standardized by state population. Finally, we examine the number of federally qualified HMOs that could seek to override restrictive state laws.

Table 6-1 suggests that HMO density bears no direct relationship to the passage of HMO enabling acts. None of the measures of HMO density considered here has a statistically significant effect, and coefficients are small in magnitude. There is little evidence that state HMO laws are driven by a mounting sense that HMOs formed a natural part of the health delivery scene or that HMO laws were constructed to meet the needs of a growing HMO constituency.

The best example of this noneffect is provided by California, since World War II the home of the largest HMOs in the country. But no state legislation was enacted until after the federal government sponsored HMOs in the early

TABLE 6–1
Organizational Ecology and Density Dependent Legitimation

	Estimate	S.E.
Any HMOs	.492	.306
HMOs	.018	.016
HMOs	−.005	.046
HMOs^2	.000	.001
Federally qualified HMOs	−.038	.116
Any HMOs	.470	.471
Log (HMOs + 1)	.015	.253
Any HMOs	.440	.324
HMOs	.010	.019
HMO enrollment	−1.20	3.80
HMO enrollment per 1000 population	−7.15	4.75

Note: Maximum likelihood estimates of the hazard of first passage of HMO enabling legislation in the states. Dashed lines indicate separate equations. N = 376 state years; 46 states passed enabling acts.

1970s. Nor was California among the first to translate federal support for HMOs into state law. And while Kaiser and some other plans had flourished in the absence of HMO legislation, there is little evidence that they were well served by more informal accommodation. An HMO survey in 1973 (before the passage of the California enabling act) showed California plans to be at least as dissatisfied with their state's legal and policy environment as were HMOs in other states (Schlenker 1973).

On the other side of the coin, many states with few HMOs moved quickly to enact legislation. In fact, seventeen states passed enabling acts when they possessed *no* operating plans. Ten states without a single HMO (Tennessee, Florida, Iowa, Utah, South Dakota, Idaho, South Carolina, Kansas, Oklahoma, and Arizona) passed HMO laws before California (with sixty-eight HMOs) did.

Structural Arguments

We next examine differences in the field structure of health care across the states. Following arguments about support for HMOs from organized health purchasers, we examine the proportion of the labor force that is unionized and a variety of measures of business coalition activity. The latter include the number of operating coalitions, whether any coalitions exist, the number of statewide coalitions, and the number of "autonomous" coalitions (groups that exclude providers). To examine the possible role of health providers with generally positive stances toward HMOs, we look at the insurance market share held by Blue Cross and Blue Shield plans, the proportion of for-profit hospital beds, and the proportion of physicians in group practice. Finally, we examine indicators of competitive pressures that might force established actors to accommodate themselves to HMOs: physicians per capita, hospital occupancy, and insurance claims ratios.

Table 6-2 indicates that states with many physicians per capita were quick

TABLE 6-2
Health Politics and the Structure of Health Care

	Estimate	S.E.
Health Care Purchasers		
Number of business health care coalitions	.07	.22
Any business health care coalitions	−.25	.47
Statewide business health care coalitions	−.25	.59
Autonomous business coalitions	.06	.31
Proportion of workforce unionized	1.38	1.66
Health Care Providers		
Blue Cross/Blue Shield market share	−.28	.94
Proportion of hospital beds in for-profit hospitals	1.57	2.35
Proportion of MDs in group practice	−1.93	1.63
Insurance claims ratio	2.95	2.39
Proportion of hospital beds unoccupied	−1.51	2.05
MDs per 1,000 population	.69*	.38

Note: Maximum likelihood estimates of the hazard of first passage of HMO enabling legislation in the states. Dashed lines indicate separate equations. N = 376 state years; 46 states passed enabling acts.
*$p < .10$

to pass HMO laws. As Starr (1982) details, physicians are historically the main opponent of prepaid practice, both in the workplace and in the legislature. But collective resistance depends upon the profession's ability to present a united front, and physician oversupply makes this difficult. As market competition tightens, the interests of generalists and specialists, group practices and solo practitioners, and younger and older physicians tend to fragment. HMOs become for many a much needed stable patient base.

Other indicators of the structure of health care have weak and statistically insignificant effects. Neither the level of unionization nor that of business coalition activity accelerate HMO legislation. These weak effects make sense given the declining political capital of organized labor and the late entrance of business interests on the health scene.[5] Similarly, differences in the composition of health providers and in the market pressures faced by insurers and hospitals do not affect the passage of state HMO acts. The overall picture is consistent with one where HMOs provoked sharp opposition from physicians at the same time that other established interests sought a piece of the action.

Discourse-Based Arguments

We do not measure variation in discourse across states, which is both difficult and less extensive than temporal variation. Instead, we examine the salience of problems that prevailing analyses of health care said HMOs would address. We look at state health costs, since federal policy discussions motivated HMOs as vehicles for health savings. We also examine state-level variation in access to health care, which was tied to HMO policy by Ted Kennedy but not theorized as a problem naturally suited to the HMO concept.

This approach suggests the close relation that can arise between discursive institutionalism and a choice-theoretic explanation. After all, rational choice arguments also imply that HMO laws would be quickly passed where the problems they were believed to address were most severe. While sometimes logics of appropriateness and efficiency are distinct or in opposition, here we see them as embedded. The case for HMOs was an efficiency argument, but one that was compelling because it was culturally appropriate. And it was culturally appropriate because it was a rational actor model. From a rational choice perspective the HMO discourse is analysis; from an institutional perspective it is data.

It is useful to note that the rich empirical literature on HMO performance (see Luft 1981 for a review) is inconclusive. Careful research documents cost savings for older, larger, more successful plans (like Kaiser or the Group Health Cooperative of Puget Sound) versus standard fee-for-service medicine. But a generic "HMO effect" is not apparent, and in fact the sorts of plans most stimulated by the new regulatory environment of the 1970s differ not at all from conventional insurance. Further, health service research was generally unable to control for consumer self-selection into plans, out-of-plan spending, and differences in health care quality. These research limitations meant that advocates began with known success stories (Strang and Macy 1999) and generalized beyond them, relying on theoretical logics that audiences found credible. We would argue that what is crucial for policy is not whether HMOs economize or fail to economize, but that a theory of their behavior arose that transcended empirical data.

Table 6-3 examines conditions tied to the policy discourse surrounding HMOs. We examine health costs both in absolute terms (standardized for inflation) and relative terms (deviations from the national mean for each year). We examine the extent to which states suffer problems of inadequate access to health care by counting the proportion of underserved counties and people via a "medical scarcity" metric developed by the federal government to administer HMO grants.

HMO acts are linked to the price rather than the availability of health care. States with high health costs are quick to pass laws. The effect is largest where costs are measured as absolute levels — other specifications have coefficients in the same direction, but are not statistically significant. By contrast, the size of the medically underserved population has no effect on the passage of legislation.

It makes good sense that HMO laws connect to health costs but not medical scarcity. First, the policy debate virtually defined HMOs as an organizational bundle of incentives that produced economizing behavior; the link to equity

TABLE 6–3
Discourse-Related Conditions and Diffusion Effects

	Estimate	S.E.
Health cost index	.32*	.18
Relative health cost index	.19	.15
Proportion of counties medically underserved	.13	2.71
Proportion of population medically underserved	.04	.47
Global diffusion	−5.71***	.41
Diffusion between neighboring states	−3.27***	.35

Note: Maximum likelihood estimates of the hazard of first passage of HMO enabling legislation in the states. Dashed lines indicate separate equations. $N = 376$ state years; 46 states passed enabling acts.

*$p < .10$, **$p < .05$, ***$p < .01$

and access was much weaker. Second, the proponents of a market strategy were politically better placed than were the proponents of a national plan centering on universal coverage. While Ted Kennedy and others were able to attach some of their concerns to HMOs, the general policy movement was toward the support of profit-oriented HMOs with few public commitments. Efforts to structure HMOs around consumer interests, exclude physician-managed models, and foster wider access to care ultimately failed and came to appear artificial.

Diffusion Processes

In addition to the lines of argument considered above, we also examine the spread of HMO legislation. Institutionalist discussions of diffusion generally argue that the way a practice spreads is strongly affected by its social meaning. Tolbert and Zucker (1983) suggest that local factors cease to influence diffusion either when central authorities mandate adoption or when a practice becomes taken for granted and politically uncontested. Strang and Meyer (1993) make the weaker claim that the development of theorized interpretations of a practice accelerate its diffusion and permit imitation without social proximity. These ideas can be contrasted with a notion of diffusion as fundamentally a social structural or network phenomenon, where practices spread between actors that are particularly close or attentive to each other (for a review of the diffusion literature see Strang and Soule 1998).

HMO enabling legislation closely matches the conditions for an institutional interpretation of diffusion. As described above, states did not begin to consider special legislation for HMOs until the federal government did. Once the federal government made HMOs the cornerstone of health reform, states risked seeming backward and unconcerned if they failed to act. And the rationale for health maintenance organizations was theorized in explicit and compelling ways by prominent health analysts like Paul Ellwood, Alain Enthoven, and Clark Havighurst.

To examine diffusion effects, we work within the heterogeneous diffusion framework proposed in Strang and Tuma (1993). This framework permits simultaneous analysis of internal factors, of differential susceptibility to influence, and of the impact of network patterns of proximity. To examine possible social networks underlying diffusion, we look for evidence of patterns of diffusion based on geographic proximity. States that are close to one another possess more information about one another's policies than do states that are far apart, and may be more likely to learn from each other. Neighbors may also share HMOs (or be concerned about sharing HMOs in the future), promoting explicit efforts at coordination.[6]

Table 6-3 indicates that the overall timing of HMO legislation is consistent with a simple diffusion model where all states influence each other. The parameter for global diffusion indicates that on average, each new law increases the baseline rate by about 10 percent.[7] By the end of the observation period, when forty-six states have passed HMO laws, the estimated rate of enactment is more than four times its level in 1970.

The impact of diffusion among geographically contiguous states is considerably larger. HMO laws passed by neighbors are estimated to more than double the hazard of adoption. Of course, most states have between three and four neighbors (and none more than seven), so the total magnitude of this effect is about the same as that of a fainter global effect. But neighborhood effects capture more fine-grained patterns of diffusion, suggesting that learning and influence operate most readily within clusters of states that share governmental or social traditions, and where communication is frequent.

Combining Institutional Arguments

Table 6-4 examines effects drawn from all the arguments posed above. We include the covariates shown to have a significant bivariate relation to HMO legislation — measures of physician density, health costs, and diffusion effects. We also incorporate a quadratic formulation of HMO density, since such an effect may operate net of other factors.

Model 1 suggests that diffusion processes dominate the passage of legislation, with weak effects of state characteristics. HMO density continues to have little impact on the passage of enabling legislation. Further, the coefficients of physician density and health costs diminish when both are included in the same equation. This occurs because the two covariates are strongly related ($r = .52$). States with many physicians tend to have high medical costs, presumably because medical prices are supply driven and because physicians are drawn to areas where costs are high and working conditions good.

Additional models examine whether state characteristics interact with diffusion influences.[8] We find that the impact of health costs can be unpacked into two components: a positive direct effect and negative susceptibility to adoptions by other states. If states have high health costs, they tend to pass legislation rapidly regardless of what other states do. If states have low health costs, they pass laws at a rate proportional to the numbers of laws passed elsewhere.

Model 4 also shows that health costs boost legislative activity most strongly in the early years (1971–73), consistent with Tolbert and Zucker's (1983) discussion of diffusion dynamics. Before HMO laws are embraced by central actors and come to be "taken for granted" as standard health policy, they are largely passed by states where health costs are very high. But once a federal HMO law is promulgated, even states with low medical costs move quickly to enact HMO laws.

TABLE 6–4
Multivariate Models of the Passage of HMO Legislation

	Model 1	Model 2	Model 3	Model 4	Model 5
B_0	-4.78	-5.02	-4.07	-3.89	-3.85
	(1.75)	(1.73)	(2.14)	(1.04)	(1.04)
HMOs	-0.10	-0.17	-0.10	-0.07	-0.07
	(0.22)	(0.35)	(0.16)	(0.08)	(0.08)
HMOs^2	0.002	0.003	0.002	0.001	0.001
	(0.003)	(0.005)	(0.002)	(0.001)	(0.001)
MDs per 1,000	3.99	4.18	3.48	1.62*	1.63
	(2.63)	(2.62)	(2.91)	(0.98)	(0.99)
Diffusion Effects					
Global diffusion	-5.22***	-5.52***	-5.26***	-5.30***	-5.53***
	(0.21)	(0.39)	(0.34)	(0.36)	(0.59)
Susceptibility to Diffusion					
HMOs		0.14			
		(0.13)			
HMOs^2		-0.01			
		(0.01)			
MDs per 1,000			-0.72		
			(1.50)		
Health cost index				-1.74***	-1.61***
				(0.57)	(0.56)
Proximity to Adopters					
Diffusion between neighboring states					1.29
					(1.54)
Likelihood ratio					
vs h(t) = exp(B_0)	16.2**	19.7**	16.8**	25.7**	26.1**
df	6	8	7	7	8
vs Model 1		3.4	0.6	9.4***	9.8**
df		2	1	1	2

Note: Maximum likelihood estimates of the hazard of first passage of HMO enabling legislation in the states. N = 376 state years; 46 states passed enabling acts.
*$p < .10$, **$p < .05$, ***$p < .01$.

Finally, model 5 reexamines the evidence for local patterns of diffusion. As shown in table 6-3, laws passed by neighbors are estimated to spur legislation more than do laws passed in geographically distant states. But this effect is not significant at conventional levels, and model 5 does not fit the data much better than model 4. Once differential susceptibility to influence across levels of health costs is captured, HMO laws are seen to have diffused nationally rather than via ties between geographically proximate states. This is consistent with Strang and Meyer's (1993) notion that theorization would allow diffusion to flow along weak ties.

The Content of State HMO Laws

Models of the diffusion of HMO laws across the American states implicitly suggest that these laws have much in common. But do states enact the same law or do they shape legislation to their own ends and situations? To address this issue, we turn from the timing to the content of HMO acts.

Provisions of state laws are taken from reports prepared under federal contract by the Aspen Systems Corporation from 1979 to 1989.[9] We supplemented this data by coding all first state laws passed prior to 1979, and their amendments where these were indicated in state legal codes. This approach yielded annual characterizations of twenty-one provisions of each state's HMO enabling act, listed in appendix B.

Routinizing the Technical

In many technical respects, there is little variation across state laws. HMO enabling acts typically require organizations to establish formal grievance procedures, institute quality assurance and utilization review, and specify the grounds for terminating enrollee participation. Minimum benefit packages are specified, HMOs are required to possess some kind of financial reserves, and nondeceptive advertising is permitted.

Taken as a whole, state laws tend to converge over time. Figure 6-2 plots heterogeneity (expressed in terms of deviation from a "modal state law") versus historical time.[10] Average distance from the modal state law declines from 14.5 in 1971 to 4.5 in 1989. The mean number of provisions in each state differing from this modal law declines from about 8.5 to 2.5.[11] The biggest reduction in heterogeneity occurs from 1971 to 1973, and is followed by a continuing, steady decline of some 40 percent from 1973 to 1989.

Two mechanisms produce homogeneity. First, acts passed in later years are closer to the "norm" than those passed early. Laws in Connecticut, Tennessee, Pennsylvania, and Minnesota that predate federal action are highly idiosyncratic;

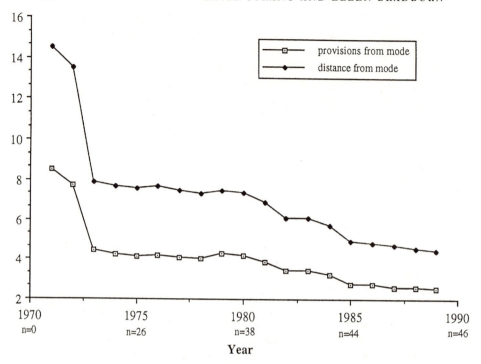

Fig. 6-2. Convergence to the "Typical" HMO Enabling Law. "Typical" HMO enabling
law contains modal set of provisions listed in app. B (excluding open enrollment). Provisions from mode = number of provisions that differ from modal law. Distance from
mode = sum of squared deviations from modal law (see text). n = number of states with
a law (Aspen Systems Corp.; state legislative codes)

laws passed in the 1980s follow well-established patterns. And second, early laws
are revised toward conventionality. Distance from the national mean and the fre-
quency of revision are strongly correlated (r = .74), and a very large percentage
of all revisions lead toward what other states do. States that passed idiosyncratic
laws in the 1970s replaced them with more typical laws in the next decade.

The emerging national norm was constructed around two salient models of
HMO regulation. One was the federal HMO Act, which was not only cognitively salient, but threatened to supersede "unfair restrictions" on HMO activity. While this threat applied only to "federally qualified" HMOs and led to no
courtroom challenges, virtually no state enabling acts include these restrictive
practices. Laws passed after the federal HMO Act thus had more in common
than those passed before it. Further, changes in federal law (such as the elimination of open enrollment) tend to be followed by changes in state laws.

A second source of national influence was a model HMO law written by the
National Association of Insurance Commissioners (NAIC).[12] The NAIC code

was designed to facilitate the lateral movement of "best practice" across states. While formally a body composed of the fifty state insurance commissioners, the NAIC provides a common forum where the voices of state health experts, the "HMO industry," and other interests can be heard. Since the 1980s, the NAIC model has also been reworked by the National Association of HMO Regulators (NAHMOR), a group that emerged from a federal training program.

The NAIC reports that twenty-seven states have enacted substantial portions of its model law (NAIC 1989). The impact of the NAIC's model law is further shown by the close relation between its 1972 code and typical state acts of the late 1970s and 1980s. Incredibly, the 1972 NAIC code is closer to the modal state law in 1989 than is the average state in 1989! This similarity is shared by none of the original state laws passed before 1973, which are extensively revised toward conventionality in later years.

Convergence thus arises through the dense associational web within which state policy makers were embedded. This web has emerged over time with growing experience in HMO regulation. Each of the components of the system is national in scope — the federal government and its sponsorship of state activity, and the NAIC and NAHMOR. While early laws could be written freehand, HMO legislation today is in most respects highly routinized and constrained.

Capturing the Contested

But while the overall trend is toward convergence, some issues remain contested. We would point to three provisions as embodying key political decisions. "Dual choice" provides HMOs with mandated access to employee groups, a potentially powerful weapon in gaining access to health care markets. "Open enrollment" requires HMOs to enroll all comers, including poor insurance risks. "Consumer representation" gives plan members a say over HMO governance, a provision that fit the ideology of community-based prepaid practices in the 1940s but not that of corporate-sponsored plans in the 1980s. While dual choice provisions were thus sought by HMOs and opposed by the enemies of managed care, open enrollment and consumer representation were opposed by HMOs and sought by consumer groups.

Table 6-5 examines the conditions promoting the passage of laws with and without dual choice, open enrollment, and consumer representation. We report a series of bivariate relations, and also utilize the "best fitting" model from table 6-4. In general, the arguments concerning the spread of HMO laws translate into predictions about provisions favorable to HMOs. For example, states with more HMOs, more business coalitions, or higher health costs are expected to quickly pass "HMO friendly" laws mandating dual choice and requiring neither open enrollment nor consumer representation.

Table 6-5 indicates two main findings. First, states with more HMOs are

TABLE 6–5
Passage of HMO Legislation Carrying Specific Provisions

	Dual Choice		Open Enrollment		Consumer Representation	
	With	*Without*	*With*	*Without*	*With*	*Without*
Bivariate Models						
HMOs	0.97**	−0.04	0.09	0.03	−0.04	0.18
HMOs^2	−0.09*	0.001	−0.02	0.00	0.001	−0.01
BC/BS market share	2.00	−0.90	−1.70	0.70	−1.10	−0.01
MDs per 1,000	1.16	0.56	−0.76	1.60**	0.17	0.87*
Business coalitions	−5.54	0.12	−6.54	0.24	−5.54	0.14
Health cost index	−0.30	0.40**	−0.50	0.70**	−0.60	0.50**
% Medically underserved	−3.30	0.30	0.60	−1.00	−0.50	−0.20
Global diffusion	−12.21	−5.51***	−13.14	−3.74***	−12.50	−5.37***
Diffusion between neighboring states	−4.41***	−3.34***	−5.14***	−2.95***	−10.47	−3.20***
Multivariate Models						
B$_0$	−7.59***	−3.97***	−23.22	−4.00***	−5.54***	−3.63***
HMOs	1.28***	0.009	−7.92	−0.08	−0.04	0.09

HMOs^2	−0.10*	0.001	0.11	0.001		−0.007
MDs per 1,000	1.05	1.37	3.38	1.99**	4.03	0.73
Health cost index	−1.35	1.25**	−6.14	1.19***	−2.52	0.91***
Diffusion Effects						
Global diffusion	−22.83	−5.29***	−5.12***	−5.84***	−5.91***	−5.32***
Susceptibility to Diffusion						
Health cost index	−20.25	−1.67**	−1.56***	−2.38	−2.29**	−1.45**
Likelihood Ratio						
vs h(t) = exp(B$_0$)	15.07	15.59	4.10	19.50	7.81	14.59
df	6	6	6	6	6	6
Number of States Passing Law	10	36	22	24	12	34

Note: Maximum likelihood estimates of the hazard of first passage of HMO enabling legislation in the states. Dashed lines indicate separate equations. The top half of this table includes just a single effect in the bivariate models except for organization density, where we include both HMOs and HMOs squared. $N = 376$ state years; 46 states passed enabling acts.

*p < .10, **p < .05, ***p < .01

more liable to include "dual choice" mandates that oblige employers to make HMOs available to their workforce. (While the relationship is nonmonotonic, the linear term dominates over the range of observed variation.) Since HMOs are highly concerned with obtaining access to employee pools, this fits well with interest-group accounts of state regulation.

Second, high health costs lead to HMO laws that are generous to HMOs and dismissive of consumer concerns. Where costs are high, states are quick to pass HMO acts that lack open enrollment provisions and ignore consumer participation, and slow to pass laws that require consumer representation on governing boards. Diffusion effects point in the same direction, indicating that open enrollment and consumer representation laws spread among states with low health costs, while states with high costs pass laws lacking these provisions. These findings mesh with a view of HMO legislation as balancing consumer protection with concerns about spiraling health costs. Where costs are high, the balance tips away from efforts to use HMOs to broaden health coverage and empower consumers, and toward laws that facilitate HMO expansion.

Inspection of the content of HMO laws thus reveals opposed dynamics of convergence and local translation. On the one hand, an interaction network has emerged around HMO policy that promotes the standardization of state laws, particularly in areas seen as technical. On the other hand, decisions about how to balance the interests of HMOs and consumers remain politically contested, and are sensitive to well-mobilized interests as well as to the problems that regulators perceive.

Discussion

While students of organizations have endeavored to theorize legitimacy, state policy makers legitimated a theory. Existing prepaid practices were not taken for granted or politically powerful, but a market model for health care was. Given mounting concerns about health care financing and the rising tide of neoliberal analysis, it is not surprising that a turn toward competitive discipline, entrepreneurship, and consumer choice surfaced in health policy. But without Paul Ellwood's insightful development of a new theory of prepaid practice, HMOs would not have been the beneficiary.

While Ellwood and other health analysts acted as rational choice theorists in arguing that HMOs correctly align incentives, we have acted as institutional theorists in treating these arguments as cultural discourse. Today the claims made on behalf of the HMO appear overblown at best, neglecting both the real difficulties of organization building and the potential for the interests of health financiers, providers, and consumers to conflict despite market competition. But what was important for empirical policy making was that a plausible theoretical logic defined the terms of political debate.

Naturalistic or interest-based arguments, we contend, are not very useful in explaining how or why HMOs gained the political stage. HMOs themselves were the product rather than the driver of federal policy. And seventeen states with no operating HMOs passed HMO enabling acts. Nor was initial legislation acutely sensitive to observable structures of interest and agency. Health purchasers showed little political muscle, and all sorts of health providers adopted flexible positions vis-à-vis HMOs. Physicians form an exception, and we see that HMO laws are passed more readily where physician "oversupply" deflated their opposition.

One can reasonably counter that the structure of interests in the health sector drew boundaries around possible HMO legislation. State and federal authorities could have given HMOs much more money, or required that all doctors be organized into HMOs, or that Medicare and Medicaid contract only with HMOs. The fact that such schemes were understood to be extravagant is undoubtedly related to the marginal status of prepaid practice before the 1970s. But if we wish to understand the laws that were enacted, we must attend to the interpretive construction of the HMO and the leverage it provided for movement beyond the status quo.

Though actual HMOs were hardly the motor of HMO policy, their reaction to the state's initiative had important consequences. At the federal level, prepaid plans mobilized to amend regulatory provisions they found inconvenient and turned them to advantage. States with more HMOs were less willing to experiment with consumer controls and more likely to write laws favorable to existing organizations.

The later evolution of HMO policy was the work of an emerging community of regulators as well as an emerging community of the regulated. Laws diffused across the states in institutional rather than network fashion. The spread of laws occurred nationally to states with low health costs rather than through regional networks. The catalyst was a national health and regulatory community that mobilized easily in the associational culture of the American polity. State laws were responsive to quasi-public agents like the National Association of Insurance Commissioners and its model law, and the National Association of HMO Regulators and its ideas about regulatory reform. It is even worth noting that much of the data utilized in this chapter were produced to contribute to policy-making discourse, from Aspen Systems reports on deviation from federal legislation to Interstudy's surveys of health maintenance organizations. In keeping with DiMaggio and Powell (1983), the result was homogenization.

While organizational institutionalists tend to agree about the strength of homogenizing forces, they disagree about why some practices are institutionalized and others are not. Hannan and Freeman (1987) see institutionalization as density dependent and thus as a self-reinforcing, natural process. DiMaggio (1982) contends that behind successful institutional projects lie the interests and capabilities of elites. While recognizing the force of both approaches, this chapter argues for the power of cultural schemas in defining models that are comprehensible, communicable, and compelling. Without a strong link to neoliberal visions of markets, entrepreneurs, and rational organization, it is unlikely that the poorly regarded prepaid practices of the 1960s could have vaulted into the important position that HMOs occupy in American health care today.

Notes

David Strang's work on this project was supported by a fellowship from the Center for Advanced Study in the Behavioral Sciences and by the National Science Foundation (SES-9213152). We thank Michael Wolfe for research assistance and Ronald Breiger, John Campbell, Neil Fligstein, Ray Liedka, John Meyer, Phyllis Moen, Ove Pedersen, Sid Tarrow, and Xueguang Zhou for their helpful comments. We also thank Rachel Rodgers of Aspen Systems Corporation, Carolyn Johnson of NAIC, and Christine Hotchkiss of NAMCR for their help in providing information on HMO laws and regulations.

1. Professional powers can be defended from an economic perspective by arguing that information asymmetry (doctors rather than patients know what's wrong) produces market failure and motivates an implicit offer from society of professional authority for occupational responsibility (Arrow 1963). For a vigorous critique taking Arrow to task for treating information asymmetries as exogenous rather than as the product of professional control, see Starr 1982, pp. 226–27.

2. Ellwood's speculations here were rather optimistic. While some kinds of prepaid plans reduce health costs, major savings come not from preventative medicine but by economizing on hospital stays (Luft 1981).

3. Where no specific enabling legislation exists, prepaid plans typically incorporate as insurers or service corporations or nonprofit corporations. Under these more general headings, HMOs may be obliged to carry capital reserves at levels designed for indemnity insurers (which they do not need because they provide rather than pay for care), and are vulnerable to claims that they constitute the corporate practice of medicine.

4. While the assumption that rates of legislative passage do not vary with time (net of covariate effects) is a strong one, results from partial likelihood models parallel those for the exponential models presented in tables 6.1–6.3. Below we examine complexities in a substantively important source of time dependence, that of diffusion processes.

5. No corporations testified in the initial federal HMO hearings, although the Committee for Economic Development, a group representing big business, did advocate HMOs in 1973. The high point of business coalition activity was 1982–85, a decade after the main wave of HMO lawmaking.

6. Very few HMOs operated across state boundaries until the development of national HMO firms in the mid-1980s, well after most initial state legislation. In 1981, when information was first collected on multistate HMOs, only 29 of the nation's 262 HMOs operated in more than one state. But all of these operated in geographically contiguous states, most often in New England.

7. $\exp(-5.71) = .003$. Since the baseline rate (where all variables are measured from

their means) is exp(-3.22) = .039, .003/.039 = .10. Note that a negative value for global diffusion does not imply a decrease in the hazard; instead, a large negative value implies a negligible increase in the hazard.

8. In a Monte Carlo study, Greve, Strang, and Tuma (1995) show that susceptibility to diffusion is easily confused with the intrinsic propensity to adopt, and that models should examine both kinds of effects simultaneously.

9. In accordance with a provision in the federal HMO Act, Aspen Systems reviewed all state laws relevant to HMOs on an annual basis. The intent of the federal government in funding this activity was to highlight to states the measures they needed to take to come into line with federal policy.

10. By modal state law we mean a law whose provisions are those most frequently found across the American states as a whole. Twenty of the twenty-one provisions retain the same mode throughout the study period (the exception is open enrollment, which is initially common but is employed by slightly fewer than half of the states by the late 1980s). For simplicity, we exclude open enrollment in computing the modal law and deviations from it.

11. Average distance measures squared deviations on a 3-point scale where values denote a provision's absence, unclear standing, or presence. Counts of the number of provisions that differ treat all deviations as having equivalent magnitude.

12. The NAIC is a body composed of the fifty state commissioners of insurance that disseminates information on the insurance industry and its regulation. HMOs are one of about two hundred domains addressed by NAIC model codes.

References

Arrow, Kenneth J. 1963. "Uncertainty and the Welfare Economics of Medical Care." *American Economic Review* 53:941–69.

Aspen Systems Corporation. 1979–89. "A Report to the Governor on State Regulation of Health Maintenance Organizations." Rockville, MD: Aspen Systems Corporation.

Berger, Peter L., and Thomas Luckmann. 1966. *The Social Construction of Reality.* Garden City, NY: Doubleday

Bergthold, Linda A. 1984. "Crabs in a Bucket: The Politics of Health Care Reform in California." *Journal of Health Politics, Policy, and Law* 9:203–22.

———. 1987. "Business and the Pushcart Vendors in an Age of Supermarkets." *International Journal of Health Services* 17:7–26.

Brown, Lawrence D. 1983. *Politics and Health Care Organization.* Washington, DC: Brookings Institution.

Campbell, John L., and Leon N. Lindberg. 1990. "Property Rights and the Organization of Economic Activity by the State." *American Sociological Review* 55:634–47.

DiMaggio, Paul J. 1982. "Cultural Entrepreneurship in Nineteenth-Century Boston: The Creation of an Organizational Base for High Culture in the United States." *Media, Culture, and Society* 4:33–50.

DiMaggio, Paul J., and Walter W. Powell. 1983. "The Iron Cage Revisited: Institutional Isomorphism and Collective Rationality in Organizational Fields." *American Sociological Review* 48:147–60.

———. 1990. Introduction. Pp. 1–38 in *The New Institutionalism in Organizational Analysis*, edited by Walter Powell and Paul DiMaggio. Chicago: University of Chicago Press.

Dobbin, Frank 1994. *Forging Industrial Policy: The United States, Great Britain, and France in the Railway Age*. New York: Cambridge University Press.

Falkson, Joseph L. 1980. *HMOs and the Politics of Health System Reform*. Chicago: American Health Association.

Fligstein, Neil. 1990. *The Transformation of Corporate Control*. Cambridge: Harvard University Press.

Friedson, Eliot. 1970. *Professional Dominance*. New York: Atherton.

Greve, Henrich R., David Strang, and Nancy B. Tuma. 1995. "Model Specification and Estimator Quality in Heterogeneous Diffusion Processes." Pp. 377–420 in *Sociological Methodology 1995*, edited by Peter V. Marsden. New York: Blackwell.

Hannan, Michael T., and John Freeman. 1987. "The Ecology of Organizational Founding: American Labor Unions, 1836–1985." *American Journal of Sociology* 92:910–43.

Imershein, Allen W., Philip C. Rond, and Mary P. Mathis. 1992. "Restructuring Patterns of Elite Dominance and the Formation of State Policy in Health Care." *American Journal of Sociology* 97:970–93.

Levinthal, Daniel, and James G. March, 1981. "A Model of Adaptive Organizational Search." *Journal of Economic Behavior and Organization* 2:307–33.

Luft, Harold 1981. *Health Maintenance Organizations: Dimensions of Performance*. New York: Wiley.

MacColl, William A. 1966. *Group Practice and Prepayment of Medical Care*. Washington, DC: Public Affairs Press.

McLaughlin, Catherine G., Wendy K. Zellers, and Lawrence D. Brown. 1989. "Health Care Coalitions: Characteristics, Activities, and Prospects." *Inquiry* 26:72–83.

McNeil, Richard, Jr., and Robert E. Schlenker. 1975. "HMOs, Competition, and Government." *Milbank Memorial Fund Quarterly/Health and Society* 53:195–224.

Meyer, John W., and Brian Rowan. 1977. "Institutionalized Organizations: Formal Structure as Myth and Ceremony." *American Journal of Sociology* 83:440–63.

Meyer, John W., and W. Richard Scott. 1983. *Organizational Environments: Ritual and Rationality*. Beverly Hills, CA: Sage.

NAIC (National Association of Insurance Commissioners). 1989. "Health Maintenance Organization Model Act." Model Regulation Service. Washington, DC: NAIC.

Schlenker, Robert E. 1973. *HMOs in 1973: A National Survey*. Minneapolis, MN: Interstudy.

Scott, W. Richard. 1987. "The Adolescence of Institutional Theory." *Administrative Science Quarterly* 32:493–511.

———. 1995. *Institutions and Organizations*. Thousand Oaks, CA: Sage.

Starr, Paul. 1982. *The Social Transformation of American Medicine*. New York: Basic.

Stigler, George. 1971. "The Theory of Economic Regulation." *Bell Journal of Economic and Management Science* 2:3–21.

Strang, David. 1994. "Institutional Accounts of Organizations as a Form of Structural Analysis." *Current Perspectives in Social Theory*, suppl., 1:51–74.

Strang, David, and Michael W. Macy. 1999. "In Search of Excellence: Success Stories,

Fads, and Adaptive Emulation." Paper presented at the Academy of Management Annual Meeting, Chicago.

Strang, David, and John W. Meyer. 1993. "Institutional Conditions for Diffusion." *Theory and Society* 22:487–512.

Strang, David, and Sarah A. Soule. 1998. "Diffusion in Organizations and Social Movements: From Hybrid Corn to Poison Pills." *Annual Review of Sociology* 24:265–90.

Strang, David, and Nancy B. Tuma. 1993. "Spatial and Temporal Heterogeneity in Diffusion." *American Journal of Sociology* 99:614–39.

Strang, David, and Tanya Uden-Holman. Forthcoming. "We Have Met the Enemy: Institutional Conditions for the Founding of Health Maintenance Organizations, 1971–1982." *Research in the Sociology of Organizations.*

Tolbert, Pamela, and Lynne Zucker. 1983. "Institutional Sources of Change in the Formal Structure of Organizations: The Diffusion of Civil Service Reform." *Administrative Science Quarterly* 28:22–39.

Torres, David L. 1988. "Professionalism, Variation, and Organizational Survival." *American Sociological Review* 53:380–94.

Tuma, Nancy Brandon, and Michael T. Hannan. 1984. *Social Dynamics: Models and Methods.* New York: Academic Press.

U.S. House of Representatives. 1972. "Health Maintenance Organizations." Hearings before the Committee on Interstate and Foreign Commerce, Subcommittee on Public Health and Environment, 92nd Congress, 2nd Session. Washington, DC: U.S. General Printing Office.

Appendix A

Descriptive Statistics and Variable Sources

	Mean	S.D.
Any HMOs[a]	0.51	—
Number of HMOs[a]	2.53	6.34
Number of federally qualified HMOs[a]	0.42	1.42
HMO enrollment (100,000s)[a]	1.05	3.45
HMO enrollment per 1,000 population[a]	22.75	46.75
Any business health care coalitions[b]	0.14	—
Number of business health care coalitions[b]	0.25	0.77
Number of statewide business health care coalitions[b]	0.08	0.12
Number of autonomous business coalitions[b]	0.12	0.44
Proportion of workforce unionized[c]	0.24	0.09
Blue Cross/Blue Shield market share[d]	0.41	0.16
Proportion of hospital beds in for-profit hospitals[e]	0.05	0.06
Proportion of MDs in group practice[f]	0.25	0.10
Insurance claims ratio[d]	0.85	0.06
Proportion of hospital beds unoccupied[g]	0.27	0.07
MDs per 1,000 population[h]	1.36	0.35
Health cost index[i]	260.59	71.40
Relative health cost index[i]	−5.06	5.42
Proportion of counties medically underserved[j]	0.39	0.31
Proportion of population in underserved counties[j]	0.20	0.21

Sources:

[a]National Census of HMOs (Interstudy, various years)

[b]*Directory of Business Coalitions for Health Care Action* (U.S. Chamber of Commerce, various years). Autonomous business coalitions are business health care coalitions with fewer than 5 percent of their members representing health care providers or insurers.

[c]*U.S. Union Sourcebook* (Leo Troy and Neil Sheflin, Industrial Relations Data and Information Services, 1985).

[d]*Sourcebook of Health Insurance Data* (HIAA, various years). Blue Cross/Blue Shield market

APPENDIX A
(Continued)

share is the ratio of premiums paid to BC/BS to premiums paid to all third-party insurers. The insurance claims ratio divides benefits paid by premiums paid, for all insurers.

eHospital Statistics (American Hospital Association, various years).

fMedical Groups in the United States (American Medical Association, various years).

gCounty Hospital File (various years).

hPhysician Masterfile (American Medical Association).

iHealth Care Financing Administration, various years. This index is calculated as mean Medicare reimbursements per enrollee, in hundreds of dollars. Relative health costs are deviations from the national mean for that year.

jComputed from the Index of Medical Underservice, Federal Register 40 (170) 1975: 40315–20. The federal HMO Act of 1973 provided for the designation of medically underserved areas, permitting certain benefits be provided to HMOs founded and operating in those areas. The index is constructed from the percetage of the population below the poverty level, the percentage of the population over age sixty-five, the infant mortality rate, and the number of primary care physicians per 1,000 population.

Appendix B

Provisions of State HMO Enabling Acts

1. all HMOs must be certified under the act
2. operation is limited to non profits
3. the State Insurance Department is the primary regulator
4. HMO reorganization and dissolution is regulated as an insurer
5. a consumer representative on the HMO governing board required
6. a policy-making role for subscribers is required
7. advertising is permitted
8. deceptive advertising is prohibited
9. dual choice is required
10. required HMO benefits are enumerated
11. physician employment is restricted
12. copayments are permitted
13. open enrollment is required
14. grounds for enrollee termination must be specified
15. a grievance mechanism is required
16. quality assurance and utilization review are required
17. state approves HMO rates
18. adequate working capital is required
19. reserves or guarantees are required
20. Certificate of Need Law applies to HMOs
21. the state law meets federal HMO Law protections for qualified HMOs

Source: Aspen Systems Corporation, state legislative codes (various).

Chapter 7

Institutional Analysis and the Role of Ideas in Political Economy

JOHN L. CAMPBELL

IN REACTION to rational choice theory, scholars have tried to better understand how ideas, such as economic theories, norms, and values, rather than self interests, influence policy making (e.g., Dobbin 1994; Goldstein and Keohane 1993a; Hall 1989a). However, critics have charged that at least two serious problems have hampered this effort (Blyth 1997; Jacobsen 1995; Yee 1996). First, the concept of ideas and their effects on policy outcomes have been poorly conceptualized. Many scholars agree that an analytic distinction should be drawn between ideas and interests as determinants of policy (e.g., Somers 1995; Thelen and Steinmo 1992), but what they mean by *ideas* has varied widely from broad notions of culture, shared belief systems, and worldviews to specific strategies of action and policy programs.[1] Second, critics maintain that proponents of the ideas perspective have not provided convincing empirical evidence to support the claim that ideas affect policy outcomes in ways that are truly independent from the effects of interests — a problem that stems in part from the poor conceptualization of ideas and their effects in the first place.

This chapter sharpens the concept of ideas and clarifies how ideas affect policy making. As a result, it rectifies the first problem and takes an important step toward resolving the second. In doing so it draws insights from and is located at the intersection of two institutionalist perspectives that have questioned the rational choice assumption that politics are driven solely by actors operating according to a self-interested cost-benefit calculus. The first view, *historical institutionalism*, has been developed by political sociologists and political scientists (e.g., Steinmo, Thelen, and Longsteth 1992), while the second, *organizational institutionalism*, stems from the work of organizational sociologists (e.g., Powell and DiMaggio 1991). I argue that each perspective has unique theoretical blind spots that create the possibility for cross-fertilization and an improved understanding of different types of ideas and how they influence policy making.

Organizational institutionalism has been interested in how ideas affect policy making longer than historical institutionalism has (Peters 1999). Nevertheless, virtually no one has tried to blend these two perspectives in ways that enhance our knowledge of these issues. Indeed, only a handful of scholars have compared these viewpoints at all, and most have either argued for one theory over the other (Dobbin 1994) or simply called for rather than provided a synthesis (Hall and Taylor 1996; W. R. Scott 1994b). Some theorists have combined certain elements from each perspective to show how material and symbolic factors simultaneously determine outcomes (e.g., Campbell and Pedersen 1996; Friedland and Alford 1991; Sewell 1992), but they have done little to refine the concept of ideas per se or to identify the unique effects that different types of ideas have on policy making.

I begin by briefly comparing how historical and organizational institutionalism treat the issue of ideas and policy making. The key insight of historical institutionalism is its theory of constraint, that is, its explanation of how ideas and institutions limit the range of possible solutions that policy makers are likely to consider when trying to resolve policy problems. More specifically, historical institutionalists hold that underlying normative structures restrict the set of policy ideas that political elites find acceptable, and formal institutions mediate the degree to which elites transport different ideas into policy-making arenas for consideration. Organizational institutionalists have a theory of constraint that focuses on underlying cognitive rather than normative structures. They also offer a theory of action, that is, an account of how actors define and articulate their policy problems and solutions, initially by utilizing the institutionalized scripts, cues, and routines that constitute their cognitive frameworks and empower them to act. Second, I extend the insights of each perspective to create a typology of ideas based on two structural dimensions. There are four distinct types of ideas, depending on whether they operate primarily at a cognitive or normative level and whether they constitute the explicit arguments or underlying assumptions of policy debates. Third, I indicate the utility of this scheme by showing how during the late 1970s and early 1980s each type of idea had important effects that helped conservative supply-side economics, rather than its chief intellectual rival, liberal industrial policy, to become the dominant conceptual framework for macroeconomic policy making in the United States. In brief, supply-side economics, a cornerstone of neoliberalism, became politically influential because it offered clearer and simpler programmatic policy guidelines for resolving important economic problems, better fit the existing cognitive and normative constraints that policy makers faced, and was more effectively framed for discursive purposes than was industrial policy. Thus, I argue that different types of ideas, identified by their structural features, had different effects on policy making. Finally, I examine the theoretical and methodological implications of the argument.

I refer to the rise of supply-side economics simply as an illustration and recognize the need to be careful about reading too much from one case, which, of course, cannot constitute unequivocal proof. Furthermore, I do not claim that ideas alone caused the rise of supply-side policies in America. Material interests and the resources backing them were important too. I will show that the relationship between interests and ideas is more complex than the interests-versus-ideas debate often acknowledges. Indeed, to ask whether *either* interests *or* ideas is the chief determinant of policy outcomes is a misleading way to pose the issue because it neglects the possibility that it is the interaction between the two that counts and that some types of ideas are endogenous to the policy process in the sense that they are influenced by policy struggles in which interests, resources, and power loom large. Hence, supply-side ideas captured the imagination of policy makers in part, but not entirely, because they were connected to the organizational resources of powerful political and economic interests.

Historical Institutionalism

Because historical institutionalism was derived from the materialist views of Marx and the comparative history of Weber, for many years it was a perspective that assumed that the material interests of political and economic actors motivated politics and that these interests were institutionally determined (e.g., Evans, Rueschemeyer, and Skocpol 1985; Hall 1986; Katzenstein 1978).[2] By in-stitutions, historical institutionalists generally meant formal and informal rules and procedures, such as those codified in the law or deployed by states and other bureaucratic organizations (Thelen and Steinmo 1992, p. 2). However, they gradually discovered that politicians as well as actors outside the state occasionally struggled for political change in order to improve government, the economy, and society in general rather than simply for the sake of personal gain (e.g., Quirk 1990; Rueschemeyer and Skocpol 1996a; Skocpol 1992; Skowronek 1982). The lesson for these scholars was that ideas as well as self-interest mattered. But how?

A handful of scholars began studying the conditions under which ideas influenced policy makers in areas such as macroeconomic policy (e.g., Hall 1989a; Weir and Skocpol 1985), international relations (e.g., Haas 1992), and the early development of social welfare policies in Europe and North America (e.g., Rueschemeyer and Skocpol 1996a). The general thrust of this literature was that the power of ideas depends largely on how much support they receive from political parties, unions, the business community and from influential political and intellectual elites and how much institutional access these actors have to critical policy-making arenas (e.g., Hall 1989b). For example, Margaret Weir and Theda Skocpol (1985) showed how different forms of Keynesianism were adopted in Sweden, Britain, and the United States during the 1930s largely as a result of Keynesian economists having different institutional opportunities to penetrate policy-making venues in each country. They concluded that institutional constraints mediated the influence of ideas on policy.

Historical institutionalists have always focused on how institutional factors, such as the relative insulation and centralization of political elites or the relationships between branches of government, constrain policy making (Ikenberry 1988, p. 242; Thelen and Steinmo 1992, p. 14), so it is not surprising that their first impulse in studying how ideas affect policy making was to explore how institutions constrained the impact of ideas on the policy process. However, they often overlooked how ideas themselves can constrain policy making.[3] Subsequent work began to address this issue. Some researchers recognized that policy makers use policy ideas as the basis for creating new policy tools, government agencies, and other formal institutions that limit policy options later (Goldstein 1993; Goldstein and Keohane 1993b; Pierson 1994), but this argument remained close to the traditional notion that institutions rather than ideas per se are the critical policy-making constraints (Jacobsen 1995, p. 294–305; Yee 1996, pp. 86–89). More importantly, a few scholars argued that in order for policies to be adopted, they must fit with the underlying norms and values of a society (e.g., Hall 1989b; Katzenstein 1993; Weir 1992, p. 169). Focusing on normative constraints was a sharper break with traditional historical institutionalism.

Despite these advances, researchers paid little attention to how ideas facilitate rather than constrain action. Their contribution in this regard was rather modest, acknowledging simply that ideas spur action by providing specific "road maps" out of policy dilemmas (Goldstein 1993, chap. 1; Weir 1992). For instance, they argued the obvious point that policy makers use economic theories as explicit guides for reducing inflation, stimulating economic growth, resolving trade imbalances, and solving other policy puzzles. In this sense, ideas push policy making in very precise directions by giving policy makers clear reasons to adopt a specific course of action. Of course, for most historical institutionalists, whether or not this happens still depends largely on whether key elites deem these ideas to be normatively acceptable and whether they can transport them through institutional channels into influential policy-making arenas.

As a result, historical institutionalists neglected how elites and other actors deliberately package and frame policy ideas in order to convince each other as well as the general public that certain policy proposals constitute plausible and acceptable solutions to pressing problems. Indeed, the ability of elites to transport an idea into influential arenas may turn on their ability to successfully package and frame it in the first place—hence, the importance of "spin doctors," media relations personnel, and other communications specialists in politics (e.g., Jamieson 1996). Furthermore, historical institutionalists ignored how the content of underlying norms and values provides the symbols and other elements that political actors use in carrying out these more explicit and deliberate manipulations (Yee 1996). For example, in an influential discussion of ideas and policy making, Peter Hall (1989b, pp. 383–86) acknowledged that national political discourse sets important normative limits on policy-making options but barely mentioned that these structures also provide participants in policy debates with a conceptual repertoire for actively framing these options and did not theorize how such framing occurs. The point is that ideas facilitate policy-making action not just by serving as road maps, but also by providing symbols and other discursive schema that actors can use to make these maps appealing, convincing, and legitimate. Organizational institutionalists have had more to say about this.

Organizational Institutionalism

Organizational institutionalism constitutes a branch of organizational sociology that is based on phenomenology. Its adherents maintain that because organizational environments are often uncertain, people's interests are ambiguous and thus their actions are motivated more by institutionalized routines, habits, rituals, scripts, and cues than by interests.[4] In order to differentiate themselves from earlier organizational theorists who stressed how behavior was normatively based, organizational institutionalists stress that routines, habits, and the like are important parts of an actor's underlying cognitive framework and that actors rarely subscribe to them self-consciously or deliberately, due to the fact that cognitive frameworks are generally so taken for granted that they are virtually invisible to the actors themselves (DiMaggio and Powell 1991; Meyer, Boli, and Thomas 1987; W. R. Scott 1995, chap. 3).

Some scholars have used this approach to theorize how ideas affect policy making and state building (e.g., Meyer et al. 1997; Thomas et al. 1987; Tolbert and Zucker 1983). For example, Frank Dobbin (1994) argued that ideas in the form of national political cultures determined how policy makers promoted railway development in the late-nineteenth century. By culture Dobbin meant the shared conceptions of reality, institutionalized meaning systems, and collective understandings that guide policy making — cognitive structures that are rationalized in the sense that policy makers take them for granted as part of the nature of reality (Dobbin 1994, pp. 9–19). Traditionally, he argued, French political culture held that centralized state institutions and state sovereignty were the keys to political order. As a result, political elites in Paris choreographed railway development with a heavy hand in order to ensure that self-interested firms did not jeopardize the development of an efficient and well-coordinated national rail system serving the public interest. Conversely, policy makers in the United States assumed that markets, local self-rule, and community sovereignty were the sources of political order. Hence, they initially based rail policies on government activism at the state and local levels and, later, on the reinforcement of market mechanisms by the Interstate Commerce Commission. Variation in cognitive frameworks was responsible for nationally unique policy outcomes.

There is a tension within organizational institutionalism insofar as cognitive structures are both constraining and enabling (Jepperson 1991, p. 146). On the one hand, structures constrain in the sense that the underlying cognitive frames and schema through which actors view and interpret the world limit the possibilities for action (W. R. Scott 1994a, pp. 66–68). Some possibilities are simply not recognized due to the cognitive blinders with which actors operate. For instance, in Dobbin's view it never would have occurred to French political elites to relinquish railway planning to local authorities and private actors because that was not part of their institutionalized political culture. On the other hand, in order to infuse their perspective with a theory of action, organizational institutionalists also claim that structures "enable" and "empower" actors to generate solutions to their problems by providing cues and scripts that "constitute" legitimate forms of action (e.g., Meyer 1994; Powell 1990, p. 304).

Action-oriented metaphors such as these are common in this literature. Critics have charged, however, that by relying on these metaphors, organizational institutionalists fail to specify the causal processes through which structures enable and empower actors and constitute action.[5] As a result, they neglect the important role of agency in policy making, and their theory of action leaves the impression that actors are institutional dopes blindly following the institutionalized scripts and cues around them (Finnemore 1996; Hirsch 1997; Hirsch and Lounsbury 1997a, 1997b). For instance, Dobbin (1994) argued that French policy makers initially employed a central state planning model to build highways and then *transposed* this model to the development of canals and then railroads, but he did not specify whether this was a conscious and thoughtful adoption of policy-making patterns inherited from the past or not; the role of agency in his account is unclear.[6] Other analyses of transposition fare better. Notably, Yasemin Soysal (1994) showed that as a new model of citizenship emerged at the world level during the latter half of the twentieth century, it was gradually adopted by many nation-states, but with significant variations across countries because local actors tailored the new model to existing national political institutions. The point is that analysts' acknowledgment of the self-conscious capacity of actors to engage in deliberate and creative transposition is one way to inject agency into structural explanations and develop a more refined and dynamic theory of action (Sewell 1992).

Mary Douglas (1986, pp. 66–67) identified a second way to do this. She maintained that actors self-consciously craft solutions to their problems through a process of *bricolage*, through which they recombine already available and legitimate concepts, scripts, models, and other cultural artifacts that they find around them in their institutional environment (see also Campbell 1997; Powell 1991, p. 199). In this view, change results from the deliberate modification and recombination of old institutional elements in new and socially acceptable ways. Ann Swidler (1986) developed a similar idea, that culture provides the "tool kit" with which actors construct their worldviews and devise strategies of action (see also Goldstone 1991; Snow et al. 1986; and Snow and Benford 1992). Ironically, although organizational institutionalists often refer to Douglas's work insofar as she recognizes that new institutions are constructed in socially appropriate ways, they pay less attention to her discussion of bricolage, although it is certainly consistent with their arguments (e.g., DiMaggio and Powell 1991, pp. 24–25; Dobbin 1994, p. 19).

In sum, compared to how historical institutionalists view the influence of ideas on policy making, the insights of organizational institutionalism are twofold. First, insofar as historical institutionalists see that ideas constrain policy making at all, they have focused almost entirely on how the background constraints underlying policy debates are normative. Organizational institutionalists have deliberately moved away from this position in a cognitive direction.[7] Second, whereas historical institutionalists have a rather static and simplistic view of how ideas constitute action by means of exogenously given road maps, at least some organizational institutionalists offer the possibility for a more dynamic theory of action that acknowledges the importance of agency through the concepts of transposition and bricolage — terms that capture the notion that actors self-consciously devise solutions to their problems by deliberately manipulating explicit, culturally given concepts that reside in the cognitive foreground.

Possibilities for Cross-Fertilization

Scholars have argued that there has been a strong tendency for excessively one-sided views to predominate in discussions of these issues, at the expense of comprehensive theoretical development (DiMaggio and Powell 1991; Jepperson 1991). Indeed, despite the fact that both historical and organizational institutionalists are concerned with ideas as determinants of policy making, there has been astonishingly little cross-fertilization between these two perspectives. This is particularly striking insofar as the insights of each one often complement the blind spots of the other. One would expect that theoretical progress could be made by blending elements of these two perspectives. How can this be done to improve our understanding of the relationship between ideas and policy making?

The comparison of historical and organizational institutionalism reveals two conceptual distinctions that are useful for identifying different types of ideas relevant for policy making. First, ideas can be underlying and sometimes taken-for-granted assumptions residing in the background of policy debates. However, ideas can also be concepts and theories located in the foreground of these debates where they are explicitly articulated by policy-making elites. Although the distinction between background and foreground is inspired by organizational institutionalism's recognition that some ideas are so taken for granted that they are invisible, the concept of background assumptions adopted here is not as strong. That is, background assumptions can be visible to actors yet taken for granted in the milder sense that they remain largely accepted and unquestioned, almost as principles of faith, whereas ideas in the foreground are routinely contested as a normal part of any policy debate. Second, ideas can be either cognitive or normative. At the cognitive level ideas are descriptions and theoretical analyses that specify cause-and-effect relationships, whereas at the normative level ideas consist of values and attitudes. Recently scholars in both camps have urged that the distinction between cognitive and normative ideas be incorporated into analysis, but have not indicated how this should be done (e.g., Rueschemeyer and Skocpol 1996b, p. 300; W. R. Scott 1994a). The typology represented by figure 7-1 shows how this can be accomplished. By combining these structural distinctions, we can identify four types of ideas: paradigms, public sentiments, programs, and frames.

Although the typology is based on structural distinctions, I will show that each type of idea exerts unique effects on policy making. Thus, the typology serves an analytic as well as taxonomic function. As elaborated below, *paradigms* are cognitive background assumptions that constrain action by limiting the range of alternatives that policy-making elites are likely to perceive as useful and worth considering. *Public sentiments* are normative background assumptions that constrain action by limiting the range of alternatives that elites

	Concepts and Theories in the Foreground of the Policy Debate	Underlying Assumptions in the Background of the Policy Debate
Cognitive Level	**Programs** Ideas as elite policy prescriptions that help policy makers to chart a clear and specific course of policy action.	**Paradigms** Ideas as elite assumptions that constrain the cognitive range of useful solutions available to policy makers.
Normative Level	**Frames** Ideas as symbols and concepts that help policy makers to legitimize policy solutions to the public.	**Public Sentiments** Ideas as public assumptions that constrain the normative range of legitimate solutions available to policy makers.

Fig. 7-1. Types of Ideas and Their Effects on Policy Making

are likely to perceive as acceptable and legitimate to the public. In the foreground of policy debates *programs*, or policy prescriptions, are cognitive concepts and theories that facilitate action among elites by specifying how to solve
specific policy problems, whereas *frames* are normative concepts that elites use
to legitimize these programs to the public through processes such as transposition and bricolage. Paradigms and public sentiments are second-order concepts insofar as they constitute the underlying ideas upon which the first-order
concepts — that is, programs and frames, respectively — rest.

Ideas and the Rise of Supply-Side Economics

In order to elaborate and illustrate the analytic utility of this scheme, I describe
in the discussion that follows how each type of idea contributed to the rise of
the supply-side approach to macroeconomic policy making in the United
States. Central to this approach was the idea that federal government expenditures and especially income taxes should be cut — an approach that culmi-
nated in passage of the Reagan administration's 1981 Economic Recovery Tax
Act, the largest tax cut in U.S. history, a bold attempt to revitalize the economy, and a radical departure from the Keynesian approach that had dominated
macroeconomic policy making since the Second World War. Because this was
a time when economists and policy makers were debating the merits of different macroeconomic policy approaches, notably supply-side economics versus
industrial policy, this case also provides valuable insights about why some ideas
have greater influence on policy making than others.

Ideas as Programs

Programmatic ideas (Weir 1992) help actors to devise concrete solutions to
their policy problems. These are often technical and professional ideas that
specify cause-and-effect relationships and prescribe a precise course of policy
action. They are often presented in policy briefs, position papers, advisory
memos to policy makers, and congressional testimony. Actors use these ideas
self-consciously and deliberately. Examples include specific supply-side and
industrial policy proposals for revitalizing the U.S. economy.

   During the late 1970s there was tremendous debate among policy-making
elites and economists as to how best to solve the nation's twin economic problems, economic stagnation and double-digit inflation (stagflation). However,
most agreed that standard Keynesian policies were failing because the inverse
relationship between unemployment and inflation, as represented by the well-
known Phillips curve that had guided Keynesian policy making for decades,
no longer held. As a result, Keynesianism fell into disrepute, and an atmo-

sphere of intellectual crisis prevailed among economists and policy makers (Heilbroner and Milberg 1995). A variety of alternatives emerged. For instance, supply-side economists urged that deep cuts in marginal income tax rates for individuals as well as in corporate income taxes would stimulate capital investment, thereby increasing economic growth and reducing unemployment. Moreover, supply-siders argued that this could be done without exacerbating inflation because these tax cuts would stimulate investment rather than consumption. Following Arthur Laffer, an economist at the University of Southern California, some also believed that tax cuts would reduce budget deficits because the increased revenues stemming from reinvigorated economic activity would more than compensate for those lost by lowering marginal tax rates (Roberts 1984, pp. 5–13).

Many liberal and conservative economists criticized supply-side economics (Krugman 1994, chaps. 2–3). However, programmatic ideas often appeal to policy makers more because they provide a clear and concise course of action than because economists agree on their theoretical rigor or empirical validity (Moore 1988; Solow 1989, p. 80). In this regard, supply-side economics had a tremendous advantage over the alternatives because neither its policy recommendations nor its account of how tax cuts would resolve the stagflation problem were complicated: just cut taxes, and everything else would automatically fall into place. In contrast, industrial policy advocates argued that stagflation was rooted in the institutional arrangement of the economy, and thus favored policies that involved complex government interventions, such as the formation of tripartite planning boards involving business, labor, and government leaders and the creation of new government agencies to channel investment capital to key industries and firms — prescriptions that called on government to build new institutions, pick industrial winners and losers, and figure out how to finance additional government spending (Graham 1992). The fact that this sort of complexity was unnecessary within the supply-side framework was an important reason why policy makers favored it (Heilbroner and Milberg 1995, p. 100; Ricci 1993, p. 179). Thus, although there were a variety of policy road maps around, the simplest and easiest to read had an edge.

Cognitive clarity was further enhanced by the fact that although some supply-siders disagreed that tax cuts would reduce the budget deficit, they all concurred that tax cuts were necessary. As a result, they constituted a united intellectual front when it came to making policy recommendations (Roberts 1984). This was not true of industrial policy advocates. While some wanted to establish a government investment bank, modeled after the New Deal's Reconstruction Finance Corporation, to revitalize old troubled industries like steel and automobiles, others favored channeling investment into new industries, such as computers, electronics, and biotechnology, at the expense of traditional manufacturing. While some wanted centralized corporatist advisory boards to coordinate research and development strategies and devise selective tax cuts and export promotion schemes, others rejected corporatism and argued for more decentralized forms of cooperative economic decision making. This dissension made it impossible to forge a clear, concise, and unified set of policy proposals and, as a result, undermined the appeal of industrial policy to policy makers (Shoch 1994, pp. 177–78).

In fact, supply-siders worked hard to package their ideas in clear and simple terms. Several popularized versions of the argument were written and disseminated widely to policy makers and the general public. Notable among them was a series of editorials written by Jude Wanniski in the *Wall Street Journal* and George Gilder's (1981) best-seller, *Wealth and Poverty*, which was serialized in several newspapers and adopted as a Book-of-the-Month Club selection. These presented the supply-side program in uncomplicated terms, often referring in particular to the so-called Laffer curve, an elementary depiction of the idea that lower tax rates increase revenues. The Laffer curve became a powerful pedagogical symbol that many supply-siders used when presenting their position. It was a symbol that generated tremendous publicity in newspapers and magazines and helped put supply-side economics at the center of the burgeoning policy debate (Roberts 1984, p. 27). Of course, politically liberal academics and journalists writing for *Business Week*, the *Washington Post*, the *New Republic*, and other publications tried to popularize the industrial policy alternatives. But as Robert Reich and Ira Magaziner, two of the most prominent industrial policy supporters, admitted later, their ideas failed to have more impact in Washington because they had not streamlined them enough for policy makers, and so industrial policy remained a vague and sometimes contradictory prescription for action (Graham 1992, p. 166). Furthermore, they failed to develop an attractive pedagogical symbol that could rivet attention like the supply-siders' Laffer curve or the Keynesians' Phillips curve before that. Such symbols often have been important in convincing politicians of the merits of a particular theoretical approach to economic policy making (Heilbroner and Milberg 1995, chap. 3).

Although the supply-side program was relatively simple in its own right, a sophisticated and well-funded organizational infrastructure helped supply-siders to package their ideas as succinctly as possible. In response to the perceived domination of Washington politics by liberals, during the 1970s, conservative think tanks such as the Heritage Foundation, the American Enterprise Institute, and the Manhattan Institute pioneered aggressive approaches to distilling academic knowledge into simple forms and disseminating them to the government through brief position papers and to the public through popular books, journal articles, radio and television appearances, and op-ed newspaper pieces. Gilder's book, for instance, was underwritten by the Manhattan Institute. In contrast to moderate and liberal think tanks, such as the Brookings Institution, where industrial policy advocates enjoyed some support, these conservative organizations specialized in packaging and marketing rather than in creating new ideas, and viewed political advising more as an exercise in intellectual salesmanship than as scholarship. The Heritage Foundation in particular pushed the supply-side argument in this way (Allen 1994; Ricci 1993, chap. 7; Smith 1989, p. 189). Industrial policy proponents were at a disadvantage without comparable organizational support. Hence the cognitive clarity and simplicity of supply-side ideas, and thus their appeal to policy makers as well as to the public depended not just on the nature of the ideas themselves, but also on the self-interested, strategic efforts of actors to deliberately render them in this way as an endogenous part of the struggle over public policy.

It is worth noting that there have also been other cases where parsimony, or the lack thereof, was important in determining the fortunes of programmatic ideas. First, despite the fact that many large corporations, unions, and other well-financed groups backed the Clinton administration's proposed health care reforms in 1993–94, the proposal was never enacted, in part because the administration presented it in excessively vague, complex, and ambiguous terms that, on the one hand, failed to unify support within the Democratic party, Congress, and the general public and, on the other hand, created an opportunity for conservative opponents to argue effectively that it was a dangerously complicated and confused proposal (Skocpol 1996). Second, regardless of fierce opposition from the dominant corporations and unions in the airline and trucking industries, economic deregulation proceeded in the United States during the late 1970s and early 1980s in both industries in part because reform was conceptually uncomplicated, logical, and thus conducive to consensus building among policy makers, academic experts, and government regulators (Derthick and Quirk 1985). In both cases, parsimony mattered in ways that were relatively independent of the alignment of material interests and resources.

Ideas as Paradigms

Paradigms constitute broad cognitive constraints on the range of solutions that actors perceive and deem useful for solving problems. In contrast to programmatic ideas, which are precise, concrete, and policy-specific courses of action articulated consciously by policy makers and experts in the cognitive foreground, paradigms generally reside in their cognitive backgrounds as underlying theoretical and ontological assumptions about how the world works. Insofar as economic policy is concerned, they are typically revealed in core economics curriculums in graduate schools, seminal theoretical texts, and other abstract academic publications written by esteemed scholars (e.g., Guillen 1994, pp. 7–20). Paradigmatic effects are profound because they define the terrain of policy discourse (Block 1990; Schön and Rein 1994). When programmatic ideas fit the dominant paradigm, they appear natural and familiar and, as a result, are more likely to appeal to policy makers than alternatives that do not (Hall 1993; Lau, Smith, and Fiske 1991).

Some paradigms are more dominant than others. Important here is the degree to which they are institutionalized within leading universities, think tanks, and professional organizations that provide policy makers with a particular cognitive worldview. During the 1970s and early 1980s, the major economics departments in the country, such as those at the University of Chicago, Harvard, and Stanford, the top economics journals like the *American Economic Review,* and virtually all of the major liberal and conservative think tanks embraced the paradigmatic principles of neoclassical economics. The heterodox paradigms like institutional economics and Marxism received more attention at less-elite schools like Michigan State University, Rutgers, and the University of Massachusetts-Amherst; less conventional journals, including the *Journal of Economic Issues* and the *Review of Radical Political Economics*; and more marginal think tanks like the left-wing Institute for Policy Studies (Canterbery and Burkhardt 1983; Ricci 1993). Insofar as the appeal of ideas is derived in part from the status of their sponsors (Goldstein 1993, p. 15), the fact that neoclassical economics was associated closest with the most prestigious departments, journals, and research institutes certainly enhanced its influence.

As a result, neoclassical principles dominated economic discourse and the paradigm's central tenets, which most policy makers and economists took for granted, limited the range of solutions to economic problems that they viewed as making sense (Earl 1983, pp. 100–101; Eichner 1983, pp. 234–35). Of particular importance were the core neoclassical assumptions that markets develop naturally; that a healthy economy depends on the ability of individual economic actors to pursue their self-interests; that competition among private actors is the source of economic innovation and growth; and that excessive government intervention undermines efficient market activity.

These assumptions took on special significance in the late 1970s. Consensus around Keynesian policy prescriptions had dissolved, and no programmatic alternative had emerged yet to replace it as the new policy-making standard (Krugman 1994). As a result, most economists and policy makers, confronted with the need to solve the stagflation riddle, fell back on their deeply held paradigmatic assumptions for guidance. Indeed, the economics profession was in theoretical disarray, had difficulty identifying appropriate policy responses to current economic problems, and, as a result, began to suspect that policy was often futile and that government should simply leave market forces alone. At the level of abstract theory, this attitude was reflected in the growing popularity among academic economists of rational expectations theory, which suggested that policy often failed because people anticipated policy moves and adjusted their behavior in advance in ways that neutralized the impact of policy, an argument thoroughly consistent with neoclassical assumptions that gov-

ernment intervention is often ineffective, if not counterproductive. At the
level of programmatic policy prescription, this idea created a situation ripe for
laissez-faire approaches like supply-side economics that fit closely with the prevailing theoretical pessimism of the economics profession and, more important, the core assumptions of the neoclassical paradigm (Heilbroner and Milberg 1995, chap. 5). In particular, supply-siders were true to these assumptions
in arguing that the country's economic problems were due to excessive government interference with the economy, notably through burdensome taxation, which undermined the individual initiative of corporations and workers.
After all, they asked, why should corporations invest and innovate in order to
increase profits and why should employees work harder to earn more money
if the government appropriates the fruits of these efforts through high taxes? In
other words, if government left these economic actors alone by reducing taxes,
their entrepreneurialism, competitive spirit, and work ethic would flourish naturally, spawning technological innovations, new markets, more jobs, greater
productivity, and a healthier economy.

In contrast, industrial policy approaches were based on institutional economics, a paradigm whose assumptions deviated sharply from neoclassical economics. In brief, institutional economics does *not* assume that markets occur
naturally; that the pursuit of individual self-interest necessarily results in a
healthy economy; that private competition is necessarily the key to economic
innovation and growth; or that government intervention always undermines
market efficiency.[8] As a result, industrial policy advocates offered programmatic ideas that contradicted the basic neoclassical paradigm. They called for
government to help create new markets and facilitate the competitiveness of
U.S. firms by providing considerable assistance through the provision of research and development funds, technology, tariff protection, worker training
programs, and infrastructure. Because these things were expensive, they might
require higher taxes and, as a result, still more government intervention. Similarly, they suggested that a healthy economy entailed long-range investment
strategies that required corporations to worry less about immediate profitabil-
ity and more about developing new products and production technologies that
would secure their long-term competitive advantage. This implied higher
taxes on short-term capital gains as a way to entice investors to develop more
patient investment strategies. Industrial policy proponents also stressed how
the key economic actors were not just self-interested individuals but organized
groups, such as trade unions, business associations, and networks of firms, that
needed to cooperate as well as compete in ways that would improve the economy's health, and would do so only if government created the proper incentives (e.g., "Reindustrialization of America" 1980; Thurow 1980).

As industrial policy supporters eventually acknowledged, one of their problems was that their programmatic ideas did not resonate well with the dominant neoclassical paradigm, whose assumptions remained largely unchal-

lenged (e.g., Piore 1995, chap. 3). Indeed, even some politically liberal economists attacked industrial policy, arguing that the nation's economic condition
stemmed from macroeconomic and cyclical problems, not institutional ones
(Shoch 1994, p. 185) — a critique that was consistent with neoclassical orthodoxy rather than the heterodox canons of institutional economics. In short, the
paradigmatic advantage went to supply-side economics.

Ideas as Public Sentiments

Whereas paradigmatic ideas constrain the cognitive range of solutions that
policy makers perceive as instrumentally useful, public sentiment constrains
the normative range of solutions that they view as politically acceptable. After
all, even if a solution is deemed instrumentally effective, it may not receive
serious consideration if it lacks political legitimacy. Public sentiment consists
of broad-based attitudes and normative assumptions about what is desirable
or not. Because public sentiment covers such a wide range of issues, it does
not necessarily constitute a coherent, consistent set of issue positions — that
is, broad-based sentiment in one issue area may contradict that in another. In
contrast to paradigms, which are assumptions held by policy makers and experts, public sentiments are assumptions held by large segments of the general public. Policy makers discern these through public opinion polls and
other forms of constituent feedback (Kingdon 1984, chap. 7; Weir 1992, p.
169). Hence, public sentiments are generally not so taken for granted that
they are invisible.

The debate over economic policy was constrained by deep suspicions about
the wasteful and corrupt ways of big government. These concerns have always
been central to national public sentiment and have long been reflected in opposition to budget deficits and high taxes (Lipset 1996, chaps. 1–2; Makin and
Ornstein 1994; Savage 1988), but they became particularly acute during the
1970s. Since the Second World War, a majority of Americans almost always
felt that their federal taxes were too high, especially if they perceived government spending as extravagant, but by the late 1970s this number had grown to
over 70 percent of Americans polled (Page and Shapiro 1992, pp. 160–63).
Furthermore, surveys indicated that by 1980, the vast majority of citizens had
become increasingly concerned about budget deficits, associated deficits with
government profligacy, and favored a balanced budget (Page and Shapiro
1992, p. 148–49). As a result, reducing deficits had become code in Washington for reducing the size and exorbitance of government (Weir 1992, p.
158). Indeed, politicians who argued that deficits were benign often outraged
their constituents and learned that proposing almost anything that might ex-
acerbate deficits was politically unacceptable. Even the liberal Democratic
black caucus, which traditionally advocated more spending on government

programs at the expense of larger deficits, began calling for budget balancing through spending cuts (Savage 1988, chap. 7).

All of this bore heavily on efforts to tackle the stagflation problem. In such an anti–big government environment, industrial policy supporters faced severe obstacles. After all, their arguments for more federal spending on research and development, infrastructure, and the like amounted to calls for *bigger* government. So did their prescriptions about how to pay for it because they generally recommended either more deficits or tax increases. Of course, funds could be redirected from other programs, notably defense, as some industrial policy advocates urged, but this was a difficult position to defend politically because public support for additional defense spending was rising sharply, especially after the Iran hostage crisis and the Soviet Union's invasion of Afghanistan in 1979 (Page and Shapiro 1992, p. 265).[9] In contrast, the supply-side program promised less government through lower taxes, smaller budget deficits, and reductions in federal spending, especially social welfare programs. Policy makers from both political parties recognized how well all of this resonated with prevailing public sentiment, which is one reason why Democrats as well as Republicans began to suggest regressive tax cuts during the late 1970s. Notably, in 1978, for the first time in over forty years, a Democratic Congress passed and a Democratic president, Jimmy Carter, signed regressive tax legislation that cut capital gains rates for the upper-middle class and the wealthy (Edsall 1984, p. 65).

It is important to remember that policy makers themselves may hold these same attitudes. Nowhere was this more evident than with Ronald Reagan. Indeed, Reagan's deep suspicion of big government was one reason he favored tax cuts so strongly (Makin and Ornstein 1994, chap. 2). Edwin Meese, one of Reagan's longtime advisors, remarked that this basic perspective was never open to question or debate in the White House, and other members of Reagan's inner circle reported that they were supposed to be keepers of this central ideological faith. For instance, when it became apparent that at least some legislative pork would have to be written into the 1981 Tax Act in order to ensure its passage through Congress, Reagan reluctantly agreed, but drew the line when it came to reducing the tax cut for individuals and ordered his lieutenants to stand firm on this principle (Weatherford and McDonnell 1990, pp. 139–40). Thus, ideas about what is socially appropriate constrain policy makers in two ways. First, and most importantly, public sentiment affects the constituent pressures to which policy makers pay close attention. Second, policy makers may also hold these sentiments, which then limit the range of policy options they themselves believe to be normatively acceptable.

Deeply held public sentiments become especially influential during policy episodes veiled in uncertainty. After all, the debate between supply-siders and industrial policy supporters was fierce precisely because there was no consensus about the causes of stagflation (Krugman 1994). When the truth is elusive and knowledge vacuums such as this arise, policy makers place greater emphasis on whether a particular policy option coincides with important social values (Rein and Winship 1997). Nonetheless, although public sentiment as well as intellectual paradigms constrain the range of options that policy makers are likely to consider, they are rarely so precise and consistent that they determine specific policy choices in their own right (Kingdon 1984, p. 70). How programmatic ideas are strategically framed is also important.

Ideas as Frames

Ideas provide actors with symbols and concepts with which to frame solutions to policy problems in normatively acceptable terms through transposition and bricolage. Indeed, in many policy areas the programmatic ideas that become most influential are those that experts, advisers and others frame in ways that most closely coincide with or seem to protect central cultural values (Brint 1994a, p. 141; Lau, Smith, and Fiske 1991, p. 670). Frames appear typically in the public pronouncements of policy makers and their aids, such as sound bites, campaign speeches, press releases, and other very public statements designed to muster public support for policy proposals. Frequently the repertoires from which framers select symbols and concepts are precisely the values and opinions that are reflected in public sentiment in the first place. In this regard, actors intentionally appropriate and manipulate public sentiments for their own purposes. Hence, policy makers are not just constrained by public sentiment; they also enjoy some leeway to mobilize it toward their own ends (Nordlinger 1981, p. 30).

Many scholars described the 1981 tax reform as the result of intense lobbying by interest groups and political factions operating through the decentralized and fragmented structure of the state (Martin 1991; Roberts 1984; Steinmo 1993). This is an important and well-known part of the story. However, historians have shown that some of the most important tax reforms, including the initial adoption of income taxes, were passed only after politicians framed them in ways that were consistent with prevailing public sentiment (Leff 1984; Stanley 1993).

Supply-siders were deft at framing their programmatic ideas in this way (Ackerman 1982, Chap. 2). First, they combined the tax-cut strategy with Jeffersonian images of a big, centralized, and expanding government whose consequences were devastating to the country and that could best be brought under control by limiting politicians' access to revenues (Savage 1988, pp. 201–4). Gilder (e.g., 1981, chaps. 1–2), for instance, often argued that high taxes jeopardized individual freedom and public safety by encouraging tax evasion and other criminal activities and undermined the traditional American family by reducing net family income, which forced wives into the labor market, threatened their husbands' manhood, and fueled higher divorce rates. Thus, his frame for justifying steep supply-side tax cuts was a bricolage that combined cherished beliefs in family and freedom with suspicions of big government. Second, supply-siders transposed historical examples to frame their arguments in ways that were intended to appeal to the American public's normative sensibilities. Among the most striking examples was when Reagan and his advisers sought to support the business tax cut strategy by arguing that this was exactly what President Kennedy had done in 1963 to combat recession — a strategy so successful, they claimed, that it generated an additional $54 million in federal revenue, as Laffer would have predicted (Jamieson 1996, p. 394). Policy makers use famous historical events, particularly if they are associated with public figures with high prestige like Kennedy as well as with broad normative principles, such as Jeffersonianism, for framing purposes. Commenting on the supply-side victory over industrial policy, one political observer noted that Reagan was a master framer, offering the public "an amalgam of images, aspirations, and expectations which resonated very powerfully with American ideas of personal and national identity. There was the challenge that liberals were unable to answer effectively" (Ricci 1993, p. 175).

Indeed, industrial policy supporters stumbled badly over framing issues and seemed always to be on the defensive, in part because conservatives were quick to frame industrial policy in negative ways. For example, conservatives attacked industrial policy as a form of state planning and, by implication, socialism (Shoch 1994, p. 108). Gilder (1981, pp. 5, 22, 51) repeatedly described industrial policy advocates of all stripes, such as Lester Thurow, John Kenneth Galbraith, and Robert Heilbroner, as socialists and crypto-Marxists. Industrial policy supporters including Reich, Magaziner, and Thurow responded by refusing to use the word *planning* at all and vehemently denied that this was what they had in mind precisely because of their concerns over this framing problem (Graham 1992, p. 102). Moreover, they searched hard for alternative language that might be more publicly palatable. For instance, industrial policy advocates advising the Carter administration tried to shift attention away from planning imagery while also appealing to blue-collar workers in traditional manufacturing industries. Thus, sociologist Amitai Etzioni suggested the phrase "reindustrialization of America," but after Carter's arch political rival, Senator Edward Kennedy, happened to advance the idea of a Reindustrialization Corporation in a speech on how to solve the country's economic woes, Etzioni's term was unacceptable in the White House. Similarly, Thurow, Reich, and others substituted terms like "competitiveness policy" and "industrial strategy" in order to avoid the stigma and normative controversy surrounding the planning imagery (Graham 1992, pp. 42, 208). In the end, however, observers agreed that because industrial policy supporters were unable to reframe their arguments in ways that were more appealing politically, industrial policy remained an ideological lightning rod of the worst kind (Graham 1992, p. 158).

Supply-siders also effectively neutralized the impact of many of the industrial policy advocates' favorite symbols. For instance, supporters of industrial policy often referred to the old Reconstruction Finance Corporation as a symbol of how the U.S. economy had enjoyed great success when government provided investment capital to businesses. However, conservatives countered by recalling that the agency had become mired in corruption, scandal, and other problems during its later years, and therefore really demonstrated the need for a laissez-faire approach. Similarly, industrial policy advocates pointed to Japan as an example of how mercantilist policies, directed by the Ministry of International Trade and Industry, could stimulate economic growth, but conservatives responded that Japan's success lay instead in private sector market forces, such as aggressive corporations, high savings rates, low capital costs, innovative management techniques, fewer lawyers, and less bureaucratic red tape (Graham 1992, chap. 7). Hence, framing was a dynamic process that evolved through struggle as one actor responded to the symbolic overtures of another, often by trying to appropriate the opponent's symbols for his or her own purposes. It was a process made possible by the malleability of symbols, historical examples, and analogies; driven by the clash of opposing frames; and involving considerable creativity and ingenuity to transpose and recombine a variety of discursive artifacts.

Two issues require further elaboration. First, the selection of symbols and rhetoric for framing purposes is often a very strategic and deliberate activity because framers are acutely aware that a frame that fits the prevailing public mood is important in generating public support for policy proposals. For example, framing tax cut proposals as representing a solution to budget deficits and big government became increasingly popular among supply-siders during the 1980 presidential campaign because Reagan's campaign advisers recognized from public opinion polls that deficits had become a particularly important public concern (Jamieson 1996, p. 416). Indeed, whether or not a frame is effective often turns on how well framers monitor public sentiment, an activity that is, of course, a function of the level of resources at their disposal. One reason why the Reagan campaign was more effective than the Democrats at framing issues such as these in 1980 was that they extensively pretested their frames with focus groups and in selected media markets before they broadcast them more widely on television and radio. They even tested their ads against Democratic ads. Because they had less money, the Democrats did very little of this and suffered in the campaign as a result (Jamieson 1996, pp. 397–98). The point is that although everyone tries to frame their policy proposals as effectively as possible, framers understand that the quality and effectiveness of frames is variable and that this can be discerned ahead of time, given adequate resources.

Second, although creativity is an important part of the framing process, so is the ability to project frames, once they have been built, to the intended audience. The supply-siders' eventual success turned in part on their ability to do this better than their opponents. Again, organizational resources were important. Conservative think tanks were more interested and sophisticated in this sort of activity and had more resources to dedicate to it than their liberal counterparts did (Ricci 1993; Smith 1989). Indeed, given the fact that deficits in 1980 were not substantially larger in real terms or as a percentage of the GNP than they had been for the previous fifteen years, this effort in conjunction with a massive conservative publicity campaign during the 1970s may have exacerbated public concern over deficits in the first place (Page and Shapiro 1992, p. 149). Moreover, during the 1980 presidential campaign, when the level of public debate over these issues was especially intense, Reagan had considerably more money for advertising his position than did Carter (Jamieson 1996, pp. 417–28).

Thus, especially insofar as frames are concerned, there is a closer and more complex relationship between interests, resources, and ideas than much of the literature on ideas and policy making suggests. Put simply, the ability to influence policy making depends in part on finding which frames are the most appropriate and projecting them to the public — tasks that are endogenous to the policy-making struggle and that often depend, in turn, on the ability of various interests to dedicate resources to them. However, this does not mean that interests and resources alone determine policy-making outcomes. If they did, then frames would not matter, policy-making elites would not dedicate nearly as much money, time, and energy as they do to figuring out which frames work best, and clever campaign advisers and spin doctors would not play such prominent roles in politics.

Conclusion

To summarize briefly, when we juxtapose the analytic strengths and weaknesses of historical and organizational institutionalism, we can disentangle what we mean by ideas and better understand how different types of ideas affect policy making. Ideas provide specific solutions to policy problems, constrain the cognitive and normative range of solutions that policy makers are likely to consider, and constitute symbols and concepts that enable actors to construct frames with which to legitimize their policy proposals.

This last point is especially important because it is the most obvious way in which my position differs from both organizational and historical institutionalism. Although organizational institutionalists focus almost exclusively on the unintended effects of largely taken-for-granted ideas (e.g., Meyer et al. 1997; Meyer, Boli, and Thomas 1987), the events depicted above show that the intentional manipulation of ideas through cognitively clear and concise packaging and normatively acceptable framing also requires theoretical attention. Most historical institutionalists who take ideas seriously also neglect how actors use ideas in this way, particularly insofar as frames are concerned (e.g., Goldstein and Keohane 1993b; Hall 1989b; Thelen and Steinmo 1992). This is particularly ironic in their case, because several prominent historical institutionalists also have contributed to a literature on social movements that speaks about the importance of cultural repertoires and idioms in framing movement issues (e.g., Skocpol 1994; Tilly 1979; see also Tarrow 1994, chap. 7; Gamson 1992). It emphasizes that broad cultural themes provide a resonant backdrop for political messages; that messages are deliberately framed for public consumption; that frames are built from the raw materials provided by the broader culture; and that this entails much contention among framed messages (Brint 1994b). Indeed, the rise of supply-side economics involved just such a process. By conceptualizing this process for policy making, this chapter elevates agency to a more prominent and appropriate position in the analysis than either organizational or historical institutionalists have done, and as a result provides a more balanced assessment of the ideational foundations of action and constraint. It also demonstrates that the ideational foundation of action has both a cognitive and normative dimension.

My argument also differs from organizational institutionalism by emphasizing that an analysis of powerful organizations and conflict must be incorporated into our theories of how ideas affect policy making. Critics have charged that organizational institutionalism rejects realist or materialist arguments, ignores the central role of conflict and struggle in institution building and policy making, and avoids discussing how powerful organizations help enact the ideas that frame governmental policies (Hirsch 1997). The rise of supply-side economics was very much an intellectually and politically contested process in which powerful think tanks and other organizations mobilized substantial financial resources to influence policy making at the ideational level. In this regard, the argument presented here resembles that of other scholars who have shown that the rise and fall of policy ideas is a highly conflictual process (e.g., Kingdon 1984).

Researchers who seek to bring ideas and culture back into the analysis of politics have been criticized for failing to develop empirically grounded causal explanations and generalizations (Brint 1994b). By comparing the political fortunes of two opposing sets of programmatic ideas, supply-side economics and industrial policy, my argument contributes to our general understanding of the causal processes whereby some programmatic ideas affect policy making more than others. Specifically, the probability that a programmatic idea will affect policy making varies in part according to the extent to which it provides clear and simple solutions to instrumental problems, fits existing paradigms, conforms to prevailing public sentiment, and is framed in socially appropriate ways (see also Kingdon 1984, pp. 131–39). Whether or not these effects are patterned and systematically related to each other remains an open question, but one might hypothesize that they operate in a hierarchically nested fashion according to the following logic, which may not always be fully apparent to policy makers: Given the perception of a problem for which policy makers seek a remedy, a programmatic idea must be credible to them in the sense that it fits the dominant policy paradigm. If it is, then they must believe that it provides an effective solution to a policy-making problem — a perception that is enhanced to the extent that the idea is packaged in simple enough terms for policy makers to understand and that it provides clear policy guidelines. If policy makers perceive an idea to be useful in this sense, then it must fit with prevailing public sentiment. If it does not, then it must be framed to improve this fit. In other words, it is the cumulative effect of different types of ideas that influences whether or not a programmatic idea carries the day. For example, it was not just the fact that supply-siders characterized industrial policy as socialism that ensured their success. After all, conservatives have been making such charges against liberals for decades. Instead, it was the combination of that frame and others combined with all the other effects described above that helped make the difference.

However, as I have stressed, the argument that ideational conditions affect policy-making outcomes does not mean that interests are unimportant. My claim is simply that simplicity and clarity, cognitive and normative fit, and proper framing are *necessary* but not inevitably sufficient conditions for policy makers to adopt and deploy a programmatic idea. Indeed, the fact that the victory of supply-side economics over industrial policy turned on the material and organizational resources of people with explicit political agendas as well as the effects of various types of ideas suggests that it is the *interaction* of ideas and interests that is ultimately the important thing for scholars to consider (e.g., Weber 1946, p. 280; 1958, p. 183; Wuthnow 1989). Thus, although my position lies at the intersection of organizational and historical institutionalism, it does not reject all aspects of rational choice institutionalism.

Nevertheless, my argument does differ from that often made by those who maintain that the ideas that influence policy making simply reflect the dominant material interests in society (e.g., Domhoff 1983, chap. 4; Dye 1995, chap. 9). In particular, although the influence of organizational resources has a heavy effect on building effective frames, actors build frames from the already existing normative elements that constitute public sentiments, which do not arise simply due to the manipulations of powerful interests (Page and Shapiro 1992, pp. 31–34). Furthermore, although the capacity to package programmatic ideas in parsimonious ways is enhanced by these programs' links to organizational resources, they must fit with underlying paradigmatic assumptions whose origins and institutionalization are not due solely to the power of political and economic interests over universities and other arenas of intellectual discourse (McCloskey 1985; Rueschemeyer and Skocpol 1996b). Indeed, the relationship between ideas, interests, and public policy is a complex one. A comprehensive analysis of the interactions among different types of ideas and interests, particularly with respect to paradigms and public sentiments, is beyond the scope of this chapter, but the specification of different types of ideas and their possible effects is an important starting point for such an investigation.

Similarly, a clearer specification of ideas and their effects is important for those who insist that interests have very *little* impact on policy-making outcomes. For instance, Dobbin (1994) maintained that national principles regarding the desirable relationship between state and economy rather than the material interests of business and political elites determined railroad policy. He based his argument on an analysis of the public pronouncements, speeches, and official congressional and parliamentary proceedings recorded at the time. However, people may say one thing publicly but another privately in order to shield their true motives from public scrutiny and otherwise legitimize their behavior (Edelman 1964; Goffman 1959, chap. 3; Kuran 1995; J. Scott 1990). Although Dobbin recognized that politicians may be committed to taken-for-granted cognitive paradigms, by focusing on public testimonies he neglected to investigate the possibility that they may also engage in much more self-conscious framing exercises in order to conceal ulterior motives, including self-interest. As a result, it is difficult to tell whether or not interests were at work in his empirical cases. Because his methodology was not sensitive to the full array of ideas and how they might have affected railroad policy making, he failed to provide the sort of "crucial experiment" (Stinchcombe 1968, pp. 24–28) that could have resolved the issue. A better test would have been to compare the public pronouncements against more private documents, such as personal diaries and correspondence, where actors are less likely to conceal their true motives if they differ from those that they express publicly. Doing so would have created an opportunity to determine the degree to which the private thoughts of actors matched their public declarations, whether or not framing had occurred in order to conceal ulterior motives and whether or not self-interests were involved. Of course, this still begs the question of how actors with particular beliefs come to occupy critical policy-making positions in the first place — a question posed by historical institutionalists and noninstitutionalists alike and one that again focuses attention on the possible interactions between interests and ideas.

John Maynard Keynes (1936, p. 383) once wrote that the ideas of economists, regardless of their empirical truth, are more powerful than is generally understood. Nevertheless, those engaged in the ideas-versus-interests debate have run into methodological problems trying to decipher how much power ideas have on policy making because they have not specified precisely enough what they mean by ideas. My purpose has been to suggest how we might think more clearly about ideas and their effects so that we can begin to overcome

these methodological hurdles. This is the only way we can determine how powerful ideas really are.

Notes

This chapter was originally published as "Institutional Analysis and the Role of Ideas
in Political Economy," *Theory and Society* 27 (1998) :377–409, © Kluwer Academic
Publishers, and is reprinted here in slightly revised form with kind permission from
Kluwer Academic Publishers. For comments on earlier versions I am indebted to Robert
Alford, Steve Brint, Bruce Carruthers, Frank Dobbin, Bill Form, Roger Friedland, Ju-
dith Goldstein, Peter Hall, Bob Jenkins, Peter Kjær, John Meyer, Ove K. Pedersen,
Frances Fox Piven, Dick Scott, Jim Shoch, Yasemin Soysal, Ann Swidler, Rosemary Taylor, Charles Tilly, the *Theory and Society* editors, and seminar participants at Stanford,
Stockholm, Harvard, and Ohio State Universities and the Copenhagen Business School.
    1. Despite this analytic separation there are, of course, important relationships be-
tween ideas and interests. Notably, there is convincing evidence that self-interest as an
important motivation in the Western world is a historically specific social construction
that emerged only after the concept of the individual gained privileged position over
the concept of community (Hirschman 1977). Thus, subjectively understood interests
are in fact a particular type of idea. Nevertheless, as Weber (1946, p. 280) recognized
in his famous reference to how ideas act as the switchmen that determine the tracks
along which interests push action, to simply dismiss the distinction between ideas and
interests in this way is to ignore important differences in types of human motivation and
determinants of political and other social outcomes.
    2. There have been very few attempts to describe the central paradigmatic features
of historical institutionalism (but see Skocpol 1985; Thelen and Steinmo 1992). Hence,
the characterization that follows is based largely on empirical work within this tradition.
    3. Whereas some scholars have attributed the historical institutionalists' problem of
undertheorizing the development and impact of ideas to excessively state-centered analytic assumptions (Friedland and Alford 1991), the problem stems more from the materialist theoretical heritage of the perspective. Indeed, many historical institutionalists
rejected the state-centered versus society-centered dichotomy but still ignored the influence of ideas on policy making (e.g., Campbell 1988; Campbell and Lindberg 1990;
Hall 1986; Katzenstein 1978).
    4. A few historical institutionalists have also acknowledged that the impact of ideas
on policy makers is heightened during times of economic or political uncertainty and
ambiguity (Goldstein 1993, p. 3).
    5. Some scholars have argued that the failure to specify the causal processes through
which structures enable and empower actors is partly due to the high level of abstrac-
tion at which organizational institutionalists often operate theoretically (Hirsch and
Lounsbury 1997a, 1997b). However, it is also due to the fact that much of the empirical work done within this tradition involves the analysis of changes in large numbers of
states or organizations that obscure the details of change that would be revealed by more
fine-grained case studies. For example, see many of the empirical studies in W. R. Scott
and Meyer 1994.

6. Elsewhere Dobbin does a much better job showing how cognitive structures are enabling. Notable is his discussion of how the failed paradigm of traditional economics — e.g., balanced budgets — guided policy innovation during the Great Depression and provided policy makers with a model of what *not* to do (Dobbin 1993).

7. Indeed, among historical institutionalists Peter Hall (1993) is probably the only one who has paid much attention to cognitive issues, and then primarily to identify the conditions under which shifts in cognitive paradigms occur rather than how they constrain policy making once they are established.

8. For comparisons of the assumptions of institutional and neoclassical economics, see Best 1990, chap. 4; Lazonick 1991; and Stevenson 1987.

9. The irony that the public was averse to deficits but willing to support a dramatic military buildup that quickly increased deficits to historically unprecedented levels underscores the fact that public sentiments are often inconsistent.

References

Ackerman, Frank. 1982. *Reaganomics: Rhetoric vs. Reality.* Boston: South End Press.

Allen, Michael Patrick. 1994. "Elite Social Movement Organizations and the State: The Rise of the Conservative Policy-Planning Network." *Research in Politics and Society* 4:87–109.

Best, Michael. 1990. *The New Competition: Institutions of Industrial Restructuring.* Cambridge: Harvard University Press.

Block, Fred. 1990. *Postindustrial Possibilities: A Critique of Economic Discourse.* Berkeley and Los Angeles: University of California Press.

Blyth, Mark M. 1997. "Any More Bright Ideas? The Ideational Turn of Comparative Political Economy." *Comparative Politics* 29(2)229–50.

Brint, Steven. 1994a. *In an Age of Experts: The Changing Role of Professionals in Politics and Public Life.* Princeton: Princeton University Press.

———. 1994b. "Sociological Analysis of Political Culture: An Introduction and Assessment." *Research on Democracy and Society* 2:3–41.

Campbell, John L. 1988. *Collapse of an Industry: Nuclear Power and the Contradictions of U.S. Policy.* Ithaca: Cornell University Press.

———. 1997. "Mechanisms of Evolutionary Change in Economic Governance: Interaction, Interpretation, and Bricolage." Pp. 10–32 in *Evolutionary Economics and Path Dependency*, edited by Lars Magnusson and Jan Ottosson. Aldershot, UK: Edward Elgar.

Campbell, John L., and Leon N. Lindberg. 1990. "Property Rights and the Organization of Economic Activity by the State." *American Sociological Review* 55:634–47.

Campbell, John L., and Ove K. Pedersen. 1996. "Theories of Institutional Change in the Postcommunist Context." Pp. 3–26 in *Legacies of Change: Transformations of Postcommunist European Economies.* New York: Aldine de Gruyter.

Canterbery, E. Ray, and Robert J. Burkhardt. 1983. "What Do We Mean by Asking Whether Economics Is a Science?" Pp. 15–40 in *Why Economics Is Not Yet a Science*, edited by Alfred S. Eichner. New York: M. E. Sharpe.

Derthick, Martha, and Paul J. Quirk. 1985. *The Politics of Deregulation.* Washington, DC: Brookings Institution.

DiMaggio, Paul J., and Walter W. Powell. 1991. Introduction. Pp. 1–38 in *The New Institutionalism in Organizational Analysis,* edited by Walter Powell and Paul DiMaggio. Chicago: University of Chicago Press.

Dobbin, Frank. 1993. "The Social Construction of the Great Depression: Industrial Policy during the 1930s in the United States, Britain, and France." *Theory and Society* 22:1–56.

———. 1994. *Forging Industrial Policy: The United States, Britain, and France in the Railway Age.* New York: Cambridge University Press.

Domhoff, G. William. 1983. *Who Rules America Now?* Englewood Cliffs, NJ: Prentice-Hall.

Douglas, Mary. 1986. *How Institutions Think.* Syracuse, NY: Syracuse University Press.

Dye, Thomas. 1995. *Who's Running America? The Clinton Years.* Englewood Cliffs, NJ: Prentice-Hall.

Earl, Peter E. 1983. "A Behavioral Theory of Economists' Behavior." Pp. 90–126 in *Why Economics Is Not Yet a Science,* edited by Alfred S. Eichner. New York: M. E. Sharpe.

Edelman, Murray. 1964. *The Symbolic Uses of Politics.* Urbana: University of Illinois Press.

Edsall, Thomas Byrne. 1984. *The New Politics of Inequality.* New York: Norton.

Eichner, Alfred S. 1983. "Why Economics Is Not Yet a Science." Pp. 205–41 in *Why Economics Is Not Yet a Science,* edited by Alfred S. Eichner. New York: M. E. Sharpe.

Evans, Peter, Dietrich Rueschemeyer, and Theda Skocpol, editors. 1985. *Bringing the State Back In.* New York: Cambridge University Press.

Finnemore, Martha. 1996. "Norms, Culture, and World Politics: Insights from Sociology's Institutionalism." *International Organization* 50(2)325–47.

Friedland, Roger, and Robert R. Alford. 1991. "Bringing Society Back In: Symbols, Practices, and Institutional Contradictions." Pp. 232–63 in *The New Institutionalism in Organizational Analysis,* edited by Paul DiMaggio and Walter Powell. Chicago: University of Chicago Press.

Gamson, William A. 1992. *Talking Politics.* New York: Cambridge University Press.

Gilder, George. 1981. *Wealth and Poverty.* New York: Basic Books.

Goffman, Irving. 1959. *The Presentation of Self in Everyday Life.* Garden City, NY: Doubleday Anchor.

Goldstein, Judith. 1993. *Ideas, Interests, and American Trade Policy.* Ithaca: Cornell University Press.

Goldstein, Judith, and Robert O. Keohane, editors. 1993a. *Ideas and Foreign Policy: Beliefs, Institutions, and Political Change.* Ithaca: Cornell University Press.

———. 1993b. "Ideas and Foreign Policy: An Analytical Framework." Pp. 3–30 in *Ideas and Foreign Policy: Beliefs, Institutions, and Political Change.* Ithaca: Cornell University Press.

Goldstone, Jack A. 1991. "Ideology, Cultural Frameworks, and the Process of Revolution." *Theory and Society* 20:405–53.

Graham, Otis L., Jr. 1992. *Losing Time: The Industrial Policy Debate.* Cambridge: Harvard University Press.

Guillen, Mauro. 1994. *Models of Management.* Chicago: University of Chicago Press.

Haas, Peter M. 1992. "Introduction: Epistemic Communities and International Policy Coordination." *International Organization* 46:1–35.

Hall, Peter A. 1986. *Governing the Economy.* New York: Oxford University Press.

———, editor. 1989a. *The Political Power of Economic Ideas.* Princeton: Princeton University Press.

———. 1989b. "Conclusion: The Politics of Keynesian Ideas." Pp. 361–91 in *The Political Power of Economic Ideas,* edited by Peter A. Hall. Princeton: Princeton University Press.

———. 1993. "Policy Paradigms, Social Learning, and the State: The Case of Economic Policymaking in Britain." *Comparative Politics* 25(3)275–96.

Hall, Peter A., and Rosemary C. R. Taylor. 1996. "Political Science and the Three New Institutionalisms." *Political Studies* 44(4)936–57.

Heilbroner, Robert, and William Milberg. 1995. *The Crisis of Vision in Modern Economic Thought.* New York: Cambridge University Press.

Hirsch, Paul. M. 1997. "Sociology without Social Structure: Neoinstitutional Theory Meets Brave New World." *American Journal of Sociology* 102(6)1702–23.

Hirsch, Paul M., and Michael Lounsbury. 1997a. "Putting the Organization Back into Organization Theory: Action, Change, and the 'New' Institutionalism." *Journal of Management Inquiry* 6:79–88.

———. 1997b. "Ending the Family Quarrel: Toward a Reconciliation of the 'Old' and 'New' Institutionalism." *American Behavioral Scientist* 40:406–18.

Hirschman, Albert O. 1977. *The Passions and the Interests.* Princeton: Princeton University Press.

Ikenberry, G. John. 1988. "Conclusion: An Institutional Approach to Foreign Economic Policy." Pp. 219–43 in *The State and American Foreign Economic Policy,* edited by G. John Ikenberry, David A. Lake, and Michael Mastanduno. Ithaca: Cornell University Press.

Jacobsen, John Kurt. 1995. "Much Ado about Ideas: The Cognitive Factor in Economic Policy." *World Politics* 47:283–310.

Jamieson, Kathleen Hall. 1996. *Packaging the Presidency.* New York: Oxford University Press.

Jepperson, Ronald. 1991. "Institutions, Institutional Effects, and Institutionalism." Pp. 143–63 in *The New Institutionalism in Organizational Analysis,* edited by Walter Powell and Paul DiMaggio. Chicago: University of Chicago Press.

Katzenstein, Peter J., editor. 1978. *Between Power and Plenty.* Madison: University of Wisconsin Press.

———. 1993. "Coping with Terrorism: Norms and Internal Security in Germany and Japan." Pp. 265–95 in *Ideas and Foreign Policy: Beliefs, Institutions, and Political Change,* edited by Judith Goldstein and Robert O. Keohane. Ithaca: Cornell University Press.

Keynes, John Maynard. 1936. *The General Theory of Employment, Interest, and Money.* London: Macmillan.

Kingdon, John W. 1984. *Agendas, Alternatives, and Public Policies.* New York: Harper-Collins.

Krugman, Paul. 1994. *Peddling Prosperity.* New York: Norton.

Kuran, Timor. 1995. *Private Truths, Public Lies.* Cambridge: Harvard University Press.

Lau, Richard R., Richard A. Smith, and Susan T. Fiske. 1991. "Political Beliefs, Policy Interpretations, and Political Persuasion." *Journal of Politics* 53(3)644–75.

Lazonick, William. 1991. *Business Organization and the Myth of the Market Economy.* New York: Cambridge University Press.

Leff, Mark. 1984. *The Limits of Symbolic Reform: The New Deal and Taxation, 1933–1939.* New York: Cambridge University Press.

Lipset, Seymour Martin. 1996. *American Exceptionalism: A Double-Edged Sword.* New York: Norton.

Makin, John H., and Norman J. Ornstein. 1994. *Debt and Taxes.* New York: Random House.

Martin, Cathy J. 1991. *Shifting the Burden: The Struggle over Growth and Corporate Taxation.* Chicago: University of Chicago Press.

McCloskey, Donald. 1985. *The Rhetoric of Economics.* Madison: University of Wisconsin.

Meyer, John W. 1994. "Rationalized Environments." Pp. 28–54 in *Institutional Environments and Organizations,* edited by W. Richard Scott and John W. Meyer. Newbury Park, CA: Sage.

Meyer, John W., John Boli, and George M. Thomas. 1987. "Ontology and Rationalization in the Western Cultural Account." Pp. 12–37 in *Institutional Structure: Constituting State, Society, and the Individual,* edited by George Thomas, John Meyer, Francisco Ramirez, and John Boli. Beverly Hills, CA: Sage.

Meyer, John W., John Boli, George M. Thomas, and Francisco O. Ramirez. 1997. "World Society and the Nation-State." *American Journal of Sociology* 103(1)144–81.

Moore, Mark H. 1988. "What Sort of Ideas Become Public Ideas?" Pp. 55–83 in *The Power of Public Ideas,* edited by Robert Reich. Cambridge: Harvard University Press.

Nordlinger, Eric A. 1981. *On the Autonomy of the Democratic State.* Cambridge: Harvard University Press.

Page, Benjamin I., and Robert Y. Shapiro. 1992. *The Rational Public: Fifty Years of Trends in Americans' Policy Preferences.* Chicago: University of Chicago Press.

Peters, B. Guy. 1999. *Institutional Theory in Political Science.* London: Pinter.

Pierson, Paul. 1994. *Dismantling the Welfare State? Reagan, Thatcher, and the Politics of Retrenchment.* New York: Cambridge University Press.

Piore, Michael J. 1995. *Beyond Individualism.* Cambridge: Harvard University Press.

Powell, Walter W. 1990. "The Transformation of Organizational Forms: How Useful Is Organization Theory in Accounting for Social Change?" Pp. 301–29 in *Beyond the Marketplace,* edited by Roger Friedland and A. F. Robertson. New York: Aldine de Gruyter.

———. 1991. "Expanding the Scope of Institutional Analysis." Pp. 183–203 in *The New Institutionalism in Organizational Analysis,* edited by Walter Powell and Paul DiMaggio. Chicago: University of Chicago Press.

Powell, Walter W., and Paul J. DiMaggio, editors. 1991. *The New Institutionalism in Organizational Analysis.* Chicago: University of Chicago Press.

Quirk, Paul. 1990. "Deregulation and the Politics of Ideas in Congress." Pp. 183–99 in *Beyond Self-Interest,* edited by Jane J. Mansbridge. Chicago: University of Chicago Press.

Rein, Martin, and Christopher Winship. 1997. "Policy Entrepreneurs and the Academic Establishment: Truth and Values in Social Controversies." Pp. 17–48 in *Intelligence, Political Inequality, and Public Policy,* edited by Elliot White. New York: Praeger.

"The Reindustrialization of America." 1980. *Business Week,* June 30 (special issue).

Ricci, David M. 1993. *The Transformation of American Politics: The New Washington and the Rise of Think Tanks.* New Haven: Yale University Press.

Roberts, Paul Craig. 1984. *The Supply-Side Revolution: An Insider's Account of Policymaking in Washington.* Cambridge: Harvard University Press.

Rueschemeyer, Dietrich, and Theda Skocpol, editors. 1996a. *States, Social Knowledge, and the Origins of Modern Social Policies.* Princeton: Princeton University Press.

———. 1996b. Conclusion. Pp. 296–312 in *States, Social Knowledge, and the Origins of Modern Social Policies.* Princeton: Princeton University Press.

Savage, James D. 1988. *Balanced Budgets and American Politics.* Ithaca: Cornell University Press.

Schön, Donald A., and Martin Rein. 1994. *Frame Reflection: Toward the Resolution of Intractable Policy Controversies.* New York: Basic Books.

Scott, James C. 1990. *Domination and the Arts of Resistance: Hidden Transcripts.* New Haven: Yale University Press.

Scott, W. Richard. 1994a. "Institutions and Organizations: Toward a Theoretical Synthesis." Pp. 55–80 in *Institutional Environments and Organizations,* edited by W. Richard Scott and John W. Meyer. Thousand Oaks, CA: Sage.

———. 1994b. "Institutional Analysis: Variance and Process Theory Approaches." Pp. 81–99 in *Institutional Environments and Organizations,* edited by W. Richard Scott and John W. Meyer. Thousand Oaks, CA: Sage.

———. 1995. *Institutions and Organizations.* Thousand Oaks, CA: Sage.

Scott, W. Richard, and John W. Meyer, editors. 1994. *Institutional Environments and Organizations.* Thousand Oaks, CA: Sage.

Sewell, William H., Jr. 1992. "A Theory of Structure: Duality, Agency, and Transformation." *American Journal of Sociology* 91:1–29.

Shoch, Jim. 1994. "The Politics of the U.S. Industrial Policy Debate, 1981–1984." Pp. 173–90 in *Social Structures of Accumulation,* edited by David Kotz, Terrence McDonough, and Michael Reich. New York: Cambridge University Press.

Skocpol, Theda. 1985. "Bringing the State Back In." Pp. 3–37 in *Bringing the State Back In,* edited by Peter Evans, Dietrich Rueschemeyer, and Theda Skocpol. New York: Cambridge University Press.

———. 1992. *Protecting Soldiers and Mothers: The Political Origins of Social Policy in the United States.* Cambridge: Harvard University Press.

———. 1994. "Cultural Idioms and Political Ideologies in the Revolutionary Reconstruction of State Power: A Rejoinder to Sewell." Pp. 199–212 in *Social Revolutions in the Modern World,* edited by Theda Skocpol. New York: Cambridge University Press.

———. 1996. *Boomerang.* New York: W. W. Norton.

Skowronek, Stephen. 1982. *Building a New American State: The Expansion of National Administrative Capacities, 1877–1920.* New York: Cambridge University Press.

Smith, James A. 1989. "Think Tanks and the Politics of Ideas." Pp. 175–94 in *The Spread of Economic Ideas,* edited by David Colander and A. W. Coats. New York: Cambridge University Press.

Snow, David, and Robert Benford. 1992. "Master Frames and Cycles of Protest." Pp. 133–55 in *Frontiers in Social Movement Theory,* edited by Aldon Morris and Carol Mueller. New Haven: Yale University Press.

Snow, David, E. Burke Rochford, Steven Worden, and Robert Benford. 1986. "Frame Alignment Processes, Micromobilization, and Movement Participation." *American Sociological Review* 51:464–81.

Solow, Robert M. 1989. "How Economic Ideas Turn to Mush." Pp. 75–85 in *The Spread of Economic Ideas*, edited by David Colander and A. W. Coats. New York: Cambridge University Press.

Somers, Margaret R. 1995. "What's Political or Cultural about Political Culture and the Public Sphere? Toward an Historical Sociology of Concept Formation." *Sociological Theory* 13(2)113–44.

Soysal, Yasemin. 1994. *Limits of Citizenship*. Chicago: University of Chicago Press.

Stanley, Robert. 1993. *Dimensions of Law in the Service of Order: Origins of the Federal Income Tax, 1861–1913*. New York: Oxford University Press.

Steinmo, Sven. 1993. *Taxation and Democracy*. New Haven: Yale University Press.

Steinmo, Sven, Kathleen Thelen, and Frank Longstreth. 1992. *Structuring Politics: Historical Institutionalism in Comparative Perspective*. New York: Cambridge University Press.

Stevenson, Rodney. 1987. "Institutional Economics and the Theory of Production." *Journal of Economic Issues* 21(4)1471–93.

Stinchcombe, Arthur. 1968. *Constructing Social Theories*. New York: Harcourt, Brace and World.

Swidler, Ann. 1986. "Culture in Action: Symbols and Strategies." *American Sociological Review* 51:273–86.

Tarrow, Sidney. 1994. *Power in Movement*. New York: Cambridge University Press.

Thelen, Kathleen, and Sven Steinmo. 1992. "Historical Institutionalism in Comparative Politics." Pp. 1–32 in *Structuring Politics: Historical Institutionalism in Comparative Analysis*, edited by Sven Steinmo, Kathleen Thelen, and Frank Longstreth. New York: Cambridge University Press.

Thomas, George M., John W. Meyer, Francisco O. Ramirez, and John Boli, editors. 1987. *Institutional Structure: Constituting State, Society, and the Individual*. Newbury Park, CA: Sage.

Thurow, Lester. 1980. *The Zero-Sum Society*. New York: Basic Books.

Tilly, Charles. 1979. "Repertoires of Contention in America and Britain, 1750–1830." Pp. 126–55 in *The Dynamics of Social Movements*, edited by John D. McCarthy and Mayer Zald. Cambridge, MA: Winthrop Publishers.

Tolbert, Pamela S., and Lynne G. Zucker. 1983. "Institutional Sources of Change in the Formal Structure of Organizations: The Diffusion of Civil Service Reform, 1880–1935." *Administrative Science Quarterly* 28:22–39.

Weatherford, M. Stephen, and Lorraine M. McDonnell. 1990. "Ideology and Economic Policy." Pp. 122–55 in *Looking Back on the Reagan Presidency*, edited by Larry Berman. Baltimore: Johns Hopkins University Press.

Weber, Max. 1946. "The Social Psychology of the World Religions." Pp. 267–301 in *From Max Weber: Essays in Sociology*, edited by Hans Gerth and C. Wright Mills. New York: Oxford University Press.

———. 1958. *The Protestant Ethic and the Spirit of Capitalism*. New York: Scribner's.

Weir, Margaret. 1992. *Politics and Jobs: The Boundaries of Employment Policy in the United States*. Princeton: Princeton University Press.

Weir, Margaret, and Theda Skocpol. 1985. "State Structures and the Possibilities for

'Keynesian' Responses to the Great Depression in Sweden, Britain, and the United States." Pp. 107–68 in *Bringing the State Back In*, edited by Peter Evans, Dietrich Rueschemeyer, and Theda Skocpol. New York: Cambridge University Press.

Wuthnow, Robert. 1989. *Communities of Discourse: Ideology and Social Structure in the Reformation, the Enlightenment, and European Socialism.* Cambridge: Harvard University Press.

Yee, Albert S. 1996. "The Causal Effects of Ideas on Policies." *International Organization* 50(1)69–108.

Part IV

DISCURSIVE INSTITUTIONALISM

Chapter 8

The "Crisis" of Keynesianism and the Rise of Neoliberalism in Britain

AN IDEATIONAL INSTITUTIONALIST APPROACH

COLIN HAY

IN THIS chapter I advance a distinctive *ideational* approach to institutional analysis — an attempted synthesis of historical and more discursive strands of neo-institutionalism. Such a perspective is sensitive to the role of ideas in the mediation of complex institutional change, yet resists the temptation to conflate the ideational and the institutional. I argue that the policy-making process is frequently informed by policy paradigms that tend to become institutionalized over time. Consequently, while policy development is generally directional, taking the form of iterative yet cumulative change within the context of an ascendant paradigm, alterations in the trajectory of institutional evolution do occur and are invariably associated with paradigm shifts arising in moments of (perceived) crisis. Such a conception allows for a recognition of the contingent processes and uneven temporalities of institutional and ideational change.

The chapter seeks further to elaborate this ideational conception of institutional change by examining the processes of crisis "narration" and paradigm-shift, which the existing literature has left largely unexplicated. In a context in which policy failures are widely identified, experienced, and associated with the dominant paradigm, a diversity of competing narratives proffering alternative new paradigms (and premised upon often incommensurate conceptions of the possible and the desirable) may emerge. In such a context, it is improbable that any successor paradigm will resolve the contradictions of the old rather than attempt to redefine the very problems that need addressing. This is illustrated and explored more systematically by way of a detailed case study — the replacement of Keynesianism by neoliberalism ("monetarism") in Britain. As I hope to demonstrate, an ideational institutionalism sensitive to the inherently (though not exhaustively) ideational aspect of the moment of crisis demonstrates the rather different and uneven temporalities of ideational and institutional change. This has important implications for our understanding of Thatcherism and the rise (and consolidation) of neoliberalism more generally. In particular, it allows us to reconcile a conception of the first Thatcher governments as ideologically radical (ushering in a new economic and political paradigm in the context of perceived state "crisis") with a more conventional institutionalist analysis (emphasizing the evolutionary and only cumulatively radical nature of neoliberalism in Britain). Crises within such a schema emerge not as revolutionary moments of instantaneous transformation, but as punctuating moments in the ongoing process of social learning and institutional evolution.

Political Time and the Temporality of Crisis

Time is to politics what space is to geometry (Debray 1973, p. 90)

It is perhaps all too enticing to begin a chapter on political time, the transformation of the state, and the temporality of crisis with this quote, written from the spatial and temporal confines of a prison cell. A certain caution is required in our interpretation of this seeming truism. If time is indeed to the process and practice of politics what space is to geometry, then it is certainly not the case that time is (or has been) to political *analysis* what space is (and has been) to geometrical analysis.

The basis then for what is to follow is the observation that political scientists in general, and Anglophone political scientists in particular, have tended to fail to develop a conceptual armory adequate to the task of dealing with political change. Clearly some perspectives are more sensitive than others to temporal considerations and the uneven texture of political time. Indeed, if there is one development within the field of contemporary political science and political economy that might lead one to challenge this observation, it is surely the emergence of a distinctive *historical* institutionalism in recent years (see, in particular, Steinmo, Thelen, and Longstreth 1992). Yet if historical institutionalism certainly has the potential to offer crucial insights into the complex and uneven processes of political change — reflected in its central prescription that political analysis should be concerned above all with "process tracing" (Katzenstein 1978; Thelen and Steinmo 1992) — that potential is still as yet largely unrealized. To date, it has been concerned perhaps too exclusively with the elucidation of the processes of institutional *formation* on the one hand and the mechanisms of institutional *constraint* and *inertia* on the other. The casualty has been a concern with the evolution and transformation of *extant* institutions (Hay and Wincott 1998a, 1998b). Given its characteristic emphasis upon the "path dependence" of institutional change, this is perhaps understandable. As Bo Rothstein (1992, p. 35) notes,

If institutions set limits on what some agents can do, and enable other agents to do things they otherwise would not have been able to do, then we need to know under what circumstances these institutions were *created*. For if political agents can design or construct institutions, they may then construe an advantage in future political battles. . . . The analysis of the *creation* and *destruction* of political institutions might thus serve as a bridge between the "men [*sic*] who make history" and the circumstances under which they are able to do so.

Enticing though this logic may seem, however, it is not unproblematic. Clearly any framework that emphasizes path dependence must give due attention to the complex interplay of strategy involved in the process of institutional design and innovation — for the initial form and social architecture of an institution, though *under*determining of its future form, does militate against certain paths of institutional evolution while facilitating others. In short, it delineates and circumscribes a space within which such path-dependent evolution may occur. Rothstein, and historical institutionalists more generally, is then surely right to underline the importance of institutional formation.

Yet to seek to derive institutional constraints, opportunities, and capacities from an analysis of institutional formation (as Rothstein seems to propose here) is to imply that the subsequent evolution and transformation of those institutions over time is insignificant. It is to subscribe to an institutional determinism that trivializes unintended consequences and path dependence at any point judged to lie outside an initial phase of institutional creation. A historically consistent view that allows for the path dependence and unintended consequences so often alluded to by historical institutionalists cannot preclude the possibility of critical junctures and "branching points" occurring *after* the initial flux of institutional creation has subsided (Thelen and Steinmo 1992; Pierson 1993, 1997). It must then give equal weight and consideration to the processes and mechanisms of nonformative institutional change. To point to institutionalism's characteristic *creational bias* is, then, to point to an *inconsistency* in the application of its theoretical premises, rather than to reveal fundamental theoretical contradictions within the approach itself.

Nonetheless, an overemphasis upon factors relating to institutional formation in the explication of institutional outcomes accounts for some of historical institutionalism's widely observed weaknesses: its difficulty in accounting for the formation of interests and the motivation of actors; its much greater facility in accounting for institutional rigidity, inertia, and stasis than for change; and its associated tendency to depict institutions as structural constraints on action rather than as the very condition of action (see, in particular, Campbell 1998; P. Hall and Taylor 1996; Hay and Wincott 1998a).

Yet if these are the characteristic limitations of historical institutionalism, then it is important to emphasize that they have not gone unnoticed by historical institutionalists themselves (see, for instance, Ikenberry 1988, p. 242; Thelen and Steinmo 1992, p. 14; Campbell 1998, pp. 379–81; P. Hall and Taylor 1996). Indeed, in recent years a distinctive literature has emerged, to some extent on the margins of institutionalism, that has concentrated on institutional change after the initial phase of institutional formation. The contributions of three authors are particularly noteworthy in this context: (1) Theda Skopcol's focus in her most recent works on the processes of policy feedback over time (1992); (2) Paul Pierson's related concern with institutional dynamics, feedback processes, and the uneven temporality of institutional change (1993, 1996, pp. 140–41, 1997); and (3) Peter Hall's focus on institutional change as a process of "social learning" within the context of an evolving paradigm punctuated by periodic paradigm-shifts (1993). It is the concern with institutional development over time animating these various contributions that is the subject of this chapter. I argue that despite the significant insights made by those who have focused explicitly upon the question of institutional change, insufficient attention has as yet been given by institutionalists to: (1) the processes and mechanism precipitating institutional change; (2) the conditions within which shifts in policy paradigm are likely to occur; and (3) the relationship between the evolution and transformation of policy paradigms on the one hand and institutional change (here the development of the state) on the other. My aim is to demonstrate the contribution that a conception of crisis as a moment of decisive intervention and paradigm shift may make to an institutionalism sensitive to the uneven temporality of political change.

In its methodological emphasis on process-tracing, its ontological rejection of both the structural-functional and intentionalist tendencies, and its concern with the role of ideas in the mediation of strategic conduct and hence political/institutional outcomes, such an approach has obvious affinities with certain currents in historical institutionalism. Indeed, in its concern with the dynamic relationship not only between context and conduct (or structure and agency) but the ideational and the material, the discursive and the political, its emphasis is perhaps closest to the recent work of Peter Hall on policy paradigms, social learning, and institutional change (1993). In the sections that follow my aim is to build on, develop, and further elaborate this instructive and provocative approach to institutional change.

Paradigms, Templates, Social Learning: Bringing Ideas (Back) In

The work of Hugh Heclo first and subsequently Peter Hall on policy paradigms and political change represents by far the most sustained, consistent, and systematic attempt within the institutionalist oeuvre to accord a key role for ideas in the determination of institutional outcomes. It is based on an analogy drawn from Thomas Kuhn's celebrated analysis, *The Structure of Scientific Revolutions* (1962). In this seminal work Kuhn argues that the development of science can be understood as a succession of more or less enduring paradigms punctuated by periodic "revolutions" in which the ascendant paradigm is challenged and ultimately replaced. During phases of "normal science," a single paradigm is ascendant and remains largely unchallenged. It provides an interpretative framework delineating a legitimate range of problems (and indeed nonproblems), techniques, and criteria of scientific adequacy. In phases of "exceptional" science, by contrast, an accumulation of anomalies within the old paradigm (principally experimental outcomes that do not conform with the predictions of current theories) lead some scientists to break from the paradigm and the constraints it imposes. They search for alternative theoretical approaches that might account for (and hence resolve) the anomalies of the old paradigm, thereby opening a space for a new phase of normal science under the dominance of a new paradigm (internalized by the scientific community).

Historical institutionalists (notably Hall) have extended Kuhn's analogy to the policy-making arena, arguing that policy is made within the context of a "policy paradigm." This interpretative schema is internalized by politicians, state managers, policy experts, and the like. As such, it comes to define a range of legitimate policy techniques, mechanisms, and instruments (and in some instances even specifies a range of appropriate instrumental settings), thereby delimiting the very targets and goals of policy itself. In short, it comes to circumscribe the realm of the politically feasible, practical and desirable. As Hall elaborates (1993, p. 279),

> [P]olicy makers customarily work within a framework of ideas and standards that specifies not only the goals of policy and the kind of instruments that can be used to attain them, but also the very nature of the problems they are meant to be addressing. . . . [T]his framework is embedded in the very terminology through which policymakers communicate about their work, and it is influential precisely because so much of it is taken for granted and unamenable to scrutiny as a whole.

The identification of such distinctive policy paradigms[1] allows us to differentiate between: (1) periods of "normal" policy making (and change) in which the paradigm remains largely unchallenged (at least within the confines of the policy-making arena) and in which change is largely incremental and evolutionary and (2) periods of "exceptional" policy making (and change) in which the very parameters that previously circumscribed policy options are cast asunder and replaced, and in which the realm of the politically possible, feasible, and desirable is correspondingly reconfigured.

Quite clearly, ideational factors are profoundly implicated in the process of social and political change. Yet we should not restrict our focus on policy change to those exceptional and intense moments in which paradigms are transcended, superseded, and replaced. As Hall notes, drawing again on the pioneering work of Heclo, "policy responds less directly to social and economic conditions than it does to the consequences of past policy" (1993, p. 277; Heclo 1974; see also Argylis and Schön 1978; Haas 1992); policy makers, as reflexive and strategic (if not utility maximizing) actors, are engaged in a constant process of evaluation and assessment of the consequences of prior policy choices — a process of *social learning*. This is partly intuitive, partly explicit. "Learning is conventionally said to occur when individuals assimilate new information, including that based on past experience, and apply it to their subsequent actions. . . . [W]e can define social learning as a deliberate attempt to adjust the goals or techniques of policy in response to past experience and new information. Learning is indicated when policy changes as the result of such a process" (Hall 1993, p. 278).

Not satisfied with this rather homogeneous and undifferentiated conception of learning, however, Hall introduces a further level of sophistication, distinguishing various "orders" of social learning. Policy making, he argues, can be understood as "a process that usually involves three central variables: the overarching goals that guide policy in a particular field, the techniques or policy instruments used to attain these goals, and the precise settings of these instruments" (1993, p. 278). This allows us to distinguish between three orders of social learning and three corresponding levels of policy change: *first-order change*, in which the specific settings of policy instruments are modified while the instruments themselves (and indeed the broad goals of policy) remain unaltered; *second-order change*, in which both the settings and instruments are altered (yet still within the context of stable goals); and *third-order change*, in which the very goals of policy itself are revised (with knock-on consequences for instruments and settings). Third-order change within this schema corresponds to a paradigm shift and hence to an exceptional mode of policy making, while first- and second-order change fall within the confines of normal policy making.

Interrogating Institutional Change: Toward a Conception of "Punctuated Evolution"

This serves to establish a point of departure for what is to follow. The perspective developed below should be viewed as an attempt both to elaborate and, at the same time, to revise this highly suggestive conception of the relationship between policy paradigms and institutional change. Whereas historical institutionalists have to date tended to concentrate on developing an abstracted, deductive, and theoretically informed periodization of the policy process that might be applied in a variety of contexts, my principal concern is to examine the processes of change that underlie this model. Instead of developing a relatively generic and abstracted conception of the policy learning process over time, into which specific events can be slotted, my aim is to ask under what conditions paradigms are consolidated, challenged, and replaced. In so doing, I emphasize the importance of the moment of crisis itself.

In bringing back a focus on the very *processes* of institutional and ideational change in this way, it is useful to consider the dynamic relationship between institutional context and institutionalized conduct. Consider a group of policy makers, conceptualized here as both strategic and reflexive. They must formulate policy in a context that is "strategically selective" (Jessop 1990, pp. 9–10), favoring certain strategies over others as means to realize intentions. That the context restricts the range of hypothetical options available to our policy makers over a particular time horizon is not lost on them. Yet the knowledge on which they must base their strategic calculations is likely to be impressionistic and incomplete at best (and in some instances demonstrably false). The context they inhabit is selective of the strategies they might deploy in a variety of ways, reflecting the institutional capacities of the state apparatus, the resources at the disposal of policy makers, the power and influence of interest and pressure groups, the nature of public opinion, and the strength of the domestic economy, to list but a few significant factors. In formulating policy within such a complex context, policy makers can rely only upon a partial and, in all likelihood, outdated knowledge of the strategic terrain. Accordingly, they become reliant upon poorly informed projections of the likely consequences of various policy options and of the responses of other actors to such initiatives. Moreover, their assessment of the range of strategic options available to them is likely to be constrained significantly by perceptions of what is feasible, possible, and desirable. These are, in turn, likely to be shaped and circumscribed by the currently dominant *policy paradigm*. The ability of state managers to formulate policies likely to prove successful in their own terms (or in terms of the paradigm) is further influenced: (1) by the cognitive frames within which policy makers operate (which are likely to privilege certain time-horizons over others in the formulation of policy); (2) by their perceptions of institutional resources and policy-making capacity; and (3) by the lessons they draw from other contexts by way of *policy transfer* and their assessment of previous policy successes and failures (on which see Dolowitz and Marsh 1996).

Yet this is perhaps to present an overly static conception of policy making, for strategic actors are reflexive, routinely monitoring the consequences of previous actions (both their own and those of others). If anything, this generic reflexivity is more acute in the case of policy makers. The process of policy evolution then tends to be characterized by successive stages or iterations of strategic learning within the broad parameters of an evolving paradigm. Policy strategists assess the consequences (both intended and unintended) of prior policy initiatives in an attempt to understand better the process of policy implementation and to gauge more accurately societal responses in the hope that by so doing they might learn how to fashion future policies more likely to realize policy goals. Of course, such exercises in strategic learning, however painstakingly conducted, cannot guarantee future policy successes: the context within which policy is formulated is not a static one. Indeed, it is under a constant process of evolution and transformation. Needless to say, not all aspects of that process of change are amenable to control by policy makers. Thus, despite the assumptions that seem to pervade much of the literature on policy evolution, strategic learning is rarely cumulative. Moreover, exercises in strategic learning conducted within the context defined by a pervasive policy paradigm will tend to associate policy failures, where they (are perceived to) occur, with relatively parochial factors such as inappropriate choices or settings of policy instruments, rather than with the obsolescence of the very policy paradigm itself. Consequently, paradigm shifts tend not to occur as a result of social or strategic learning on the part of experts, policy makers, bureaucrats, or civil servants. Instead, they are generally associated (at least within advanced liberal capitalist democracies) with highly politicized and public debates about the desirability and feasibility of contending political goals. Such open political contestation, I suggest, tends in turn to be associated with moments of widely perceived institutional and state crisis (for further elaboration see Hay 1999a, 1999b). The conception of policy change and institutional transformation that thus emerges is one not of "punctuated equilibrium,"[2] but of "punctuated evolution" — of policy evolving through the iterative unfolding and adaptation of a paradigm to changing circumstances, punctuated periodically by crisis and paradigm shift.[3]

Such a formulation is outlined schematically in figure 8-1. Within this schema, policy making is located in the context of an evolving policy paradigm. This, in some sense, defines what is considered legitimate, feasible and desirable within the policy arena, thereby circumscribing and delimiting the realm of the politically possible. Policy making within such a context, as we have already noted, yields consequences, both intended and unintended. Policy outcomes are both monitored by policy makers within the state apparatus and experienced (whether directly, through their consequences, or in mediated form) by the public, on whose life chances they impinge. Within complex political systems, such as those that characterize contemporary liberal democracies, policy outcomes are likely to include significant policy failures. These too are monitored internally and experienced externally. In the absence of wide-scale public debate about such policy failures and fiascoes that manages to link policy contradictions to a more generic sense of crisis (and, as in the case of the "winter of discontent" considered below, stimulated generally by intense media scrutiny), the narration and definition of the problem is likely to remain internal to the state apparatus itself.[4] Under such circumstances the likely consequence is iterative (as opposed to fundamental) policy modifications within the parameters defined by the existing policy paradigm — strategic or social learning. This then is an *evolutionary* conception of policy (and institutional) change. It is represented in figure 8-1 by the cycle 1-2-3a-4a-5a-1.

Yet as the diagram suggests, this is not the only, nor indeed the most significant, way in which policy development occurs.[5] In a highly politicized policy making climate, an accumulation of perceived policy failures, contradictions,

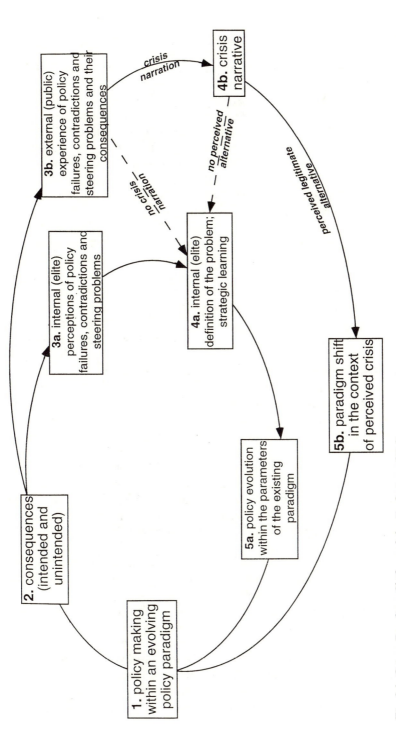

Fig. 8-1. Crises, Paradigm Shifts, and the Evolution of Policy

and steering problems may well give rise to a profusion of "crisis" narratives from political entrepreneurs and the media alike. This may take the identification and definition of the problem out of the hands of civil servants and the state elite and into the public arena (2-3b-4b in fig. 8-1). Nonetheless, in the absence of a widely disseminated and widely accepted crisis narrative and a widely perceived alternative in the form of a new policy-making paradigm, it is still likely that policy revisions will be made within the confines of the existing paradigm, as guided by strategic learning on the part of policy makers (3b-4b-4a-5a in fig. 8-1). Thus, only in exceptional circumstances (such as those of the war years 1940–44 and the late 1970s in Britain) can a genuine crisis be said to exist, announcing the obsolescence of the dominant paradigm (laissez-faire and Keynesian, respectively) and heralding its replacement (by Keynesian and neoliberal paradigms, in turn).

Once such paradigm shifts are taken into account, then, the model of policy development presented here can be seen as one of *punctuated evolution*. Two policy development cycles can be identified: (1) an *incremental (yet developmental) cycle* within which policy changes iteratively within the parameters of the existing paradigm in response to strategic learning on the part of policy makers (presented schematically in figure 8-1 in the form of the inner circle, 1-2-3a-4a-5a-1); and (2) a *punctuating cycle* of paradigmatic transcendence, by which the very parameters of the policy-making process are periodically redefined (presented in fig. 8-1 in the form of the outer circle, 1-2-3b-4b-5b-1). Clearly there may be many iterations of the incremental/evolutionary cycle before a punctuating crisis narrative emerges.

As should by now be clear, such a perspective ascribes a crucial role to ideas in any understanding of complex institutional change. As suggested above, governments mobilizing state power may usefully be conceived of as strategic actors. Yet as we have also already noted, the formulation of strategy itself implies particular perceptions of the strategic context — more specifically, particular perceptions of what is considered politically and economically feasible, possible, and desirable. This would suggest that the ability to impose a new evolutionary trajectory upon the institutions of the state may reside precisely in the ability to shape and reshape the ideational parameters that circumscribe what governments consider politically possible, feasible, and desirable. Such an analysis then places great emphasis on political-economic *paradigms* (such as Keynesian social democracy or neoliberalism) — the cognitive and ideational filters through which notions of the political "good" and the politically possible are constructed. Moreover, it suggests that *paradigm shifts*, which I will argue tend to occur in moments of *perceived crisis*, are truly strategic moments in the transformation of the state, for once institutionalized within the state apparatus, paradigms continue to inform strategic calculations and decisions at all levels of government. In so doing they may come to circumscribe not only the parameters of the politically possible, but in some sense the very parameters of the evolution and transformation of the state. Paradigms once established and internalized by the personnel of the state (and often more broadly by societal actors) thus provide the immediate discursive and cognitive context within which strategic learning and hence the cumulative unfolding of the state as an institution occurs.

In placing such a great emphasis upon political-economic *paradigms* in the shaping of strategic conduct and, in particular, upon paradigm-*shifts* as strategic moments in the evolutionary, yet cumulatively radical, transformation of the state, this perspective suggests a highly differentiated and uneven conception of political time. Time within this framework is textured and contoured, alternating (though in no preordained or predetermined manner) between decisive, intense, and contested moments of crisis and paradigm shift on the one hand, and longer, slower, more drawn-out periods of iterative change and path-dependent institutional evolution on the other.

Conceptualizing Crisis: A Material or Ideational Condition?

At this point it is perhaps worth emphasizing the implications of this theoretical schema for our conceptualization and analysis of crisis. Is the identification of a situation as one of crisis an objective, analytical, or even empirical claim or does it necessarily imply a subjective and hence a normative judgment? Should we define crisis in terms of objective factors such as the "weight" of contradictions within a given system or in more subjective terms such as the perception of the need for rapid and decisive intervention in the context of widely experienced political and economic contradiction?

"Crisis," from the Greek *Krino* (to decide) means, literally, "a moment of decisive intervention." Yet in most contemporary accounts it has come to refer simply to an accumulation of contradictions. While intuitively appealing, the suggestion that a particular weight of contradictions necessarily precipitates a decisive or structural response gives us little insight into the process of change itself (indeed, it assumes a simplistic theory of change for which there is scant evidence). To make a decisive intervention requires a *perception of the need to make a decisive intervention*. Thus, although the weight of accumulated contradictions may render more likely a decisive intervention, it is at best a necessary but *insufficient* condition for such an intervention.[6] For "objective" contradictions to motivate a structural response requires an awareness and an understanding of current political and economic circumstances as indicative of contradictions and as indicative of contradictions that not only *must* be dealt with but that *can* be dealt with. The narration of crisis here plays a crucial role.

This has important implications for the analysis that follows. If we wish to understand the making of decisive interventions and hence the transformation of social and political systems that such decisive interventions may initiate, then we must consider the mechanisms and processes by which perceptions of crisis and indeed of the responses that such crises necessitate are mobilized and shaped. If we wish to analyze the mechanisms of institutional development, we have little choice but to acknowledge the perceptual or discursive quality of the moment of crisis and hence to consider the processes through which competing narratives of crisis struggle for ascendancy in a battle to shape the course of subsequent institutional development.

This suggests the importance of maintaining a clear and unambiguous distinction between contradiction and failure (an accumulation of contradictions) on the one hand and crisis on the other — for if it is narratives of crisis that are responded to and not the contradictions themselves, we cannot in any sense (theoretical or otherwise) derive the response to crisis from a static analysis of the contradictions of the existing system. A given constellation of contradictions can sustain a multitude of differing and incommensurate conceptions of crisis, apportioning responsibility and culpability very differently and calling forth wildly divergent decisive interventions. Moreover, crisis narratives do not compete in terms of the sophistication or indeed accuracy of their understanding of the crisis context. Indeed, their "success" as narratives generally resides in their ability to provide a simplified account sufficiently flexible to "narrate" a great variety of morbid symptoms while unambiguously apportioning blame. To become sufficiently ascendant to alter the trajectory of institutional change in the "postcrisis" world, crisis narratives must make sense to individuals of their experiences of the crisis (whether direct or mediated); they must also be sufficiently general and simple to identify clear paths of responsibility and an unambiguous sense of the response that *must* be made if catastrophe is to be averted. This is nowhere clearer than in the case of economic policy making in Britain in the 1970s and 1980s. It is to an analysis of this case to which we now turn.

The Crisis of Keynesianism and the Rise of Neoliberalism in Britain

These points can be well illustrated if we turn in some detail to the transition from Keynesianism to neoliberalism (or, in some accounts, "monetarism") in Britain in the late 1970s. In fact, in order to reveal the complex and contested process(es) of change during this period, it is instructive to extend the timeframe to include the whole of the 1970s. Before doing so, however, it is perhaps worth considering what is at stake, by focusing on the implications of the above model for the literature on Thatcherism and, in particular, for our assessment of the extent of the break with the past that the election of Thatcher marked in May 1979.

It is the argument of this chapter that an ideational institutionalist analysis (such as that developed here) offers the potential to transcend the rather un-helpful and polarizing dualism that has tended to characterize the debate on the impact of Thatcherism in Britain. This literature is fundamentally divided over the question of the extent, scale, reversibility, and (if less explicitly) the temporality of the Thatcherite "revolution." Thus, on the one hand, a number of authors, drawing on an implicitly incremental, gradualist, and evolutionary institutionalism, stress continuity rather than discontinuity, incremental evo-lution rather than punctuating crisis and revolution, inertia rather than dy-namism (Jessop et al. 1988; Marsh and Rhodes 1992, 1995; Dolowitz et al. 1996; Kerr and Marsh 1999). In so doing, these "revisionists" emphasize the rather unexceptional character of successive Thatcher administrations in the face of what they see as exaggerated claims to the contrary by Thatcherite apol-ogists (strategic or unwitting). On the other hand, an equally influential group of authors emphasize what they see as the specificity, singularity, and excep-tional character of the Thatcher governments, arguing that the election of Margaret Thatcher in 1979 marked a path-shaping moment of largely irre-versible institutional and ideational transformation (Jenkins 1988; S. Hall 1988; Moon 1993, 1994; Savage, Atkinson, and Robbins 1994). Unsurpris-ingly, this polarity of views has generated a series of often confrontational ex-changes, and arguably rather more heat than light. Thus, as is so often the case, the differences between the protagonists in the exchange have tended to in-crease as the debate has passed through successive "rounds," as the authors in-volved have first resorted to caricature, then come to reflect the caricatures pre-sented of themselves, and in some cases have ultimately degenerated into self-parody. This is reflected, perhaps most clearly, in the titles of the multi-round "contest" between Jeremy Moon on the one hand and David Marsh and Rod Rhodes on the other in the pages of *Politics*.[7] A similar point might also be made of the exchange, though not perhaps prone to quite the excesses of this debate, between Stuart Hall and the self-styled "gang of four" in the pages of *New Left Review* (S. Hall 1983, 1985; Jessop et al. 1988; Jessop, Bon-nett, and Bromley 1990; Leys 1990; for a review see Hay 1996b, pp. 140–47). The point of this, however, is only to suggest that what is absent from such ex-changes is much of an appreciation of the other "side" of the debate. In both these cases, the protagonists quite simply talk past one another, failing to ap-preciate that rather different objects of analysis are being appealed to. Thus, al-though Moon, Marsh and Rhodes, Jessop and colleagues, and Hall all refer to "Thatcherism," arguably they mean rather different things by it. Herein lies the difficulty.

For Hall, as indeed for Moon, Thatcherism is understood, defined, and hence periodized in terms of its distinctiveness. For Hall, in particular, that distinctiveness resides in its invocation of new right ideology (a flexible and often contradictory articulation of neoliberalism and neoconservatism). For Jessop and his colleagues as for Marsh and Rhodes, Thatcherism is understood in more classically institutional terms. It is periodized, accordingly, in terms of its political and economic effects. In all cases, the relationship between ideas and institutions (between paradigms and policy) is left untheorized and unspecified.

Once this is acknowledged, and once an explicitly dialectical understanding of the relationship between ideas and institutions is introduced into the equation, the possibility of some reconciliation and rapprochement between these seemingly contending and incommensurate views emerges. Given the argument developed above, it should come as no surprise that those who concern themselves principally with the realm of ideas tend to emphasize the radicalism, exceptionalism, and relatively rapid nature of the Thatcherite "break" with the past (S. Hall 1988; Wolfe 1991; O'Shea 1984; Letwin 1992), nor that those who focus on the consequences of policy and institutional outcomes and effects more generally should emphasize continuity, incrementalism and either enduring inertia (Marsh and Rhodes 1992; Dolowitz et al. 1996) or, at best, cumulative radicalization (Kerr and Marsh 1999; Kerr 2000). As argued above, the process of institutional change following a period of crisis is likely to be much slower than the process by which the ideas animating and informing policy may change. Thus, even if a new paradigm becomes ascendant relatively swiftly within the corridors of Westminster and Whitehall, it may take an extremely long period of time before its consequences are reflected to any significant extent in the institutional architecture of the state itself. The institutions of the state did not look remarkably different six months, or even five years, after Mrs Thatcher entered Downing Street, despite her obvious commitment to a radically different conception of the political "good" from that of her predecessor. The transformation of the state, then, is neither simply evolutionary nor simply stepwise. As argued above, and clearly revealed in the British case from the 1970s to the present day, it takes the form of a "punctuated evolution" — of iterative yet cumulative change animated and informed by particular political-economic paradigms. During moments of crisis, these may be challenged and replaced to alter the trajectory, if not necessarily the pace, of institutional change.

A dualism in the interpretation of Thatcherism's radicalism thus reflects a dualism in the understanding of the relationship between ideas and institutions. The transcendence of the latter dualism proposed here thus offers the potential for a reconciliation between previously divergent and polarized strands in the literature on Thatcherism.

Yet at this point a note of caution should perhaps be sounded, for the debate on Thatcherism reflects, in however distorted a fashion, an empirical reality. Tempting though it might seem, disputes within the existing literature cannot be resolved entirely by theoretical fiat. The theoretically informed account presented above is, at best, suggestive of an interpretation of Thatcherism; it is not an interpretation in its own right. For that, an operationalization of the notion of "punctuated evolution" in and through the moment of crisis is required. It is to this task, and to the development of a theoretically informed historical narrative of the rise of neoliberalism, that we turn in the final section of this chapter (see also Kjær and Pedersen, this volume).

From "Monetarily Constrained Keynesianism" to Monetarism and Beyond

In what follows, I present first an overview of the transition from Keynesianism to neoliberal supply-side economics (via "monetarily constrained Keynesianism" and monetarism).[8] I conclude by relating such developments to the ideational institutionalist theoretical schema developed above.

Even the most cursory of reflections on the catalog of events leading to the exhaustion of the long "golden age" of economic growth that had characterized the postwar period and, seemingly inexorably, to the crisis of the British state of the late 1970s, reveals the significance and interconnectedness of political, economic, and ideational factors (Marsh 1995; Marsh et al. 1999).

The first, and perhaps most widely identified of these, is the Yom Kippur War of October 1973. This was to result in the Organization of Petroleum-Exporting Countries (OPEC) limiting the production and export of crude oil and quadrupling its prices virtually overnight (Cairncross 1992, pp. 182–87; Claever 1997, pp. 177–78). The "oil shock" became the catalyst, if not the direct cause, of the longest and deepest world economic recession since the Great Depression. Its economic consequences were devastating for the (Fordist) phase of growth that had characterized the postwar years in Western Europe and, ultimately, for the ascendancy of the Keynesian economics widely held to be responsible for that sustained growth phase (Glyn et al. 1990, pp. 98–113). The rise in the cost of crude led to price explosions across the economies of the advanced capitalist world, further escalating already rising inflation and generating higher wage pressure from trade unions anxious to protect real incomes in the face of such inflationary pressures. The result was to set in place an "accelerating cost-price-wage-spiral" (Scharpf 1987, p. 42). Moreover, the increase in oil prices significantly eroded the buying power of the advanced industrialized nations at the same time massive surpluses accrued to the OPEC countries. As Scharpf notes, "These OPEC surpluses corresponded with equivalent reductions in aggregate demand in the industrial nations. . . . [I]n the absence of effective remedial action, the consequence . . . had to be decreased production and rising unemployment" (p. 42). The Yom Kippur War, then, in the context of the transition to a system of flexible exchange rates since 1971 (which rendered unilateral reflationary responses much more difficult), served to bring about the desperate combination of high and rising inflation on the one hand, and high and rising unemployment on the other. To this inauspicious constellation of circumstances Keynesianism had neither an explanation nor a solution.

The Yom Kippur War could scarcely have come at a worse moment for the incumbent Conservative government of Edward Heath. It was, at the time, engaged in delicate wage negotiations with the National Union of Miners (NUM), negotiations whose strategic context was altered significantly by the quadrupling of oil prices, to say nothing of the (further) inflationary pressures this injected into the domestic economy (Kavanagh 1996; Taylor 1996). Predictable intransigence on both sides, combined with the rapidly deteriorating fuel situation, led to the government declaring a State of Emergency on November 13 and, later, to the infamous "three-day Week" (during which electricity was supplied to industry for only three specified days per week) starting on New Year's Day 1974. Heath resisted the mounting pressure (from within his own party and from the media alike) for a General Election early in the New Year, but could only delay the inevitable, as the NUM balloted for an all-out strike for early in February. The election was called for February 28, 1974 and was fought, perhaps inevitably, over the issue of "who ran the country" — the trade unions or the government. The electorate decided, though by no means unequivocally, that whoever ran the country, it was not to be the Conservatives, and restored Labour to power (with Wilson once again as prime minister) as the largest single party but without an overall majority.

That Labour won the general election (and indeed won again six months later), was testimony to the impression (an impression that it had done much to cultivate) that Labour was better placed to keep the unions on board. This was undoubtedly the case and was reflected in its Social Contract with the unions (negotiated in opposition but taken with it into government). Yet it was to help little in managing the contradictory economic settlement that Labour inherited from the Conservatives (Coates 1980). In the early years, the incoming Labour administration followed the broadly Keynesian strategy of the Heath government, engaging in reflationary policies by increasing social expenditures and public sector wages. Consumer spending rose, restoring economic growth, but only at the cost of heightened inflation (peaking at 25 percent in the spring of 1975) and an escalating balance-of-payments crisis. In late 1975 and 1976 matters came to a head. Open, if unguarded, speculation about the need for a competitive devaluation (though never really actively contemplated) led to a disinvestment of the OPEC countries' funds from sterling, bolstering a wave of self-reinforcing speculation against the pound. The consequence was to increase massively the cost of imports, generating further inflationary pressures and hence undermining the government's Social Contract with the unions. The Bank of England's attempts to defend the pound on the international exchanges failed to convince investors of the government's commitment not to devalue the currency while at the same time it was exhausting regular lines of credit from the International Monetary Fund (Barnett 1992, pp. 97–117; Burk and Cairncross 1992, pp. 20–58; Scharpf 1987, p. 80). It was in this context that the government was forced to contemplate a longer-term "special loan" from the IMF. Yet this came with strings attached and only after a detailed investigation of Britain's predicament by the IMF's monetarist converts. As Scharpf notes, the government's "reluctant conversion to monetarism," though already evidenced in the Treasury's moderately restrictive stance since the winter of 1975, was reaffirmed and reinforced here (1987, p. 82; see also Epstein and Schor 1990, p. 147).

Yet if monetarism was already being deployed as a *technique or instrument* of economic management by the Labour government even prior to the IMF loan (with its rather punitively anti-Keynesian conditions), then it is important to note that the conversion to monetarism as an economic doctrine was, at this stage, by no means secured (Epstein and Schor 1990; Kenway 1998; Scharpf 1987, p. 239). Monetarism, like corporatism (and the incomes policies and compulsory wage restraint on the part of the unions that they facilitated), was deployed by Labour as a crisis-management technique. As such, the Labour government of 1974–79 never abandoned its overarching (indeed, *paradigmatic*) policy commitment to full employment, a mixed economy, and a comprehensive welfare state, even if the instruments and techniques it deployed were hardly compatible with such goals. From 1973 to 1979, a clear gulf opened up between the instruments of economic management deployed by the British state, which were increasingly monetarist in inspiration, and the governing economic paradigm (and attendant political goals), which continued to be broadly Keynesian and welfarist (Panitch and Leys 1997, pp. 121–23; Tomlinson 1986, p. 8).

It was only with the election of Margaret Thatcher in 1979 that the paradigm shift was completed, as economic and political goals were brought up to date with the monetarist techniques that had increasingly come to characterize the management of the economy since the 1970s in Britain as elsewhere.[9] Arguably this was, in turn, dependent upon the events, the humiliation, and the ignominy of the "winter of discontent," in which a wave of industrial stoppages shattered the Social Contract with the trade unions, bringing Britain to a standstill during the worst winter in living memory (Hay 1996a). All hopes for a corporatist (far less monetarist) solution to the problems of Britain's peculiar Keynesianism were abruptly terminated. If there is one single point in postwar British political development that can be referred to as a cathartic moment of crisis, it is surely this.

It is in this context that the appeal of the new right's account of a crisis of an overextended, overloaded, and ungovernable state "held to ransom" by the trade unions must be sought. It was this narrative and the resonance that it found and constructed that brought Thatcher to Downing Street in May 1979, promising, in the words of St. Francis of Assisi, "harmony" where there had been "discord." The victory of monetarism (however temporary in textbook terms) and of neoliberal economics, more generally, was now secured.

Periodizing Macroeconomic Policy Making in the Transition to Neoliberalism

The above account, however generalized, is highly compatible with the theoretical schema presented above. It is also suggestive of a theoretically informed periodization of macroeconomic policy over this period.[10] It is with such a periodization that I conclude.

Here, as suggested above, we might usefully consider the whole decade of the 1970s. The period from June 1970 (and the election of the Heath government) to May 1979 (and the election of Margaret Thatcher) might usefully be periodized into three cycles of second-order policy change or strategic learning: (1) a contradictory "proto-Thatcherite Keynesianism" from 1970 until 1971; (2) a restoration of more "orthodox Keynesianism" from 1971 until 1976; and (3) the emergence of a hybrid "monetarily constrained Keynesianism" from 1976 until 1979.

The first, abortive, phase of monetarist experimentation from 1970 to 1971 is frequently cast as a "disengagement" (however temporary) from the (peculiarly British) Keynesian orthodoxies of much of the postwar period.[11] Certainly, Heath's "Selsdon man" speech marked a radical departure from the more interventionist tone of economic management that had come to characterize the late 1960s. Fiscal policy was tightened severely and, in 1970 at least, a restrictive monetary stance adopted.[12] More significantly still, the emphasis of economic policy making switched from demand-side measures toward less interventionist supply-side policies that might help to curb inflation and stimulate growth. Nonetheless, as Coopey and Woodward note (1996, p. 10),

> we should be careful not to exaggerate the switch in direction that took place. For one thing, there was much less emphasis on monetary policy than in 1979–81. At the same time there was never any intention of abandoning discretionary demand management in favor of a regime of policy rules, while on the supply-side the Heath government remained firmly committed to the mixed economy and the welfare state. Finally, the Heath government never had any intention of allowing unemployment to become the major weapon of inflation control.

In Hall's terms, this was quite clearly an exercise in second-order policy change (in which the instruments, if not the pervasive goals, of policy were revised). As such, however, it was exceedingly short-lived, as unemployment rose alarmingly in late 1971.

Policy would now revert to a classically Keynesian stance, with the Heath government quickly making amends for its proto-Thatcherite adventure of the previous years, with the active pursuit of discretionary demand management. Planned increases in public expenditure in autumn 1971, followed by an expansionary tax-cutting budget in May 1972, launched the so-called Heath-Barber boom. This was subsequently sustained by the floating of sterling only a month later, leading to significant wage inflation, a return to formal incomes policy, and the threat of a severely overheating economy. The expansionary fiscal and monetary stance was only partially reversed in 1973, and the Heath government fell in the wake of the first oil shock as the incomes policy introduced less than two years earlier disintegrated, precipitating the "three-day week." Labour inherited something of a poison chalice, but the broad thrust of its macroeconomic policy remained Keynesian (if rather more conservatively so [Artis and Cobham 1991]). The government's strategy, in the context of pervasive "stagflation" and a world economy already spiraling into a precipitous nosedive, was to retain a relatively expansionary stance (and to encourage other governments to do likewise) to mitigate the almost inevitable increase in unemployment. This proved, in practice, perhaps remarkably successful. Nevertheless, the combination of exhortations to multilateral expansionism, a tighter monetary stance, and initially voluntary but subsequently statutory wage restraint were only ever likely to delay the inevitable. Whenever possible, as in February 1976 following the economic upturn in the latter half of the previous year, Labour increased public expenditure in an ultimately vain attempt to reduce unemployment. Its April budget was also expansionary, introducing a series of tax cuts conditional upon wage restraint. However, as Coopey and Woodward note, its strategy to promote an export-led recovery was decidedly less successful. "[I]nterest rates were reduced and attempts were made to nudge sterling down on the foreign exchange markets" (1996, p. 13). Unfortunately, its effects were only to precipitate the sterling crisis that would sound the first (of several) death knells for Keynesianism in Britain, driving the government cap-in-hand to the IMF.

The terms of the IMF's loan were severe, requiring that Labour now render more substantive its rhetorical (and highly strategic) invocations of monetarist doctrine that had been trotted out at every available opportunity since it became apparent that the government would indeed be dependent upon cash from the IMF's coffers. Thus, as Thain and Wright observe, Callaghan's famous "monetarist" conversion in front of the Labour Party Conference in 1976 was "a tactical political attempt to achieve multiple objectives: to appease the financial markets, to frighten the Labour Party into accepting the need for tough economic measures, and to make the right impression on the US Treasury Secretary whose support would be vital for the UK to obtain IMF support" (1995, p. 20). Labour's convictions, motivations, aspirations, and, indeed, its basic mode of operation, however, remained essentially Keynesian-corporatist. Thus, incomes policy rather than monetary targeting remained the central instrument of the government's counterinflationary strategy. As such, Thain and Wright are surely right to conclude, "Healey as Chancellor presided over a major shift in the emphasis of macro-economic policy, but one which fell short of an outright repudiation of the post-war consensus. His approach was to use whatever means were at hand to shore up that consensus while responding to the particular crises of the time" (p. 16).

As such, the label "monetarily constrained Keynesianism" is far more appropriate to capture the mindset of a crisis-beset Labour administration between 1976 and 1979, rather than monetarism itself. As Robert Skidelsky has recently suggested, "The reluctance to put the whole burden of the fight against inflation on monetary policy reflect both a vestigial political commitment to full employment and an analytic commitment to the cost-push theory of inflation. It was the collapse of the incomes policy in the 'winter of discontent' in 1978–9, leading to the election of the much more ideologically intransigent Conservative Party under Mrs Thatcher, which finally put policy Keynesianism to sleep" (1997, p. 62). Similarly, as Coopey and Woodward conclude in their admirable analysis, "with the continuous adherence to incomes policy and the use — albeit the less enthusiastic use — of fiscal policy as a weapon of demand management, it cannot be realistically claimed that monetarism came to Britain in 1976" (1996, p. 13).

It was then, only, in May 1979, with Mrs. Thatcher on the steps of Downing Street, that the paradigm shift was secured. Keynesianism, albeit in a peculiarly constrained form, would now yield to neoliberalism, initially in its rather ephemeral textbook monetarist guise, as the dominant paradigm informing economic policy making in Britain.

Conclusion

As the above analysis has hopefully demonstrated, the historical institutionalist conception of paradigmatically mediated institutional change provides a powerful heuristic devise, sensitizing us to the uneven temporality of institutional change. Yet it remains essentially that — a heuristic devise — for while it is premised upon a highly sophisticated and dynamic conception of the dynamic relationship between ideas and institutions it, in the end, lacks a theory of crisis and institutional transformation, telling us little about the process by which a paradigm emerges, accumulates anomalies, is challenged and ultimately replaced. My aim in this chapter has been to begin to rectify that oversight.

Historical institutionalism's rather instantaneous depiction of the moment of paradigm shift, as well as its neat and differentiated view of first-, second- and third-order change, is perhaps overly parsimonious. As the above example illustrates, the process of paradigm shift is complex, involved, and hardly instantaneous. Paradigms become entrenched both culturally and institution-ally. They are difficult to transcend and, arguably, their traces and attendant legacies can never be totally erased. The institutionalization of a paradigm within the state apparatus and the translation of that paradigm into policy are protracted, unpredictable, and often contested processes. Moreover, the rela-tionship between ideas, policy, and the institutional effects of such policy is more complex still, suggesting that any periodization of the ideas animating policy needs to be supplemented by a somewhat different periodization of the institutional effects of such paradigmatic change. My aim here has been to contribute, in the most modest way, to this further development and elabora-tion of this theoretical heuristic.

In so doing I hope to have demonstrated the utility of a distinctly ideational institutionalist perspective in developing some of undoubted insights of its more historical variant. It is not only ideational institutionalism, however, that might contribute to this development and working through of suggestive themes thrown up by a more historical approach to institutional analysis. Un-likely though it might at first seem, there are certain affinities between the approach developed here and (variants of) rational choice institutionalism. Certainly, there are epistemological and ontological differences (of a fairly pro-found nature) between these perspectives (see Hay and Wincott 1998a, 1998b). Similarly, the shared emphasis of historical and ideational institutionalism on process tracing over time is somewhat at odds with the more synchronic (or "snapshot") approach adopted by rational choice theorists. Nonetheless, one might plausibly imagine the development by rational choice institutionalists, within the context of this general approach, of game-theoretical scenarios to model those situations in which opposition parties and interests might seek to mobilize perceptions of systemic crisis requiring a decisive intervention and a change in the ascendant economic paradigm. Thus, while rational choice and ideational institutionalists might continue to disagree over the more or less ma-terial determinants of the interests motivating such strategic action and on the extent to which demonstrable rationality is a guide to anticipated behavior, there is much to be gained by more systematically exploring the affinities be-tween such seemingly diverse positions. This, surely, is the way forward for in-stitutional analysis.

Notes

This paper has undergone a rather lengthy and complex process of gestation. Earlier versions of aspects of the argument have been presented at the Eleventh Conference of Europeanists, Baltimore, February 1998; at the European Consortium of Political Research, Warwick, April 1998; at the Conference on Institutionalism, Sophienberg Castle, Denmark, August 1997; and in seminars at Columbia University, York University (UK), and Birmingham University. I have benefited immeasurably from discussions with a number of people over the years on its principal themes. In particular, I would like to thank the following for their insight, encouragement, and, above all, patience: Mark Blyth, John Campbell, Josef Esser, Peter Hall, Jane Jenson, Peter Kerr, Dave Marsh, Ove K. Pedersen, Paul Pierson, Hugh Ward, Matthew Watson, Daniel Wincott, and an anonymous reader for Princeton University Press.

1. In the context of postwar economic policy-making in Britain, Keynesianism and neoliberalism/monetarism.

2. The term was first used in this context by Stephen D. Krasner to refer to accounts positing "short bursts of rapid institutional change followed by long periods of stasis" (1990, pp. 240–44). It was originally coined, however, by Stephen Jay Gould and Niles Eldredge in an attack on conventional Darwinian notions of evolution (1977; see also Eldredge 1989; Gould 1989). It must be emphasized that the notion of "punctuated evolution" developed in this paper implies a significantly different conception of political time and change from that implied by Krasner in the work of the authors he describes.

3. After a warning of the dangers of analogies drawn from the philosophy of the natural sciences, it is perhaps appropriate to sound a note of caution about the use of biological analogy in this context. The notion of evolution is, and has proved, a dangerous one in the hands of social scientists. Nonetheless, recent development in paleobiology in particular have had the effect of liberating the notion of evolution from Darwinian conceptions of progress. It is in this latter sense that the notion of evolution is deployed here to refer to incremental, path-dependent, and directional change that is circumscribed in some way (in this case by a dominant paradigm within which policy is framed). See in particular Gould 1989; Levins and Lewontin 1985.

4. This point is also made by Hall (1993; see also 1986, 1992).

5. It is, however, by far the most common, associated as it is with nonexceptional moments of political time.

6. Whether a certain accumulation of contradictions is in any sense a necessary condition for a crisis narrative capable of motivating a decisive intervention (and paradigm shift) is a complex issue. For a more detailed discussion see Hay 1999a.

7. On the basis of the titles alone, a narrow points victory would seem to have gone to the former. In order of appearance, they are "Explaining Thatcherism" (Moon 1994); "Over the Moon or Sick as a Parrot" (Marsh and Rhodes 1995); and "Evaluating Thatcher: Did the Cow Jump Over?" (Moon 1995).

8. On "monetarily constrained Keynesianism" see Fforde 1983; Artis and Cobham 1991; Smith 1987; Thain and Wright 1995, p. 19; Tomlinson 1986. In this section I expand and develop the argument first advanced in Hay 1999a, pp. 102–5.

9. Moreover, it might be noted that many senior civil servants within the Treasury remained (more or less staunch) Keynesians until relatively late in the Thatcherite first term.

10. In developing such a periodization I have dawn extensively upon the similar accounts presented by Begg (1987); Coopey and Woodward (1996); Thompson (1996); Thain and Wright (1995).

11. The term is, in fact, Coopey and Woodward's.

12. This, however, would be weakened somewhat with the introduction of Competition and Credit Control in 1971.

References

Argylis, Chris, and Donald Schön. 1978. *Organizational Learning*. Reading, England: Addison-Wesley.

Artis, Michael, and David Cobham, editors. 1991. *Labour's Economic Policy, 1974–1979*. Manchester, England: Manchester University Press.

Barnett, J. 1992. *Inside the Treasury*. London: André Deutsch.

Begg, D. 1987. "Fiscal Policy." In *The Performance of the British Economy*, edited by R. Dornbusch and R. Layard. Oxford: Oxford University Press.

Burk, Kathleen, and Sir Alec Cairncross. 1992. *"Goodbye, Great Britain": The 1976 IMF Crisis*. New Haven: Yale University Press.

Cairncross, Sir Alec. 1992. *The British Economy since 1945*. Oxford: Blackwell.

Campbell, John L. 1998. "Institutional Analysis and the Role of Ideas in Political Economy." *Theory and Society* 27:377–409.

Claever, Tony. 1997. *Understanding the World Economy*. London: Routledge.

Coates, David. 1980. *Labour in Power? A Study of the Labour Government, 1974–1979*. London: Longman.

Coopey, Richard, and Nicholas Woodward. 1996. "The British Economy in the 1970s: An Overview." Pp. 1–33 in *Britain in the 1970s: The Troubled Economy*, edited by R. Coopey and N. Woodward. London: Palgrave.

Debray, Regis. 1973. "Time and Politics." Pp. 87–160 in *Prison Writings*. New York: Random House.

Dolowitz, David, and Marsh, David. 1996. "Who Learns What from Whom? A Review of the Policy Transfer Literature," *Political Studies* 44:343–57.

Dolowitz, David, Stuart McAnulla, David Marsh, and David Richards. 1996. "Thatcherism and the Three 'R's: Radicalism, Realism, and Rhetoric in the Third Term of the Thatcher Government." *Parliamentary Affairs* 49:455–70.

Eldredge, Niles. 1989. "Punctuated Equilibrium, Rates of Change, and Large-Scale Entities in Evolutionary Systems." Pp. 103–20 in *The Dynamics of Evolution: The Punctuated Equilibrium Debate in the Natural and Social Sciences*, edited by A. Somit and S. A. Peterson. Ithaca: Cornell University Press.

Epstein, Gerald A., and Juliet B. Schor. 1990. "Macropolicy in the Rise and Fall of the Golden Age." Pp. 126–52 in *The Golden Age of Capitalism: Reinterpreting the Postwar Experience*, edited by S. Marglin and J. Schor. Oxford: Clarendon Press.

Fforde, J. S. 1983. "Setting Monetary Objectives." *Bank of England Quarterly Bulletin* (June) 200–209.

Glyn, Andrew, Alan Hughes, Alain Lipietz, and Ajit Singh. 1990. "The Rise and Fall of the Golden Age." Pp. 39–125 in *The Golden Age of Capitalism: Reinterpreting the Postwar Experience*, edited by S. Marglin and J. Schor. Oxford: Clarendon Press.

Gould, Stephen Jay. 1980. "On Replacing the Idea of Progress with an Operational Notion of Directionality." Pp. 319–38 in *Evolutionary Progress*, edited by M. H. Nitecki. Chicago: University of Chicago Press.

———. 1989. "Punctuated Equilibrium in Fact and Theory." Pp. 54–84 in *The Dynamics of Evolution: The Punctuated Equilibrium Debate in the Natural and Social Sciences*, edited by A. Somit and S. A. Peterson. Ithaca: Cornell University Press.

Gould, Stephen Jay, and Niles Eldredge. 1977. "Punctuated Equilibria: The Tempo and Mode of Evolution Reconsidered." *Paleobiology* 3:115–51.

Haas, Ernst B. 1992. *When Knowledge Is Power*. Berkeley and Los Angeles: University of California Press.

Hall. Peter A. 1986. "The State and Economic Decline." Pp. 266–302 in *The Decline of the British Economy*, edited by B. Elbaum and W. Lazonick. Oxford: Clarendon Press.

———. 1992. "The Movement from Keynesianism to Monetarism: Institutional Analysis and British Economic Policy in the 1970s." Pp. 90–113 in *Structuring Politics*, edited by S. Steinmo, K. Thelen, and F. Longstreth. New York: Cambridge University Press.

———. 1993. "Policy Paradigms, Social Learning, and the State: The Case of Economic Policy-Making in Britain." *Comparative Politics* 25:175–96.

Hall, Peter A., and Rosemary C. R. Taylor. 1996. "Political Science and the Three New Institutionalisms." *Political Studies* 44:936–57.

Hall, Stuart. 1983. "The Great Moving Right Show." Pp. 19–39 in *The Politics of Thatcherism*, edited by S. Hall and M. Jacques. London: Lawrence and Wishart.

———. 1985. "Authoritarian Populism: A Reply." *New Left Review* 151:115–24.

———. 1988. *The Hard Road to Renewal: Thatcherism and the Crisis of the Left*. London: Verso.

Hay, Colin. 1996a. "Narrating Crisis: The Discursive Construction of the Winter of Discontent." *Sociology* 30:253–77.

———. 1996b. *Re-Stating Social and Political Change*. Buckingham: Open University Press.

———. 1999a. "Crisis and British Political Development." Pp. 87–106 in *Postwar British Politics in Perspective*, edited by David Marsh, Jim Buller, Colin Hay, et al. Cambridge: Polity.

———. 1999b. "Crisis and the Structural Transformation of the State: Interrogating the Process of Change." *British Journal of Politics and International Relations* 1:317–44.

Hay, Colin, and Daniel Wincott. 1998a. "Structure, Agency, and Historical Institutionalism." *Political Studies* 46:951–57.

———. 1998b. *Interrogating Institutionalism, Interrogating Institutions: Beyond "Calculus" and "Cultural" Approaches*. Program for the Study of Germany and Europe Working Paper 8.3. Cambridge: Harvard University.

Heclo, Hugh. 1974. *Modern Social Politics in Britain and Sweden*. New Haven: Yale University Press.

Ikenberry, G. John. 1988. "Conclusion: An Institutional Approach to Foreign Economic Policy." Pp. 219–43 in *The State and American Foreign Economic Policy*, edited by G. J. Ikenberry, David Lake, and Michael Mastanduno. Ithaca: Cornell University Press.

Jenkins, Patrick. 1988. *The Thatcher Revolution: The Post-Socialist Era*. Cambridge: Harvard University Press.

Jessop, Bob. 1990. *State Theory: Putting Capitalist States in their Place*. Cambridge: Polity.

Jessop, Bob, Kevin Bonnett, and Simon Bromley. 1990. "Farewell to Thatcherism? Neo-Liberalism and New Times." *New Left Review* 179:81–102.

Jessop, Bob, Kevin Bonnett, Simon Bromley, and Tom Ling. 1988. *Thatcherism: A Tale of Two Nations*. Cambridge: Polity.

Katzenstein, Peter J., editor. 1978. *Between Power and Plenty*. Madison: University of Wisconsin.

Kavanagh, Dennis. 1996. "The Fatal Choice: The Calling of the February 1974 Election." Pp. 351–70 in *The Heath Government, 1970–1974*, edited by S. Ball and A. Seldon. London: Longman.

Kenway, Peter. 1998. *From Keynesianism to Monetarism: The Evolution of UK Macroeconometric Models*. London: Routledge.

Kerr, Peter. 2000. *From Conflict to Consensus: The Evolution of Post-War British Politics, 1945–1997*. London: Routledge.

Kerr, Peter, and David Marsh. 1999. "Explaining Thatcherism: Towards a Multi-Dimensional Approach." Pp. 168–88 in *Postwar British Politics in Perspective*, David Marsh, Jim Buller, Colin Hay, et al. Cambridge: Polity.

Krasner, Stephen J. 1984. "Approaches to the State: Alternative Conceptions and Historical Dynamics." *Comparative Politics* 37:231–43.

Kuhn, Thomas S. 1962. *The Structure of Scientific Revolutions*. Chicago: University of Chicago Press.

Letwin, Sophie. 1992. *The Anatomy of Thatcherism*. London: Fontana.

Levins, Richard, and Richard C. Lewontin. 1985. *The Dialectical Biologist*. Cambridge: Harvard University Press.

Leys, Colin. 1990. "Still a Question of Hegemony." *New Left Review* 181:119–28.

Marsh, David. 1995. "Explaining 'Thatcherite' Policies: Beyond Uni-Dimensional Explanation." *Political Studies* 43:595–613.

Marsh, David, and R. A. W. Rhodes, editors. 1992. *Implementing Thatcherite Policies: Audit of an Era*. Buckingham: Open University Press.

——. 1993. "Implementing Thatcherism: Policy Change in the 1980s." *Parliamentary Affairs* 45:33–51.

——. 1995. "Evaluating Thatcherism: Over the Moon or Sick as a Parrot." *Politics* 15:49–54.

Marsh, David, Jim Buller, Colin Hay, Jim Johnstone, Peter Kerr, Stuart McAnulla, and Matthew Watson. 1999. *Postwar British Politics in Perspective*. Cambridge: Polity.

Moon, Jeremy. 1993. *Innovative Leadership in Democracy: Policy Change under Thatcher*. Aldershot, England: Dartmouth.

——. 1994. "Explaining Thatcherism: Skeptical versus Synthetic Approaches." *Politics* 14:43–49.

——. 1995. "Evaluating Thatcher: Did the Cow Jump Over? A Reply to Marsh and Rhodes." *Politics* 15:113–17.

O'Shea, Alan. 1984. *Formations of Nations and People*. London: Routledge.

Panitch, Leo, and Colin Leys. 1997. *The End of Parliamentary Socialism*. London: Verso.

Pierson, Paul. 1993. "When Effects Become Cause: Policy Feedback and Policy Change." *World Politics* 45:595–628.

——. 1996. "The Path to European Integration: A Historical Institutionalist Analysis." *Comparative Political Studies* 29:123–63.

——. 1997. "Increasing Returns, Path Dependence, and the Study of Politics." Jean Monnet Chair Papers, 44.

Rothstein, Bo. 1992. "Labour-Market Institutions and Working-Class Strength." Pp.

33–56 in *Structuring Politics*, edited by S. Steinmo, K. Thelen, and F. Longstreth. New York: Cambridge University Press.

Savage, Stephen P., Robert Atkinson, and Lynton Robins. 1994. *Public Policy in Britain*. London: Macmillan.

Scharpf, Fritz. 1987. *Crisis and Choice in European Social Democracy*. Ithaca: Cornell University Press.

Skidelsky, Robert. 1997. "The Fall of Keynesianism." Pp. 41–66 in *The Ideas That Shaped Post-War Britain*, edited by D. Marquand and A. Seldon. London: Fontana.

Skocpol, Theda. 1992. *Protecting Soldiers and Mothers: The Political Origins of Social Policy in the United States*. Cambridge: Harvard University Press, Belknap Press.

Smith, David. 1987. *The Rise and Fall of Monetarism: The Theory and Politics of an Economic Experiment*. Harmondsworth, England: Penguin.

Steinmo, Sven, Kathleen Thelen, and Frank Longstreth, editors. 1992. *Structuring Politics: Historical Institutionalism in Comparative Analysis*. New York: Cambridge University Press.

Taylor, Robert. 1996. "The Heath Government and Industrial Relations: Myth and Reality." Pp. 161–90 in *The Heath Government, 1970–1974*, edited by S. Ball and A. Seldon. London: Longman.

Thain, Colin, and Maurice Wright. 1995. *The Treasury and Whitehall*. Oxford: Oxford University Press.

Thelen, Kathleen, and Sven Steinmo. 1992. "Historical Institutionalism in Comparative Politics." Pp. 1–32 in *Structuring Politics*, edited by S. Steinmo, K. Thelen, and F. Longstreth. New York: Cambridge University Press.

Thompson, Noel. 1996. "Economic Ideas and the Development of Economic Opinion." Pp. 55–80 in *Britain in the 1970s: The Troubled Economy*, edited by R. Coopey and N. Woodward. London: UCL Press.

Tomlinson, Jim. 1986. *Monetarism: Is There an Alternative? Non-Monetarist Strategies for the Economy*. Oxford: Blackwell.

Wolfe, Joel. 1991. "State Power and Ideology in Britain: Mrs Thatcher's Privatization Programme." *Political Studies* 39:237–52.

Chapter 9 _____

Translating Liberalization

NEOLIBERALISM IN THE DANISH NEGOTIATED ECONOMY

PETER KJÆR AND OVE K. PEDERSEN

WHEN researchers and policy makers discuss the global spread of neoliberalism, they tend to understand the role of neoliberal ideas in the following way: After three decades of Keynesianism and following the stagflation crisis of the mid-1970s, there was a resurgence of neoliberal ideas and models of organization that challenged existing policy ideas and, to varying degrees, resulted in the implementation of reforms based on neoliberal principles.[1] They assume that a significant change has diffused across countries; that this change has involved a shift toward neoliberalism; and that we now have only to ascertain how much has changed and why neoliberal ideas came to have this impact. We challenge this understanding of neoliberalism.

First, we question its empirical and analytical point of departure. We contend that the phenomenon of neoliberalism must be analyzed in terms of how it was *translated* in particular contexts and in particular historical situations. In other words, the empirical challenge is to identify national (or subnational) translations rather than to generalize about diffusion processes across countries and across history. Translation is a process whereby concepts and conceptions from different social contexts come into contact with each other and trigger a shift in the existing order of interpretation and action in a particular context. By phrasing the issue as one of translation rather than diffusion, we stress that the story of neoliberalism should be analyzed as a process in which actors within a particular national context *select* various relevant neoliberal concepts and conceptions from ideas available to them and use them in ways that *displace* the existing order of interpretation and action and *trigger* a shift in policy attention, preferred policy models, and opportunities for political action. In contrast to diffusion, translation does not assume that there exists a fully developed and easily identifiable idea (or paradigm) that is transferred unchanged over time and from one country to another. The problem with the notion of diffusion is that it represents ideas as frozen cultural objects that are transferred from one context to another without being altered. In translation, the process is an *ongoing* production of meaning in a particular social context in which an idea may be articulated and then stabilized.[2] To illustrate this process, we will focus on the development of Danish structural policy since the mid-1970s, a time during which neoliberal concepts were translated into structural policy in ways that were heavily conditioned by the particular discursive and institutional order of Danish economic policy making.

Second, we question some of the theoretical conceptions underlying the thesis of the spread of neoliberalism, and in particular the key concepts of *ideas* and *change*. Scholars often see the spread of neoliberalism as an example of how a particular set of powerful economic ideas come to determine political strategies and policy outcomes in various contexts. In other words, neoliberalism becomes an important example of how ideas influence politics and cause policies to change (e.g., Campbell 1998; Goldstein and Keohane 1993a; Hall 1989a). In these approaches, the power of particular ideas stems from their association with various institutional or structural conditions, such as the position of economists as bearers of ideas in policy making, the institutionalization of particular conceptions in the legal structure of a country, or the adoption of an idea by a powerful group in the polity. We argue that these approaches to ideas and political change have problems in conceptualizing and analyzing the role of ideas because they do not embed ideas in broader theories of meaning. As a result there is a tendency to ascribe universal properties to ideas and, in analytical terms, a tendency to conflate ideas with individuals (as beliefs) or with institutions (as outcomes).

Starting from the concept of *discourse*, we develop a more contextual and complex understanding of the role of ideas. Discourse is a system of meaning that orders the production of conceptions and interpretations of the social world in a particular context. In this view, ideas are always embedded in discourses and become meaningful only by being interpreted as part of a particular discursive system of meaning. Furthermore, ideas become stabilized only by being institutionalized as parts of particular institutional arrangements that systematically link particular expectations to particular actors and actions in discursive processes. Instead of assuming that ideas are exogenous forces with autonomous causal powers or conflating them with individuals or with institutions, we want to know how ideas become significant social phenomena in the first place.

Similarly, we argue that the approaches mentioned above have problems in analyzing change insofar as they assume that change in ideas, environments, and the like, including the rise of neoliberalism, *has* occurred rather than taking this as an empirical question and object of analysis in itself. Usually the theoretical question has been how changes on one level (i.e., the international level or ideational level) cause change on another level (i.e., in national policy making). Here there have been intense debates on the sources of change as well as the nature of change, such as whether lower-level changes should be theorized in terms of abrupt or punctuated shifts alternating with long periods of relative stability, or in terms of periods of slow, incremental evolution alternating with periods of rapid or revolutionary change (e.g., Hay this volume; Krasner 1984). The problem with these views is that change, like ideas, tends to be taken for granted as a point of departure for a causal analysis and therefore exogenized from the empirical analysis. The question for us is, how are we equipped to make sense of events as something that constitutes a change, such as a shift from Keynesianism to monetarism? Our approach views change as an internal aspect of a discourse, so another critical analytical question is, what constitutes a change in a particular context? Our point is that rather than assuming that neoliberalism has in fact led to a change in Keynesian ideas, this assumption ought to be an empirical question. Conceptions of change are part of existing discourses in at least two ways. First, discourses involve conceptions of what is to be understood as change. For example, as a result of the focus on demand-side policies in Keynesianism, a reorientation toward supply-side policies will automatically be interpreted as a change toward another reading of Keynesianism. Second, in every discourse there is a place for innovation. Keynesianism furnishes its own rules concerning how to experiment with concepts and conceptions. Indeed, Keynesian ideas have changed dramatically over the years in ways that led to experimentation with a range of policy programs, policy settings, and the like that involved changes in the interpretation and understanding of modern economies, including the Danish economy (e.g., Ricoeur 1983, pp. 64–70).

To summarize, we claim that neoliberalism should not be conceived as a universally meaningful totality of ideas that diffused across nations and through time, but as a more loosely connected set of concepts, distinctions, and ideas that gained meaning as they were selected, articulated, and then stabilized in unique ways depending on the particular discursive and institutional contexts in which this occurred. Thus, our project is not one of ascertaining the causal links between changes in the broader environment and local changes in ideas and organization, nor of theorizing the generic nature of social and political change. Instead it is one of empirically mapping the particular transformations in ideas, discourses, institutions and the processes that came to be understood as a change in the unique Danish context.

Our approach to this analysis is a *discursive institutionalist* one that combines elements of current debates in historical institutionalism with theories of discourse and meaning frequently associated with organizational institutionalism (see chap. 1). We will describe this approach after a discussion of how historical institutionalism deals with ideas and change. This discussion is followed by a two-step empirical analysis of the Danish case. First, we outline the institutional history of the Danish polity after 1945 in order to present the broader context within which neoliberalism developed. Second, we describe the development of structural policy in Denmark between 1975 and 1995 and how neoliberal conceptions were translated into this particular context. By structural policy we mean efforts to restructure the Danish economy through various public and private means. We conclude with a brief outline of our analytical strategy, based on discursive institutionalism, and a discussion of the empirical, conceptual, and methodological implications of our study.

Discourse analysis generally involves detailed textual analysis. However, for lack of space in this chapter, we base our argument on closer textual analyses of documents, reports, blueprints, and the like published elsewhere. We refer to these analyses and some of the original texts as we go along. The idea here is to *illustrate* in a general way how discursive institutionalism goes about its work, rather than to present a full-blown text-analytic discursive analysis (e.g., Pedersen et al. 1992).

Ideas and Change: Historical and Discursive Institutionalism

Institutional theory is usually concerned with accounts of behavior and organization that emphasize explanations in which actors, individuals, or collectives are seen as constrained and sometimes enabled by institutions that in a wide sense constitute an endogenous source of order. Institutions, be they formal contractual arrangements, organizational routines and conventions, or taken-for-granted normative or cognitive structures, are key explanatory variables in that they influence choices, regulate behavior, and generally order social interaction. Different institutional theories start from different assumptions about individual motivations and rationality, the nature of institutions, and the causal mechanisms linking institutional structure and individual choice. However, they all emphasize the role of institutions as historically evolved social patterns that shape social behavior in important ways.[3]

A number of institutionalists have also attempted recently to integrate the notion of *ideas* into institutional accounts of political, economic, and organizational change. They describe ideas as important explanatory variables in addition to the already recognized categories of institutional structure, individual rationality, and individual and collective interests. There are at least two typical ways of dealing with ideas and change in this literature: the *causal* approach and the *dialectical* approach. To these we add our *discursive institutionalist* approach.

Ideas as Causes

Some institutionalists have criticized the neglect of ideas in causal analyses of political and institutional change. They have argued that ideas are not just "hooks" or ex post rationalizations of behavior, but that ideas also play causal roles in politics in ways that need to be conceptualized and tested in empirical analysis, particularly against rational choice and structural arguments (e.g.,

Goldstein and Keohane 1993a). Indeed, when ideas are viewed as causes, it is often part of the critique of rational choice theory. Notably, Douglass North (1990, p. 23) argued that when we allow for imperfect information, knowledge of the world will influence how people make choices. In turn, this knowledge will be influenced by ideas or ideologies, that is, the subjective perceptions (i.e., models and theories) that people possess to explain the world around them and that play an important part in people's choices. Ideas and ideologies are linked to institutions in the sense that institutions make it possible to express ideas and ideologies. North (pp. 85–86) admits that he does not provide an elaborate theory of ideas as they relate to institutions and change, but simply introduces the theme.

Judith Goldstein and Robert Keohane (1993b, pp. 3–5) provided some conceptual elaboration of this theme. They defined ideas as "beliefs held by individuals" and contended that "ideas matter for policy, even when human beings behave rationally to achieve their ends." Ideas serve to clarify the causal maps of decision makers; serve as coordinating focuses in social interaction; and become embodied in institutional arrangements that structure outcomes in particular ways. However, they emphasized that "ideas often become politically efficacious only in conjunction with other changes, either in material interests or in power relationships" (p. 25). In other words, ideas can provide only a *supplement* to more conventional rational and structural explanations of change.

Peter Hall (1989b) took a similar approach. He claimed that the notion of ideas is an important supplement to the structural analysis of policy change. Ideas are important to the development of policy because they constitute the knowledge base of state action. He suggested, however, that ideas are too often treated as an exogenous variable in accounts of policy making and are imported into the analysis to explain outcomes without much attention to why certain ideas, rather than others, matter. As a result, he argued that we need to know more about the conditions that enable one set of ideas to matter more than another in a particular historical setting. Indeed, he specified through comparative historical analysis four structural conditions that accounted for the efficacy of a particular body of ideas, namely Keynesianism, after the Second World War: the orientation of the governing party; the structure of the state and state-society relations; the nature of national political discourse; and events associated with the war. Conditioned by these factors, Keynesian ideas influenced national policies by providing concepts, rationales for state action, and policy prescriptions.

Paradoxically, the causal approach illustrated by these authors introduced the concept of ideas only to conflate it with institutions or structure in the empirical analysis. Ideas were thought to have an existence and force of their own, but they exerted that force only when associated with institutions or interests. Similarly, it was assumed that ideas have distinct identities (i.e., that there is a distinct body of ideas such as Keynesianism) but can be analyzed only when objectified as institutions or beliefs. In other words, ideas were given a unique creative status as a source of change, but a status that remained unresolved theoretically. Moreover, in analyses of change ideas were treated as external, causal variables and were not themselves treated as something that constantly has to be interpreted and given meaning and that may, in fact, be subject to change during the process being studied.

The Dialectics of Ideas and Institutions

More recently, Hall (1992, 1993) developed an analysis of ideas in which he introduced the concept of *learning* in order to gain a more dynamic understanding of policy change. Rather than reducing ideas to causes, his aim was to ascertain how ideas condition policy learning and how changes in ideas entail changes in the nature of the politics of economic policy making. In addition, he introduced the concept of *paradigm*:

> [P]olicymakers customarily work within a framework of ideas and standards that specifies not only the goals of policy and the kinds of instruments that can be used to attain them, but also the very nature of the problems they are meant to be addressing. *Like a Gestalt, this framework is embedded in the very terminology through which policymakers communicate about their work, and it is influential precisely because so much of it is taken for granted* and unamenable to scrutiny as a whole. I am going to call this interpretive framework a policy paradigm. (Hall 1993, p. 279, our emphasis).

With the help of the concept of paradigm, he outlined different types of changes in policy, that is, different types of learning. First-order change involves adjusting the settings of policy instruments; second-order change involves changing the instruments themselves; and third-order change involves changing the very characteristics of the learning process. This typology not only complicated the question of the relationship between ideas and change, but also implied a more complex relationship between ideas and institutions in which policy paradigms are an important part of political discourse because they can structure the policy-making process much as formal institutions can. Indeed, he argued that the two reinforce each other due to the fact that the way policy-making routines are designed reflects ideas about what policy makers can and should do. He also pointed out that ideas that are embodied in policy paradigms have a status somewhat autonomous from institutions that actors can use to induce or reinforce changes in institutional routines (p. 290). Rather than a simple causal relationship between ideas, institutions, and change, the relationship between ideas and institutions was now construed as a dialectical one, which could be disentangled only as part of a longitudinal analysis that relates the policy paradigm to mutually dependent shifts in ideas and institutions. This approach is developed further by Colin Hay (in this volume).

The dialectical approach constitutes a theoretical advance in terms of dealing with ideas and change. Yet some of the problems of the causal approach remain. First, although advocates of the dialectical approach introduce the concept of policy paradigm, which to some degree is similar to our notion of discourse, and do so in order to supplement the institutional analysis of policy change, they do not describe paradigms as historically constituted, situated, and contingent phenomena. Whereas they assume that paradigms, such as Keynesianism or neoliberalism, have the same easily identified core meaning everywhere, we contend that they must be understood as concrete historical discourses, specific to certain times and places such that British and Scandinavian readings of neoliberalism, for example, may be quite different. Second, although the dialectical approach attempts to theorize the relationship *between* paradigms and institutions, in the end both are given the same theoretical status. That is, both are viewed as part of a particular stabilized policy-making framework. We argue that paradigms (or discourses) should be given a different theoretical status from that of institutions. Finally, the dialectical approach develops a typology of change in which different levels of change are theorized from the perspective of learning. Both Hall and Hay seek to develop generalizable theories of the processes and mechanisms of change without considering whether what constitutes a change in one context also counts as a change in another. We suggest that change cannot be ascertained outside a particular discursive and institutional context precisely because the meaning of change — that is, what local actors interpret as a significant change — may vary from one context to another according to the conceptions of change embedded in particular paradigms and to the rules governing experimentation with ideas within the paradigm.[4]

These are problems that challenge the epistemology and ontology of historical institutionalism. Our claim is that once historical institutionalism begins to deal with questions of ideas, change, and discourse, the approach faces problems that cannot be dealt with simply by expanding theoretical agendas or relaxing behavioral assumptions. The question of ideas challenges more fundamental points of departure because it introduces the question of *meaning* into social analysis. In this sense, our approach more closely resembles organizational institutionalism (see chap. 1). The question of ideas poses three challenges to the analyst: How do we distinguish ideas from other phenomena? How do we observe ideas? How do we describe ideas? Historical institutionalism's answer has been to proceed along the path of theory construction and causal explanation. Our answer is to develop an analytical approach that makes questions of ideas and change empirical questions that can be dealt with only in particular discursive and institutional contexts.

Discursive Institutionalism

Discursive institutionalism may be characterized in terms of three points that distinguish it from other types of institutional theory, notably rational choice and historical institutionalism. To begin with, it takes discourse as its object of analysis and thereby considers discourse as a social phenomenon in its own right. Discourse is a symbolic order involving concepts and conceptions that have a common form due to a regulative principle relating concepts and conceptions. This form structures in advance actors' experiences of things, people, events, and ideal entities by establishing the modes of thematizing what counts as real or relevant (Kögler 1999, p. 180). In other words, a discourse is a *symbolic order* or social ontology in the sense that it establishes the conditions of possibility of experience (of observation and interpretation) in a particular social setting. At the same time, a discourse constitutes a *rationality context* in the sense that it constitutes social actors, motivations, and the rules according to which actions may be validated and consequences identified. Accordingly, discourse analysis attempts to ascertain both the space of possibility of social action (i.e., which actions count as rational) and the horizon of meaning (i.e., which interpretations count as valid and acceptable) in a particular context. As a social phenomenon, discourse is treated as a textual phenomenon, and accordingly discourse may be analyzed empirically as textual practice. Thus, when we analyze discourse, we analyze texts as cultural and linguistic artifacts in their own right. To make discourse an object of analysis requires a particular analytical approach that avoids reducing discourse to an epiphenomenon of other aspects of social organization.

Second, making discourse the object of analysis has consequences for our conceptualization of institutions. At the most fundamental level, we define *institution* from a Saussurian perspective in terms of a distinction between linguistic structure (*langue*) and linguistic practice (*parole*) — that is, a distinction between the rules of discourse and the articulation of these rules in discursive practice. Any discursive practice is seen as preconditioned, but not necessarily determined, by a particular set of linguistic or discursive rules. This is why a discourse only constitutes the "grammar" that governs the composition of any discursive practice and why, for example, to speak the language of economics there must be an institutionalized set of rules pertaining to that particular type of discursive practice. As a result, the concept of institution can be elaborated in terms of three types of preconditioning aspects of any discursive practice. First, following Kuhn, the institution can be viewed as a formalization of discursive practice in systems of knowledge production and maintenance, such as libraries, archives, reference systems, and models, including macroeconomic models. Second, following Foucault, institutions are socially sanctioned speech acts governed by a particular set of rules of acceptance and validity, such as scientific arguments based on particular rules of empirical validation and truth claims. Third, following Wittgenstein, the institutional merges with discursive language games to constitute a particular context of meaning and rationality that operates with particular definitions of problems, solutions, causation, and temporal and spatial concepts. Discursive institutionalism thus develops the concept of institution starting from the concept of discourse and views the relationship between discourse and institution as historically contingent — as the outcome of historically specific ways of situating and organizing discursive practices in a society.[5]

Third, making discourse the object of analysis conditions our approach to the concept of change. Change is not an objective phenomenon but something that is contingent on the choice of the object of analysis, the choice of time periods over which change is examined, and thus the choice of conceptual categories available to us for understanding change (Ricoeur 1983). Furthermore, discourses embody particular norms of what counts as change; particular rules of experimentation with existing concepts and conceptions; and particular stories of their own emergence and development. For example, Keynesianism as a discourse constitutes a particular set of concepts and categories that distinguish it from other discourses and thus define what counts as change (i.e., what distinguishes a Keynesian from a monetarist or neoliberal argument). It also constitutes a set of rules that govern experimentation with Keynesian ideas, such as by sanctioning certain forms of economic fine-tuning, policy reforms, and the management of conjunctural (as opposed to structural) crises. Finally, it embodies particular stories of its rise, its transformation, and its linkages to the emergence of modern welfare states and macroeconomic regulation — stories that vary across countries (Wagner, Wittrock, and Whitley 1991). Thus, whereas others theorize general processes of change or the relationships between ideas and institutions, we take the discursive and institutional construction of change as an object of analysis. This implies an interpretive approach that analyzes processes of creating and stabilizing systems of knowledge. Discourse in this perspective is a process of making social phenomena visible, meaningful, and communicable by articulating them as part of particular orders of knowledge, that is, as part of a particular set of rules for the production of acceptable statements in an institutionalized process of articulation. In the discursive perspective, meaning is made possible by these rules of acceptance (Fairclough 1992, pp. 39–49; Foucault 1972).

The Rise of Neoliberalism in Denmark

We will use this approach to examine the role of neoliberalism in Danish economic policy making. Neoliberalism in this context was a loose discursive ensemble of which certain elements came to be seen as especially influential. First, it was distinguished from Keynesian demand-side politics by an emphasis on the supply-side as an ideal point of departure for economic policy making. Second, it was understood as focusing on the boundary between public and private and emphasized liberalization, that is, restoring market relations and removing obstacles to free competition. Third, it was understood as entailing attempts to introduce market principles of organization, either by moving functions from the public to the private sector and removing restrictions on the operation of private markets or by marketizing the public sector through reforms that created or simulated competition among public institutions or depoliticized or individualized decision making in and around public institutions.

Neoliberalism became part of Danish politics but in a rather selective fashion. There were no radical neoliberal reforms of public policy making. The process was both gradual and partial, and the overall degree of liberalization in the Danish public sector was less than that in some other countries, such as Britain. There was no *withdrawal* of the state, but rather a process of *reform* in which both governments and certain parts of the central administration, in collaboration with particular interest organizations, initiated liberalization in particular sectors (Jessop 1990). Also, only certain neoliberal notions were introduced and only in certain policy areas. Notably, privatization and deregulation played only a limited role, partly because there were very few nationalized enterprises to privatize in the first place and because Danish industrial policy in general never involved drastic state intervention. However, even those neoliberal ideas that did gain prominence in Danish reform initiatives were interpreted and implemented in very selective ways. Marketization, for instance, was interpreted as part of a process of strengthening the overall coordination of the public and private sector rather than as a process of dismantling or weakening public or political control of the production of services.

What accounts for this selectivity in the Danish political context? The most obvious explanation is the peculiar parliamentary situation with many small parties and few possibilities to establish majority governments. Indeed, the parliamentary basis of the bourgeois coalition governments from 1982 to 1993 was extremely weak. Minority coalition governments were the rule. This not only weakened the ideological profile of the government but also forced it to compromise with parties outside government, most commonly the Social Democratic Party. In fact, minority governments or coalition governments have been a persistent trait of Danish policy making since the Second World War. Not even the Social Democrats, the largest party in Denmark, have ever had a majority of their own but have depended routinely on the support of at least one bourgeois party. As a result, any Danish government has to orient its policy toward a liberal but socially oriented middle ground — a situation that has usually precluded radical reform in the areas of welfare, industrial, and economic policy. Yet while this parliamentary situation explains the *lack* of radical reform, it does little to explain the *presence* and *unique character* of neoliberal reform in Denmark.

Certainly, part of this story entails the usual political struggles that involve a variety of actors, including political parties, business associations, labor unions, and the like. However, to fully account for the unique interpretation and implementation of neoliberal ideas, we must examine the conditions of translation in the Danish context. It is this part of the story that we are concerned with here. We must locate the mechanisms of selection in the particular discursive order of the Danish polity, and particularly the discursive order that emerged as a result of the institutionalization of structural policy. Our argument is that neoliberal ideas, policies, and forms of organization were translated into the Danish context in ways that were enabled and constrained by the discursive mechanisms operating in the field of economic policy but also in ways that reflected the broader historical and institutional characteristics of the Danish polity. This does not mean that neoliberalism had no consequences. Translation means not only selection but also a possible displacement in the existing system of interpretation and the triggering of new forms of political and social action. In other words, even the Danish interpretation of Keynesianism changed over time and was gradually displaced in the sense that some of its elements obtained slightly different meanings. Moreover, the translation of neoliberal ideas created new forms of political attention, new policies, and new possibilities for political action.

Thus, the development of Danish neoliberalism must be seen as part of the discursive history of the Danish polity after 1945, and particularly the history of structural policy after 1975. In the following two sections we account for this discursive and institutional history. First, we describe briefly the creation of the broader discursive order shaping economic policy making in Denmark, namely the "negotiated economy" that emerged as a result of the institutionalization of socioeconomic problems of coordination in the postwar era. Second, we outline the development of structural policy and describe how neoliberal distinctions became part of the formulation of that policy.

Discursive and Institutional History of the Danish Polity after 1945

The institutionalization of structural policy was part of the gradual articulation and stabilization of a broader socioeconomic frame of meaning in Danish politics and the establishment and transformation of an institutional ordering of political and economic relations that we call the negotiated economy. This frame of meaning is a particular Danish economic policy discourse built around an ideal conception of socioeconomic balance through negotiated coordination of policy among various autonomous actors in the national economy. This discourse constitutes a blend of liberal and social democratic principles. It is liberal in the sense that it respects the autonomy of economic actors and organized interests; that it downplays direct state intervention into the economy, preferring negotiated settlements instead; and that it views the Danish economy as an open economy that is exposed to international competition and that must find ways to become and remain internationally competitive. It is social democratic in the sense that it portrays the national economy as a "community of fate" of a multiplicity of social interests and that it attempts to secure the interests of the whole by inducing the parts to act responsibly with respect to the overall socioeconomic balance (Pedersen 1999). To illustrate briefly, the process of articulation and stabilization of this socioeconomic frame of meaning is reflected in three overlapping phases of policy articulation and institution building (Pedersen 1993).

First, from 1945 through the 1960s wage formation and labor markets were of concern. In this phase, the key problem of the Danish economy was conceptualized not only as a problem of macroeconomic management, but as one of socioeconomic coordination between wage formation and the overall development of the national economy. Wage structures and labor markets, it was believed, needed to be maintained in ways that better facilitated economic growth. In this view, responsibility for economic coordination lay both with the state and with the peak organizations in the Danish labor market. This problem was articulated in a series of public investigations and official blueprints that defined labor market organizations as responsible for the resolution of the wage and labor market coordination problem but also emphasized the autonomous status of these organizations, thus pointing to the need for voluntary coordination and mutual restraint in the labor market.[6] From the early 1960s, there was gradual institution building in relation to this coordination problem, such as the creation of an Economic Advisory Council of economic experts designed to create a common awareness of coordination problems in the economy. There was also experimentation with active labor market and incomes policies that became stable parts of Danish economic policy making during the 1970s.

Second, from the late 1960s through the 1980s there was concern with the increasing size and growth of the public sector. This problem was first articulated in two major reports on long-term planning in 1971 and 1973 and was further articulated in later publications from the Ministry of Finance (Finansministeriet 1971, 1972). These reports called for a significant degree of public-sector decentralization by granting the municipalities responsibility for a constantly growing part of public expenditures. The question was how to ensure fiscally responsible municipalities while maintaining their autonomous status vis-à-vis the national government. This was resolved by defining public expenditures as a problem and gradually institutionalizing this idea through the creation and use by the state of new economic models and budgetary systems, and through the creation of a system of budget negotiations between the Ministry of Finance and the municipalities that was governed by the goal of limiting total public expenditures. This system was implemented during the late 1970s and early 1980s.

Third, beginning in the mid-1970s Danish economic problems were conceptualized as stemming from the structure of the Danish economy itself. The
structural problem entailed a concern with the competitiveness of the national
economy, a preoccupation with the supply-side (i.e., the conditions of production rather than demand and consumption), and a focus on structural as
opposed to conjunctural barriers to competitiveness. Initially, the competitiveness problem was viewed as having to do with a large public sector that put
severe constraints on the cost-competitiveness of exporting firms. However, it
gradually came to be associated with a number of problems inherent in the
structure and organization of the private sector, such as low levels of technological development and an inability of firms to adequately adapt and innovate. During the 1980s a more coherent structural policy framework was articulated that first involved industrial policy and later public expenditure
policy. The emergent conception of structural policy was one that emphasized
the continuous and voluntary restructuring of the Danish economy through
the creation of various private and public policy-making and implementing
bodies. This approach was gradually institutionalized in industrial, labor market, educational, and administrative policy areas.

In the course of these processes of problem formulation, articulation, and
institutionalization a new institutional order emerged. In a number of policy areas the organizing principles shifted from those of either a mixed or
market economy to those of a negotiated economy (Nielsen and Pedersen
1991). Whereas both the mixed and market economy were based on a clear
division of labor between the sovereign state and an autonomous market—
a clear distinction between public and private decisions—the negotiated
economy entailed political and economic processes and relations that were
neither public nor private but situated between public authority and private
autonomy. Thus, the negotiated economy was a system of governance where
economic coordination was achieved through institutionalized games of negotiation among autonomous actors in both the public and the private sector and was conditioned by an overarching, shared socioeconomic frame of
meaning.

Furthermore, whereas policy formation and implementation in both market and mixed economies were centered around the state hierarchy, notably
the legislature and the executive branches, policy formation and implementation in the negotiated economy took place in a more complex set of complementary institutions. *Policy institutions* (e.g., public commissions) identified socioeconomic problems, related them to particular policies (e.g., wage or
labor-market policy problems) and formulated general guidelines for their resolution. *Campaign institutions* (e.g., the Economic Advisory Council) com-
municated socioeconomic conceptions to the broader public and engaged in
processes of persuasion to create a focus on particular socioeconomic problems
in order to get them on the political agenda. *Discourse institutions* (e.g., ana-

lytical units in the Ministry of Finance) created the theoretical and empirical
language of socioeconomic problem solving through the development of socioeconomic theories and models that could depict and predict causal relations and dependencies in the economy as a systematic basis for the ongoing
identification of socioeconomic problems. *Negotiation and arbitration institutions* (e.g., the biannual wage negotiations between employer federations and
the organizations of labor) facilitated policy negotiations, adjudicated settlements, and resolved disputes. In this institutional network shared problems
were formulated, common policy frames were articulated, and procedures
were stabilized that entailed problem solving via institutionalized learning
through which interests and actions could be developed and coordinated
through knowledge production, campaigning and negotiations without automatic recourse to authoritative state intervention.

    Two points are important. On the one hand, these arrangements did not pre-
vail in all aspects of economic policy making, nor did they erase the institutions and mechanisms of the market or the mixed economy. Rather, when
negotiated arrangements were introduced in a policy area, they tended to repo-
sition the existing institutions so that, for instance, state legislation or intervention became articulated and institutionalized as part of more complex
games of negotiation.(Kjær, Pedersen, and Andersen 1996). On the other
hand, these changes eventually entailed the translation of certain neoliberal
ideas and concepts into the Danish context. In wage formation, neoliberal
ideas favoring voluntary rather than state-mandated bargaining as well as the
autonomy of private actors vis-à-vis the state were translated into a prevailing
socioeconomic discourse that did *not* accept that wages should be set by unbridled market forces. In the public sector, neoliberal notions of limiting public expenditures and decentralizing state authority were translated into a prevailing socioeconomic discourse that did *not* accept the outright dismantling
of state authority, just its negotiated devolution to lower levels of government
and labor market organizations. In structural policy, the neoliberal emphasis
on supply-side policies was translated into a prevailing socioeconomic discourse that did *not* reject the significance of various "interventionist" industrial
and expenditure policies, but rather favored their negotiated devolution to
lower levels of the public administration. Finally, insofar as institution building in general was concerned, the neoliberal idea that economic policy making should be removed from the traditional legislative and executive hierarchies of the state was translated into a prevailing socioeconomic discourse that
did *not* reject the facilitative role of the state in economic affairs, but rather favored its negotiated devolution into a more complex and decentralized set of
institutional links between the government, local authorities, and private organizations. In this case, the result was that the adoption of neoliberal concepts
occurred at a time of extensive institution building. This resulted in the development of a *negotiated* economic model — an institutional arrangement far

from the sort of *free market* model that neoliberalism generally favors. Let us look more closely at the translation of neoliberalism in the area of structural policy.

Structural Policy and Neoliberalism in Denmark, 1975–1995

The development of structural policy in the last twenty years is one of the most conspicuous aspects of modern Danish economic policy making. What began as a complement to existing forms of policy and policy making has gradually come to constitute an overarching political project in the context of which other ideals, policies, and institutional arrangements are positioned and given meaning.

Although neoliberal ideas have been part of the history of structural policy in varying ways since the late 1970s, liberal ideas were evident in Danish economic policy making long before 1975. As we have already indicated, there were important liberal elements in the institutionalization of the socioeconomic discourse early during the postwar period. Therefore, when neoliberal ideas began to be articulated in the context of structural policy, the effect was not so much a total shift in policy orientation as a displacement in the relation between the existing elements of the discourse. Here we describe the development of structural policy in terms of three phases of policy formation and institutionalization. In each one we characterize the manner in which neoliberal ideas were translated in the context of structural policy. We then describe the changing institutional order of structural policy and attempt to identify the emergent institutional processes that account for the way neoliberalism was translated into the Danish context.

The Formulation of a Structural Problem: Structural Policy as Sector Policy (1975–1985)

Danish economic policy making was traditionally viewed as involving a trade-off between employment and balanced budgets that could be solved through the management of aggregate demand. In this perspective, economic imbalance first and foremost reflected conjunctural trends in the economy, notably vacillation in the business cycle, that could be dealt with effectively through fiscal or incomes policies.

However, in the latter half of the 1970s this conjunctural interpretation of the economic crisis was challenged by a view that stressed that Denmark's economic problems were rooted in the structure of the economy itself. This structural conception was formulated in response to the evident failure of various short-term and demand-oriented policy responses to the international recession. In particular, several actors, including organized labor and the Danish Federation of Industry, saw the problems of crisis management as an expression of structural problems on the supply-side rather than on the demand-side of the Danish economy. Whereas labor saw the problem as having to do with the basic organization and orientation of Danish industry, the Federation of Industry viewed the problem as stemming from the constraints on export-oriented firms caused by a large public sector that tended to favor industries oriented primarily toward domestic markets. As a result, labor called for stronger industrial policy, but capital called for wage restraint and public expenditure policies designed to improve the international competitiveness of Danish industry. The key implication of the debate, however, was a common focus on structural problems in the national economy and a common linking of macroeconomic problems and problems of industrial competitiveness (Pedersen et al. 1992).

As it turned out, the formulation of a more structural view of the problems of Danish industry led quickly to a revitalization of industrial policy, which was now seen as a tool for socioeconomic reconstruction. This led to attempts to formulate a technology policy aimed at improving the technological competitiveness of Danish firms through programs targeted at particular industries or technologies or at public-private cooperation in the area of technological development. In the technology policy interpretation of structural problems, the key problem was the low level of technological development in industry, partly due to the small size and limited financial strength of Danish firms. The key actors in this strategy were the Ministry of Industry and the network of public and semipublic research and development (R&D) institutions under the auspices of the Ministry.

In this early phase of structural policy development, neoliberal concepts and ideas were important but rather limited in terms of their impact on policy-making discourse and institutional development overall. The questioning of demand-oriented macroeconomic policies was certainly inspired by the international debate on supply-side economics and the neoliberal critique of state planning and economic intervention. At the same time, however, the idea of using industrial policy, which was abhorred by neoliberals, to foster structural adjustment and thus international competitiveness, even if it was tempered by concerns about controlling the growth of public expenditures, was of foremost importance. Moreover, the development of sectorally oriented technology policy signaled a move *away* from a traditional nonselective and noninterventionist industrial policy toward industrial policy that involved a greater directive role for the government—again, something that was antithetical to neoliberalism. This shift was also reflected institutionally in the fact that significant changes had been made in the Ministry of Industry and elsewhere that led directly to new, more active, and project-oriented policy programs, such as in the areas of information technology and "new materials."

Structural Policy as Cross-Sector Policy (1985–1990)

In the mid-1980s a broader definition of structural problems developed whereby the Ministries of Finance and Industry adopted the concept of "structural competitiveness," in which the competitiveness of Danish industry was seen as being dependent on a much wider variety of structural problems in the Danish economy that resulted not just in low R&D but in an orientation toward producing for low-growth markets and a general lack of adaptative and innovative capacities in Danish industry. It was argued that in order to resolve these problems, coordinated efforts were needed in areas other than just industrial policy. There was also a need to reform state administrative and regulatory structures in several policy areas (Nielsen 1991).

The Ministries of Industry and Finance as well as the Economic Advisory Council took active parts in formulating a framework for structural policy that transcended the area of industrial policy. Industrial policy had preoccupied policy makers during the previous period, and entailed the coordination of industrial policy with other policy areas, such as labor-market and R&D policy. A series of policy publications linked the need for economic growth and structural adjustment to initiatives that emphasized much closer coordination between various policy areas and between public and private actors with respect to industrial development, research, and education. The key problem of Danish industry in this interpretation was not only its low degree of technological development but also its inability to adjust to new positions of strength in the international competitive environment. Increased dialogue between various public and private actors was called for in order to develop policy to facilitate this end. The key actors in this regard were several sector ministries and a variety of firms, industries, and other private actors.

Furthermore, in 1986 a process of reorganization started in the Ministry of Industry. Several subsidy programs were terminated and the administrative structure of the Ministry was changed to more closely approximate a corporate structure — that is, an administrative form based on the management principles of private corporations and intended in part to improve the efficiency of industrial policy. A few years later and in tandem with these changes at the Ministry, several private and semipublic industrial and structural policy organizations began to emerge in an effort to expand the scope of structural policy. For instance, the Forum for Industrial Development was founded in 1988 and comprised representatives from firms, institutional investors, trade unions, and other private organizations. It sought to put issues of industrial restructuring on the agenda and later also pushed broader issues, such as welfare reform. Indeed, during the late 1980s there was an explosive growth in local and regional industrial and structural policy initiatives like this that were favored by groups representing a broad selection of actors, including public agencies, industrial associations, R&D institutions, and private firms (Amin and Thomas 1996).

Throughout this period a number neoliberal ideas and distinctions were introduced into the structural policy debate. One was the notion that state subsidies to industry presented "barriers" to adaptability and therefore to competitiveness. Another was the idea that public regulation had adverse effects on private firms. Still, it was not public regulation per se that was seen as the problem, as conventional neoliberal discourse maintained, but rather a particular form of regulation that posed barriers to industrial adaptation and competitiveness. As a result, ministries, policy agencies, and other administrative bodies relevant to industrial performance were not to *withdraw* from their activities, as neoliberals would have had it, but to *reorganize* according to the needs and practices of industry and other relevant economic actors. Thus, on the one hand, implementation of the corporate model in the Ministry of Industry was designed not so much to liberalize or deregulate industrial policy but to improve its efficiency — a clear case where an important neoliberal concept was translated into public administrative practice by fitting it to the Danish context. On the other hand, public bodies were to become more goal- and market-oriented, professional, and open to dialogue with a more inclusive group of private actors as well as with other public bodies.

Structural Policy as a Macro Policy (the 1990s)

Around 1990 the conception of structural problems shifted from an orientation toward barriers to growth and adaptation in Danish industry to one toward the adaptation of Danish society as a whole — both the public and private sectors — to a challenging future in a world of European integration and economic globalization. The new conception of structural policy was one of a much more continuous, simultaneous, and, importantly, *integrated* structural adaptation of the public and private sectors. This was foreshadowed by the development of public-sector and structural policies since 1985. Insofar as the public sector was concerned, specifically public expenditure policy and public sector modernization, the long-term development of the public sector was now seen increasingly as being connected with the overall structural development of Danish society. Neither one could develop effectively without the development of the other. For instance, it was no longer enough to limit public expenditures and to make the public sector more efficient; one also had to consider the relationship between the public and private sector and the overall dynamics of development of society. In the context of structural policy, one became increasingly aware of the role of the public sector in facilitating the restructuring of industry.

As a result, structural policy gradually became more macro-oriented in the sense that it entailed not only coordination and restructuring in and between policy sectors, but also a continuous restructuring of the entire Danish economy. Structural policy now merged with public sector modernization policies and became oriented toward the restructuring of the *boundaries* both between policy fields and institutions, on the one hand, and between the public and private sectors, on the other. The goal of creating an efficient and adaptive public sector, which had been articulated in 1984 through the Modernization Program of the bourgeois government, was now linked to the goal of creating an adaptive and future-oriented industrial structure in the private sector. The key problem and object of attention became the adaptation of Danish society to future developments in the European Union and the international economy. The key actors were a multitude of both public and private actors at the national and local level that all shared responsibility for the continuous development and adaptation of the Danish economy.

This was perhaps clearest in the area of public sector modernization policy. Here policies were institutionalized that attempted to consider the role and boundaries of the entire public sector. First, starting in 1990, Fiscal Policy Statements that were published by the Ministry of Finance began to treat questions of structural transformation and structural policy making as the over-arching consideration toward which most other policies were oriented, including stabilization policies. Second, several programs and plans were initiated to promote experimentation with new types of public sector governance and new relations between public and private bodies. For example, at the regional level new forms of dialogue and problem solving were tried that involved local authorities, trade organizations, and private companies.

In this third phase of structural policy development, drawing attention to and problematizing the existing boundaries between state and economy — a common theme in neoliberalism — became a key ingredient in the formulation of structural problems and, consequently, in policy and institutional reform. Of course, a change in boundaries was usually seen as part of the new problem of improving structural competitiveness vis-à-vis European political and economic integration. Still, although the neoliberal emphasis on state-economy boundaries was paramount in assessing structural problems, within the Danish context it was often more an issue of how to better coordinate and *integrate* policies and structures on each side of the boundary rather than *sharpen* and *deepen* the divide between public and private, as neoliberalism favored.

Nevertheless, neoliberal ideas and distinctions were especially pronounced during this period. Indeed, the rise of neoliberal ideas helped initiate the debate about the need to rethink the established boundary between public and private sectors in the first place, but also about the need to improve the general environment for market activity not only by introducing new governance principles into the public sector, but also by limiting public regulation, improving public services and transferring activities from the public to the private sector. Eventually, these themes were institutionalized to a degree through ex-

periments in contracting out the provision of public services to the private sector, in various forms of public utility privatization, and in the establishment
of contractual arrangements between ministries and government agencies.
Again, however, these initiatives were articulated not as goals in themselves, as
neoliberalism does, but as part of a broad program to resolve structural problems by improving the adaptive capacity of Danish society as it coped with increased European integration and competition. For example, the need to
liberalize particular regulated industries was motivated by the problem of competitiveness and the potential for development in related industries as well as
by the anticipated trend toward liberalization that would eventually be required by the European community. Furthermore, experiments with contracting out were not seen as ends in themselves but as part of a broader set of
structural policies (Andersen 1997).

The Institutional Order: The Early 1980s and the Early 1990s Compared

We have seen that the translation of neoliberal ideas and themes into the Danish context was conditioned by the already existing discourse and institutional
arrangements of the negotiated economy. Throughout this twenty-five year period, three rather basic mechanisms played a particularly important role in all
the developments we have described above: problem formation, codification,
consensus building. Recall that the negotiated economy is an institutional
order that builds on and makes possible collective learning. These three
mechanisms facilitate this. However, each underwent significant change during the 1980s. These changes are best revealed by contrasting certain fundamental features of the discursive and institutional orders of the early 1980s
with those of the early 1990s, periods that marked different organizing principles before and after the institutionalization of structural policy as well as the
beginning and end points of the bourgeois coalition governments in Denmark. Overall, this was a period of increasing elaboration and complexity not
only in the general organizational principles but also, importantly, in the
learning processes of the negotiated economy — a transformation that was
linked, in part, to the gradual translation of neoliberal ideas into Danish discourse and practice.

First, the collective construction and articulation of socioeconomic problems is a central feature of the Danish negotiated economy and one that leads
to the institutionalization of taken-for-granted understandings of what these
problems are. We refer to this as the *problem formation* mechanism. During
the 1980s and early 1990s there was a fundamental change in how problems
were perceived and formulated. During the early 1980s problems were defined
in terms of the past. For example, it had long been assumed that policy ought

to be directed toward maintaining an ideal socioeconomic balance reflected in measures such as balanced budgets. Under these discursive conditions what was perceived as problematic and requiring explanation, evaluation, and policy management were the factors that moved the economy away from the desired balance. However, during the early 1990s problems were defined much more in terms of the future. Specifically, the concern was how the national economy and its position vis-à-vis other national economies related to the future development of markets and political structures, including the development of the unified European market project as well as the more general globalization of economic activity. What had to be articulated now was an imagined future and the associated problems that might be anticipated with it. Consequently, the policy process became more preoccupied with definitions, predictions, and anticipatory strategies for future problems than with descriptions and explanations of past and present conditions.

Second, actors in the negotiated economy verbalize conflicts and disagreements, articulate interests, coordinate behavior, modify courses of action, create strategies for actions, and ultimately codify decisions through negotiation. We refer to this simply as the *codification* mechanism. Two important developments occurred here. On the one hand, whereas codification initially occurred within fairly stable cognitive and institutional frameworks, it now took place within more open-ended bounds due partly to the more future-oriented nature of problem formation. On the other hand, codification became professionalized. For example, in order to become a participant in the structural policy debate, actors now had to legitimize themselves by reference to being familiar and comfortable, if not masterful, with particular and somewhat exclusive bodies of scientific knowledge. Among other things, this professionalization had been mirrored since the late 1980s in the sharply increasing number of secretariats and specialist functions in ministries and interest organizations. The form of writing in many reports published by these secretariats and organizations increasingly resembled the style of more scientific publications (Pedersen and Pedersen 2000).

Third, a key element of the negotiated economy is, of course, the *consensus* mechanism. Here the formulation of problems and coordination of behavior is made possible and constrained by the continuous production of a basic and widely shared understanding of the situation — the socioeconomic frame of meaning — among all participants engaged in the articulation and negotiation of problems and solutions. In the early 1980s this process was closely linked to a corporatist type of institutional arrangement that included bipartite or tripartite consultations in various policy fields. During this time a consensus on substantive policy prescriptions was a precondition for joint action. In other words, only those prescriptive measures to which all parties could agree were enacted as official policy. However, beginning in the early 1990s there was less emphasis on consensus over substantive matters and more on methods and procedures for devising policy prescriptions. Hence, there has been a shift from substantive to a kind of procedural consensus.

In sum, although the negotiated economy has always been a unique form of collective learning that contributed directly to policy and institutional change, key elements of this learning process — the mechanisms of problem formation, codification and consensus — changed as neoliberalism was translated into the Danish context. However, it is important to recognize that these changes were themselves driven, at least in part, by this translation. In other words, as neoliberal concepts were incorporated into discourse, they began to have significant effects on these mechanisms. This involved the selection and displacement of ideas and concepts as well as the triggering of shifts in policy orientations and reform plans.

For example, these three mechanisms contributed to the *selection* of neoliberal ideas in the sense that they determined what ideas and issues could fit into or become part of the learning process. Notably, the problem-formation mechanism ensured that only issues and ideas that could be defined as socioeconomic problems could become part of the discussions about structural policy. Thus, the issue of supply-side structural barriers to industrial growth became part of the existing economic policy discourse because it was possible to formulate this issue as a socioeconomic problem. Conversely, the issue of preserving or extending individual rights vis-à-vis the state, another important neoliberal theme in other countries, was not selected as important for consideration because it did not fit the prevailing conception of what was an "acceptable" socioeconomic problem. Once the supply-side orientation had been translated, it transformed the problem-formation mechanisms by opening up a whole new range of possibilities for defining and formulating economic problems.

The translation of neoliberal ideas into the Danish policy discourse also *displaced* certain elements of the discursive and learning process. For example, the consensus mechanism was altered by the introduction of a neoliberal emphasis on structural rather than conjunctural problems. This led to the expansion of formal procedures of participation in policy negotiation and consensus building. The initial conjunctural perspective on socioeconomic problems, especially that which focused on problems associated with business-cycle fluctuations, entailed a stable pattern of bipartite or tripartite interest representation in negotiation because these were problems that could be dealt with through well-established wage-negotiation institutions. However, problems of structural competitiveness were more complex, involved a multiplicity of structural difficulties that could not be handled in one negotiation arena or policy area, and required a more integrated approach spanning several arenas as well as multiple levels and departments of government. This precipitated a revision of the procedures for consensus building, notably the inclusion of a wider and often shifting set of participants, such as representatives from R&D institutes and new government agencies and municipalities, as noted earlier.

Finally the translation of neoliberalism triggered a *shift in attention* toward new aspects of reality, made possible new ways of conceptualizing problems and solutions, and created possibilities for new types of political action and intervention. For example, neoliberalism's emphasis on structural competitiveness shifted policy makers' attention to current and future structural and organizational constraints in the economy. This led to changes in codification mechanisms, which increasingly emphasized the importance of supply-side professionalization and training strategies. In terms of labor market policy, attention shifted from demand-side job creation strategies to supply-side human resource strategies, where the idea was to improve worker competence and skills in order to facilitate greater flexibility and efficiency in the labor market.

Conclusion

The preceding analysis entailed two parts.[7] First was a diachronic analysis that described the gradual articulation and institutionalization of a socioeconomic frame of meaning with the creation of a negotiated economy, particularly with respect to the development of structural policy. This involved a description of how ideal conceptions were formulated and became part of a process of articulation and institutionalization; how a new discourse or order of knowledge was constructed; and how this discourse became institutionalized or embodied in a particular set of institutions, thereby lending them an important degree of authority and stability.[8] Second was a synchronic analysis that described the selection of neoliberal ideals, the displacement in horizons of meaning, and the triggering of new ways of conceptualizing problems, and therefore considered what was politically possible. This depicted the emergent order of the negotiated economy as a system of institutionalized collective learning and described the displacements and changes in the problem formation, codification, and consensus mechanisms that it experienced in connection with the rise of neoliberalism. Whereas the diachronic analysis was an account of the gradual articulation and institutionalization of particular ideal conceptions, the synchronic analysis was an attempt to account for change in some of the overarching learning processes through which emergent institutional orders were stabilized and transformed.[9]

Through this approach we described the development of structural policy vis-à-vis neoliberalism as one of translation rather than diffusion. More specifically, we insisted that ideas should not be considered as external sources of change, but as part of a contextually specific process of articulation and institutionalization. Ideas help constitute different conceptions of change within a discursive and institutional order. Through their translation into institutionalized collective learning processes, they displace already existing discursive arrangements as a result of their effects on policy conceptions, political economic agendas, and political strategies.

These findings both resonate with and diverge from analyses in the tradition of historical institutionalism. In many ways, our empirical story supports the historical institutionalist thesis of national specificity in the response to neoliberalism, what Steven Vogel (1996, p. 260) calls "differential responses to common challenges." Our research design does not involve comparative analysis. Nevertheless, although neoliberal ideas were articulated in several national contexts, our study suggests that one should not expect convergence on a single neoliberal model of policy making. Here we agree with much of the comparative historical institutionalist research that stresses that national institutions or orientations mediate the way neoliberalism is incorporated into specific practices.[10] In line with these studies, we would emphasize that in Denmark a particular socioeconomic frame of meaning, the institutions of the negotiated economy, and certain processes of institutionalized learning played key roles in determining how neoliberalism was translated into practice. We would also prefer the notion of translation to that of diffusion, which is implied in some historical institutionalist analysis insofar as change is attributed to "common challenges." With the notion of translation we avoid the idea of a common challenge to particular systems — an idea that tends to exaggerate the continuity, stability, and universal identity of the phenomenon of neoliberalism. In the translation approach "common challenges" are always local discursive constructions. Although we may find similar distinctions and models across discursive and institutional settings, the meaning and identity of neoliberalism is always local.[11]

Historical institutionalists have begun to address the important problem of ideas in institutional analysis. One central line of argument here is that ideas may be seen as causal factors that influence political behavior by shaping perceptions of decision makers, providing rationales for action, or filtering interpretations of the external world. In more elaborate versions the question of ideas involves more complex concepts. Notably, Hall introduced the concept of policy paradigm that describes how ideas are part of more complex learning and knowledge systems. Similarly, Sheri Berman (1998, p. 21) discusses programmatic beliefs that, like ideologies, "are abstract; systematic and coordinated; and marked by integrated assertions, theories and goals . . . [which provide] mutual expectations and a mutual predictability of intention."

Our approach to the analysis of ideas, discourse, and institutions differs from theirs mainly in the sense that we do not see causal explanation as the chief purpose of the analysis. Rather, our discursive institutionalist strategy aims at contextual understanding of particular cases. In other words, our approach does not attempt to provide an ex ante specification of variables and causal relations among them, but aims at describing processes of discursive and institutional construction that constitute social relations and interests. Hence, our

analysis of the Danish case described the history of neoliberalism as a history
through which certain discursive distinctions were articulated, stabilized, and
displaced in ways that have constituted particular horizons of meaning and
spaces of possibility for political action.

Discursive institutionalism also bears some resemblance to the so-called
narrative turn in social science, such as the "analytic narrative" approach represented by Robert Bates and his colleagues (1998). Their approach is narrative in the sense that it pays close attention to detailed stories and accounts,
and the contexts within which they unfold. Moreover, their analytic narratives
are explorations of concrete historical cases that are "problem driven, not theory driven; they are motivated by a desire to account for particular events or
outcomes. They are devoted to the exploration of cases" (p. 11). Similar to
discursive institutionalism, their approach starts from a thick description of a
historical case rather than a specification and operationalization of variables.
The purpose of the analysis in both approaches is to "cut deeply into the
specifics of time and space, and to locate and trace the processes that generate outcomes of interest" (p. 12). Indeed, we have tried to develop a contextual understanding of the role of neoliberalism in the Danish case through an
analysis that accounts for the complexity of the local discursive and institutional context.

However, the analytic narrative approach differs from ours in its attempt to
use advanced rational choice models to account for the logic of the processes
described in narrative form. In contrast, we focus on the notions of translation,
selection, displacement, and the like through synchronic and diachronic
analysis. Furthermore, our conceptualization of mechanisms of change does
not draw on a formalized and generalized theoretical model but rather constitutes a preliminary reconstruction of local discursive and institutional patterns.
Hence, we are much less interested in theoretical prediction than in understanding the particularities of historically specific cases. Finally, we differ even
more fundamentally in the way we conceive of and use narratives. Bates and
his colleagues construct a coherent narrative account through a multiplicity of
sources, which is then subjected to logical, game-theoretical analysis and thus
abstracted from reality. We reconstruct a historically specific discourse as something that is in this world — not an abstract analytical construct — and that has
attained its own degree of logical coherence and narrativity. In this sense our
approach is one that sees "narratives as viable realities (i.e., a social phenomenon) in themselves" (Abbott 1992, p. 440).

A few additional comments about the relationship between discursive and
rational choice institutionalism are in order. Discursive institutionalism entails
a rethinking of both the notion of ideas and the notion of change, but does it
also entail a rejection of explanations starting from a notion of rational behavior? There is both an empirical and a theoretical aspect to this question. First,
we have selected as our primary object of analysis the creation of macroframes

of action, rather than choosing microgames of negotiation and policy making as rational choice theorists tend to do. The story of neoliberalism could no doubt have been told "from below," that is, as microgames of coordination and resource allocation in the public sector involving individual political actors, institutions, and organizations. Indeed, there have been several interesting case studies of the microprocesses of Danish policy making, negotiation, and institution building. Our lack of emphasis on microbehavior does not so much reflect a theoretical stance as it reflects a conscious choice of level of analysis.

Second, the question of rational behavior also raises a more theoretical problem from the perspective of discursive institutionalism. In our view, rational choice models may provide fruitful rationalizations of the behavior of individual actors engaging in concrete games of policy making and negotiation. Here we embrace the idea that several logics of action, including those of rational choice, may coexist and provide us with relevant explanations of behavior. Following James March and Johan P. Olsen (1989), "logics of appropriateness," or rule-governed behavior, may coexist with "logics of consequentiality," or intentionally rational behavior. However, rather than viewing rationality as a comprehensive or constitutive aspect of behavior as such, the discursive institutionalist approach is interested in *the conditions of rationality*, that is, the historical emergence and stabilization of conditions under which rational behavior becomes possible in the first place. In other words, we see rationality not as a given but as an *outcome* of historical processes of discursive construction and institutionalization. Thus, logics of consequentiality are always embedded in and made possible by particular stable social conceptions that identify who is expected to engage in certain types of behaviors; what behaviors are appropriate; and what motives are acceptable in order for individuals, groups, and organizations to act *as if* they were rational. In our society instrumentally rational behavior has come to be valued and conceptions of rational behavior are now something that are continually produced and reshaped as part of broader discursive frames of meaning. Indeed, the creation of rational actors has been a chief concern of administrative policy in Denmark and elsewhere during the last twenty years. Shifting our attention toward the discursive and institutional preconditions of rationality is therefore an attempt to highlight a fundamental aspect of neoliberalism as a broad political project — namely, that it is not so much about freeing particular "natural forces" of society as it is about constructing these forces in the first place.

In sum, the discursive institutional approach is case- and problem-oriented, both synchronic and diachronic, and takes discourse as a social phenomenon in its own right. The purpose of discursive institutionalism is twofold. On the one hand, it seeks to describe and account for displacements in the horizons of meaning and spaces of possibility constituted by a particular institutional order. On the other hand, it addresses questions of ideas and change — and rationality — in such a manner that they are not reduced to ontological givens, black boxes, or epiphenomena, but become objects of empirical analysis in their own right.

Notes

The authors wish to express their gratitude for comments on earlier versions of this chapter to John L. Campbell, Tore Hafting, James G. March, John Hall, and the participants at the Second Conference on Institutional Analysis at Dartmouth College, 1998, and at seminars at SCANCOR, Stanford University, 1999.

1. Examples of the broad literature on neoliberalism include Wilensky 1991; Baldwin 1993; Pierson 1994; Berger and Dore 1996; Boyer and Drache 1996; and Vogel 1996.

2. For further discussion of the concept of diffusion, see Rogers 1962; Burt 1987; and Strang and Meyer 1994. For discussion of the distinction between diffusion and translation (or the related concepts of imitation and translation), see Latour 1996 and Czarniawska and Sevon 1996.

3. For overviews of various schools of institutional analysis, see Scott 1995; DiMaggio and Powell 1991; and Thelen and Steinmo 1992.

4. A similar point is discussed by Miller (1997).

5. This entails that the difficult question of the autonomy of discourse should be considered a historical and not a theoretical question.

6. One key publication was the official report on problems of cooperation in the Danish economic policy: Betænkning 154. 1956. *Samarbejdsproblemer I den danske Økonomiske politik*, Copenhagen.

7. For an elaboration of this analytical strategy under the heading of "institutional history," see Andersen and Kjær 1996.

8. In other versions, we have elaborated two more steps in the diachronic analysis following the three outlined here: *organization*, which designates the creation of various types of organizational actors and interorganizational patterns of relations, and *transformation*, which designates the formation of a set of strategies of transformation in a particular field.

9. The diachronic and the synchronic analysis constitute two different perspectives on change. The two perspectives differ in much the same way as the approach of the historian differs from that of many sociologists. Diachronic analysis considers change as historical variation over time and, like the historian, emphasizes the uniqueness and discontinuous nature of the processes under study. Synchronic analysis considers change as the dynamics (e.g., of selection and displacement) of a set of mechanisms built into and structuring processes at particular points in time.

10. Other examples of such comparative analyses of national responses to international or global developments are Gourevitch 1986; Hall 1989a; Steinmo, Thelen, and Longstreth 1992; and Guillen 1994.

11. See also Locke and Thelen 1995. This focus on context as a local construction is also a key feature in the work of Bruno Latour (1996).

References

Abbott, Andrew. 1992. "From Causes to Events: Notes on Narrative Positivism." *Sociological Methods and Research* 20(4)428–55.

Amin, Ash, and Damian Thomas. 1996. "The Negotiated Economy: State and Civic Institutions in Denmark." *Economy and Society* 25:255–81.

Andersen, Niels Å. 1997. *Udlicitering: Strategi og historie.* Copenhagen: Nyt fra Samfundsvidenskaberne.

Andersen, Niels Å., and Peter Kjær. 1996. "Institutional Change: An Analytical Strategy of Institutional History." COS Research Report. Copenhagen: Copenhagen Business School, May.

Betænkning 154. 1956: *Samarbejdsproblemer I Den Danske Økonomiske Politik.* Copenhagen.

Baldwin, David A., editor. 1993. *Neorealism and Neoliberalism: The Contemporary Debate.* New York: Columbia University Press.

Bates, Robert H., Avner Greif, Margaret Levi, Jean-Laurent Rosenthal, and Barry R. Weingast. 1998. *Analytic Narratives.* Princeton: Princeton University Press

Berger, Suzanne, and Ronald Dore, editors. 1996. *National Diversity and Global Capitalism.* Ithaca: Cornell University Press.

Berman, Sheri. 1998. *The Social Democratic Moment: Ideas and Politics in the Making of Interwar Europe.* Cambridge: Harvard University Press.

Boyer, Robert, and Daniel Drache. 1996. *States against Markets: The Limits of Globalization.* London: Routledge.

Burt, Ron S. 1987. "Social Contagion and Innovation: Cohesion versus Structural Equivalence." *American Journal of Sociology* 92:1287–1335.

Campbell, John L. 1998. "Institutional Analysis and the Role of Ideas in Political Economy." *Theory and Society* 27:377–409.

Czarniawska, Barbara, and Guje Sevon. 1996. *Translating Organizational Change.* Berlin: Aldine de Gruyter.

DiMaggio, Paul, and Walter Powell. 1991. Introduction. Pp. 1–40 in *The New Institutionalism in Organizational Analysis,* edited by Walter Powell and Paul DiMaggio. Chicago: University of Chicago Press.

Fairclough, Norman. 1992. *Discourse and Social Change.* London: Polity Press.

Finansministeriet. 1971. *Perspektivplanloegning 1970–1985.* Copenhagen.

———. 1973. *Perspektivplanloegning 1972–1987.* Copenhagen.

Foucault, Michel. 1972. *The Archaeology of Knowledge and the Discourse on Language.* New York: Pantheon Books.

Goldstein, Judith, and Robert O. Keohane, editors. 1993a. *Ideas and Foreign Policy: Beliefs, Institutions, and Political Change.* Ithaca: Cornell University Press.

———. 1993b. "Ideas and Foreign Policy: An Analytical Framework." Pp. 3–30 in *Ideas and Foreign Policy: Beliefs, Institutions, and Political Change,* edited by Judith Goldstein and Robert O. Keohane. Ithaca: Cornell University Press.

Gourevitch, Peter. 1986. *Politics in Hard Times: Comparative Responses to International Economic Crises.* Ithaca: Cornell University Press.

Guillen, Mauro F. 1994. *Models of Management: Work, Authority, and Organization in Comparative Perspective.* Chicago: University of Chicago Press.

Hall, Peter A., editor. 1989a. *The Political Power of Economic Ideas: Keynesianism across Nations.* Princeton: Princeton University Press.

———. 1989b. "Conclusion: The Politics of Keynesian Ideas." Pp. 361–92 in *The Political Power of Economic Ideas,* edited by Peter A. Hall. Princeton: Princeton University Press.

———. 1992. "The Movement from Keynesianism to Monetarism: Institutional Analysis and British Economic Policy in the 1970s." Pp. 90–113 in *Structuring Politics: Historical Institutionalism in Comparative Analysis,* edited by Sven Steinmo, Kathleen Thelen, and Frank Longstreth. New York: Cambridge University Press.

———. 1993. "Policy Paradigms, Social Learning, and the State: The Case of Economic Policymaking in Britain." *Comparative Politics* 25(3)275–96.

Jessop, Bob. 1990. *State Theory.* London: Polity Press.

Kjær Peter, Ove K. Pedersen, and Niels Å. Andersen. 1996. "On the Critique of Negotiated Economy." *Scandinavian Political Studies* 19(2)167–77.

Kögler, Hans Herbert. 1999. *The Power of Dialogue: Critical Hermeneutics after Gadamar and Foucault.* Cambridge: MIT Press.

Krasner, Stephen D. 1984. "Approaches to the State: Alternative Conceptions and Historical Dynamics." *Comparative Politics* 16(2)223–46.

Latour, Bruno. 1996. *Aramis, or The Love of Technology.* Cambridge: Harvard University Press.

Locke, Richard, and Kathleen Thelen. 1995. "Apples and Oranges Revisited: Contextualized Comparisons and the Study of Comparative Labor Politics." *Politics and Society* 23(3)337- 67.

March, James G., and Johan P. Olsen. 1989. *Rediscovering Institutions. The Organizational Basis of Politics.* New York: Free Press.

Miller, Peter. 1997. "The Multiplying Machine." *Accounting, Organizations and Society.* 22(3/4)355–36.

Nielsen, Klaus. 1991. "Learning to Manage the Supply-Side: Flexibility and Stability in Denmark." COS Research Report 7. Copenhagen: Copenhagen Business School, July.

Nielsen, Klaus, and Ove K. Pedersen. 1991. "From the Mixed Economy to the Negotiated Economy: The Scandinavian Countries." Pp. 145–68 in *Morality, Rationality, and Efficiency: New Perspectives on Socio-Economics,* edited by R. M. Coughlin. New York: M. E. Sharpe.

North, Douglass C. 1990. *Institutions, Institutional Change, and Economic Performance.* New York: Cambridge University Press.

Pedersen, Ove K. 1993. "The Institutional History of the Danish Polity: From a Market and Mixed Economy to a Negotiated Economy." Pp. 277–300 in *Institutional Change: Theory and Empirical Findings,* edited by Sven-Erik Sjøstrand. New York: M. E. Sharpe.

Pedersen, Ove K. 1999. "Den Samfundsøkonomiske Forvaltning — Om Forvaltning og Interesseorganisationer." Pp. 127–50 in *Stat, Forvaltning, og Samfund efter 1950,* edited by Peter Bogason. Dansk Forvaltningshistorie, Bind 3, Copenhagen: Jurist- og Økonomforbundets Forlag.

Pedersen, Ove K., Niels Å. Andersen, Peter Kjær and John Elberg. 1992. *Privat Politik: Projekt Forhandlingsøkonomi.* Copenhagen: Samfundslitteratur.

Pedersen, Ove K., and Dorthe Pedersen. 2000. "The Europeanization of Local Inter-

est in Denmark: The Strategic Choice of 'Go Through' vs. 'By-Pass' National Institutions." Pp. 51–76 in *Local and Regional Governance in Europe*, edited by Janerik
Gidlund and Magnus Jerneck. Aldershot, England: Edward Elgar.

Pierson, Paul. 1994: *Dismantling the Welfare State*. Cambridge: Cambridge University
Press.

Ricoeur, Paul. 1983. *Time and Narrative*. Vol. 1. Chicago: University of Chicago Press.

Rogers, Everett M. 1962. *Diffusion of Innovations*. New York: Free Press.

Scott, W. Richard. 1995. *Institutions and Organizations*. Thousand Oaks, CA: Sage.

Strang, David, and Meyer, John W. 1994. "Institutional Conditions for Diffusion." Pp.
100–112 in *Institutional Environments and Organizations: Structural Complexity
and Individualism*, edited by W. Richard Scott and John W. Meyer. Thousand Oaks,
CA: Sage.

Steinmo, Sven, Kathleen Thelen, and Frank Longstreth, editors. 1992. *Structuring Politics: Historical Institutionalism in Comparative Analysis*. New York: Cambridge University Press.

Thelen, Kathleen, and Sven Steinmo. 1992. "Historical Institutionalism in Comparative Politics." Pp. 1–32 in *Structuring Politics: Historical Institutionalism in Comparative Analysis*, edited by Sven Steinmo, Kathleen Thelen, and Frank Longstreth.
New York: Cambridge University Press.

Vogel, Steven K. 1996. *Freer Markets, More Rules: Regulatory Reform in Advanced Industrial Countries*. Ithaca: Cornell University Press.

Wagner, Peter, Björn Wittrock, and Richard Whitley, editors. 1991. *Discourses on Society: The Shaping of Social Science Disciplines*, Sociology of Science series, vol. 15.
New York: Kluwer Academic.

Wilensky, Harold L. 1991. *The Nation-State, Social Policy, and Economic Performance*,
Institute of Industrial Relations, University of California, Berkeley, Research Series
no. 69.

Chapter 10

Conclusion

THE SECOND MOVEMENT IN INSTITUTIONAL ANALYSIS

JOHN L. CAMPBELL AND OVE K. PEDERSEN

THE MAIN purpose of this project has been to present work by scholars representing the state of the art in institutional analysis in order to assess the prospects for theoretical development and synthesis. As such, the preceding chapters have analyzed the rise of neoliberalism, our common point of departure, from all four of the theoretical paradigms typically employed by scholars who are interested in studying political and economic institutions: rational choice, historical, organizational, and discursive institutionalism (see chapter 1). This chapter evaluates these analyses in order to compare, contrast, and draw conclusions about current institutional analysis as well as the phenomenon of neoliberalism. We argue that a *second movement* in institutional analysis is emerging. By second movement we mean an effort to stimulate dialogue among paradigms in order to explore the possibilities for theoretical cross-fertilization, rapprochement, and integration. This is not to say that all of the chapters in this volume illustrate or contribute directly to this second movement. Some deliberately explore the possibilities for integration, while others are more centrally located within a particular paradigm. However, as a whole they point toward the sort of dialogue that can facilitate a second movement in institutional analysis.

This chapter consists of several parts, each based on comparisons of the preceding chapters. The points of comparison are those discussed in chapter 1 (see table 1-1) as particularly important for institutional analysis. First, we examine the underlying and wide-ranging *methodological* approaches that these chapters represent, and we argue, contrary to other scholars, that these differences do not preclude the possibility of a second movement in institutional analysis. Second, we explore how different approaches account for *institutional change*, where potential for paradigmatic cross-fertilization and integration may be, and what some of the payoffs might be for pursuing such rapprochement. We argue that attempts at integration can reveal a wider, more complex range of causal processes than each paradigm alone generally does, as well as areas in which paradigms overlap or complement each other. Third, we suggest that these comparisons point toward a second movement in institutional analysis and that there are four *analytic strategies* being used to advance this movement in the literature. These are evident in the contributions to this volume. Scholars link paradigms by specifying more closely the context in which each one's causal processes operate; blend insights from different paradigms by showing how the causal factors of one paradigm interact or are nested with those of another; identify common analytic problems shared by paradigms in order to expose areas of convergence; and subsume the arguments of one paradigm into those of another. Finally, we assess what we have learned from the papers in this volume about the phenomenon of *neoliberalism* itself. Taken together, the papers reveal that it is a mistake to assume that all policy makers interpret and cope with the neoliberal project in the same way, and it is a significant exaggeration to argue that the advanced capitalist economies are converging on a standard package of neoliberal institutions and policy prescriptions. Furthermore, neoliberalism does not necessarily undermine nation-state authority or guarantee more efficient economic outcomes.

Much of the discussion that follows focuses on the important differences among the chapters in this volume. However, it is important at the outset to explain what they have in common. To begin with, all of the authors adhere to the very basic idea that markets, including markets organized according to neoliberal principles, do not emerge naturally or inevitably, even in the face of increased levels of international trade, capital flows, and other forms of global economic activity, as other scholars have argued (e.g., Strange 1997, p. 190).[1] Instead, our contributors agree that markets are socially constructed by actors in various ways. They also recognize that economic organization, including the market, is quite heterogeneous in character and that this heterogeneity is largely the result of the underlying institutional context within which it is embedded. That is, markets are not necessarily the dominant mechanism of economic governance in capitalist societies; others, including the state, may play an equal if not greater role in organizing economic activity (see also Campbell, Hollingsworth, and Lindberg 1991; Hollingsworth, Schmitter, and Streeck 1994; Hollingsworth and Boyer 1997).

Furthermore, the chapters collectively provide a general definition of neoliberalism that consists of three dimensions. First, there is a *normative* dimension that applauds the virtues of unregulated markets and revolves around the idea that neoliberalism is the most desirable way to organize economic activity. Second, there is a *positive* dimension that makes predictive claims about the effects neoliberalism has on economic performance. Specifically, it holds that market deregulation facilitates more efficient economic outcomes than do other forms of economic organization. Third, there is a *regulatory* dimension that consists of economically consequential rules for action. In this case, these are rules, such as property rights and labor-capital accords, that govern the market and that can be described empirically in terms of how they emerge and shape economic allocation. This three-dimensional definition bears directly on one of the sharpest differences among the analyses in this volume — differences in methodological approach.

Do Methodological Differences Preclude a Second Movement?

Some scholars have suggested that there may be inherent methodological differences among paradigms that present serious obstacles to a second movement in institutional analysis. In particular, they maintain that although there has been some creative borrowing among paradigms, there is significant divergence among them in how they construct theory, organize research findings, and approach the issue of falisifiability and in what they accept as convincing explanation, and that these differences may derail any second movement that begins to develop (e.g., Hall 1997; Levi 1997a, p. 36; Somers 1998; Kiser and Hechter 1998). We are more optimistic. Even if paradigms tend to be associated with certain methodologies, as suggested in chapter 1, this does not inevitably preclude cross-fertilization among paradigms. To defend this claim we assess the methodological approaches used in the chapters in this volume.

These chapters represent a broad array of methodologies and can be located along two continuums representing different methodological means and ends. On the one hand, the goal of some authors is to develop more generalizable, parsimonious, and sometimes formal theories of institutional change, whereas others seek to establish more historically and contextually specific empirical descriptions. On the other hand, in order to pursue these goals some chapters rely more on a conventional positivist approach that involves deduction, hypothesis testing, and well-established principles of falsifiability (e.g., Stinchcombe 1968), including statistical analysis, while others use more interpretive means, including induction, process tracing, thick description, and principles of grounded theory (e.g., Glaser and Strauss 1967). The intersection of these continuums generates a methodological map that is useful for identifying each chapter's approach and comparing them to one another (see figure 10-1).

To begin with, Jack Knight uses rational choice game theory to deduce an account of the rise of neoliberalism in Latin America. He also derives and tests hypotheses from several other theories by exploring how well they predict Latin American outcomes. This approach is typical of the positivism frequently used by rational choice institutionalists who seek to develop highly generalizable theories. Similarly, Edgar Kiser and Aaron Laing use rational choice theory to explain the degree to which neoliberalism affected budgetary policies in advanced capitalist countries. They deduce hypotheses about how taxation and spending policies should have changed throughout the advanced capitalist world and then test them with time-series data. Whereas Knight emphasizes formal modeling, Kiser and Laing are more empirically oriented and descrip-

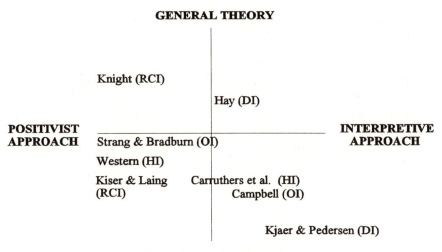

(OI) Organizational institutionalism
(DI) Discursive institutionalism
(HI) Historical institutionalism
(RCI) Rational choice institutionalism

Fig. 10-1. Methods and Goals of Institutional Analysis

tive, even though they aspire in principle to theoretical generalization (e.g., Kiser and Hechter 1998, 1991). Their chapter is also less parsimonious than Knight's insofar as they acknowledge that to a limited degree ideational factors as well as rational choice theory are required to fully explain their data. Moreover, their arguments are less generalizable than Knight's to the extent that they document substantially different outcomes in different groups of countries — specifically, more government spending for business in Scandinavia than in Britain or the United States — and theorize somewhat different political processes for each. Knight briefly acknowledges country-specific differences but does not theorize them.

David Strang and Ellen Bradburn's chapter tests competing theories within organizational institutionalism to explain the conditions under which state-level health care systems became more market oriented in the United States. Similarly, Bruce Western's analysis tests competing hypotheses from historical institutionalism about the degree to which neoliberal, corporatist, and other institutional systems of labor market coordination buffered national economies from the effects of shifting investment flows on unemployment rates. These chapters share a positivist orientation but are closer to Knight than are Kiser and Laing because they develop explicit causal models, although ones that are statistically descriptive rather than formal in nature. However, they are less inclined than Knight toward broad theoretical generalizations, at least insofar as their statistical techniques yield more probabilistic and, therefore, qualified theoretical conclusions than those typical of game theorists. The chapters by Kiser and Laing, Strang and Bradburn, and Western are also all much more empirically based than Knight's, and as a result, their approaches are more historically sensitive, given that they try to explain how outcomes vary across time and space. In particular, Strang and Bradburn's techniques show how the adoption of neoliberal health care reform varied across states according to the timing of reform and the geographical proximity of states to each other.

Peter Kjær and Ove K. Pedersen's chapter is an example of discursive institutionalism. They show how discourse mediated the impact of neoliberalism on Danish economic adjustment. Of all the analyses in this volume, theirs is the most interpretive and empirically descriptive. It emphasizes thick description of a single case instead of a causal analysis based on comparisons of several cases or aggregate-level data; focuses on process tracing and narrative history instead of formal modeling; favors the reconstruction of discourse instead of hypothesis testing and falsification; and seeks to understand the historical and national specificity of neoliberal reform in a particular country instead of its general patterning.

The chapter by Bruce Carruthers, Sarah Babb, and Terence Halliday represents historical institutionalism and is also inclined toward empirical description, but lies somewhat closer to the middle of the positivist-interpretive continuum. They use cross-national and historical comparisons to show that central banking reform emulated neoliberal principles but that reforms in bankruptcy law did not. Their use of detailed case studies of France and Mexico is more typical of an interpretive approach, while their use of aggregate cross-national data to test whether institutional change results in greater economic efficiencies reflects a degree of positivism. They also suggest that while trends in banking and bankruptcy institutions are occurring in a large number of countries, thus demonstrating their sensitivity toward theoretical generalization, they emphasize that the causes for these trends are historically and empirically specific, differing from the advanced capitalist countries, where the rise of the European Union was especially important, to postcommunist Europe, where the need to attract foreign investment capital was critical, to the Third World, where debt crisis was important.

John Campbell's chapter draws primarily from organizational institutionalism but deliberately blends elements from this school with others from historical institutionalism. He argues that in order for neoliberal, supply-side policies to be adopted in the United States during the early 1980s, they had to fit within prevailing cognitive and normative constraints, be framed so as to resonate with public opinion, and serve the pragmatic interests of policy makers who needed solutions to the stagflation problem. Because neoliberalism achieved these goals better than the industrial policy alternative did, supply-side economics was institutionalized. He derives concepts but not hypotheses from his paradigms, and uses thick empirical description to illustrate but not test his arguments. As a result, his approach is somewhat more interpretive and less generalizable than the paper by Carruthers and his colleagues. However, because he systematically analyzes two cases (e.g., the fate of industrial policy as well as of supply-side policy) and suggests hypotheses for future research based on his analysis, he is more inclined toward theoretical generalities than Kjær and Pedersen in their discursive approach.

Finally, Colin Hay's paper is another example of discursive institutionalism, albeit one also informed by historical institutionalism, that resides somewhat closer to the interpretive than the positivist position insofar as he relies extensively on thick historical description of a single case to carefully map the processes through which British policy makers took their neoliberal turn. Nevertheless, in contrast to other discursive institutionalists, notably Kjær and Pedersen, he also engages in hypothesis testing by using historical evidence to assess alternative theories regarding the influence of ideas on policy making, evolutionary and punctuated theories of institutional change, and specific debates about the rise of neoliberalism in Britain. Moreover, similar to Knight, he strives to construct a more generalizable causal model of institutional change than do many of the other authors in the volume. Where the two differ in this regard is that Hay's generalizations are restricted empirically because they are based on one country, whereas Knight's are based on all of Latin America. In fact, Hay's use of thick historical description to delineate a schematic causal model is perhaps most characteristic of historical institutionalists, even if most of them favor larger numbers of cases for comparative purposes (e.g., Campbell and Lindberg 1991; Hall 1989b; Weir and Skocpol 1985).

One caveat is required. Although it is not apparent in figure 10-1, all of these chapters, when compared to other noninstitutionalist paradigms, tend to cluster around the intersection of the two axes. If these axes were extended, other paradigms would be located farther away from the intersection than the institutionalist paradigms would be. For instance, whereas structural functionalism, Marxism, and noninstitutional versions of rational choice theory seek to provide truly universal theories of social change that hold across time and space, institutional approaches are generally careful not to make such sweeping claims. Similarly, postmodernism is a paradigm that is substantially more descriptive, historically specific, and often radically interpretive than any of the perspectives represented in this volume. The point is that all the institutionalist paradigms are dedicated more to middle-range theorizing and analysis than to other approaches. In this sense, they stand apart from other perspectives.

Nevertheless, the methodological similarities and differences among our chapters are important. Some chapters from *different* paradigms share *common* methodological ground. For instance, the work by Strang and Bradburn, Western, and Kiser and Laing represents organizational, historical and rational choice institutionalism, respectively, but cluster within the same quadrant in figure 10-1. Conversely, the two rational choice papers (Knight; Kiser and Laing) are located in *different* quadrants, as are the two discursive institutionalist papers (Hay; Kjær and Pedersen) and the two organizational institutionalist papers (Strang and Bradburn; Campbell). If different paradigms are not as tightly linked to a specific and unique methodology, then it is hard to understand how methodological differences per se will necessarily block theoretical or conceptual cross-fertilization or undermine movement toward some sort of integration among paradigms.

Of course, in some cases methodological differences may be so extreme, at least on epistemological and ontological grounds, as to be irreconcilable (e.g., Hay and Wincott 1998). In particular, some who adopt the positivist approach would question whether an extreme interpretive position constitutes good social science at all insofar as strict interpretivists often avoid testing competing hypotheses or making empirically based causal arguments, but make descriptive statements or explanations (e.g., Kiser and Hechter 1998). Conversely, some interpretivists would argue that one cannot fully understand how institutional change occurs without recognizing the shifts in cognition, cultural scripts, and discourse that underlie how actors interpret economic situations and thus motivate change. They maintain that this is fundamentally important because these things organize action just as surely as do more formal institutional structures and because actors defend, legitimize, and institutionalize action at least in part by invoking concepts and causal arguments from particular scripts and discourses (e.g., Alexander and Smith 1993; Blyth 1998; Somers 1998, 1995).[2] However, it is worth remembering that any paradigm consists of contributions from a *range* of scholars, some taking more extreme, radical, or pure paradigmatic positions on methodological and other matters than others (Hall and Taylor 1998; Ruggie 1998, pp. 880–85; Schneiberg and Clemens forthcoming; Yonay 1998, chap. 1). Indeed, our methodological map reveals this. The possibility for methodological obstacles to impede a second movement may be greatest in these more extreme cases, whereas moderates are likely to be more flexible methodologically and, therefore, more inclined toward a synthetic dialogue.

All of this is important in light of the earlier discussion of the three-dimensional view of neoliberalism. In general, those contributors who were primarily concerned with explaining the *normative* underpinnings of neoliberalism resorted to a more interpretive approach. This makes sense. After all, if you want to study the normative aspect of social change, then you need to understand how people view and interpret their social world. Notably, Kjær and Pedersen use this approach to examine the translation of neoliberalism into the Danish normative context. However, if you study the positive claims of theory, focusing on how people interpret their world will not be a principal concern and researchers more typically will use a positivist approach. Indeed, Western takes this approach because he is concerned with examining the *positive* neoliberal claim that less-regulated labor markets facilitate the most efficient allocation of labor as reflected in low unemployment rates. Finally, those contributors who try to explain the emergence of neoliberalism's *regulatory* structure tended to adopt a more eclectic approach, mixing positivist and interpretive techniques. For example, Carruthers and his colleagues use both methods in varying degrees to explain the development of neoliberal rules and regulations. In short, the choice regarding which dimension of neoliberalism to investigate seems to have significantly motivated the methodological approach used.

The point is twofold. On the one hand, the object of analysis — that is, the normative, positive, or regulatory dimension of neoliberalism — seems to have influenced each author's methodological choices more than their paradigmatic orientation did. Certainly, a paradigm often affects the questions we ask and the subjects about which we are interested, which may then bear on our methodological choices. But this is not inevitable, because the connection between theory and method is often loose. For example, several historical institutionalists have studied how ideational factors as well as the pursuit of self-interest affect institutional change. Some of them have used a standard positivist approach (e.g., McDonough 1997), while others have used a more interpretive one (e.g., Locke and Thelen 1995; Ziegler 1997). Thus, a single theoretical issue can be investigated by means of a variety of methodological approaches.[3] On the other hand, and perhaps more importantly for those who are concerned that methodological differences divide paradigms, scholars who pay attention to work done in competing paradigms may expand their range of questions and objects of investigation and in doing so may also become more open-minded, if not eclectic, in their methodological approach. That is, *theoretical* cross-fertilization may also facilitate *methodological* diversity. Notably, rational choice and historical institutionalists who have become interested in how actors interpret their situations and interests, a central concern of organizational institutionalism for years, now advocate blending positivist deduction and hypothesis testing with thick description in order to better understand this process and refine their theories of strategic action (e.g., Bates et al. 1998, chap. 1; Goldstein 1993; Hattam 1993; Levi 1997b). In sum, there is no inherent reason why different paradigms necessarily cluster around different methods and, thus, no reason why methodological differences necessarily threaten a second movement in institutional analysis. What follows is a more direct discussion of the possibilities and payoffs for such a movement.

Possibilities and Payoffs for a Second Movement

The chapters in this volume are generally concerned with explaining the shift toward neoliberal institutions in different political-economic systems and the variation in the degree to which neoliberalism penetrated and was institutionalized in them. This occurred very unevenly across countries and cases. We have chapters documenting that neoliberalism penetrated more substantially in some countries than others (Kiser and Laing; Western); that the development of neoliberal institutions in one area was compensated for by institutions based on different principles in other areas (Carruthers, Babb, and Halliday); and that the adoption of neoliberalism was heavily mediated by other institutional principles (Campbell; Hay; Kjær and Pedersen; Knight; Strang and Bradburn). Furthermore, the chapters illustrate considerable variation in how all of this occurred. Notably, contributors identify several levels of determination that need to be sorted out in order to understand the full complexity of the rise of neoliberalism in particular and, by implication, institutional change in general.

To begin with, virtually every contributor, regardless of theoretical or methodological orientation, argues that fundamental problems in political economic performance, such as stagflation, investment volatility, debt crisis, unemployment, international competition, or cost escalation, initially *triggered* efforts to change institutional arrangements. In effect, they agree that some sort of exogenous shock provided this initial stimulus for change. However, all of this occurred in conjunction with a major political-cultural shift, that is, the increasing salience of neoliberal ideas, models, and prescriptions. The reason for the initial appearance of the neoliberal vision is explored in only a few of our chapters (Campbell; Hay), but all the authors agree that the rise of this political-cultural model in conjunction with various economic problems launched searches for new institutional arrangements.

Furthermore, many authors argue that a variety of historically given factors — many of them institutional, such as formal political institutions (Hay; Western; Kjær and Pedersen) and discourse institutions (Campbell; Kjær and Pedersen; Hay; Strang and Bradburn), but also resource endowments (Campbell; Knight) — subsequently limited the range of solutions that were either politically available or discursively imaginable to policy makers. In other words, a variety of institutional and other constraints *mediated* the spread or incursion of neoliberalism within a particular context, system, or field.

Finally, within these constraints several mechanisms eventually *determined* the degree to which neoliberalism penetrated and was institutionalized. Authors theorized this process in various ways. First, many indicated that this process was highly contested and involved much political *struggle, bargaining,* and *negotiation.* This is clearest in Knight's chapter, which theorizes bargaining among Latin American actors as they adopted neoliberalism, but it is also evident in Hay's analysis of the struggles over neoliberal reform in Britain; Carruthers, Babb and Halliday's assessment of France's decision to relax bankruptcy law; and Kjær and Pedersen's discussion of the negotiated adoption of reforms in Denmark. Strang and Bradburn argue that political struggles affected the adoption of neoliberal health care reform in federal as well as state-level legislation. Campbell shows that neoliberalism had to overcome a challenge from left-wing industrial policy advocates before being institutionalized as public policy. Notably, chapters spanning the paradigmatic spectrum showed that struggle, bargaining, and negotiation were important mechanisms for change. It is an important way in which institutional analysis differs from structuralist, functionalist, and efficiency oriented theories that invoke much more inevitability, if not teleology, to the process of institutional change.

Second, Strang and Bradburn show that the technical aspects of legislation enabling health maintenance organizations (HMOs) *diffused* across state governments, resulting in relatively homogeneous institutional outcomes that were tightly coupled with the advent of neoliberal discourse, particularly the establishment of federal standards for HMO legislation that were followed by many state governments. Such diffusion stemmed largely from different governments *imitating* what they perceived to be appropriate innovations in health care. Similarly, Carruthers and his colleagues argue that the rise of neoliberal central bank policies diffused across countries in part due to the tight coupling among central banks and between central banks and financial markets.

Third, Kjær and Pedersen suggest that in Denmark bits and pieces of a general conglomeration of neoliberal concepts were *translated* into institutional practices that were characteristically Danish. Their very fine-grained analysis of a single case reveals a more loosely coupled relationship between discourse and institutional change than that shown in many of the other chapters. Similarly, Campbell shows that in order for neoliberalism to be adopted in the United States, it had to be framed in ways that fit the prevailing normative and cognitive context. Finally, Hay notes that the evolution of neoliberalism in Britain began with the Labour government's attempt to link more austere monetary policies to conventional Keynesianism in the mid-1970s, but that neoliberalism did not emerge full-blown until the political climate was disrupted by economic crisis and the election of Margaret Thatcher's Conservative government. Even then, he argues, the adoption of neoliberal policy ideas did not change state institutions as much as one might have expected had policy ideas and institutions been more tightly coupled. In effect, Hay's story describes how neoliberalism was translated into practice in different ways at different historical moments. Although both Campbell's and Hay's chapters most clearly represent other institutionalist paradigms, they also reveal how historical institutionalists have paid increasing attention to how neoliberal programs were translated into practice in unique ways, depending on the identities and worldviews of different political and technical elites, rather than diffused uniformly across nation-states (e.g., Locke and Thelen 1995; Premfors 1998; Ziegler 1997, chap. 3).

Fourth, Hay also maintains that the adoption of neoliberalism in Britain involved policy makers *learning* slowly what institutional solutions were best suited to the problems of stagflation. Consequently, policies and institutions evolved in response to the feedback that policy makers received as they *experimented* with different solutions. Kjær and Pedersen make a similar argument about Denmark. Carruthers and his colleagues describe a learning process insofar as their policy makers discovered that granting more autonomy to central banks created a more competitive economic climate, increased the number of business failures, and, in turn, required that they develop more lenient bankruptcy policies in order to mitigate the political fallout. Similarly, Knight recognizes that in some Latin American countries, politicians rescinded some reforms after learning that the consequences of neoliberalism were politically explosive.

This may be a situation akin to the old parable of the elephant being examined by three blind men — each offering a different description because they had located much different parts of a large and complex beast. Indeed, the rise of neoliberalism is so large and complex a process that different analysts may examine and thus theorize different parts of it with dramatically different results. Considered as a whole, these chapters suggest that there were a variety of economic and political-cultural factors that triggered changes in institutional arrangements; a variety of mechanisms that determined the extent to which neoliberalism penetrated and was institutionalized in different contexts; and a variety of factors that mediated this change process. When these pieces are combined, the theoretical "elephant" that emerges resembles that shown in figure 10-2. Heuristic models like this have been used to describe other sorts of sweeping institutional changes (e.g., Campbell and Lindberg 1991; Hall 1999). Of course, they are not particularly satisfying if one aspires to parsimonious theory, which offers the benefits of being concise, elegant, and powerful insofar as it provides relatively simple explanations that account for a wide variety of phenomena. But parsimony is not always possible when dealing with large and very complex issues like this one (Hall 1997, p. 189; Hirschman 1992).

Obviously, this model implies that theoretical integration is required in order to fully account for the rise of neoliberalism, if not for other examples of institutional change. In particular, recall that in chapter 1 we showed that different institutionalist paradigms tend to focus on different mechanisms of change. The fact that some chapters actually incorporate *several* of these mechanisms into their analysis underscores not only the desirability but the possibility for theoretical cross-fertilization. Notably, Strang and Bradburn identify the effects of all four types of change mechanisms reviewed in chapter 1 and

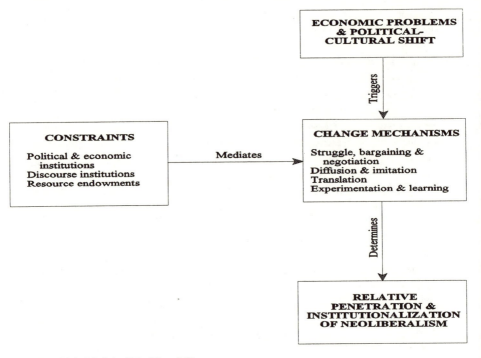

Fig. 10-2. Model of Neoliberal Change

noted in figure 10-2. In addition to recognizing how political struggles and diffusion affected the adoption of HMO legislation, they show that the less technical aspects of the HMO idea were translated into practice and institutionalized in different ways in different states. They also identify learning effects insofar as health care providers and others found that they needed to strategically frame the HMO solution in the language of neoliberalism and efficiency in order for it to be accepted. Later, state governments learned that this new institutional form of health care had become politically acceptable and, as a result, they began to imitate it. In sum, struggle, diffusion, translation, and learning are all important mechanisms of institutional change in their analysis. Certainly, one of the most important payoffs for developing a synthetic analysis that considers several causal mechanisms is that it yields a more nuanced account of change and reveals the truly *complex, multidimensional* nature of the change process.

Beyond the sheer complexity of neoliberal reform, there are two additional reasons why scholars might focus on different parts of the elephant. First, it seems that the empirical and theoretical insights they make about how change occurs depend in part on how analytically fine-grained their analysis is. For instance, when considering mechanisms of change, the fine-grained analyses are more likely to identify and theorize relatively complex causal processes, such as translation or social learning, through which new ideas are institutionalized in practice. Less detailed analyses are more likely to attribute change to a generic process, like diffusion, that often remains a theoretical black box whose internal dynamics await further inspection pending the development of more refined cases. After all, it is only when Kiser and Laing shift from an aggregate analysis of all OECD countries to a disaggregated examination of clusters of neoliberal and social democratic ones that they discover that the effects of increased capital mobility do not diffuse uniformly across advanced capitalist countries, but are translated into budgetary practice in different ways in different countries according to their political institutions. It is only when Carruthers and his colleagues shift from an analysis of aggregate level data from many countries to detailed case studies of France and Mexico that they see how politicians learn about the consequences of increasing central bank autonomy and consider easing bankruptcy law in response. It is only when Strang and Bradburn disaggregate different dimensions of HMO legislation that they detect that the less technical aspects of reform do not diffuse uniformly across states, but are translated into practice differently from one state to another.

Operating with different degrees of detail may obscure the possibility that scholars who appear to be talking about very different processes may actually be talking about the same thing. For instance, Yasemin Soysal (1994), who shares the organizational institutionalist orientation of Strang and Bradburn but focuses on a much smaller number of cases, showed that a new institutional form of citizenship diffused across several European countries during the 1970s and 1980s. However, in each case the generic form was translated into practice in unique ways that depended on prevailing national political institutions (see also Keck and Sikkink 1998). In other words, translation rather than imitation was the primary mechanism by which diffusion occurred. Similarly, Kjær and Pedersen do *not* reject the idea that the neoliberal discourse diffused across countries, but they are quick to point out, echoing Kiser and Laing, that the way it was translated into Danish practice may have been much different from how it was translated in other countries given the character of Danish institutions. Historical institutionalists have recently made similar arguments based on very detailed case studies (e.g., Locke and Thelen 1995). As Kiser and Laing note, there may be more overlap among institutional theories than is often recognized. Identifying points of *overlap* and *similarity* among paradigms is another payoff to be gained from developing integrative heuristics like ours and exploring the possibilities of theoretical synthesis.

The second reason why scholars might pay more attention to some parts of the elephant than others is that different paradigms are preoccupied with different theoretical problematics (see chapter 1). For example, most of the papers represented in this volume take for granted the problems that trigger transformations of institutional arrangements. That is, they view these problems as things that actors cannot help but recognize and respond to. However, discursive and some organizational institutionalists ask why some phenomena are defined as problems in the first place while others are not (e.g., Bourdieu 1998, 1993; Dobbin 1994b; Fligstein 1990; Pedersen 1995). Why were inflation and low productivity defined as the most pressing problems in Britain during the 1970s, whereas high unemployment and centralized state bureaucracy were the key issues in Denmark, when all of these conditions obtained in both countries? The answer, they suggest, lies in how political-cultural institutions constitute people's perceptions of problems. As Kjær and Pedersen document, the Danes identified unemployment as particularly troublesome because they interpreted their situation through a certain "socioeconomic frame of meaning," that is, a set of social democratic concepts, theories and worldviews that "naturally" made unemployment a major concern. Hay's discussion of how important the local construction of a particular "crisis narrative" was to the rise of British neoliberalism is another good example. Historical institutionalists who have become enamored recently with how ideas and culture as well as interests cause shifts in policy-making paradigms make similar arguments (e.g., Blyth 1998; Goldstein and Keohane 1993; Hall 1993; Locke and Thelen 1995).

Traditionally, however, the problematic of historical institutionalism asks how formal institutions constrain, mediate, and limit the range of choices available to actors and how these limits persist over time (Hall 1993; Pierson 1993; Steinmo, Thelen, and Longstreth 1992). Hence, Western investigates how cross-national variation in institutional constraints affects employment outcomes in the face of increased international capital mobility. Rational choice theorists are also interested in how institutions constrain and shape behavior (e.g., Garrett and Lange 1996). Knight argues that actors' bargaining strategies are influenced by their resource endowments, which presumably could include a variety of institutional capacities like access to different policy makers and policy-making arenas where bargaining games occur in the first place (e.g., Levi 1997b). However, the rational choice problematic is concerned primarily with how institutions emerge to solve exchange and collective goods problems. Consequently, Knight pays closest attention to how bargaining games among social classes, parties, political elites, and other organized actors reform institutions.

There are real and important differences among theoretical paradigms. But the point is that because different paradigms tend to employ different problematics and thus raise different theoretical questions, their insights may be more complementary to one another than is often recognized (e.g., Fiorina 1995; Skocpol 1995). Heuristic models, such as figure 10-2, can reveal this complementarity and help scholars avoid excessive intellectual myopia and the possibility of talking past one another. Significantly, Strang and Bradburn

CONCLUSION   263

were initially concerned only with investigating the degree to which HMO legislation diffused across state governments, but after reflecting on Kjær and Pedersen's chapter decided to explore whether state governments translated parts
of the general HMO model into practice in unique ways. In the end, they
found evidence for both homogenous diffusion and heterogeneous translation,
depending on which parts of the legislation they tracked. So, instead of arguing about whether one or another part of the heuristic model best explains
a particular institutional outcome, it may be more productive to ask under
what conditions different parts of the model seem to have greater effects on
outcomes than others do. Does the relatively widespread or deep penetration
of neoliberalism require several of the causal mechanisms identified here to
be operating in unison? Does the initial penetration tend to involve certain
mechanisms, such as imitation, diffusion, or translation, whereas struggle or
bargaining might be more important in cases where neoliberal reforms were
eventually modified or reversed? Hence, another payoff from exploring the
possibilities of theoretical integration in institutional analysis is that by identifying *complementarities* among paradigms we can generate these sorts of questions, foster new research agendas, and, as a result, advance our understanding of institutional change.

   Overall, then, it is apparent that at a very basic level all the new institutionalist paradigms share a *common project*. All seek to better understand the nature of institutional change by articulating the complex, multidimensional processes and mechanisms through which it occurs; all seek to understand how
already existing institutional arrangements affect these processes; all seek to
ground their arguments in the middle-range analyses of empirical cases. Certainly each paradigm approaches this project from a different direction, but it
should be clear now that these approaches are not entirely incompatible with
each other. We are *not* arguing that all approaches can necessarily be synthe-
sized so thoroughly that all of the distinctions among them are obliterated.
What we are suggesting is that given the complexity of their common project,
paradigms can benefit in significant ways by considering the possibility that
there may be some areas in which there is enough complementarity among
views to facilitate cross-fertilization. At the very least, we should recognize that
despite their differences, all institutionalist paradigms are bound together by
virtue of the fact that they share this common project.

Strategies for a Second Movement in Institutional Analysis

So far we have argued two points. First, there is no a priori reason why methodological differences should prevent the development of a second movement in
institutional analysis. Second, there are key points at which different institutionalist paradigms may overlap or complement each other in ways that can

provide significant theoretical payoffs, including a more nuanced understanding of the complexities of institutional change (see also Hall and Taylor 1996; Thelen 1999). This suggests that if you want to understand institutional change in specific empirical settings, then you may have to weave together an analysis that draws together a lot of ideas that are sometimes viewed as competitors. Hence, the real challenge for scholars interested in understanding institutional change and its effects is *not* choosing among ideal-typical paradigms, but elaborating the connections among the phenomena that these paradigms highlight — an enterprise that could in the long run dramatically transform current paradigmatic distinctions and debates. In fact, there are several analytic strategies that scholars may use to do this and advance a second movement in institutional analysis. These can be found in the contributions to this volume as well as in the broader literature.

First, scholars can *link* the causal arguments of different paradigms by specifying the different contexts within which each holds the greatest explanatory power. One way to do this is to specify the *scope conditions* under which aspects of different paradigms obtain in empirical situations. For example, some scholars have studied the conditions under which ideas such as worldviews, symbolic frames, and intellectual theories, as opposed to material interests, affect the development of institutions and the public policies that constitute them (e.g., Blyth 1998, 1997; Goldstein and Keohane 1993; Hall 1993; Rueschemeyer and Skocpol 1996b). Colin Hay's chapter contributes to this debate insofar as he argues that ideas and worldviews affect policy making and institutional change, but especially during moments of crisis, when political elites perceive that dominant policy ideas no longer yield satisfactory results and political and intellectual space opens in which new ideas and theories become influential and fundamental shifts in policy and institutions occur. Similarly, others have argued that ideas, cognitive frames, and normative structures have their greatest effects under conditions of great uncertainty (Goldstein 1993) or when the costs of pursuing them are relatively low (Knight and Ensminger 1998; North 1990, pp. 43–44).

Another way to link arguments from different paradigms is to consider the *stages* through which institutional development occurs and determine the degree to which aspects of different paradigms explain each stage (e.g., Tolbert and Zucker 1983). Strang and Bradburn, for example, show that state governments experiencing high health care costs quickly passed laws enabling HMOs regardless of what other states were doing, but that states with lower costs tended to adopt legislation later and in order to keep up with the actions taken by other states. In the first stage, economic interests and a "logic of instrumentality," reminiscent of rational choice institutionalism, drove institution building; in the second stage, concerns with organizational legitimacy and a "logic of appropriateness," central to organizational institutionalism, motivated the process (March and Olsen 1989, chap. 2). Similarly, Kjær and Pedersen argue that an important step in examining rational action is determining what constitutes an appropriate definition of rationality in the first place.

Second, whereas linking strategies preserve the integrity of each paradigm and carefully identify the contextual boundaries separating them, scholars can also *blend* insights from different paradigms in ways that suggest the possibility of transcending or at least blurring these boundaries. A few rational choice theorists have examined the interplay of cognition and institution building: how people learn, how they incorporate beliefs and mental models with preferences to reach decisions, and how they interpret their uncertain worlds through culturally and historically given frames (Knight and North 1997; North 1990; Piore 1995). This is an intriguing effort to blend the microfoundations of rational choice institutionalism with the cognitive microfoundations of organizational institutionalism (see also DiMaggio 1997; Zerubavel 1997). Others have tried to blend insights from historical and organizational institutionalism to show that material interests as well as identities or worldviews influence action (Fligstein 1990; Hattam 1993; Keck and Sikkink 1998; Locke and Thelen 1995; Ziegler 1997). In this volume, Campbell blends elements of organizational and historical institutionalism to show that cognitive and normative perspectives mediate how actors articulate and pursue their political interests. Kjær and Pedersen modify organizational institutionalism's concept of diffusion with the idea of translation from discursive institutionalism. Hay explains how strategically calculating political elites seek policy solutions within constraints posed by formal institutional contexts as well as by more cognitive policy paradigms, and how these paradigms affect their perceptions of interests, resources, and capacities for action in the first place. This is an ambitious attempt to blend insights from discursive institutionalism with those from historical and rational choice institutionalism. Hay, then, manages both blending and linking strategies, thereby indicating that these are not mutually exclusive approaches.

A particularly fruitful approach to blending paradigms may be to *nest* concepts and causal arguments from one paradigm within those of another. For instance, Steven Vogel (1996) showed that neoliberal regulatory reforms varied across countries depending on the nested effects of nationally specific ideas and institutionally defined interests. Some reforms were deemed unacceptable or unthinkable due to the regulatory orientation of policy makers, that is, their normative and cognitive assumptions about the appropriate role for government in the economy. Within these limits, policy makers struggled over the specifics of reform according to their institutionally and organizationally defined interests. Thus, a long history of British liberalism combined with a fragmented array of regulatory bureaucracies made coordinated and carefully planned regulatory reform impossible, so Thatcher pushed for privatization and liberalization. By contrast, the Japanese had long believed in a strong managerial role for government in the economy, and within this normative and cognitive framework developed a centralized bureaucracy that was more insulated from interest groups than that in Britain. As a result, Japanese policy makers found British style deregulation unacceptable and instead redefined regulatory reform in terms of limiting the growth of bureaus and reorganizing — not reducing — the degree of governmental authority over the private sector. Similarly, in this volume Campbell argues that in order for institutional change to occur, policy makers must first find new policy ideas that fit their cognitive assumptions, serve their interests, and, finally, resonate with the public's norms and values.

Blending can also involve recognizing the importance for change of *interactions* among factors highlighted by different paradigms. Carruthers and his colleagues, for instance, argue that the increasing institutional autonomy enjoyed by central banks around the world was triggered by the interaction of new ideas, specifically the rise of monetarist and rational expectations theories in economics, and the transformation of formal institutions, especially the collapse of the Bretton Woods accords, the fall of communism in Eastern Europe, and the development of the European Union project. Moreover, they show how central banking was transformed as a result of the diffusion of a model that stressed bank autonomy but that the problems associated with adopting this model generated political contradictions that triggered counterbalancing changes in bankruptcy laws. Thus, mechanisms and conditions of change stressed by different paradigms — that is, organizational and historical institutionalism, respectively — were blended by showing how their interactions precipitated change. Similarly, Marc Schneiberg (1998) demonstrated that institutional arrangements in the U.S. fire insurance industry evolved as a result of interactions between shifting prices, which receive much attention from rational choice institutionalists, and concerns about maintaining political and institutional legitimacy within a field of organizations, a concern of organizational institutionalism.

Third, scholars may try to *identify* the common analytic problems that are central to all paradigms. For example, Kathleen Thelen (1999) cataloged a number of commonalities among institutionalist paradigms, including concerns with theorizing the micro-foundations of action, the preference formation process, and the evolutionary or path-dependent nature of institutional change. More abstractly, Ellen Immergut (1998) argued that historical, organizational, and rational choice institutionalism share a common theoretical core, that is, a vehement rejection of behavioralism, which leads them all to theorize how interests are shaped, aggregated, and expressed as a result of the institutional contexts within which behavior occurs. Recognizing this, she maintained, will help proponents of these paradigms see that they are much closer to each other on certain theoretical issues than they might otherwise realize, regardless of whether they view institutions as cognitive structures, formal procedures, or something else. The fact that some scholars are trying to blend the insights from different paradigms on common problems — such as how interests are defined (e.g., Knight and North 1997), how institutional constraints consist of both strategic contexts and shared understandings (e.g., Katzenstein 1993; Keck and Sikkink 1998), or how ideas affect institutional change (Campbell and Hay in this volume) — suggests that identification of common analytic problems may be the critical precursor to a second movement in institutional analysis.

Of course, this chapter distills insights from all the chapters in this volume in order to identify problems shared by different paradigms. As noted earlier, most of the authors are concerned with identifying the conditions that trigger shifts toward neoliberal institutions in the first place. They are also concerned with identifying the mechanisms that subsequently determine the degree to which this shift occurs and the factors that mediate this process. In doing so, several analyses from different paradigms focus on the same factors, notably the onset of some sort of political economic crisis and political-cultural shift as key triggers, and bargaining, struggle, negotiation, and learning as change mechanisms. Some chapters also identify complementary processes, such as resource and discursive legacies that mediate this process. As we have suggested, these insights might be gathered together to form the basis for an integrated and generic model of neoliberal reform and, more generally, institutional change.

Finally, some scholars have argued that elements of one institutionalist paradigm can be *subsumed* under another. For instance, Margaret Levi's (1997b) analysis of military conscription subsumes normative effects into a rational choice framework. She suggests that conscription works only if citizens believe that it is a fair system, that is, a system based on norms of "ethical reciprocity," the belief that all citizens are eligible to be drafted and will serve when called. Yet such a belief is based on individuals' rational evaluations of information concerning who receives exemptions, how many people evade the draft, and whether the draft operates according to equitable procedures. Thus, the government's normative claims per se that the system is fair are not sufficient; they must be rationally verified by actions in the world external to the government. Similarly, some organizational institutionalists have tried to subsume rational choice theory by arguing that both instrumental and noninstrumental rationalities are socially constructed and, therefore, vary across time and space (Dobbin 1994a; Fligstein 1998). In this volume, Knight adopts the subsumption strategy by arguing that bargaining models contain the core elements of several different theories of neoliberal change in Latin America, including some that rely on common arguments about coercive, normative, and mimetic isomorphism often found in organizational institutionalism (DiMaggio and Powell 1983). He also invokes arguments about self-interested politicians and class struggle, central elements in both his own rational choice view and historical institutionalism (e.g., Skocpol 1985).

There is a fundamental distinction between the first three strategies and the last one. Linking, blending, and identifying common problems are strategies that imply the possibility of better integrating paradigms — an exercise that involves retaining in various ways useful parts of different approaches. However, subsuming one paradigm into another is an approach that implies the generality, if not the superiority, of one over the other. In other words, the first three approaches imply paradigmatic *complementarity*; the fourth implies paradigmatic *competition*. There is certainly disagreement as to which one is most desirable. Some would argue that subsumption is antithetical to institutional explanation. If the premise of institutional explanation is that action is heterogeneous and contextually specific, then explanations must also be heterogeneous, utilizing different conceptual tools according to context. Hence, linking and blending are more desirable strategies if one is interested in exploring the possibilities of theoretical integration. In other words, those who aspire to a more comprehensive understanding of the rich complexities of institutional phenomenon (and a comprehensive critique of the neoclassical account of market organization and action) would prefer the complementary strategies. On the other hand, the more competitive subsumption approach has more appeal for those who yearn for a less comprehensive but more parsimonious understanding of institutions that emphasizes breadth over depth, that is, for those who believe that understanding 90 percent of the variance in one case is less important than understanding 10 percent of the variance in several cases, particularly if the cases vary widely across time and place (see also Fiorina 1995, pp. 110–11).

Of course, there is another, much different approach to adjudicating paradigms: the creation of some sort of grand theory consisting of vast and abstract conceptual schemes (e.g., Parsons 1951; Althusser and Balibar 1970). The essays in this volume, including this chapter, do *not* aspire to grand theory, for widely recognized reasons. First, contributors are trying to make sense of real-world phenomena by building their arguments on empirical analysis. Even in the case of Knight's game theory — the most theoretically abstract essay in the volume and one that seeks to clear the theoretical terrain of several theories of institutional change by subsuming them under the rational choice rubric — the task is to identify the best theoretical explanation by seeing how well competing arguments fit the data. As others have argued forcefully, this is a much different and more scientifically sensible task than simply trying to create conceptual schemes and theoretical arguments with little connection to empirical reality, as grand theorists tend to do (Bates et al. 1998; Mills 1959, chap. 2; Thompson 1978).

Second, contributors are not claiming that the theoretical arguments they make necessarily hold across time and space. Indeed, as noted in chapter 1, if there is one thing that unites institutional theorists, it is their commitment to middle-range theory. Although several authors are searching for an explanation that accounts for the rise of neoliberalism across several countries, no one suggests that their accounts can be generalized universally to all cases of market making, state deregulation, and the like. Even the chapters by Knight and by Kiser and Laing, which begin from rational choice assumptions that are occasionally said to constitute the foundation for a universal theory of social change (e.g., Kiser and Hechter 1991), make no claims about being able to explain the development of more market oriented societies everywhere. Indeed, Knight is explicitly interested in developing middle-range rather than grand theory.

In sum, by advocating that scholars explore the possibilities for bridge building and cross-fertilization among institutionalist paradigms, we intend only that they seek to recognize and understand the complex, historical character of institutions and institutional change and acknowledge that each paradigm may offer insights that could benefit the others. We are *not* suggesting that a full-blown synthesis of paradigms is imminent. All we are arguing is that movement toward cross-fertilization is evident insofar as scholars are trying to push the boundaries of their paradigms toward each other; that this movement involves a variety of analytic strategies; and that these strategies have various advantages and disadvantages. Whether all of this results in some sort of paradigmatic reconciliation remains to be seen. However, we are convinced that the attempt will generate benefits even if there is no reconciliation because, in addition to the payoffs noted above, it will yield *new insights* about real-world phenomenon, such as the rise of neoliberalism.

The Rise of Neoliberalism

A basic assumption underlying this project is that institutional analysis is important because it can improve our understanding of the empirical world. The chapters in this volume provide many insights about the rise of neoliberalism, but a few stand out as being particularly important.

First, some contributors see neoliberalism as a loose conglomeration of ideas and formal institutions. For instance, Kjær and Pedersen regard neoliberalism as a set of concepts from which political elites and others pick and choose in ways that suit their unique political and historical traditions. As a result, neoliberalism can take different forms depending on how actors interpret and construct it—a view of institution building that is consistent with theories emphasizing the importance of culture and discourse as key parts of institutional change (e.g., Alexander and Smith 1993; Goldstone 1991; Swidler 1986; Somers 1995). Hay also recognizes the loose, multidimensional nature of neoliberalism by showing how the monetarist dimension of the neoliberal package captured the imagination of British policy makers long before other dimensions, such as privatization or state decentralization. Furthermore, much as Kjær and Pedersen do, Hay draws an important distinction between the ideas and formal institutions of neoliberalism. He explains that the acceptance of neoliberal ideas preceded the neoliberal overhaul of formal state institutions and that there continues to be a significant temporal lag between the two (see also Pierson 1994). Carruthers and his colleagues also view neoliberalism as a rather complex set of institutions, some of which do not appear to be very neoliberal at all — that is, softer bankruptcy laws — and some of whose development is lagged. Even Strang and Bradburn, who come from a theoretical tradition that seeks to explain how institutional forms diffuse homogeneously across organizational fields (e.g., Thomas et al. 1987; Scott and Meyer 1994), find that certain parts of HMO legislation were translated into practice in different ways in different states.

However, two contributors view neoliberalism as more of a monolithic whole. Western assumes that all neoliberal societies are similar institutionally, as have other comparativists (e.g., Goldthorpe 1984; Zysman 1983), but has little choice if he wants to compare the quantitative effects of neoliberal and other broad types of capitalist regimes on economic performance. Knight assumes that neoliberal reform packages were basically the same throughout Latin America, but does so because he is much less interested in cross-national variation than in the general bargaining process through which neoliberal institutional change occurred — a theory, he might argue, that could account for cross-national variation if it were applied to a more fine-grained comparison of different countries.

The point is that the basic concept of neoliberalism is itself contested in this volume, as it is in the general literature on neoliberalism and the political world itself. This has important implications for theories of neoliberal change. After all, if one assumes that neoliberalism is a unified and coherent set of ideas and institutional prescriptions, then it is perfectly acceptable to simply attend to the general circumstances or processes, such as the globalization of finance capital or economic competition, whereby it diffuses across political economies (e.g., Ohmae 1990; Strange 1997). However, if we suspect that neoliberalism is a loose and malleable aggregation of concepts and practices, then it is incumbent upon us to examine how political actors pick and choose from this aggregation and construct different forms of neoliberalism depending on their unique, historically given, political, economic, and institutional situations (e.g., King and Wood 1999; Locke and Thelen 1995; Pierson 1994; Vogel 1996). In this case, scholars need to attend to the unevenness of institutional change. Furthermore, if we assume that neoliberalism is a monolithic whole, then we tend to view change as rather revolutionary in the sense that the shift to neoliberalism as a totality occurs rather rapidly in any given time and place. But if we assume that neoliberalism is an aggregation, then the possibility exists that we may detect a more evolutionary process of change toward neoliberalism, where one piece is put into place at a time, as Hay describes in the British case and Kjær and Pedersen discuss for Denmark.

A second empirical insight gleaned from these chapters regards the question of whether or not there is a convergence toward some common set of neoliberal institutions. Some of the literature suggests that there is a neoliberal juggernaut rolling across the advanced capitalist countries, for better or worse, that will probably force such a convergence. In this view, neoliberalism is an inevitable response to international capital mobility, trade, economic competition, and technological change (e.g., Crouch and Streeck 1997; Lash and Urry 1987; Ohmae 1990; Reich 1991; Strange 1997). Several papers in this volume provide evidence to the contrary. Western documents that despite increased capital mobility and the potential for capital disinvestment, insofar as labor market institutions are concerned substantial variation remains among OECD countries in terms of the degree to which they approximate the neoliberal model and, in fact, some clearly do not (see also Garrett 1998). Moreover, Kiser and Laing do not find a race to lower corporate tax rates in the OECD as a result of increased capital mobility. Nor do they see a convergence in government subsidies to business. Western, Kiser and Laing, and others (Doremus et al. 1998; Kitschelt et al. 1999; Weiss 1998) continue to identify distinct clusters of countries that have retained unique institutional profiles despite the pressures for neoliberal reform often associated with the globalization of economic activity.

This is not to say that convergence is an illusion. Carruthers and his colleagues find evidence for convergence, but with an engaging twist. While some institutions, specifically central bank regulations, were deregulated and thus shifted in a neoliberal direction — a finding that is entirely consistent with the view that financial markets are among the most likely sites for neoliberal reform due to the increasing volatility of capital flows (Cerny 1997) — a corresponding shift *away* from neoliberalism has occurred in bankruptcy law. As a result, neoliberal convergence is contingent on the institutional arena in question. This supports those who have argued that policy making and institution building often consist of seemingly contradictory changes in rules, regulations, and formal bureaucratic procedures (Skowronek 1995, p. 95). However, the contradiction is reconciled when it is understood that when it comes to reforming economic regulation, neoliberalism is often more a matter of *re-regulating* economic activity and shifting the basis of state capacities, as occurred in bankruptcy law, than *deregulating* it and abandoning these capacities entirely (e.g., Vogel 1996; Weiss 1998, p. 40). This suggests that scholars ought to pay more attention to determining which institutions and areas of public policy are most susceptible to neoliberal reform and why.

Certainly, the intellectual backlash against the convergence thesis has been substantial (e.g., Doremus et al. 1998; Fligstein 1998; Hirst and Thompson 1996; Wade 1996). What the papers in this volume suggest, however, is that although the thesis, at least as originally posed (e.g., Ohmae 1990; Reich 1991), was a profound exaggeration, we should not throw the baby out with the bathwater. It is certainly dangerous to assume that all the important institutional dimensions of national political economies are converging on a neoliberal ideal, or even that there is a single neoliberal ideal in the first place. Nevertheless, convergent tendencies may be at work, but in much subtler, more complex, and less overwhelming ways than previously recognized. Here the notions that there may be counterbalancing tendencies both toward and away from neoliberalism; that the ideas of neoliberalism may spread and find acceptance faster than more formal and substantive institutional responses; that different aspects of the neoliberal model may be translated into practice in different ways in different national contexts and at different times; and that neoliberal institutional change may occur for different reasons at different times and places are all important insights found in this volume.

Third, this volume raises questions about whether neoliberalism has been fundamentally misunderstood as a political-institutional phenomenon. Several scholars on both the left and right have argued that nation-states are increasingly incapacitated or hollowed out as a result of their inability to cope with the globalization of economic activity and, thus, are forced to pursue neoliberal policies (Crouch and Streeck 1997; Jessop 1997; Ohmae 1990; Reich 1991). Others have disagreed (Hall 1998; Garrett 1998; Mann 1996; Soskice 1999; Weiss 1998). Taken as a whole, our contributors suggest that states respond to shifting international economic pressures in various ways that prevent them from being incapacitated by neoliberal currents.

More specifically, states can *block* pressures for neoliberalism for long periods of time (e.g., Evangelista 1996; Shirk 1996). Kiser and Laing's description of Scandinavia as a region that has persistently maintained high levels of business taxation and government spending is a case in point and one that is supported by others who have shown that countries with strong unions and social democratic governments have held out against the neoliberal juggernaut, sometimes even managing to strengthen traditional social democratic policies insofar as they provide the security and stability businesses seek in the face of rising international economic competition and risk (Garrett 1998). States can also *adapt* neoliberalism to their own long-standing existing institutions without abandoning them entirely, as Kjær and Pedersen describe the translation of neoliberal ideas into Danish corporatist practices. Recall that Vogel (1996) identified the same process in other countries when neoliberal pressures for deregulation emerged and policy makers tailored regulatory changes to fit the political interests as well as institutional and normative configurations of prevailing regulatory bureaucracies. Of course, even when states experiment with neoliberal programs, it is entirely possible that they may *reverse* course in order to correct for the political fallout that results. Knight noted that this occurred in some Latin American countries, and Carruthers and his colleagues argued that softening bankruptcy law was a similar kind of midcourse correction. All of these arguments support the view that states have not succumbed to neoliberal trends in ways that have necessarily debilitated them to the point where they are incapable of regulating economic activity within their borders (Hall 1995; Weiss 1998). Indeed, Western shows that states continue to *mediate* the effects of global capital flows on domestic economic performance, specifically unemployment, through the different labor market institutions they support. Warnings about the neoliberal juggernaut are exaggerated in part because they neglect the stickiness or path-dependence of institutional legacies that institutionalists from all paradigmatic orientations emphasize (e.g., North 1990; Pierson 1994; Dobbin 1994b).

Finally, proponents of neoliberalism argue that the political deregulation of markets will spur the development of more efficient economic activity (Ohmae 1990). The contributors in this volume who test this proposition disagree. For instance, Western finds that unemployment is actually lower on average in countries whose labor markets do not fit the neoliberal model. If clearing the labor market, that is, reducing unemployment, is indicative of economic efficiency, then Western's evidence suggests that other institutional arrangements are more efficient insofar as this market is concerned. Furthermore, the easing of bankruptcy law in response to increased central bank autonomy, documented by Carruthers and his colleagues, is an outcome that makes it easier for unprofitable firms to remain in business. If weeding out unprofitable firms is indicative of economic efficiency, then neoliberal reform in one arena may actually increase inefficiency in another. All of this suggests that institutions and their effects are far more important, complex and at least in some cases potentially beneficial to economic performance than the neoliberal account generally grants, and that the imposition of political controls on economic behavior may in the long run yield greater efficiencies than removing them (Amsden, Kochanowicz, and Taylor 1994; Best 1990; Hall 1998; Soskice 1999; Streeck 1997). Again, this underscores how important it is to pursue institutional analysis in all of its forms.

Conclusion

We have suggested that a second movement in institutional analysis is emerging in which some scholars are less concerned now with establishing and defending their intellectual turf than in finding ways to connect their turf to others'. We do not detect insurmountable methodological barriers to this effort. We have also argued that this movement employs a variety of theoretical strategies and that the payoffs from using them and institutional analysis in general can be substantial in terms of better understanding the empirical world, as our contributors have done by analyzing the rise of neoliberalism. Nevertheless, at least three things will likely play important roles in determining the degree to which the second movement flourishes or not.

First, different approaches will be judged to a degree on *empirical* grounds. Those that are able to demonstrate greater explanatory power, resolve empirical anomalies, and explain the greatest proportion of variance in the data will be at an advantage, at least within the scholarly community (Kuhn 1962). Indeed, this is an approach that several of our contributors have employed to resolve debates within and between institutionalist paradigms, notably Strang and Bradburn, Kiser and Laing, Western, and Knight. There is also evidence to suggest that the relative influence of a theoretical perspective among the broader population turns, at least in part, on its ability to account for empirical outcomes. The fall of Keynesianism is a notable example where, during the 1970s, many academics and policy makers no longer believed that Keynesianism could account for the simultaneous problems of inflation and unemployment and, as a result, rejected it in favor of more conservative approaches, such as monetarism. The same thing happened during the 1930s and 1940s when Keynesianism replaced orthodox economic theory (Hall 1989a, 1993; Heilbroner and Milberg 1995). Of course, this is not to say that monetarism resolved all the anomalies left unexplained by Keynesianism or that it was somehow a "better" theory, just that Keynesianism's demise in both academic and policy-making circles was rooted in its inability to account for certain empirical trends.

Second, insofar as institutional analysis generally seeks to understand and explain important political and economic phenomena that concern public and private policy makers, *normative* considerations will also be involved. Certainly, normative criteria weigh heavily in policy debates where the empirical evidence on different sides of the argument is inconclusive. But recent scholarship indicates that even when the vast body of empirical evidence is clear, the analytic perspective that eventually captures the imagination of policy makers may be the one that resonates more with their normative views than with the data. Indeed, the outcome often has much to do with the ability of different intellectual and policy entrepreneurs to frame their arguments in ways that provide normative resonance (Rein and Winship 1997; Schön and Rein 1994).

Finally, *political* criteria will surely come into play. There is ample evidence showing that those paradigmatic views that came to dominate the intellectual landscape at different moments in history did so in part because they were backed by substantial material resources and intellectual elites who were able to gain footholds in important institutional arenas where they could articulate their ideas, train protégés, and establish influential intellectual and professional networks for the propagation of their views (Rueschemeyer and Skocpol 1996a; Wuthnow 1989; Yonay 1998). Of course, this is the bread and butter of intellectual politics, and we have no reason to doubt that it will affect the manner in which the paradigmatic debates discussed above and illustrated throughout this volume eventually play out. If for no other reason than this, we are not so naive to assume that these debates will inevitably result in a complete reconciliation and synthesis of views. To do so would be utopian. Nevertheless, we hold out hope that scholars will be open-minded enough to take seriously the possibilities offered by a second movement in institutional analysis and reap whatever insights it may yield.

Regardless of how these things turn out, this project was undertaken recognizing that important intellectual advances have occurred throughout history as a result of scholars from different perspectives engaging one another's ideas directly. In this spirit, we hope that the volume will promote dialogue, identify areas of commonality and difference among paradigms, and with luck generate insights, if not breakthroughs, by stimulating others who read it.

Notes

Thanks go to Colin Hay, Edgar Kiser, Peter Kjær, Jim March, Woody Powell, Marc Schneiberg, Dick Scott, David Strang, and Bruce Western for comments and suggestions.

1. For reviews of the literature that maintains that economic globalization necessarily precipitates the development of relatively unfettered markets, see Garrett 1998, chap. 1; Gilpin 2000, chap. 10; and Weiss 1998, chap. 1.

2. Indeed, when our contributors met to discuss the papers in this volume such a debate occurred between Western and Kiser, on the positivist side, and Hay, Kjær, and Pedersen, on the other. For detailed discussions of these methodological debates and their ontological and epistemological roots, see Benton 1977 and Keat and Urry 1975.

3. We do not deny that some methodologies may be better suited to the investigation of certain theoretical issues than others; however, the range of methodological options may be broader than typically assumed. For further discussion, see Schneiberg and Clemens (forthcoming).

References

Alexander, Jeffrey C., and Philip Smith. 1993. "The Discourse of American Civil Society: A New Proposal for Cultural Studies." *Theory and Society* 22:151–207.

Althusser, Louis, and Etienne Balibar. 1970. *Reading Capital*. London: New Left Books.

Amsden, Alice H., Jacek Kochanowicz, and Lance Taylor. 1994. *The Market Meets Its Match: Restructuring the Economies of Eastern Europe*. Cambridge: Harvard University Press.

Bates, Robert H., Avner Greif, Margaret Levi, Jean-Laurent Rosenthal, and Barry R. Weingast. 1998. *Analytic Narratives*. Princeton: Princeton University Press.

Benton, Ted. 1977. *Philosophical Foundations of the Three Sociologies*. London: Routledge and Kegan Paul.

Best, Michael. 1990. *The New Competition*. Cambridge: Harvard University Press.

Blyth, Mark. 1997. "Any More Bright Ideas? The Ideational Turn of Comparative Political Economy." *Comparative Politics* 29:229–50.

——. 1998. "From Ideas and Institutions to Ideas and Interests: Beyond the Usual Suspects?" Paper presented at the Conference of Europeanists, Baltimore.

Bourdieu, Pierre. 1993. *The Field of Cultural Production.* Cambridge: Polity Press.

——. 1998. *Acts of Resistance: Against the Tyranny of the Market.* New York: New Press.

Campbell, John L., J. Rogers Hollingsworth, and Leon N. Lindberg, editors. 1991. *Governance of the American Economy.* New York: Cambridge University Press.

Campbell, John L., and Leon N. Lindberg. 1991. "The Evolution of Governance Regimes." Pp. 319–55 in *Governance of the American Economy*, edited by John L. Campbell, J. Rogers Hollingsworth and Leon N. Lindberg. New York: Cambridge University Press.

Cerny, Philip C. 1997. "International Finance and the Erosion of Capitalist Diversity." Pp. 173–81 in *Political Economy of Modern Capitalism*, edited by Colin Crouch and Wolfgang Streeck. Thousand Oaks, CA: Sage.

Crouch, Colin, and Wolfgang Streeck. 1997. "Introduction: The Future of Capitalist Diversity." Pp. 1–18 in *Political Economy of Modern Capitalism*, edited by Colin Crouch and Wolfgang Streeck. Thousand Oaks, CA: Sage.

DiMaggio, Paul J. 1997. "Culture and Cognition." *Annual Review of Sociology* 23: 263–87.

DiMaggio, Paul J., and Walter W. Powell. 1983. "The Iron Cage Revisited: Institutional Isomorphism and Collective Rationality in Organizational Fields." *American Sociological Review* 48:147–60.

Dobbin, Frank. 1994a. "Cultural Models of Organization: The Social Construction of Rational Organizing Principles." Pp. 117–42 in *The Sociology of Culture*, edited by Diana Crane. Cambridge, MA: Blackwell.

——. 1994b. *Forging Industrial Policy.* New York: Cambridge University Press.

Doremus, Paul N., William W. Keller, Louis W. Pauly, and Simon Reich. 1998. *The Myth of the Global Corporation.* Princeton: Princeton University Press.

Evangelista, Matthew. 1996. "Stalin's Revenge: Institutional Barriers to Internationalization in the Soviet Union." Pp. 159–85 in *Internationalization and Domestic Politics*, edited by Robert O. Keohane and Helen V. Milner. New York: Cambridge University Press.

Fiorina, Morris. 1995. "Rational Choice and the New(?) Institutionalism." *Polity* 28(1)107–15.

Fligstein, Neil. 1990. *The Transformation of Corporate Control.* Cambridge: Harvard University Press.

——. 1998. "Ruling Markets: An Economic Sociology of Capitalist Economies." Department of Sociology, University of California–Berkeley. Manuscript.

Gamson, William A. 1992. *Talking Politics.* New York: Cambridge University Press.

Garrett, Geoffrey. 1998. *Partisan Politics in the Global Economy.* New York: Cambridge University Press.

Garrett, Geoffrey, and Peter Lange. 1996. "Internationalization, Institutions, and Political Change." Pp. 48–78 in *Internationalization and Domestic Politics*, edited by Robert O. Keohane and Helen V. Milner. New York: Cambridge University Press.

Gilpin, Robert. 2000. *The Challenge of Global Capitalism*. Princeton: Princeton University Press.

Glaser, Barney G., and Anselm L. Strauss. 1967. *The Discovery of Grounded Theory*. New York: Aldine de Gruyter.

Goldstein, Judith. 1993. *Ideas, Interests, and American Trade Policy*. Ithaca: Cornell University Press.

Goldstein, Judith, and Robert O. Keohane, editors. 1993. *Ideas and Foreign Policy: Beliefs, Institutions, and Political Change*. Ithaca: Cornell University Press.

Goldstone, Jack A. 1991. "Ideology, Cultural Frameworks, and the Process of Revolution." *Theory and Society* 20:405–53.

Goldthorpe, John H., editor. 1984. *Order and Conflict in Contemporary Capitalism*. London: Clarendon Press.

Gourevitch, Peter. 1986. *Politics in Hard Times*. Ithaca: Cornell University Press.

Hall, John A. 1995. "The State of Post-Modernism." Pp. 206–13 in *Coercion and Consent: Studies on the Modern State*. London: Polity.

Hall, Peter A. 1993. "Policy Paradigms, Social Learning, and the State: The Case of Economic Policymaking in Britain." *Comparative Politics* 25(3)275–96.

———. 1997. "The Role of Interests, Institutions, and Ideas in the Comparative Political Economy of Industrialized Nations." Pp. 174–207 in *Comparative Politics: Rationality, Culture, and Structure*, edited by Mark Lichbach and Alan Zuckerman. New York: Cambridge University Press.

———. 1998. "Organized Market Economies and Unemployment in Europe: Is It Finally Time to Accept Liberal Orthodoxy?" Paper presented at the Eleventh International Conference of Europeanists, Baltimore.

———. 1999. "The Political Economy of Europe in an Era of Interdependence." Pp. 135–63 in *Continuity and Change in Contemporary Capitalism*, edited by Herbert Kitschelt, Peter Lange, Gary Marks, and John D. Stephens. New York: Cambridge University Press.

Hall, Peter A., editor. 1989a. *The Political Power of Economic Ideas*. Princeton: Princeton University Press.

———. 1989b. Conclusion. Pp. 361–92 in *The Political Power of Economic Ideas*, edited by Peter A. Hall. Princeton: Princeton University Press.

Hall, Peter A., and Rosemary C. R. Taylor. 1996. "Political Science and the Three New Institutionalisms." *Political Studies* 64:936–57.

———. 1998. "The Potential of Historical Institutionalism: A Response to Hay and Wincott." *Political Studies* 48(5)958–62.

Hattam, Victoria C. 1993. *Labor Visions and State Power*. Princeton: Princeton University Press.

Hay, Colin, and Daniel Wincott. 1998. "Structure, Agency, and Historical Institutionalism." *Political Studies* 46(5)951–57.

Heilbroner, Robert, and William Milberg. 1995. *The Crisis of Vision in Modern Economic Thought*. New York: Cambridge University Press.

Hirschman, Albert O. 1992. "Against Parsimony: Three Easy Ways of Complicating Some Categories of Economic Discourse." Pp. 142–60 in *Rival Views of Market Society*. Cambridge: Harvard University Press.

Hirst, Paul, and Grahame Thompson. 1996. *Globalization in Question*. London: Polity.

Hollingsworth, J. Rogers, and Robert Boyer, editors. 1997. *Contemporary Capitalism: The Embeddedness of Institutions.* New York: Cambridge University Press.

Hollingsworth, J. Rogers, Philippe C. Schmitter, and Wolfgang Streeck, editors. 1994. *Governing Capitalist Economies.* New York: Oxford University Press.

Immergut, Ellen M. 1998. "The Theoretical Core of the New Institutionalism." *Politics and Society* 26(1)5–34.

Jessop, Bob. 1997. "The Future of the National State: Erosion or Reorganization?" Paper presented at the Conference on Globalization: Critical Perspectives, University of Birmingham, United Kingdom.

Katzenstein, Peter J. 1993. "Coping with Terrorism: Norms and Internal Security in Germany and Japan." Pp. 265–96 in *Ideas and Foreign Policy: Beliefs, Institutions, and Political Change.* Ithaca: Cornell University Press.

Keat, Russell, and John Urry. 1975. *Social Theory as Science.* London: Routledge and Kegan Paul.

Keck, Margaret E., and Kathryn Sikkink. 1998. *Activists beyond Borders: Advocacy Networks in International Politics.* Ithaca: Cornell University Press.

King, Desmond, and Stewart Wood. 1999. "The Political Economy of Neoliberalism: Britain and the United States in the 1980s." Pp. 371–97 in *Continuity and Change in Contemporary Capitalism,* edited by Herbert Kitschelt, Peter Lange, Gary Marks, and John D. Stephens. New York: Cambridge University Press.

Kiser, Edgar, and Michael Hechter. 1991. "The Role of General Theory in Comparative-Historical Sociology." *American Journal of Sociology* 97:1–30.

———. 1998. "The Debate on Historical Sociology: Rational Choice and Its Critics." *American Journal of Sociology* 104(3)785–816.

Kitschelt, Herbert, Peter Lange, Gary Marks, and John D. Stephens. 1999. "Convergence and Divergence in Advanced Capitalist Democracies." Pp. 427–60 in *Continuity and Change in Contemporary Capitalism,* edited by Herbert Kitschelt, Peter Lange, Gary Marks, and John D. Stephens. New York: Cambridge University Press.

Knight, Jack, and Jean Ensminger. 1998. "Conflict over Changing Social Norms: Bargaining, Ideology, and Enforcement." Pp. 105–26 in *The New Institutionalism in Sociology,* edited by Mary Brinton and Victor Nee. New York: Russell Sage Foundation.

Knight, Jack, and Douglass North. 1997. "Explaining Economic Change: The Interplay between Cognition and Institutions." *Legal Theory* 3:211–26.

Kuhn, Thomas S. 1962. *The Structure of Scientific Revolutions.* Chicago: University of Chicago Press.

Lash, Scott, and John Urry. 1987. *The End of Organized Capitalism.* Madison: University of Wisconsin Press.

Levi, Margaret. 1997a. "A Model, a Method, and a Map: Rational Choice in Comparative and Historical Analysis." Pp. 19–41 in *Comparative Politics: Rationality, Culture, and Structure,* edited by Mark Lichbach and Alan Zuckerman. New York: Cambridge University Press.

———. 1997b. *Consent, Dissent, and Patriotism.* New York: Cambridge University Press.

Locke, Richard M., and Kathleen Thelen. 1995. "Apples and Oranges Revisited: Contextualized Comparisons and the Study of Comparative Labor Politics." *Politics and Society* 23(3)337–67.

Mann, Michael. 1996. "Has Globalization Ended the Rise of Nation-States?" Paper presented at the National Conference in Sociology, Bergen, Norway.

March, James G., and Johan P. Olsen. 1989. *Rediscovering Institutions*. New York: Free Press.

McDonough, John E. 1997. *Interests, Ideas, and Deregulation*. Ann Arbor: University of Michigan Press.

Mills, C. Wright. 1959. *The Sociological Imagination*. New York: Oxford University Press.

North, Douglass. 1990. *Institutions, Institutional Change, and Economic Performance*. New York: Cambridge University Press.

Ohmae, Kenichi. 1990. *The Borderless World*. New York: HarperCollins.

Parsons, Talcott. 1951. *The Social System*. New York: Free Press.

Pedersen, Ove K. 1995. "Problemets Anatomi: Eller Problemet, der er et Problem." *Copenhagen Tendens* 7(1)1–11.

Pierson, Paul. 1993. "When Effect Becomes Cause: Policy Feedback and Political Change." *World Politics* 45:595–628.

———. 1994. *Dismantling the Welfare State?* New York: Cambridge University Press.

Piore, Michael. 1995. *Beyond Individualism*. Cambridge: Harvard University Press.

Premfors, Rune. 1998. "Reshaping the Democratic State: Swedish Experiences in a Comparative Perspective." *Public Administration* 76(1)141–59.

Reich, Robert. 1991. *The Work of Nations*. New York: Vintage.

Rein, Martin, and Christopher Winship. 1997. "Policy Entrepreneurs and the Academic Establishment: Truth and Values in Social Controversies." Pp. 17–47 in *Intelligence, Political Inequality, and Public Policy*, edited by Elliot White. New York: Praeger.

Rochefort, D. A., and R. W. Cobb. 1994. *The Politics of Problem Definition: Shaping the Policy Agenda*. Lawrence: University Press of Kansas.

Rueschemeyer, Dietrich, and Theda Skocpol. 1996a. Conclusion. Pp. 296–312 in *States, Social Knowledge, and the Origins of Modern Social Policies*. Princeton: Princeton University Press.

———, editors. 1996b. *States, Social Knowledge, and the Origins of Modern Social Policies*. Princeton: Princeton University Press.

Ruggie, John Gerard. 1998. "What Makes the World Hang Together? Neo-Utilitarianism and the Social Constructivist Challenge." *International Organization* 52(4)855–85.

Schneiberg, Marc. 1998. "From Associations and States to Markets and Hierarchies: Endogenous Price Shifts, Models of Rational Order, and Institutional Change." Department of Sociology, University of Arizona. Manuscript.

Schneiberg, Marc, and Elisabeth Clemens. Forthcoming. "The Typical Tools for the Job: Research Strategies in Institutional Analysis." In *How Institutions Change*, edited by Walter W. Powell and Dan L. Jones. Chicago: University of Chicago Press.

Schön, Donald A., and Martin Rein. 1994. *Frame Reflection*. New York: Basic.

Scott, W. Richard, and John W. Meyer. 1994. *Institutional Environments and Organizations*. Thousand Oaks, CA: Sage.

Shirk, Susan. 1996. "Internationalization and China's Economic Reforms." Pp. 186–208 in *Internationalization and Domestic Politics*, edited by Robert O. Keohane and Helen V. Milner. New York: Cambridge University Press.

Skocpol, Theda. 1985. "Bringing the State Back In: Strategies of Analysis in Current Research." Pp. 3–37 in *Bringing the State Back In*, edited by Peter Evans, Dietrich Rueschemeyer, and Theda Skocpol. New York: Cambridge University Press.

———. 1995. "Why I Am an Historical Institutionalist." *Polity* 28(1)103–6.

Skowronek, Stephen. 1995. "Order and Change." *Polity* 28(1)91–96.

Somers, Margaret R. 1995. "What's Political or Cultural about Political Culture and the Public Sphere? Toward an Historical Sociology of Concept Formation." *Sociological Theory* 13(2)113–44.

———. 1998. "We're No Angels: Realism, Rational Choice, and Relationality in Social Science." *American Journal of Sociology* 104(3)722–84.

Soskice, David. 1999. "Divergent Production Regimes: Coordinated and Uncoordinated Market Economies in the 1980s and 1990s." Pp. 101–34 in *Continuity and Change in Contemporary Capitalism*, edited by Herbert Kitschelt, Peter Lange, Gary Marks, and John D. Stephens. New York: Cambridge University Press.

Soysal, Yasemin. 1994. *Limits of Citizenship*. Chicago: Chicago University Press.

Steinmo, Sven, Kathleen Thelen, and Frank Longstreth, editors. 1992. *Structuring Politics: Historical Institutionalism in Comparative Analysis*. New York: Cambridge University Press.

Stinchcombe, Arthur L. 1968. *Constructing Social Theories*. Chicago: University of Chicago Press.

Strange, Susan. 1997. "The Future of Global Capitalism; or, Will Divergence Persist Forever?" Pp. 182–191 in *Political Economy of Modern Capitalism*, edited by Colin Crouch and Wolfgang Streeck. Thousand Oaks, CA: Sage.

Streeck, Wolfgang. 1997. "Beneficial Constraints: On the Economic Limits of Rational Voluntarism." Pp. 197–219 in *Contemporary Capitalism: The Embeddedness of Institutions*, edited by J. Rogers Hollingsworth and Robert Boyer. New York: Cambridge University Press.

Swidler, Ann. 1986. "Culture in Action: Symbols and Strategies." *American Sociological Review* 51:273–86.

Thelen, Kathleen. 1999. "Historical Institutionalism in Comparative Politics." *Annual Review of Political Science* 2:369–404.

Thomas, George M., John W. Meyer, Francisco O. Ramirez, and John Boli. 1987. *Institutional Structure*. Newbury Park, CA: Sage.

Thompson, E. P. 1978. "The Poverty of Theory of an Orrery of Errors." Pp. 1–210 in *The Poverty of Theory and Other Essays*. London: New Left Books.

Tolbert, Pamela, and Lynn Zucker. 1983. "Institutional Sources of Change in the Formal Structures of Organization: The Diffusion of Civil Service Reform, 1880–1935." *Administrative Science Quarterly* 28:22–39.

Vogel, Steven K. 1996. *Freer Markets, More Rules: Regulatory Reform in Advanced Countries*. Ithaca: Cornell University Press.

Wade, Robert. 1996. "Globalization and Its Limits: Reports of the Death of the National Economy Are Greatly Exaggerated." Pp. 60–88 in *National Diversity and Global Capitalism*, edited by Suzanne Berger and Ronald Dore. Ithaca: Cornell University Press.

Weir, Margaret, and Theda Skocpol. 1985. "State Structures and the Possibilities for 'Keynesian' Responses to the Great Depression in Sweden, Britain, and the United States." Pp. 107–67 in *Bringing the State Back In*, edited by Peter Evans, Dietrich Rueschemeyer, and Theda Skocpol. New York: Cambridge University Press.

Weiss, Linda. 1998. *The Myth of the Powerless State*. Ithaca: Cornell University Press.

Wuthnow, Robert. 1989. *Communities of Discourse*. Cambridge: Harvard University Press.

Yonay, Yuval P. 1998. *The Struggle over the Soul of Economics: Institutionalist and Neo-classical Economists in America between the Wars*. Princeton: Princeton University Press.

Zerubavel, Eviatar. 1997. *Social Mindscapes: An Invitation to Cognitive Sociology*. Cambridge: Harvard University Press.

Ziegler, J. Nicholas. 1997. *Governing Ideas: Strategies for Innovation in France and Germany*. Ithaca: Cornell University Press.

Zysman, John. 1983. *Governments, Markets and Growth*. Ithaca: Cornell University Press.

Index

Alchian, Armen, 37
Allen, Michael Patrick, 65
American Enterprise Institute, 169
American Medical Association, 134
analytic narrative approach, 13, 243
Asian financial crisis, 8
Aspen Systems Corporation, 145, 151
Australia, bankruptcy law, 120n9

Babb, Sarah, 253–54, 256, 258–59, 261, 266, 270–73
Banco de México, 112–14
bankruptcy laws: compared to central banks, 95–97, 107–8, 116–20; changing to soften market discipline, 105–8; convergence and divergence across nations, 117–18; France, 109–12, 117; function of, 102–5; Mexico, 114–17; socialist economies, 120n4
banks, central. *See* central banks
Banque de France, 108–10
bargaining and institutional change, explanation of, 37–39, 42–43
Bates, Robert, 243
Bergthold, Linda, 131
Berman, Sheri, 242
Block, Fred, 53
Blue Cross/Blue Shield, 134, 139
Boudon, Raymond, 27
Bradburn, Ellen, 252–53, 255, 258–64, 270, 274
bricolage, 164–65
Britain: bankruptcy law, 106–7; economic crisis and the rise of monetarism, 207–10; neoliberalism, supplanting of Keynesianism by, 193–94; periodizing the transition to neoliberalism, 210–12; Thatcherism, 204–7
Brookings Institution, 169
Brown, Lawrence, 134
Bundesbank, 99–100
business: government spending for, 58–63; influence of, 53–55; insolvency (*see* bankruptcy laws); and neoliberal public health policy, 131

business taxes: convergence across states, 55–58, 63–64; rational choice explanations, 54; stability, 51–52; theoretical explanations, 52–55, 63–65

California, health maintenance organizations (HMOs), 137–38
Campbell, John, 65, 96, 253–58, 265–66
capital mobility, 56–58, 66nn8 and 9
Carruthers, Bruce, 253–54, 256, 258–59, 261, 266, 270–73
Carter, Jimmy, 174
central banks: bankruptcy laws, compared to, 95–97, 107–8, 116–20; convergence and divergence across states, 118; France, 108–9; functions and development of, 97–98; independence, shift toward, 98–102, 108; Mexico, 112–14
change: diachronic and synchronic perspectives, 245n9; institutional (*see* institutional change)
Coase, Ronald, 36
codification mechanism, 239
cognitive structures: effects on institution building, 17n5
Coleman, James, 28
collective action, states and business taxes, 56–58
Committee for Economic Development, 152n5
competitive selection, 37, 41, 44
Conaghan, Catherine, 43
consensus mechanism, 239–40
contracts and institutional change: explanation of, 35–37, 40–42
Coopey, Richard, 210–12
coordination theory: and unemployment, 74, 76–78, 80–81, 87
corporate taxation. *See* business taxes
corporatism: economic performance and institutions, 5–7; failure of British, 209; organized labor and unemployment, 75–81, 85–87
crisis: conceptualizing, 203–4; and institutional change, 194–96, 202–3

cultural institutionalism. *See* organizational
institutionalism

Deane, Marjorie, 101
debt: foreign and Mexico, 112–15; Third
World, 100–1. *See also* investment
democratization: and neoliberalism, 30
Demsetz, Harold, 95
Denmark: 1980s and 1990s compared, 238–
41; codification mechanism, 239; consensus mechanism, 239–40; negotiated economy, development of, 229–33; neoliberalism in, 227–29; problem formation
mechanism, 238–40; structural policy as
cross-sector policy, 235–36; structural policy as macro policy, 236–38; structural policy as sector policy, 233–34
DiMaggio, Paul, 96, 130, 151
discursive institutionalism: and the analytic
narrative approach, 243; change, conditions
and mechanisms of, 10–12; crisis and (*see*
crisis); discourse defined, 220; distinguished from other institutionalisms, 226–
27; emergence of, 2, 6; epistemological and
methodological conventions of, 10, 12; and
health maintenance organizations (HMOs),
140–42; and historical institutionalism,
242–43; ideational approach, 193–94,
200–3; and neoliberalism in Denmark (*see*
Denmark); and organizational forms, 131–
32; and organizational institutionalism,
225; problematic of, 9–10; purpose of,
244–45; and rational choice institutionalism, 243–44; theoretical roots, 13. *See also*
second movement
Dobbin, Frank, 163–64, 181
Douglas, Mary, 13, 164–65
Durkheim, Emile, 14

Eastern Europe: bankruptcy laws, 105–6;
central bank independence, 101
ECB. *See* European Central Bank
ecological institutionalism, 130, 136–38
economic performance: and institutional
structure, 5–6; and neoliberalism, 273
economic theory: Britain, transition from
Keynesian to neoliberal in (*see* Britain);
Denmark, transition from Keynesian to
neoliberal in (*see* Denmark); monetarist
and rational expectations schools, 98–99;
paradigms of, 170–73; supply-side, 160–61,

167–170, 172, 174–78, 228; unemploy-
ment, explanation of, 81–83
Eggertsson, Thrainn, 36
Eldredge, Niles, 214n2
Ellwood, Paul, 132–34, 142, 150
Elster, Jon, 27
Enthoven, Alain, 142
epistemic communities, institutional change,
explanation of, 44–45
ERM. *See* European Exchange Rate Mecha-
nism
Esping-Andersen, Gosta, 58
Etzioni, Amitai, 176
European Central Bank (ECB), 99–100
European Exchange Rate Mechanism
(ERM), 82, 90
European Monetary Union, 99–101
European Union: convergence of business
taxes, 56–58; monetary policy, 82–83; un-
employment, 74

Fobaproa, 114
Forum for Industrial Development, 235
Foucault, Michel, 13, 226
frames, ideas as, 175–78
France: central bank, 108–9; economic pol-
icy and bankruptcy law, 109–12, 117
Freeman, John, 130, 151
Frieden, Jeffry, 100

Galbraith, John Kenneth, 176
Gambetta, Diego, 27
game theory: two-person strategic game, 33–
35. *See also* rational choice institutionalism
Garrett, Geoffrey, 54, 58, 61
Germany, bankruptcy law, 107
Gilder, George, 169, 175–76
globalization: and business taxation, 53–55,
63–65; convergence of business taxes, 55–
58; and labor markets, 76; monetary policy
and central banks, 98–102; and pressures
for neoliberalism, 272–73; spending for
business, 58–63
Goldstein, Judith, 223
Gomes, Leonard, 82
Goodman, John, 99, 108
Gould, Stephen Jay, 214n2

Haas, Peter, 45
Hall, Peter, 162–63, 183n7, 196–98, 223–25,
242